British Historical Facts, 1830–190[0]
comes as an original and pioneering
attempt to provide within a single v[olume]
a comprehensive yet readily accessi[ble]
source-book of facts and figures on [the]
Victorian period. Like its companion
volume, *British Political Facts,
1900–1968*, the book covers almost
every area of interest to the historian and
political scientist. There are full facts and
figures on such diverse subjects as treaties
and trade unions, elections and
parliaments, churches and newspapers,
armed forces and the Crown, the Empire
and the economy.

In addition, complete lists of every
Victorian cabinet are included, with
useful biographical details of their
members. The book has been designed to
be as useful for schools as for research
students and for journalists as well as for
reference libraries.

Few previous published works on
Victorian history have attempted to
provide quite so much detail and wealth
of information as is encompassed here.

*For a note on the authors, please see the back
flap*

BRITISH HISTORICAL FACTS

1830–1900

BRITISH
HISTORICAL FACTS
1830–1900

CHRIS COOK

AND

BRENDAN KEITH

First published 1975 by
THE MACMILLAN PRESS LTD
London and Basingstoke
Associated companies in New York
Dublin Melbourne Johannesburg and Madras

SBN 333 13220 3

Printed and bound in Great Britain by
REDWOOD BURN LIMITED
Trowbridge & Esher

To
Sir Norman Chester
Warden of Nuffield College, Oxford

Contents

Preface

This is a book about people at the top. It lists almost all those who held high political, judicial, military or administrative office in Britain between 1830 and 1900; and provides basic information about their institutions and the world in which they moved. We hope that it will provide the serious student with a useful work of reference, bringing within the covers of one volume details previously inaccessible or widely scattered. We hope too that the book will excite the curiosity of the general reader and lead him to investigate further some of the people mentioned in these pages.

This book owes much to David Butler of Nuffield College, Oxford, whose pioneering work on a similar compilation of factual information for the period after 1900 inspired the idea behind this volume.

We are indebted to many people for assistance in preparing the book for publication. Nuffield College was for a time the home of the authors; we are particularly indebted to the Warden, Fellows and students, who offered much advice and encouragement. Substantial contributions on individual chapters were made by: Stephen Brooks (Armed Forces); Tim Congdon (Economy); Edgar Feuchtwanger (Political Parties); Martin Happs (Press); David Philips (Justice); Mrs Zara Steiner (Foreign Affairs); Mrs Gillian Sutherland (Education). Alan Gilbert wrote the whole of the section on Religion. The Index of Ministers was compiled by Susan Paton.

Among others we must thank are: Jean Ali, Mary Barker, Geoffrey Block, John Brooke, Perry Butler, Caroline Harvey, Jacqueline Johns, John Paxton, John Ramsden, John Sainty, John Stevenson, Philip Woods, and the Library Staff of: the Bodleian, British Library, Nuffield College, Oxford Union Society and Worcester College, Oxford. A particular debt is due to the British Academy who generously provided financial help to assist with part of the research expenses involved in compiling this volume.

Our thanks also go to Macmillans, especially to Tim Farmiloe and Ray Martin, and to Marion Brickell for her work on the Index of Ministers.

CHRIS COOK
BRENDAN KEITH

1* Ministries

WHIG GOVERNMENT, 1830–1834

MINISTERS IN CABINET				JUNIOR MINISTERS ATTACHED		

MINISTERS IN CABINET

P.M.	**Earl Grey**	
	22 Nov 30–9 Jul 34[1]	
	Vt Melbourne	
	16 Jul 34–14 Nov 34	
Ld Chanc.	**Ld Brougham & Vaux**	
	22 Nov 30	
Ld Pres.	**M of Lansdowne**	22 Nov 30
Privy S.	**Ld Durham (E)**	22 Nov 30
	E of Ripon	3 Apr 33
	E of Carlisle	5 Jun 34
	E of Mulgrave	30 Jul 34
Home O.	**Vt Melbourne**	22 Nov 30
	Vt Duncannon	19 Jul 34
For. O.	**Vt Palmerston**	22 Nov 30
War & Cols	**Vt Goderich**	22 Nov 30
	E. G. Stanley	3 Apr 33
	T. Spring-Rice	5 Jun 34
Exch.	**Vt Althorp**	22 Nov 30
Admir.	**Sir J. Graham**	22 Nov 30
	Ld Auckland	7 Jun 34
Bd Control	**C. Grant**	1 Dec 30

JUNIOR MINISTERS ATTACHED

P.S. to Treasury:

E. Ellice	26 Nov 30
Sir C. Wood	10 Aug 32

U-S.	G. Lamb	22 Nov 30
	Vt Howick	13 Jan 34
	E. J. Stanley	23 Jul 34
U-S.	Sir G. Shee	26 Nov 30
	Vt Fordwich	13 Nov 34
U-S.	Vt Howick	23 Nov 30
	Sir J. Shaw-Lefevre	13 Jan 34
	Sir G. Grey	16 Jul 34

F.S. to Treasury:

	T. Spring-Rice	26 Nov 30
	F. T. Baring	6 Jun 34
1st Sec.	G. Elliot	29 Nov 30
Civil Ld	H. Labouchere	8 Jun 32
Sec. to	Vt Sandon	18 Dec 30
Bd	T. H. Villiers	18 May 31
Control	T. B. Macaulay	19 Dec 32
	R. Gordon[2]	
		26 Dec 33–14 Nov 34
	J. A. S. MacKenzie	
		22 Apr 34–14 Nov 34

Chief Sec.	*(office not in cabinet)*	
Ireland	**E. G. Stanley**	16 Jun 31
	(Sir J. C. Hobhouse 29 Mar 33)	
	(office not in cabinet)	
D. Lanc.	**Ld Holland**	25 Nov 30

*For problems involved in compiling the following lists see Bibliographical Note.
[1]The Government resigned 8 May 32, but resumed 17 May 32.
[2]Joint Secretary from 22 Apr 34.

1

WHIG GOVERNMENT, 1830–1834 (*contd.*)

MINISTERS IN CABINET			JUNIOR MINISTERS ATTACHED		
Master of	(*office not in cabinet*)				
Mint	**J. Abercromby**	13 Jun 34			
Paym.-Gen.	(*office not in cabinet*)				
	Ld J. Russell	16 Jun 31			
Min.	**E of Carlisle**				
without		22 Nov 30–5 Jun 34			
Portfolio					
Postm.-Gen.	**D of Richmond**	11 Dec 30			
	(*M of Conyngham* 5 *Jul* 34)				
	(*office not in cabinet*)				
B.o.T.	(*office not in cabinet*)		*V. Pres.*	C. P. Thomson	22 Nov 30
	C. P. Thomson	5 Jun 34		H. Labouchere	5 Jun 34
Sec. at War	(*office not in cabinet*)				
	E. Ellice	20 Jun 34			
1st Comm.	(*office not in cabinet*)				
Woods	**Sir J. C. Hobhouse**	22 Jul 34			

MINISTERS NOT IN CABINET			JUNIOR MINISTERS ATTACHED		
Chief Sec.	E. G. STANLEY	29 Nov 30			
Ireland	(*office in cabinet* 16 *Jun* 31)				
	SIR J. C. HOBHOUSE				
		29 Mar 33			
	E. J. LITTLETON	17 May 33			
Ld Lieut.	M OF ANGLESEY	4 Dec 30			
Ireland	M OF WELLESLEY	12 Sep 33			
Master of	LD AUCKLAND	14 Dec 30			
Mint	(*J. Abercromby* 13 *Jun* 34)				
	(*office in cabinet*)				
Treas. of	C. P. THOMSON	30 Nov 30			
Navy					
Master-	SIR J. KEMPT	11 Dec 30	*Surveyor-*	W. L. Maberley	12 Jan 31
Gen. of			*Gen.*	C. R. Fox	30 Nov 32
Ordnance			*Clerk*	C. Trevelyan	30 Dec 30
				T. F. Kennedy	8 Feb 32
				W. L. Maberley	30 Nov 32
				A. L. Hay	19 Jun 34
			Store-	H. Duncan	30 Dec 30
			keeper		
Paym.-Gen.	LD J. RUSSELL	16 Dec 30			
	(*office in cabinet* 16 *Jun* 31)				
Postm.-Gen.	(*office in cabinet*)				
	M OF CONYNGHAM	5 Jul 34			
B.o.T.	LD AUCKLAND	22 Nov 30		(*for Junior Ministers see above*)	
	(*C. P. Thomson* 5 *Jun* 34)				
	(*office in cabinet*)				
Sec at War	C. W. WILLIAMS WYNN				
		30 Nov 30			
	SIR H. PARNELL	4 Apr 31			

WHIG GOVERNMENT, 1830–1834 *(contd.)*

MINISTERS NOT IN CABINET			JUNIOR MINISTERS ATTACHED

	SIR J. C. HOBHOUSE		
		1 Feb 32	
	E. ELLICE	6 Apr 33	
	(office in cabinet 20 Jun 34)		
1st Comm.	G. J. W. A. ELLIS	2 Dec 30	
Woods	VT DUNCANNON	7 Feb 31	
	(Sir J. C. Hobhouse 22 Jul 34)		
	(office in cabinet)		

Law Officers:			*Junior Lds of Treasury:*
Att.-Gen.	SIR T. DENMAN	24 Nov 30	Ld Nugent
	SIR W. HORNE	26 Nov 32	22 Nov 30–22 Nov 32
	SIR J. CAMPBELL	1 Mar 34	R. V. Smith
Sol.-Gen.	SIR W. HORNE	24 Nov 30	22 Nov 30–14 Nov 34
	SIR J. CAMPBELL	26 Nov 32	F. T. Baring
	SIR C. C. PEPYS	25 Feb 34	22 Nov 30–6 Jun 34
	R. ROLFE	6 Nov 34	G. Ponsonby
Judge	R. GRANT	24 Nov 30	22 Nov 30–14 Nov 34
Advoc. Gen.	R. FERGUSSON	19 Jun 34	T. F. Kennedy
Ld Advoc.	F. JEFFREY	3 Dec 30	22 Nov 32–9 Apr 34
	J. MURRAY	17 May 34	R. Graham
Sol.-Gen.	H. COCKBURN	3 Dec 30	9 Apr 34–14 Nov 34
Scotland	A. SKENE	5 Nov 34	G. S. Byng
Att.-Gen.[1]	E. PENNEFATHER	23 Dec 30	20 Jun 34–14 Nov 34
Ireland	F. BLACKBURNE	11 Jan 31	
Sol.-Gen.[1]	P. CRAMPTON	23 Dec 30	
Ireland	M. O'LOGHLEN	21 Oct 34	

H.M. Household:		
Ld Steward	M OF WELLESLEY	23 Nov 30
	D OF ARGYLL	11 Sep 33
Ld Chamb.	D OF DEVONSHIRE	22 Nov 30
V. Chamb.	E OF BELFAST	24 Jul 30
Master of Horse	E OF ALBEMARLE	24 Nov 30
Treas.	SIR W. H. FREMANTLE	27 May 26
		contd. in office
Comptr.	LD R. GROSVENOR	23 Nov 30
Capt. Gents	LD FOLEY (3rd)	8 Dec 30
Pensioners	LD FOLEY (4th)	1 May 33
	(became Capt. Gents at Arms 17 Mar 34)	
Capt.	M OF CLANRICARDE	1 Dec 30
Yeomen of Guard	E OF GOSFORD	16 Jul 34
Master of Buckhounds	VT ANSON	24 Nov 30
	(1st E of Lichfield, 1831)	

[1] It proved impossible to obtain complete information about Irish Law appointments. Many Irish Law Officers did not sit in Parliament.

CONSERVATIVE PROVISIONAL GOVERNMENT, 1834

P.M.	**D of Wellington**	17 Nov 34–9 Dec 34
Ld Chanc.	**Ld Lyndhurst**	21 Nov 34
Sec. of State[1]	**D of Wellington**	17 Nov 34

Lds Commissioners for executing the office of Ld High Treasurer:

D of Wellington (1st Ld)	21 Nov 34
E of Rosslyn	21 Nov 34
Ld Ellenborough	21 Nov 34
Ld Maryborough	21 Nov 34
Sir J. Beckett	21 Nov 34
J. Planta	21 Nov 34

CONSERVATIVE GOVERNMENT, 1834–1835

MINISTERS IN CABINET			JUNIOR MINISTERS ATTACHED		
P.M.	**Sir R. Peel**		*P.S. to Treasury:*		
		10 Dec 34–8 Apr 35		Sir G. Clerk	19 Dec 34
Ld Chanc.	**Ld Lyndhurst**	21 Nov 34			
Ld Pres.	**E of Rosslyn**	15 Dec 34			
Privy S.	**Ld Wharncliffe**	15 Dec 34			
Home O.	**H. Goulburn**	15 Dec 34	*U-S.*	W. Gregson	3 Jan 35
For. O.	**D of Wellington**	17 Nov 34	*U-S.*	Vt Mahon	17 Dec 34
War & Cols	**E of Aberdeen**	20 Dec 34	*U-S.*	J. S. Wortley	20 Dec 34
				W. E. Gladstone	27 Jan 35
Exch.	**Sir R. Peel**	10 Dec 34	*F.S. to Treasury:*		
				Sir T. F. Fremantle	20 Dec 34
Admir.	**Earl de Grey**	22 Dec 34	*1st Sec.*	G. R. Dawson	24 Dec 34
			Civil Ld	Ld Ashley	22 Dec 34
Bd Control	**Ld Ellenborough**	18 Dec 34	*Jt Secs*	W. M. Praed	
					20 Dec 34–8 Apr 35
				S. Herbert	
					8 Jan 35–8 Apr 35
Master-Gen. of Ordnance	**Sir G. Murray**	18 Dec 34	*Surveyor-Gen.*	Ld R. Somerset	22 Dec 34
			Clerk	Sir E. Owen	22 Dec 34
			Store-keeper	F. R. Bonham	22 Dec 34
Paym.-Gen.	**Sir E. Knatchbull**	23 Dec 34			
B.o.T.	**A. Baring**	15 Dec 34	*V. Pres.*	Vt Lowther	20 Dec 34
Sec. at War	**J. C. Herries**	16 Dec 34			

[1]Constitutionally speaking, the appointment of one Secretary of State is sufficient, since each Secretary of State has full power to transact the business of any or all of the departments into which the office is divided.

CONSERVATIVE GOVERNMENT, 1834–1835 (contd.)

MINISTERS NOT IN CABINET

Chief Sec. *Ireland*	SIR H. HARDINGE	16 Dec 34
Ld Lieut. *Ireland*	E OF HADDINGTON	1 Jan 35
D. Lanc.	C. W. WILLIAMS WYNN	26 Dec 34
Master of *Mint*	A. BARING	23 Dec 34
Treas. of *Navy*	VT LOWTHER	22 Dec 34
Postm.-Gen.	LD MARYBOROUGH	23 Dec 34
1st Comm. *Woods*	LD G. SOMERSET	23 Dec 34

Law Officers:

Att.-Gen.	SIR F. POLLOCK	17 Dec 34
Sol.-Gen.	SIR W. FOLLETT	20 Dec 34
Judge *Advoc. Gen.*	SIR J. BECKETT	18 Dec 34
Ld Advoc.	SIR W. RAE	19 Dec 34
Sol.-Gen. *Scotland*	D. MCNEILL	7 Jan 35
Att.-Gen. *Ireland*	(*vacant*)	
Sol.-Gen. *Ireland*	E. PENNEFATHER	27 Jan 35

H.M. Household:

Ld Steward	E OF WILTON	2 Jan 35
Ld Chamb.	E OF JERSEY	15 Dec 34
V. Chamb.	VT CASTLEREAGH	29 Dec 34
Master of *Horse*	D OF DORSET	1 Jan 35
Treas.	SIR W. H. FREMANTLE	contd. in office
Comptr.	H. T. L. CORRY	29 Dec 34
Capt. Gents *at Arms*	VT HEREFORD	29 Dec 34
Capt. *Yeomen* *of Guard*	E OF COURTOWN	5 Jan 35
Master of *Buckhounds*	E OF CHESTERFIELD	30 Dec 34

JUNIOR MINISTERS ATTACHED

Junior Lds of Treasury:

W. Y. Peel
    26 Dec 34–8 Apr 35
E of Lincoln
    26 Dec 34–8 Apr 35
Vt Stormont
    26 Dec 34–8 Apr 35
C. Ross   26 Dec 34–8 Apr 35
W. E. Gladstone
    26 Dec 34–27 Jan 35
J. Nicholl 14 Mar 35–8 Apr 35

WHIG GOVERNMENT, 1835–1841

MINISTERS IN CABINET

P.M.	**Vt Melbourne**	
	18 Apr 35–30 Aug 41[1]	
Ld Chanc.	in Commission	23 Apr 35
	Ld Cottenham	16 Jan 36
Ld Pres.	**M of Lansdowne**	18 Apr 35
Privy S.	**Vt Duncannon**	23 Apr 35
	E of Clarendon	15 Jan 40
Home O.	**Ld J. Russell**	18 Apr 35
	M of Normanby	30 Aug 39
For. O.	**Vt Palmerston**	18 Apr 35
War & Cols	**C. Grant**	18 Apr 35
	(1st *Ld Glenelg* 1835)	
	M of Normanby	20 Feb 39
	Ld J. Russell	30 Aug 39
Exch.	**T. Spring-Rice**	18 Apr 35
	F. T. Baring	26 Aug 39
Admir.	**Ld Auckland**	22 Apr 35
	E of Minto	15 Sep 35
Bd Control	**Sir J. C. Hobhouse**	
		23 Apr 35

Chief Sec.	(*office not in cabinet*)	
Ireland	**Vt Morpeth**	20 Feb 39
D. Lanc.	**Ld Holland**	23 Apr 35
	E of Clarendon	31 Oct 40
	Sir G. Grey	23 Jun 41
B.o.T.	**C. P. Thomson**	18 Apr 35
	H. Labouchere	29 Aug 39
Sec. at War	**Vt Howick**	18 Apr 35
	T. B. Macaulay	27 Sep 39
1st Comm.	**Vt Duncannon**	28 Apr 35
Woods		

MINISTERS NOT IN CABINET

Chief Sec.	Vt MORPETH	22 Apr 35
Ireland	(*office in cabinet* 20 *Feb* 39)	
Ld Lieut.	E OF MULGRAVE	29 Apr 35
Ireland	Vt EBRINGTON	13 Mar 39

JUNIOR MINISTERS ATTACHED

P.S. to Treasury:		
	E. J. Stanley	21 Apr 35
	Sir D. Le Marchant	19 Jun 41
U-S.	F. Maule	18 Apr 35
	Ld Seymour	15 Jun 41
U-S.	W. F. Strangeways	15 Aug 35
	Vt Leveson	7 Mar 40
U-S.	Sir G. Grey	18 Apr 35
	H. Labouchere	28 Feb 39
	R. V. Smith	31 Aug 39
F.S. to Treasury:		
	F. T. Baring	21 Apr 35
	R. Gordon	6 Sep 39
	R. M. O'Ferrall	9 Jun 41
1st Sec.	C. Wood	27 Apr 35
	R. M. O'Ferrall	4 Oct 39
	J. Parker	9 Jun 41
Civil Ld	Ld Dalmeny	23 Apr 35
Jt Secs	R. Gordon	
	21 Apr 35–30 Sep 39	
	R. V. Smith	
	21 Apr 35–30 Sep 39	
	Ld Seymour	
	30 Sep 39–15 Jun 41	
	(Sir) W. Clay	
	30 Sep 39–30 Aug 41	
	C. Buller 21 Jun 41–30 Aug 41	

V. Pres.	H. Labouchere	6 May 35
	R. L. Sheil	29 Aug 39
	F. Maule	28 Jun 41

JUNIOR MINISTERS ATTACHED

[1] The Government resigned 7 May 39, but resumed 10 May 39.

WHIG GOVERNMENT, 1835–1841 *(contd.)*

MINISTERS NOT IN CABINET			JUNIOR MINISTERS ATTACHED		
Master of Mint	H. LABOUCHERE	25 Apr 35			
Treas. of Navy	SIR H. PARNELL (*office abolished* 1 *Dec* 36)	20 Apr 35			
Master-Gen. of Ordnance	SIR R. H. VIVIAN (LD)	4 May 35	*Surveyor-Gen.*	Sir R. S. Donkin C. R. Fox	20 Apr 35 5 May 41
Paym.-Gen.	SIR H. PARNELL E. J. STANLEY	27 Apr 35 19 Jun 41	*Clerk*	A. L. Hay J. W. D. Dundas G. Anson	20 Apr 35 21 Mar 38 23 Jun 41
Postm.-Gen.	M OF CONYNGHAM E OF LICHFIELD	30 Apr 35 22 May 35	*Store-keeper*	G. Anson J. H. Plumridge	25 Apr 35 23 Jun 41

Law Officers:

Att.-Gen.	SIR J. CAMPBELL SIR T. WILDE	30 Apr 35 3 Jul 41	
Sol.-Gen.	SIR R. ROLFE SIR T. WILDE	4 May 35 2 Dec 39	
Judge Advoc. Gen.	R. FERGUSSON W. ST J. ARABIN SIR G. GREY R. L. SHEIL	20 Apr 35 24 Nov 38 15 Feb 39 23 Jun 41	

Junior Lds of Treasury:
Ld Seymour
    18 Apr 35–2 Nov 39
W. H. Ord
    18 Apr 35–18 Jul 37
R. Steuart
    18 Apr 35–26 May 40
R. M. O'Ferrall
    16 May 35–28 Aug 39
J. Parker
    18 Jul 37–23 Jun 41
T. Wyse 28 Aug 39–30 Aug 41
H. Tufnell
    2 Nov 39–30 Aug 41
E. Horsman
    26 May 40–30 Aug 41
W. F. Cowper
    23 Jun 41–30 Aug 41

Ld Advoc.	J. MURRAY A. RUTHERFURD	20 Apr 35 20 Apr 39
Sol.-Gen. Scotland	J. CUNNINGHAME A. RUTHERFURD J. IVORY T. MAITLAND	22 Apr 35 9 Feb 37 20 Apr 39 9 May 40
Att.-Gen. Ireland	L. PERRIN M. O'LOGHLEN J. RICHARDS S. WOULFE N. BALL M. BRADY D. PIGOT	29 Apr 35 31 Aug 35 10 Nov 36 3 Feb 37 11 Jul 38 23 Feb 39 11 Aug 40
Sol.-Gen. Ireland	M. O'LOGHLEN J. RICHARDS S. WOULFE M. BRADY D. PIGOT R. MOORE	29 Apr 35 21 Sep 35 10 Nov 36 3 Feb 37 11 Feb 39 14 Aug 40

Lds in Waiting (to Queen Victoria):
M of Headfort
    17 Jul 37–30 Aug 41
M of Queensberry
    17 Jul 37–30 Aug 41
Vt Falkland
    17 Jul 37–4 Feb 40
Vt Torrington
    17 Jul 37–30 Aug 41
Ld Byron
    17 Jul 37–31 Mar 60
    (*perm.*)
Ld Gardner
    17 Jul 37–1 Jul 40
Ld Lilford
    17 Jul 37–30 Aug 41
Ld Templemore
    17 Jul 37–26 Sep 37
E of Uxbridge
    11 Oct 37–6 May 39

WHIG GOVERNMENT, 1835–1841 (contd.)

	MINISTERS NOT IN CABINET	
Ld Steward	D OF ARGYLL	23 Apr 35
	E OF ERROLL	21 Nov 39
Ld Chamb.	M OF WELLESLEY	23 Apr 35
	M OF CONYNGHAM	
		22 May 35
	E OF UXBRIDGE	6 May 39
V. Chamb.	LD C. FITZROY	29 Jun 35
	E OF BELFAST	27 Apr 38
Master of Horse	E OF ALBEMARLE	25 Apr 35
Treas.	SIR W. H. FREMANTLE	
	contd. in office	
	E OF SURREY	17 Jul 37
	G. S. BYNG	23 Jun 41
Comptr.	G. S. BYNG	6 May 35
	LD M. HILL	23 Jun 41
Capt. Gents at Arms	LD FOLEY	6 May 35
Capt. Yeomen of Guard	E OF GOSFORD	23 Apr 35
	E OF ILCHESTER	5 Aug 35
	E OF SURREY	6 Jul 41
Master of Buckhounds	E OF ERROLL	30 Apr 35
	LD KINNAIRD	21 Dec 39
Mistress of Robes	DUCH OF SUTHERLAND (*to Queen Victoria*)	29 Aug 37

Lds in Waiting (contd.):

E of Fingall
　　　　11 Dec 37–30 Aug 41
E of Listowel
　　　　4 Feb 40–30 Aug 41
E of Aboyne
　　　　1 Jul 40–30 Aug 41

CONSERVATIVE GOVERNMENT, 1841–1846

	MINISTERS IN CABINET			JUNIOR MINISTERS ATTACHED	
P.M.	Sir R. Peel			*P.S. to Treasury:*	
	30 Aug 41–27 Jun 46[1]			Sir T. F. Fremantle	8 Sep 41
Ld Chanc.	Ld Lyndhurst	3 Sep 41		J. Young	21 May 44
Ld Pres.	Ld Wharncliffe	3 Sep 41			
	D of Buccleuch	21 Jan 46			
Privy S.	D of Buckingham	3 Sep 41			
	D of Buccleuch	2 Feb 42			
	E of Haddington	21 Jan 46			
Home O.	Sir J. Graham	3 Sep 41	*U.-S.*	J. Manners-Sutton	3 Sep 41
For. O.	E of Aberdeen	3 Sep 41	*U.-S.*	Vt Canning	4 Sep 41
				G. Smythe	27 Jan 46
War & Cols	Ld Stanley	3 Sep 41	*U.-S.*	G. Hope	8 Sep 41
	W. E. Gladstone	23 Dec 45		Ld Lyttelton	8 Jan 46

[1]Peel resigned 6 Dec 45, but resumed office 20 Dec 45.

CONSERVATIVE GOVERNMENT, 1841–1846 (contd.)

MINISTERS IN CABINET			JUNIOR MINISTERS ATTACHED		
Exch.	**H. Goulburn**	4 Sep 41	*F.S. to Treasury:*		
				Sir G. Clerk	8 Sep 41
				E. Cardwell	4 Feb 45
Admir.	**E of Haddington**	6 Sep 41	*1st Sec.*	S. Herbert	10 Sep 41
	E of Ellenborough	8 Jan 46		H. T. L. Corry	4 Feb 45
			Civil Ld	H. T. L. Corry	6 Sep 41
				H. Fitzroy	10 Feb 45
Bd Control	**Ld Ellenborough (E)**		*Jt Secs*	J. E. Tennent	
		4 Sep 41		8 Sep 41–5 Aug 45	
	Ld Fitzgerald	23 Oct 41		W. B. Baring	
	E of Ripon	17 May 43		8 Sep 41–17 Feb 45	
				Vt Jocelyn	
				17 Feb 45–27 Jun 46	
				Vt Mahon	
				5 Aug 45–27 Jun 46	
D. Lanc.	*(office not in cabinet)*				
	Ld G. Somerset	May 44			
Paym.-Gen.	**Sir E. Knatchbull**	8 Sep 41			
	W. B. Baring	1 Mar 45			
Min. without Portfolio	**D of Wellington**	3 Sep 41			
B.o.T.	**E of Ripon**	3 Sep 41	*V. Pres.*	W. E. Gladstone	3 Sep 41
	W. E. Gladstone	15 May 43		E of Dalhousie	10 Jun 43
	E of Dalhousie	5 Feb 45		Sir G. Clerk	5 Feb 45
Sec. at War	**Sir H. Hardinge**	4 Sep 41			
	(Sir T. F. Fremantle 17 May 44)				
	(office not in cabinet)				
	S. Herbert	May 45			
1st Comm. Woods	*(office not in cabinet)*				
	E of Lincoln	Feb 45			
	(Vt Canning 2 Mar 46)				
	(office not in cabinet)				

MINISTERS NOT IN CABINET			JUNIOR MINISTERS ATTACHED
Chief Sec. Ireland	Lᴅ Eʟɪᴏᴛ	6 Sep 41	
	Sɪʀ T. F. Fʀᴇᴍᴀɴᴛʟᴇ	1 Feb 45	
	E ᴏꜰ Lɪɴᴄᴏʟɴ	14 Feb 46	
Ld Lieut. Ireland	Eᴀʀʟ ᴅᴇ Gʀᴇʏ	11 Sep 41	
	Lᴅ Hᴇʏᴛᴇꜱʙᴜʀʏ	17 Jul 44	
D. Lanc.	Lᴅ G. Sᴏᴍᴇʀꜱᴇᴛ	3 Sep 41	
	(office in cabinet May 44)		
Master of Mint	W. E. Gʟᴀᴅꜱᴛᴏɴᴇ	9 Sep 41	
	Sɪʀ G. Cʟᴇʀᴋ	12 Feb 45	

CONSERVATIVE GOVERNMENT, 1841–1846 (contd.)

MINISTERS NOT IN CABINET

Master- Gen. of Ordnance	SIR G. MURRAY	9 Sep 41

Postm.-Gen.	VT LOWTHER	9 Sep 41
	(2nd E of Lonsdale 1844)	
	E OF ST GERMANS	30 Dec 45
Sec. at War	(office in cabinet)	
	SIR T. F. FREMANTLE	
		17 May 44
	S. HERBERT	4 Feb 45
	(office in cabinet May 45)	
Chief	E OF LINCOLN	16 Sep 41
Comm.	(office in cabinet Feb 45)	
Woods	VT CANNING	2 Mar 46

Law Officers:

Att.-Gen.	SIR F. POLLOCK	
		6 Sep 41
	SIR W. W. FOLLETT	
		15 Apr 44
	SIR F. THESIGER	29 Jun 45
Sol.-Gen.	SIR W. W. FOLLETT	6 Sep 41
	SIR F. THESIGER	15 Apr 44
	SIR F. KELLY	17 Jul 45
Judge	J. NICHOL	8 Sep 41
Advoc. Gen.	J. STUART-WORTLEY	
		24 Jan 46
Ld Advoc.	SIR W. RAE	4 Sep 41
	D. MCNEILL	26 Oct 42
Sol.-Gen.	D. MCNEILL	9 Sep 41
Scotland	A. ANDERSON	8 Nov 42
Att.-Gen.	F. BLACKBURN	23 Sep 41
Ireland	T. SMITH	1 Nov 42
	R. GREEN	21 Sep 42
Sol.-Gen.	E. PENNEFATHER	2 Feb 46
Ireland	J. D. JACKSON	23 Sep 41
	T. SMITH	10 Nov 41
	R. GREEN	1 Nov 42
	A. BREWSTER	2 Feb 46

H.M. Household:

Ld Steward	E OF LIVERPOOL	3 Sep 41
Ld Chamb.	EARL DE LA WARR	8 Sep 41
V. Chamb.	LD E. BRUCE	7 Sep 41
Master of Horse	E OF JERSEY	4 Sep 41

JUNIOR MINISTERS ATTACHED

Surveyor- Gen.	J. Peel	9 Sep 41
Clerk	H. G. Boldero	9 Sep 41
	Ld A. Lennox	7 Aug 45
Store- keeper	F. R. Bonham	9 Sep 41
	Sir T. Hastings	25 Jul 45[1]

Junior Lds of Treasury:

J. M. Gaskell
    6 Sep 41–11 Mar 46
H. B. Baring
    6 Sep 41–27 Jun 46
A. Perceval
    6 Sep 41–16 Sep 41
A. Pringle
    6 Sep 41–26 Apr 45
J. Young
    16 Sep 41–21 May 44
Ld A. Lennox
    21 May 44–8 Aug 45
W. F. Mackenzie
    26 Apr 45–11 Mar 46
W. Cripps
    8 Aug 45–27 Jun 46
S. T. Carnegie
    11 Mar 46–27 Jun 46

R. Neville
    11 Mar 46–27 Jun 46

Lds in Waiting:

M of Ormonde
    10 Sep 41–27 Jun 46
E of Warwick
    10 Sep 41–27 Jun 46
E of Morton
    10 Sep 41–27 Jun 46

[1]Hastings retained the office until it was abolished in 1855.

WHIG GOVERNMENT, 1846–1852 *(contd.)*

MINISTERS NOT IN CABINET

Treas.	E OF JERMYN	9 Sep 41
Comptr.	G. DAWSON-DAMER	9 Sep 41
Capt. Gents at Arms	LD FORESTER	8 Sep 41
Capt. Yeomen of Guard	M OF LOTHIAN	8 Sep 41
	E OF BEVERLEY	15 Jan 42
Master of Buckhounds	E OF ROSSLYN	10 Sep 41
Chief Equerry & Clerk Marshal	LD C. WELLESLEY	10 Sep 41
Mistress of Robes	DUCH OF BUCCLEUCH	10 Sep 41

Lds in Waiting (contd.):

E of Hardwicke
    10 Sep 41–31 jan 46

    10 Sep 41–27 Jun 46
Ld Rivers
    10 Sep 41–27 Jun 46
Vt Hawarden
    15 Sep 41–27 Jun 46
Ld Glenlyon
    31 Jan 46–27 Jun 46

WHIG GOVERNMENT, 1846–1852

MINISTERS IN CABINET

P.M.	**Ld J. Russell (E)**	30 Jun 46–21 Feb 52[1]
Ld Chanc.	**Ld Cottenham**	6 Jul 46
	in Commission	19 Jun 50
	Ld Truro	15 Jul 50
Ld Pres.	**M of Lansdowne**	6 Jul 46
Privy S.	**E of Minto**	6 Jul 46
Home O.	**Sir G. Grey**	6 Jul 46
For. O.	**Vt Palmerston**	6 Jul 46
	Earl Granville	26 Dec 51
War & Cols	**Earl Grey**	6 Jul 46
Exch.	**Sir C. Wood**	6 Jul 46
Bd Control	**Sir J. C. Hobhouse**	8 Jul 46
	F. Maule	5 Feb 52

JUNIOR MINISTERS ATTACHED

P.S. to Treasury:

	H. Tufnell	7 Jul 46

U-S.	Sir W. Somerville	5 Jul 46
	Sir D. Le Marchant	22 Jul 47
	G. C. Lewis	15 May 48
	E. P. Bouverie	9 Jul 50
U-S.	E. J. Stanley	6 Jul 46
	A. H. Layard	12 Feb 52
U-S.	B. Hawes	6 Jul 46
	F. Peel	1 Nov 51

F.S. to Treasury:

	J. Parker	7 Jul 46
	W. G. Hayter	22 May 49
	Sir G. C. Lewis	9 Jul 50

Jt Secs	G. S. Byng	6 Jul 46–30 Nov 47
	T. Wyse	6 Jul 46–26 Jan 49
	G. C. Lewis	30 Nov 47–16 May 48
	J. Wilson	16 May 48–21 Feb 52
	J. Elliot	26 Jan 49–21 Feb 52

[1] The Government resigned 22 Feb 51, but resumed 3 Mar 51.

WHIG GOVERNMENT, 1846–1852 (contd.)

MINISTERS IN CABINET   JUNIOR MINISTERS ATTACHED

Admir.	**E of Auckland**	7 Jul 46	
	Sir F. T. Baring	15 Jan 49	

1st Sec.	H. G. Ward	13 Jul 46
	J. Parker	21 May 49
Civil Ld	W. F. Cowper	7 Jul 46

Chief Sec.	**H. Labouchere**	6 Jul 46
Ireland	(*Sir W. Somerville*	
	22 *Jul* 47)	
	(*office not in cabinet*)	
D. Lanc.	**Ld Campbell**	6 Jul 46
	E of Carlisle	6 Mar 50
Paym.-Gen.	**T. B. Macaulay**	7 Jul 46
	(*Earl Granville* 8 *May* 48)	
	(*office not in cabinet*)	
	Earl Granville	Oct 51
	(*Ld Stanley of Alderley*	
	12 *Feb* 52)	
	(*office not in cabinet*)	
Postm.-Gen.	**M of Clanricarde**	7 Jul 46

B.o.T.	**E. of Clarendon**	6 Jul 46
	H. Labouchere	22 Jul 47

V. Pres.	T. M. Gibson	8 Jul 46
	Earl Granville	8 May 48
	Ld Stanley of Alderley	
		11 Feb 52

1st Comm.	**Vt Morpeth**	7 Jul 46
Woods[1]	(*7th E of Carlisle* 1848)	
	(*Ld Seymour* 17 *Apr* 49)	
	(*office not in cabinet*)	
1st C.	(*office not in cabinet*)	
Works[1]	**Ld Seymour**	Oct 51

MINISTERS NOT IN CABINET   JUNIOR MINISTERS ATTACHED

Chief Sec.	(*office in cabinet*)	
Ireland	SIR W. SOMERVILLE	
		22 Jul 47
Ld Lieut.	E OF BESSBOROUGH	8 Jul 46
Ireland	E OF CLARENDON	22 May 47
Master of	R. L. SHEIL	7 Jul 46
Mint	SIR W. HERSCHELL	13 Dec 50
Master-	M OF ANGLESEY	8 Jul 46
Gen. of		
Ordnance		

Surveyor-	C. R. Fox	8 Jul 46
Gen.		
Clerk	G. Anson	8 Jul 46
Store-	Sir T. Hastings	
keeper		contd. in office

[1] By Act of Parliament (1 Aug 51) the 1st Commissioner of the old Board of Woods, Forests and Land Revenues was to be 1st Commissioner of the new Board of Works and Public Buildings.

WHIG GOVERNMENT, 1846–1852 *(contd.)*

MINISTERS NOT IN CABINET		JUNIOR MINISTERS ATTACHED	

Paym.-Gen.   (*office in cabinet*)

EARL GRANVILLE   8 May 48
(*office in cabinet Oct* 51)
LD STANLEY OF ALDERLEY
          12 Feb 52

Poor Law	C. BULLER	23 Jul 47	*P.S.*	Vt Ebrington	23 Jul 47
Bd	M. T. BAINES	1 Jan 49		R. W. Grey	28 Jan 51

Sec. at War F. MAULE   6 Jul 46
        R. V. SMITH   6 Feb 52

1st Comm.   (*office in cabinet*)
Woods   LD SEYMOUR
          17 Apr 49–1 Aug 51

1st C.   LD SEYMOUR   1 Aug 51
Works   (*office in cabinet Oct* 51)

Law Officers: *Junior Lds of Treasury:*

Att.-Gen.	SIR T. WILDE	7 Jul 46
	SIR J. JERVIS	17 Jul 46
	SIR J. ROMILLY	11 Jul 50
	SIR A. COCKBURN	28 Mar 51

Vt Ebrington
          6 Jul 46–22 Dec 47

Sol.-Gen.	J. JERVIS	7 Jul 46
	SIR D. DUNDAS	18 Jul 46
	SIR J. ROMILLY	4 Apr 48
	SIR A. COCKBURN	11 Jul 50
	SIR W. PAGE WOOD	
		28 Mar 51

The O'Conor Don
          6 Jul 46–2 Aug 47
(Sir) W. G. Craig
          6 Jul 46–21 Feb 52
H. Rich   6 Jul 46–21 Feb 52
R. M. Bellew
          2 Aug 47–21 Feb 52
E of Shelburne
          22 Dec 47–Aug 48[1]

Judge	C. BULLER	8 Jul 46
Advoc. Gen.	W. G. HAYTER	22 Dec 47
	SIR D. DUNDAS	26 May 49

Ld Advoc.	A. RUTHERFURD	6 Jul 46
	J. MONTCREIFF	7 Apr 51

Sol.-Gen.	T. MAITLAND	6 Jul 46
Scotland	J. MONTCREIFF	7 Feb 50
	J. COWAN	18 Apr 51
	G. DEAS	28 Jun 51

Att.-Gen.	R. MOORE	16 Jul 46
Ireland	J. H. MONAHAN	21 Dec 47
	J. HATCHELL	23 Sep 50

Sol.-Gen.	J. H. MONAHAN	16 Jul 46
Ireland	J. HATCHELL	24 Dec 47
	H. G. HUGHES	26 Sep 50

H.M. Household: *Lds in Waiting:*

Ld Steward	EARL FORTESCUE	8 Jul 46
	M OF WESTMINSTER	
		22 Mar 50

E of Morley
          24 Jul 46–21 Feb 52
E of Ducie
          24 Jul 46–1 Dec 47

[1] The number of Junior Lordships was reduced from four to three in 1848.

WHIG GOVERNMENT, 1846–1852 (contd.)

MINISTERS NOT IN CABINET

Ld Chamb.	EARL SPENCER	8 Jul 46
	M OF BREADALBANE	
		5 Sep 48
V. Chamb.	LD E. HOWARD	8 Jul 46
Master of Horse	D OF NORFOLK	11 Jul 46
Treas.	LD R. GROSVENOR	3 Aug 46
	LD M. HILL	23 Jul 47
Comptr.	LD M. HILL	6 Jul 46
	W. S. LASCELLES	23 Jul 47
	E OF MULGRAVE	23 Jul 51
Capt. Gents at Arms	LD FOLEY	24 Jul 46
Capt. Yeomen of Guard	VT FALKLAND	24 Jul 46
	M OF DONEGAL	11 Feb 48
Master of Buckhounds	EARL GRANVILLE	9 Jul 46
	E OF BESSBOROUGH	
		16 May 48
Chief Equerry & Clerk Marshal	LD A. PAGET	7 Jul 46
Mistress of Robes	DUCH OF SUTHERLAND	
		4 Jul 46

Lds in Waiting (contd.):

Ld Waterpark
     24 Jul 46–21 Feb 52
Ld Camoys
     4 Aug 46–21 Feb 52
E of Listowel
     4 Aug 46–21 Feb 52
E of Morton
     10 Sep 41–26 Jun 49
M of Ormonde
     10 Sep 41–21 Feb 52
Ld Elphinstone
     1 Dec 47–21 Feb 52
Ld Dufferin & Clandeboye
     26 Jun 49–21 Feb 52

CONSERVATIVE GOVERNMENT, 1852

MINISTERS IN CABINET

P.M.	**E of Derby**	
	23 Feb 52–17 Dec 52	
Ld Chanc.	**Ld St Leonards**	27 Feb 52
Ld Pres.	**E of Lonsdale**	27 Feb 52
Privy S.	**M of Salisbury**	27 Feb 52
Home O.	**S. Walpole**	27 Feb 52
For. O.	**E of Malmesbury**	27 Feb 52
War & Cols	**Sir J. Pakington**	27 Feb 52
Exch.	**B. Disraeli**	27 Feb 52
Admir.	**D of Northumberland**	
		28 Feb 52
Bd Control	**J. C. Herries**	28 Feb 52
Postm.-Gen.	**E of Hardwicke**	1 Mar 52

JUNIOR MINISTERS ATTACHED

P.S. to Treasury:		
	W. F. Mackenzie	2 Mar 52
U-S.	Sir W. Jolliffe	27 Feb 52
U-S.	Ld Stanley	18 May 52
U-S.	Earl Desart	2 Mar 52
F.S. to Treasury:		
	G. A. Hamilton	2 Mar 52
1st Sec.	A. Stafford	3 Mar 52
Civil Ld	A. Duncombe	28 Feb 52
Jt Secs	H. J. Baillie	
	1 Mar 52–17 Dec 52	
	C. Bruce 1 Mar 52–17 Dec 52	

CONSERVATIVE GOVERNMENT, 1852 (contd.)

MINISTERS IN CABINET			JUNIOR MINISTERS ATTACHED		
B.o.T.	**J. W. Henley**	27 Feb 52	*V. Pres.*	Ld Colchester	27 Feb 52
1st C. Works	**Ld J. Manners**	4 Mar 52			

MINISTERS NOT IN CABINET			JUNIOR MINISTERS ATTACHED		
Chief Sec. Ireland	LD NAAS	1 Mar 52			
Ld Lieut. Ireland	E OF EGLINTON	1 Mar 52			
D. Lanc.	R. A. CHRISTOPHER	1 Mar 52			
Master-Gen. of Ordnance	VT HARDINGE	5 Mar 52	*Surveyor-Gen.*	Sir G. H. Berkeley	18 Jun 52
	LD F. SOMERSET	30 Sep 52	*Clerk*	F. Dunne	5 Mar 52
	(1*st Ld Raglan* 1852)		*Store-keeper*	Sir T. Hastings contd. in office	
Paym.-Gen.	LD COLCHESTER	28 Feb 52			
Poor Law Bd	SIR J. TROLLOPE	1 Mar 52	*P.S.*	F. W. Knight	3 Mar 52
Sec. at War	W. BERESFORD	28 Feb 52			
Law Officers:			*Junior Lds of Treasury:*		
Att.-Gen.	SIR F. THESIGER	27 Feb 52	M of Chandos		
Sol.-Gen.	SIR F. KELLY	27 Feb 52		28 Feb 52–17 Dec 52	
Judge Advoc. Gen.	G. BANKES	28 Feb 52	Ld H. Gordon-Lennox		
Ld Advoc.	A. ANDERSON	28 Feb 52		28 Feb 52–17 Dec 52	
	J. INGLIS	19 May 52	T. Bateson		
Sol.-Gen. Scotland	J. INGLIS	28 Feb 52		28 Feb 52–17 Dec 52	
	C. NEAVES	24 May 52			
Att.-Gen. Ireland	J. NAPIER	Feb 52			
Sol.-Gen. Ireland	J. WHITESIDE	Feb 52			
H.M. Household:			*Lds in Waiting:*		
Ld Steward	D OF MONTROSE	27 Feb 52	E of Morton		
Ld Chamb.	M OF EXETER	27 Feb 52		2 Mar 52–17 Dec 52	
V. Chamb.	VT NEWPORT	5 Mar 52	E of Verulam		
Master of Horse	E OF JERSEY	1 Mar 52		2 Mar 52–17 Dec 52	
			Vt Hawarden		
Treas.	LD C. HAMILTON	27 Feb 52		2 Mar 52–17 Dec 52	
Comptr.	G. FORESTER	27 Feb 52	Vt Galway		
Capt. Gents at Arms	E OF SANDWICH	27 Feb 52		2 Mar 52–17 Dec 52	
			Ld Crofton		
Capt. Yeomen of Guard	LD DE ROS	27 Feb 52		2 Mar 52–17 Dec 52	
			Ld Polwarth		
				2 Mar 52–17 Dec 52	
			Earl Talbot		
				2 Mar 52–17 Dec 52	

CONSERVATIVE GOVERNMENT, 1852 (contd.)

MINISTERS IN CABINET

Master of Buckhounds	E OF ROSSLYN	28 Feb 52
Chief Equerry & Clerk Marshal	LD COLVILLE OF CULROSSE	28 Feb 52
Mistress of Robes	DUCH OF ATHOLL	16 Mar 52

ABERDEEN COALITION, 1852–1855

MINISTERS IN CABINET			JUNIOR MINISTERS ATTACHED		
P.M.	**E of Aberdeen**	19 Dec 52–30 Jan 55	*P.S. to Treasury:* W. G. Hayter		5 Jan 53
Ld Chanc.	**Ld Cranworth**	28 Dec 52			
Ld Pres.	**Earl Granville**	28 Dec 52			
	Ld J. Russell	12 Jun 54			
Privy S.	**D of Argyll**	4 Jan 53			
Home O.	**Vt Palmerston**	28 Dec 52	*U-S.*	H. Fitzroy	28 Dec 52
For. O.	**Ld J. Russell**	28 Dec 52	*U-S.*	Ld Wodehouse	28 Dec 52
	E of Clarendon	21 Feb 53			
War & Cols[1]	**D of Newcastle**	28 Dec 52	*U-S.*	F. Peel	28 Dec 52
War O.	**D of Newcastle**	12 Jun 54	*U-S.*	H. Roberts	12 Jun 54
Col. O.	**Sir G. Grey**	12 Jun 54	*U-S.*	F. Peel	12 Jun 54
			F.S. to Treasury:	J. Wilson	5 Jan 53
Exch.	**W. E. Gladstone**	30 Dec 52			
Admir.	**Sir J. Graham**	30 Dec 52	*1st Sec.*	R. Bernal Osborne	6 Jan 53
			Civil Ld	W. F. Cowper	30 Dec 52
Bd Control	**Sir C. Wood**	30 Dec 52	*Jt Secs*	R. Lowe	30 Dec 52
				T. Redington (*perm.*)	30 Dec 52
D. Lanc.	(*office not in cabinet*) **Earl Granville**	21 Jun 54			
Min. without Portfolio	**M of Lansdowne** 28 Dec 52–21 Feb 58 **Ld J. Russell** 26 Feb 53–8 Jun 54				
Sec. at War	**S. Herbert**	30 Dec 52			
1st C. Works	**Sir W. Molesworth**	5 Jan 53			

MINISTERS NOT IN CABINET			JUNIOR MINISTERS ATTACHED
Bd Health	SIR B. HALL	14 Aug 54	
Chief Sec. Ireland	SIR J. YOUNG	6 Jan 53	

[1] War & Colonies were separated 10 Jun 54.

ABERDEEN COALITION, 1852–1855 (*contd.*)

MINISTERS NOT IN CABINET

Ld Lieut. Ireland	E OF ST GERMANS	5 Jan 53
D Lanc.	E. STRUTT	3 Jan 53
	(*Earl Granville* 21 *Jun* 54)	
	(*office in cabinet*)	
Master- Gen. of Ordnance	LD RAGLAN	contd. in office
Paym.-Gen.	LD STANLEY OF ALDERLEY	5 Jan 53
Postm.-Gen.	VT CANNING	5 Jan 53
Poor Law Bd	M. T. BAINES	30 Dec 52
B.o.T.	E. CARDWELL	28 Dec 52

Law Officers:

Att.-Gen.	SIR A. COCKBURN	28 Dec 52
Sol.-Gen.	SIR R. BETHELL	28 Dec 52
Judge Advoc. Gen.	C. P. VILLIERS	30 Dec 52
Ld Advoc.	J. MONTCREIFF	30 Dec 52
Sol.-Gen. Scotland	R. HANDYSIDE	17 Jan 53
	J. CRAUFURD	16 Nov 53
	T. MACKENZIE	11 Jan 55
Att.-Gen. Ireland	A. BREWSTER	Apr 53
Sol.-Gen. Ireland	W. KEOGH	Apr 53

H.M. Household:

Ld Steward	D OF NORFOLK	4 Jan 53
	EARL SPENCER	10 Jan 54
Ld Chamb.	M OF BREADALBANE	15 Jan 53
V. Chamb.	LD E. BRUCE	30 Dec 52
Master of Horse	D OF WELLINGTON	21 Jan 53
Treas.	E OF MULGRAVE	4 Jan 53
Comptr.	VT DRUMLANRIG	4 Jan 53
Capt. Gents at Arms	LD FOLEY	30 Dec 52
Capt. Yeomen of Guard	VT SYDNEY	30 Dec 52
Master of Buckhounds	E OF BESSBOROUGH	30 Dec 52

JUNIOR MINISTERS ATTACHED

Surveyor- Gen.	L. Maule	5 Jan 53
Clerk	W. Monsell	13 Jan 53
Store- keeper	Sir T. Hastings	contd. in office
P.S.	G. C. Berkeley	7 Jan 53
V. Pres.	Ld Stanley of Alderley	4 Jan 53

Junior Lds of Treasury:

Ld A. Hervey
    1 Jan 53–7 Mar 55
Ld Elcho 1 Jan 53–7 Mar 55
J. Sadleir
    1 Jan 53–6 Mar 54
C. S. Fortescue
    6 Mar 54–16 Apr 55

Lds in Waiting:

M of Ormonde
    11 Jan 53–25 Sep 54
Earl Somers
    13 Jan 53–22 Feb 57
Ld Camoys
    13 Jan 53–21 Feb 58
Ld Elphinstone
    13 Jan 53–1 Oct 53
Ld Rivers
    13 Jan 53–21 Feb 58
Ld Waterpark
    13 Jan 53–21 Feb 58
Ld de Tabley
    13 Jan 53–21 Feb 58
E of Listowel
    1 Oct 53–4 Feb 56
Ld Dufferin & Clandeboye
    28 Nov 54–21 Feb 58

ABERDEEN COALITION, 1852–1855 (contd.)

MINISTERS NOT IN CABINET

Chief	LD A. PAGET	30 Dec 52
Equerry		
& Clerk		
Marshal		
Mistress	DUCH OF SUTHERLAND	
of Robes		15 Jan 53

PALMERSTON GOVERNMENT, 1855–1858

MINISTERS IN CABINET   JUNIOR MINISTERS ATTACHED

P.M.	**Vt Palmerston**		*P.S. to Treasury:*		
	6 Feb 55–21 Feb 58			W. G. Hayter	contd. in office
Ld Chanc.	**Ld Cranworth**				
	contd. in office				
Ld Pres.	**Earl Granville**	8 Feb 55			
Privy S.	**D of Argyll** contd. in office				
	E of Harrowby	7 Dec 55			
	M of Clanricarde	3 Feb 58			
Home O.	**Sir G. Grey**	8 Feb 55	*U-S.*	H. Fitzroy	contd. in office
				W. F. Cowper	16 Feb 55
				W. Massey	13 Aug 55
For. O.	**E of Clarendon**		*U-S.*	Ld Wodehouse	
	contd. in office				contd. in office
				E of Shelburne	5 Jul 56
War O.	**Ld Panmure**	8 Feb 55	*U-S.*	F. Peel	
				Sir J. Ramsden	
Col. O.	**S. Herbert**	8 Feb 55	*U-S.*	J. Ball	8 Feb 55
	Ld J. Russell	23 Feb 55		C. S. Fortescue	Jun 57
	Sir W. Molesworth	21 Jul 55			
	H. Labouchere	21 Nov 55			
Exch.	**W. E. Gladstone**		*F.S. to Treasury:*		
	contd. in office			J. Wilson	contd. in office
	Sir G. C. Lewis	5 Mar 55			
Admir.	**Sir J. Graham**		*1st Sec.*	R. Bernal Osborne	
	contd. in office				contd. in office
	Sir C. Wood	13 Mar 55	*Civil Ld*	Sir R. Peel	13 Mar 55
				T. G. Baring	27 May 57
Bd Control	**Sir C. Wood** contd. in office		*Jt Sec.*	H. D. Seymour	3 Apr 55
	R. V. Smith	3 Mar 55			
D. Lanc.	(*vacant*)				
	E of Harrowby	31 Mar 55			
	M. T. Baines	7 Dec 55			
Min.	**M of Lansdowne**				
without	28 Dec 52–21 Feb 58				
Portfolio					
Postm.-Gen.	**Vt Canning** contd. in office				
	D of Argyll	30 Nov 55			

PALMERSTON GOVERNMENT, 1855–1858 (contd.)

MINISTERS IN CABINET	JUNIOR MINISTERS ATTACHED

B.o.T.　　　　(office not in cabinet)
　　　　　Ld Stanley of Alderley
　　　　　　　　　27 Nov 55

V. Pres.　Ld Stanley of Alderley
　　　　　　　　contd. in office
　　　　E. P. Bouverie　　31 Mar 55
　　　　R. Lowe　　　　　13 Aug 55

1st C.　**Sir W. Molesworth**
Works　　　　　contd. in office
　　　(Sir B. Hall　21 Jul 55)
　　　(office not in cabinet)

MINISTERS NOT IN CABINET	JUNIOR MINISTERS ATTACHED

Educ.　　W. F. COWPER　　　5 Feb 57
Bd Health　SIR B. HALL　contd. in office
　　　　W. F. COWPER　　13 Aug 55
　　　　W. MONSELL　　　9 Feb 57
　　　　W. F. COWPER　　24 Sep 57

Chief Sec.　SIR J. YOUNG
Ireland　　　　contd. in office
　　　　E. HORSMAN　　　1 Mar 55
　　　　H. A. HERBERT　　27 May 57

Ld Lieut.　E OF CARLISLE　　7 Mar 55
Ireland

Master-　LD RAGLAN　contd. in office
Gen. of　　　(office abolished
Ordnance　　　25 May 55[1])

Surveyor-　L. Maule　　contd. in office
Gen.[1]

Clerk　　W. Monsell　contd. in office
Store-　　Sir T. Hastings
keeper[1]　　　　contd. in office

Paym.-Gen.　LD STANLEY OF ALDERLEY
　　　　　　contd. in office
　　　　E. P. BOUVERIE　　31 Mar 55
　　　　R. LOWE　　　　28 Aug 55

Poor Law　M. T. BAINES
Bd　　　　　contd. in office
　　　　E. P. BOUVERIE　　13 Aug 55

P.S.　　G. C. Berkeley
　　　　　　contd. in office
　　　　R. W. Grey　　　9 May 56
　　　　(for Junior Ministers see above)

B.o.T.　　E. CARDWELL
　　　　　　contd. in office
　　　　LD STANLEY OF ALDERLEY
　　　　　　　31 Mar 55
　　　(office in cabinet　27 Nov 55)

1st C.　　(office in cabinet)
Works　SIR B. HALL　　21 Jul 55

Law Officers:
Att.-Gen.　SIR A. COCKBURN
　　　　　　contd. in office
　　　SIR R. BETHELL　　15 Nov 56

Junior Lds of Treasury:
　Ld A. Hervey
　　　　　　1 Jan 53–7 Mar 55
　Ld Elcho
　　　　　　1 Jan 53–7 Mar 55

[1]The Letters Patent of the Master Gen., Surveyor Gen. and Storekeeper of the Ordnance were revoked 25 May 55 and the duties of the Board were vested in the Secretary of State for War. The Clerkship of the Ordnance was abolished 1857.

PALMERSTON GOVERNMENT, 1855–1858 *(contd.)*

MINISTERS NOT IN CABINET		JUNIOR MINISTERS ATTACHED
Sol.-Gen.	SIR R. BETHELL	C. S. Fortescue
	contd in office	6 Mar 54–16 Apr 55
	J. S. WORTLEY 22 Nov 56	Vt Monck
	SIR H. KEATING 28 May 57	7 Mar 55–21 Feb 58
Judge	C. P. VILLIERS	Vt Duncan
Advoc. Gen.	contd. in office	7 Mar 55–21 Feb 58
Ld Advoc.	J. MONTCREIFF	H. B. Brand
	contd. in office	16 Apr 55–21 Feb 58
Sol.-Gen.	E. F. MAITLAND 14 Feb 55	
Scotland		
Att.-Gen.	A. BREWSTER	
Ireland	contd. in office	
	W. KEOGH Mar 55	
	J. D. FITZGERALD Mar 56	
Sol.-Gen.	W. KEOGH contd. in office	
Ireland	J. D. FITZGERALD Mar 55	
	J. CHRISTIAN Mar 56	

H.M. Household:		*Lds in Waiting:*
Ld Steward	EARL SPENCER	Earl Somers
	contd. in office	13 Jan 53–22 Feb 57
	E OF ST GERMANS 23 Nov 57	Ld Camoys
Ld Chamb.	M OF BREADALBANE	13 Jan 53–21 Feb 58
	contd. in office	Ld Rivers
V. Chamb.	LD E. BRUCE contd. in office	13 Jan 53–21 Feb 58
Master of	D OF WELLINGTON	Ld Waterpark
Horse	contd. in office	13 Jan 53–21 Feb 58
Treas.	E OF MULGRAVE	Ld de Tabley
	contd. in office	13 Jan 53–21 Feb 58
Comptr.	VT DRUMLANRIG	E of Listowel
	contd. in office	1 Oct 53–4 Feb 56
	VT CASTLEROSSE	Ld Dufferin & Clandeboye
	25 Jul 56	28 Nov 54–21 Feb 58
Capt. Gents	LD FOLEY	E of Caithness
at Arms	contd. in office	15 Apr 56–21 Feb 58
Capt.	VT SYDNEY	Ld Cremorne
Yeomen	contd. in office	22 Feb 57–21 Feb 58
of Guard		
Master of	E OF BESSBOROUGH	
Buckhounds	contd. in office	
Chief	LD A. PAGET	
Equerry	contd. in office	
& Clerk		
Marshal		
Mistress	DUCH OF SUTHERLAND	
of Robes	contd. in office	

CONSERVATIVE GOVERNMENT, 1858–1859

MINISTERS IN CABINET			JUNIOR MINISTERS ATTACHED		
P.M.	E of Derby		P.S. to Treasury:		
		21 Feb 58–11 Jun 59		Sir W. Jolliffe	2 Mar 58
Ld Chanc.	Ld Chelmsford	26 Feb 58			
Ld Pres.	M of Salisbury	26 Feb 58			
Privy S.	E of Hardwicke	26 Feb 58			
Home O.	S. Walpole	26 Feb 58	U-S.	G. Hardy	26 Feb 58
	T. H. S. Sotheron Estcourt				
		3 Mar 59			
For. O.	E of Malmesbury	26 Feb 58	U-S.	W. V. Fitzgerald	26 Feb 58
War O.	J. Peel	26 Feb 58	U-S.	Vt Hardinge	8 Mar 58
				E of Rosslyn	3 Mar 59
Col. O.	Ld Stanley	26 Feb 58	U-S.	E of Carnarvon	26 Feb 58
	Sir E. Bulwer-Lytton				
		5 Jun 58			
India O.	Ld Stanley	2 Sep 58	U-S.	H. J. Baillie	30 Sep 58
Exch.	B. Disraeli	26 Feb 58	F.S. to Treasury:		
				G. W. Hamilton	2 Mar 58
				Sir S. Northcote	21 Jan 59
Admir.	Sir J. Pakington	8 Mar 58	1st Sec.	H. T. L. Corry	9 Mar 58
			Civil Ld	Ld Lovaine	8 Mar 58
				F. Lygon	9 Mar 59
Bd	E of Ellenborough	6 Mar 58	Jt Sec.	H. J. Baillie	6 Mar 58
Control[1]	Ld Stanley	5 Jun 58			
B.o.T.	J. W. Henley	26 Feb 58	V. Pres.	E. of Donoughmore	6 Apr 58
	E of Donoughmore	3 Mar 59		Ld Lovaine	3 Mar 59
1st C. Works	Ld J. Manners	26 Feb 58			

· MINISTERS NOT IN CABINET			JUNIOR MINISTERS ATTACHED		
Educ.	C. B. ADDERLEY	12 Mar 58			
Bd Health[2]	C. B. ADDERLEY	8 Mar 58			
Chief Sec. Ireland	LD NAAS	4 Mar 58			
Ld Lieut. Ireland	E OF EGLINTON	8 Mar 58			
D. Lanc.	D OF MONTROSE	26 Feb 58			
Paym.-Gen.	E OF DONOUGHMORE				
		6 Apr 58			
	LD LOVAINE	3 Mar 59			
Poor Law Bd	T. H. S. SOTHERON ESTCOURT	6 Mar 58	P.S.	F. W. Knight	12 Mar 58
	E OF MARCH	7 Mar 59			
Postm.-Gen.	LD COLCHESTER	13 Mar 58			

[1]Bd of Control was abolished 2 Aug 58.
[2]Bd Health was abolished 1858.

CONSERVATIVE GOVERNMENT, 1858–1859 (contd.)

MINISTERS NOT IN CABINET

Law Officers:

Att.-Gen.	SIR F. KELLY	26 Feb 58
Sol.-Gen.	SIR H. CAIRNS	26 Feb 58
Judge Advoc. Gen.	J. R. MOWBRAY	13 Mar 58
Ld Advoc.	J. INGLIS	1 Mar 58
	C. BAILLIE	10 Jul 58
	D. MURE	15 Apr 59
Sol.-Gen. Scotland	C. BAILLIE	17 Mar 58
	D. MURE	12 Jul 58
	G. PATTON	3 May 59
Att.-Gen. Ireland	J. WHITESIDE	Feb 58
Sol.-Gen. Ireland	H. G. HUGHES	Feb 58
	E. HAYES	1859

H.M. Household:

Ld Steward	M OF EXETER	26 Feb 58
Ld Chamb.	EARL DE LA WARR	26 Feb 58
V. Chamb.	VT NEWPORT	26 Feb 58
Master of Horse	D OF BEAUFORT	26 Feb 58
Treas.	LD C. HAMILTON	26 Feb 58
Comptr.	G. FORESTER	26 Feb 58
Capt. Gents at Arms	EARL TALBOT	26 Feb 58
Capt. Yeomen of Guard	LD DE ROS	17 Mar 58
Master of Buckhounds	E OF SANDWICH	26 Feb 58
Chief Equerry & Clerk Marshal	LD COLVILLE OF CULROSSE	26 Feb 58
Mistress of Robes	DUCH OF MANCHESTER	26 Feb 58

JUNIOR MINISTERS ATTACHED

Junior Lds of Treasury:

Ld H. Gordon-Lennox
                1 Mar 58–14 Mar 59
T. Taylor
                1 Mar 58–11 Jun 59
H. Whitmore
                1 Mar 58–11 Jun 59
P. Blackburn
                15 Mar 59–11 Jun 59

Lds in Waiting:

E of Verulam
                26 Feb 58–11 Jun 59
E of Sheffield
                26 Feb 58–11 Jun 59
Vt Strathallan
                26 Feb 58–11 Jun 59
Ld Polwarth
                26 Feb 58–11 Jun 59
Ld Crofton
                26 Feb 58–11 Jun 59
Ld Bateman
                26 Feb 58–11 Jun 59
Ld Raglan
                26 Feb 58–11 Jun 59

LIBERAL GOVERNMENT, 1859–1866

MINISTERS IN CABINET

P.M.	**Vt Palmerston**	
	12 Jun 59–18 Oct 65	
	Earl Russell	
	29 Oct 65–26 Jun 66	
Ld Chanc.	**Ld Campbell**	18 Jun 59

JUNIOR MINISTERS ATTACHED

P.S. to Treasury:

H. B. Brand   24 Jun 59

LIBERAL GOVERNMENT, 1859–1866 (contd.)

MINISTERS IN CABINET			JUNIOR MINISTERS ATTACHED		
	Ld Westbury	26 Jun 61			
	Ld Cranworth	7 Jul 65			
Ld Pres.	**Earl Granville**	18 Jun 59			
Privy S.	**D of Argyll**	18 Jun 59			
Home O.	**Sir G. C. Lewis**	18 Jun 59	*U-S.*	G. Clive	18 Jun 59
	Sir G. Grey	25 Jul 61		H. A. Bruce	14 Nov 62
				T. G. Baring	25 Apr 64
				E. Knatchbull-Hugessen	
					25 May 66
For. O.	**Ld J. Russell (E)**	18 Jun 59	*U-S.*	Ld Wodehouse	19 Jun 59
	E of Clarendon	3 Nov 65		A. H. Layard	15 Aug 61
War O.	**S. Herbert (Ld)**	18 Jun 59	*U-S.*	Earl de Grey & Ripon	
	Sir G. C. Lewis	22 Jul 61			18 Jun 59
	Earl de Grey & Ripon			T. G. Baring	21 Jan 61
		28 Apr 63		Earl de Grey & Ripon	
	M of Hartington	16 Feb 66			31 Jul 61
				M of Hartington	28 Apr 63
				Ld Dufferin	17 Feb 66
Col. O.	**D of Newcastle**	18 Jun 59	*U-S.*	C. S. Fortescue	18 Jun 59
	E. Cardwell	7 Apr 64		W. E. Forster	25 Nov 65
India O.	**Sir C. Wood**	18 Jun 59	*U-S.*	T. G. Baring	25 Jun 59
	Earl de Grey & Ripon			Earl de Grey & Ripon	
		16 Feb 66			21 Jan 61
				T. G. Baring	31 Jul 61
				Ld Wodehouse	25 Apr 64
				Ld Dufferin	16 Nov 64
				J. Stansfeld	17 Feb 66
Exch.	**W. E. Gladstone**	18 Jun 59	*F.S. to Treasury:*		
				S. Laing	24 Jun 59
				F. Peel	2 Nov 60
				H. C. E. Childers	19 Aug 65
Admir.	**D of Somerset**	27 Jun 59	*1st Sec.*	Ld C. Paget	30 Jun 59
				T. G. Baring	30 Apr 66
			Civil Ld	S. Whitbread	27 Jun 59
				M of Hartington	23 Mar 63
				J. Stansfeld	2 May 63
				H. C. E. Childers	21 Apr 64
				H. Fenwick	22 Jan 66
				Ld J. Hay	7 Apr 66
				G. Shaw-Lefevre	8 May 66
Chief Sec.	**E. Cardwell**	24 Jun 59			
Ireland	(*Sir R. Peel* 29 *Jul* 61)				
	(*office not in cabinet*)				
D. Lanc.	**Sir G. Grey**	22 Jun 59			
	E. Cardwell	25 Jul 61			
	E of Clarendon	7 Apr 64			
	(*vacant* 3 *Nov* 65)				
	G. J. Goschen	26 Jan 66			

LIBERAL GOVERNMENT, 1859–1866 (contd.)

MINISTERS IN CABINET			JUNIOR MINISTERS ATTACHED		
Poor Law	**T. M. Gibson**	24 Jun 59	*P.S.*	C. Gilpin	28 Jun 59
Bd	**C. P. Villiers**	9 Jul 59		G. Byng	22 Feb 65
Postm.-Gen.	**E of Elgin**	24 Jun 59			
	D of Argyll	11 May 60			
	Ld Stanley of Alderley				
		17 Aug 60			
B.o.T.	(*vacant*)		*V. Pres.*	J. Wilson	18 Jun 59
	T. M. Gibson	6 Jul 59		W. F. Cowper	12 Aug 59
				(Sir) W. Hutt	22 Feb 60
				G. J. Goschen	29 Nov 65
				W. Monsell	12 Mar 66

MINISTERS NOT IN CABINET			JUNIOR MINISTERS ATTACHED
Educ.	R. LOWE	24 Jun 59	
	H. A. BRUCE	26 Apr 64	
Chief Sec.	(*office in cabinet*)		
Ireland	SIR R. PEEL	29 Jul 61	
	C. S. FORTESCUE	7 Dec 65	
Ld Lieut.	E OF CARLISLE	24 Jun 59	
Ireland	LD WODEHOUSE	1 Nov 64	
Paym.-Gen.	J. WILSON	18 Jun 59	
	W. F. COWPER	12 Aug 59	
	(SIR) W. HUTT	22 Feb 60	
	G. J. GOSCHEN	29 Nov 65	
	W. MONSELL	12 Mar 66	
1st C.	H. FITZROY	18 Jun 59	
Works	W. F. COWPER	9 Feb 60	

Law Officers:			Junior Lds of Treasury:
Att.-Gen.	SIR R. BETHELL	18 Jun 59	E. Knatchbull-Hugessen
	SIR W. ATHERTON	4 Jul 61	24 Jun 59–21 Apr 65
	SIR R. PALMER	2 Oct 63	Sir W. Dunbar
Sol.-Gen.	SIR H. KEATING	18 Jun 59	24 Jun 59–21 Apr 65
	SIR W. ATHERTON	16 Dec 59	J. Bagwell
	SIR R. PALMER	8 Jul 61	24 Jun 59–25 Mar 62
	SIR R. COLLIER	2 Oct 63	L. White 25 Mar 62–2 Jun 66
Judge	T. HEADLAM	24 Jun 59	W. P. Adam
Advoc. Gen.			21 Apr 65–26 Jun 66
Ld Advoc.	J. MONTCREIFF	24 Jun 59	J. B. Carter
Sol.-Gen.	E. F. MAITLAND	27 Jun 59	2 Jun 66–26 Jun 66
Scotland	G. YOUNG	11 Nov 62	J. Esmonde
Att.-Gen.	J. D. FITZGERALD	Jun 59	2 Jun 66–26 Jun 66
Ireland	R. DEASY	Feb 60	
	T. O'HAGAN	1861	
	J. LAWSON	1865	
Sol.-Gen.	J. GEORGE	Jun 59	
Ireland	R. DEASY	1859	
	T. O'HAGAN	Feb 60	
	J. LAWSON	1861	
	E. SULLIVAN	1865	

LIBERAL GOVERNMENT, 1859–1866 *(contd.)*

MINISTERS NOT IN CABINET		
Ld Steward	E OF ST GERMANS	18 Jun 59
	E OF BESSBOROUGH	
		20 Jan 66
Ld Chamb.	VT SYDNEY	23 Jun 59
V. Chamb.	VT CASTLEROSSE	23 Jun 59
Master of Horse	M OF AILESBURY	24 Jun 59
Treas.	VT BURY	23 Jun 59
	LD O. FITZGERALD	8 May 66
Comptr.	LD PROBY	23 Jun 59
Capt. Gents at Arms	LD FOLEY	28 Jun 59
Capt. Yeomen of Guard	E OF DUCIE	28 Jun 59
Master of Buckhounds	E OF BESSBOROUGH	18 Jun 59
	E OF CORK	23 Jan 66
Chief Equerry & Clerk Marshal	LD A. PAGET	1 Jul 59
Mistress of Robes	DUCH OF SUTHERLAND	22 Jun 59
	DUCH OF WELLINGTON	25 Apr 61

Lds in Waiting:

E of Caithness
  23 Jun 59–26 Jun 66
Ld Camoys
  23 Jun 59–26 Jun 66
Ld Rivers
  23 Jun 59–28 Apr 66
Ld de Tabley
  23 Jun 59–26 Jun 66
Ld Cremorne
  23 Jun 59–26 Jun 66
Ld Methuen
  23 Jun 59–26 Jun 66
Vt Torrington
  23 Jun 59–27 Apr 84
  (perm.)
Ld Byron
  17 Jul 37–31 Mar 60
Ld Harris
  31 Mar 60–4 May 63
Ld Talbot de Malahide
  4 May 63–26 Jun 66
M of Normanby
  8 May 66–26 Jun 66

Extra Ld in Waiting:
Ld Byron
  31 Mar 60–3 Mar 68

CONSERVATIVE GOVERNMENT, 1866–1868

MINISTERS IN CABINET		
P.M.	**E of Derby**	
		28 Jun 66–25 Feb 68
	B. Disraeli	
		27 Feb 68–1 Dec 68
Ld Chanc.	**Ld Chelmsford**	6 Jul 66
	Ld Cairns	29 Feb 68
Ld Pres.	**D of Buckingham**	6 Jul 66
	D of Marlborough	8 Mar 67
Privy S.	**E of Malmesbury**	6 Jul 66
Home O.	**S. Walpole**	6 Jul 66
	G. Hardy	17 May 67
For. O.	**Ld Stanley**	6 Jul 66
War O.	**J. Peel**	6 Jul 66
	Sir J. Pakington	8 Mar 67

JUNIOR MINISTERS ATTACHED		
P.S. to Treasury:		
	T. E. Taylor	14 Jul 66
	G. J. Noel	11 Nov 68
U-S.	E of Belmore	10 Jul 66
	Sir J. Fergusson	1 Aug 67
	Sir M. Hicks Beach	10 Aug 68
U-S.	E. Egerton	6 Jul 66
U-S.	E of Longford	7 Jul 66

CONSERVATIVE GOVERNMENT, 1866–1868 (contd.)

MINISTERS IN CABINET			JUNIOR MINISTERS ATTACHED		
Col. O.	E of Carnarvon	6 Jul 66	U-S.	C. B. Adderley	6 Jul 66
	D of Buckingham	8 Mar 67			
India O.	Vt Cranborne	6 Jul 66	U-S.	Sir J. Fergusson	6 Jul 66
	Sir S. Northcote	8 Mar 67		Ld Clinton	31 Jul 67
Exch.	B. Disraeli	6 Jul 66	F.S. to Treasury:		
	G. W. Hunt	29 Feb 68		G. W. Hunt	14 Jul 66
				G. Sclater-Booth	4 Mar 68
Admir.	Sir J. Pakington	12 Jul 66	1st Sec.	Ld H. Gordon-Lennox	
	H. T. L. Corry	8 Mar 67			16 Jul 66
			Civil Ld	C. du Cane	12 Jul 66
				F. A. Stanley	29 Aug 68
Chief Sec.	Ld Naas	10 Jul 66			
Ireland	(J. Wilson-Patten 29 Sep 68)				
	(office not in cabinet)				
Poor Law	G. Hardy	12 Jul 66	P.S.	R. A. Earle	12 Jul 66
Bd	(E of Devon 21 May 67)			G. Sclater-Booth	1 Mar 67
	(office not in cabinet)			M. Hicks Beach	28 Feb 68
Min.	S. Walpole				
without	17 May 67–1 Dec 68				
Portfolio					
B.o.T.	Sir S. Northcote	6 Jul 66	V. Pres.[1]	S. Cave	10 Jul 66
	D of Richmond	8 Mar 67			
1st C.	Ld J. Manners	6 Jul 66			
Works					

MINISTERS NOT IN CABINET			JUNIOR MINISTERS ATTACHED
Educ.	H. T. L. CORRY	12 Jul 66	
	LD R. MONTAGU	19 Mar 67	
Chief Sec.	(office in cabinet)		
Ireland	J. WILSON-PATTEN 29 Sep 68		
Ld Lieut.	M OF ABERCORN	13 Jul 66	
Ireland			
D. Lanc.	E OF DEVON	10 Jul 66	
	J. WILSON-PATTEN	26 Jun 67	
	T. E. TAYLOR	7 Nov 68	
Paym.-Gen.	S. CAVE	10 Jul 66	
Poor Law	(office in cabinet)		(for Junior Ministers see above)
Bd	E OF DEVON	21 May 67	
Postm.-Gen.	D OF MONTROSE	19 Jul 66	
Law Officers:			Junior Lds of Treasury:
Att.-Gen.	SIR H. CAIRNS	10 Jul 66	G. Noel 12 Jul 66–2 Nov 68
	SIR J. ROLT	29 Oct 66	Sir G. G. Montgomery
	SIR J. KARSLAKE	18 Jul 67	12 Jul 66–1 Dec 68

[1]On 12 Aug 67 the office of V. Pres. of the B.o.T. was abolished and a Parl. Sec. was substituted "as from the next vacancy."

CONSERVATIVE GOVERNMENT, 1866–1868 (contd.)

MINISTERS NOT IN CABINET

Sol.-Gen.	SIR W. BOVILL	10 Jul 66
	SIR J. KARSLAKE	29 Nov 66
	SIR C. SELWYN	18 Jul 67
	SIR W. BRETT	10 Feb 68
	SIR R. BAGGALLAY	16 Sep 68
Judge Advoc. Gen.	J. R. MOWBRAY	12 Jul 66
Ld Advoc.	G. PATTON	12 Jul 66
	E. GORDON	28 Feb 67
Sol.-Gen. Scotland	E. GORDON	12 Jul 66
	J. MILLAR	6 Mar 67
Att.-Gen. Ireland	J. WALSH	25 Jul 66
	M. MORRIS	1 Nov 66
	H. CHATTERTON	1867
	R. WARREN	1867
	J. BALL	1868
Sol.-Gen. Ireland	M. MORRIS	3 Aug 66
	H. CHATTERTON	8 Nov 66
	R. WARREN	1867
	M. HARRISON	1867
	J. BALL	1868
	H. ORMSBY	1868

JUNIOR MINISTERS ATTACHED

H. Whitmore
 12 Jul 66–1 Dec 68
Ld. C. Hamilton
 2 Nov 68–1 Dec 68

H.M. Household:

Ld Steward	D OF MARLBOROUGH	
		10 Jul 66
	E OF TANKERVILLE	
		19 Mar 67
Ld Chamb.	E OF BRADFORD	10 Jul 66
V. Chamb.	LD C. HAMILTON	10 Jul 66
Master of Horse	D OF BEAUFORT	18 Jul 66
Treas.	LD BURGHLEY	10 Jul 66
	P. HERBERT	27 Feb 67
Comptr.	VT ROYSTON	10 Jul 66
Capt. Gents at Arms	E OF TANKERVILLE	10 Jul 66
	M OF EXETER	20 Mar 67
Capt. Yeomen of Guard	EARL CADOGAN	10 Jul 66
Master of Buckhounds	LD COLVILLE OF CULROSSE	
		10 Jul 66
Chief Equerry & Clerk Marshal[1]	LD A. PAGET	contd. in office
Mistress of Robes	DUCH OF WELLINGTON	contd. in office

Lds in Waiting:

Vt Strathallan
 13 Jul 66–1 Dec 68
Vt Hawarden
 13 Jul 66–1 Dec 68
Ld Bagot
 13 Jul 66–1 Dec 68
Ld Polwarth
 13 Jul 66–16 Aug 67
Ld Crofton
 13 Jul 66–1 Dec 68
Ld Skelmersdale
 13 Jul 66–1 Dec 68
Ld Raglan
 13 Jul 66–1 Dec 68
E of Haddington
 7 Sep 67–1 Dec 68

[1] From 1866 the office of Chief Equerry cannot be considered political. It was held by Ld A. Paget until 1892.

LIBERAL GOVERNMENT, 1868–1874

MINISTERS IN CABINET | JUNIOR MINISTERS ATTACHED

P.M.	**W. E. Gladstone**		*P.S. to Treasury:*		
		3 Dec 68–17 Feb 74[1]		G. G. Glyn	9 Dec 68
				A. W. Peel	1 Aug 73
Ld Chanc.	**Ld Hatherley**	9 Dec 68			
	Ld Selborne	15 Oct 72			
Ld Pres.	**Earl de Grey & Ripon (M)**				
		9 Dec 68			
	H. A. Bruce	9 Aug 73			
	(*1st Ld Aberdare* 1873)				
Privy S.	**E of Kimberley**	9 Dec 68			
	Vt Halifax	6 Jul 70			
Home O.	**H. A. Bruce**	9 Dec 68	*U-S.*	E. Knatchbull-Hugessen	
	R. Lowe	9 Aug 73			10 Dec 68
				G. J. Shaw-Lefevre	11 Jan 71
				H. Winterbotham	17 Mar 71
For. O.	**E of Clarendon**	9 Dec 68	*U-S.*	A. J. Otway	12 Dec 68
	Earl Granville	6 Jul 70		Vt Enfield	9 Jan 71
War O.	**E. Cardwell**	9 Dec 68	*U-S.*	Ld Northbrook	10 Dec 68
				M of Lansdowne	26 Apr 72
			F.S.	J. C. W. Vivian	5 Aug 70
				H. Campbell-Bannerman	
					15 Nov 71
			Surveyor-	Sir H. Storks	5 Aug 70
			Gen.		
			Ordnance		
Col. O.	**Earl Granville**	9 Dec 68	*U-S.*	W. Monsell	10 Dec 68
	E of Kimberley	6 Jul 70		E. Knatchbull-Hugessen	
					14 Jan 71
India O.	**D of Argyll**	9 Dec 68	*U-S.*	M. E. Grant Duff	10 Dec 68
Exch.	**R. Lowe**	9 Dec 68	*F.S. to Treasury:*		
	W. E. Gladstone	11 Aug 73		A. S. Ayrton	9 Dec 68
				J. Stansfeld	2 Nov 69
				W. E. Baxter	17 Mar 71
				J. G. Dodson	11 Aug 73
Admir.	**H. C. E. Childers**	9 Dec 68	*1st (P.)*	W. E. Baxter	18 Dec 68
	G. J. Goschen	24 Mar 71	*Sec.*	G. J. Shaw-Lefevre	17 Mar 71
			Civil Ld	G. O. Trevelyan	21 Dec 68
				E of Camperdown	11 Jul 70
Educ.	(*office not in cabinet*)				
	W. E. Forster	Jul 70			
Chief Sec.	**C. S. Fortescue**	16 Dec 68			
Ireland	**M of Hartington**	12 Jan 71			
D. Lanc.	(*office not in cabinet*)				
	H. C. E. Childers	9 Aug 72			
	J. Bright	30 Sep 73			

[1]The Government resigned 13 Mar 73, but resumed 19 Mar 73.

LIBERAL GOVERNMENT, 1868–1874 (*contd.*)

MINISTERS IN CABINET

JUNIOR MINISTERS ATTACHED

Loc. Govt Bd	**J. Stansfeld**	19 Aug 71	*P.S.*	J. Hibbert	19 Aug 71
Poor Law Bd[1]	**G. J. Goschen**	9 Dec 68	*P.S.*	A. W. Peel	
	J. Stansfeld	24 Mar 71		10 Dec 68–14 Aug 71	
Postm.-Gen.	**M of Hartington**	9 Dec 68			
	(*W. Monsell* 14 *Jan* 71)				
	(*office not in cabinet*)				
B.o.T.	**J. Bright**	9 Dec 68	*P.S.*	G. J. Shaw-Lefevre	9 Dec 68
	C. S. Fortescue	14 Jan 71		A. W. Peel	14 Jan 71

MINISTERS NOT IN CABINET

JUNIOR MINISTERS ATTACHED

Educ.	W. E. FORSTER	9 Dec 68
	(*office in cabinet Jul* 70)	
Ld Lieut. Ireland	EARL SPENCER	18 Dec 68
D. Lanc.	LD DUFFERIN (E)	12 Dec 68
	(*H. C. E. Childers*	
	9 *Aug* 72)	
	(*office in cabinet*)	
Paym.-Gen.	LD DUFFERIN	12 Dec 68
	H. C. E. CHILDERS	9 Aug 72
	W. P. ADAM	30 Sep 73
Postm.-Gen.	(*office in cabinet*)	
	W. MONSELL	14 Jan 71
	L. PLAYFAIR	18 Nov 73
1st C. Works	A. H. LAYARD	9 Dec 68
	A. S. AYRTON	26 Oct 69
	W. P. ADAM	11 Aug 73

Law Officers:

Att.-Gen.	SIR R. COLLIER	12 Dec 68
	SIR J. COLERIDGE	10 Nov 71
	SIR H. JAMES	20 Nov 73
Sol.-Gen.	SIR J. COLERIDGE	12 Dec 68
	SIR G. JESSEL	10 Nov 71
	SIR H. JAMES	26 Sep 73
	SIR W. V. HARCOURT	
		20 Nov 73
Judge Advoc. Gen.	SIR C. O'LOGHLEN	16 Dec 68
	J. DAVISON	28 Dec 70
	SIR R. PHILLIMORE	
		17 May 71
	A. S. AYRTON	21 Aug 73
Ld Advoc.	J. MONTCREIFF	10 Dec 68
	G. YOUNG	14 Oct 69
Sol.-Gen. Scotland	G. YOUNG	14 Dec 68
	A. CLARK	14 Oct 69

Junior Lds of Treasury:

J. Stansfeld
16 Dec 68–2 Nov 69
M of Lansdowne
16 Dec 68–25 Apr 72
W. P. Adam
16 Dec 68–8 Aug 73
J. C. W. Vivian
16 Dec 68–4 Aug 70
W. H. Gladstone
2 Nov 69–17 Feb 74
Ld F. Cavendish
8 Aug 73–17 Feb 74
A. F. Greville
8 Aug 73–17 Feb 74

[1] Poor Law Bd became Local Govt Bd, 14 Aug 71.

LIBERAL GOVERNMENT, 1868–1874 (*contd.*)

MINISTERS NOT IN CABINET			JUNIOR MINISTERS ATTACHED
Att.-Gen.	E. SULLIVAN	12 Dec 68	
Ireland	C. BARRY	26 Jan 70	
	R. DOWSE	13 Jan 72	
	C. PALLES	5 Nov 72	
Sol.-Gen.	C. BARRY	12 Dec 68	
Ireland	R. DOWSE	14 Feb 70	
	C. PALLES	6 Feb 72	
	H. LAW	18 Nov 72	

H.M. Household:

Lds in Waiting:

Ld Steward	E OF BESSBOROUGH		M of Normanby
		12 Dec 68	17 Dec 68–27 Dec 69
Ld Chamb.	VT SYDNEY	9 Dec 68	E of Camperdown
V. Chamb.	VT CASTLEROSSE	12 Dec 68	17 Dec 68–11 Jul 70
	(*4th E of Kenmare* 1871)		Ld Camoys
	LD R. GROSVENOR	25 Feb 72	17 Dec 68–17 Feb 74
Master of	M OF AILESBURY	12 Dec 68	Ld Suffield
Horse			17 Dec 68–25 Feb 72
Treas.	LD DE TABLEY	12 Dec 68	Ld Methuen
	LD POLTIMORE	1 Mar 72	17 Dec 68–17 Feb 74
	LD MONSON	1 Jan 74	E of Morley
Comptr.	LD O. FITZGERALD	12 Dec 68	22 Dec 68–17 Feb 74
Capt. Gents	LD FOLEY	12 Dec 68	Ld Lurgan
at Arms	M OF NORMANBY	27 Dec 69	27 Jan 69–17 Feb 74
	EARL COWPER	20 Apr 71	Ld Wrottesley
	E OF ILCHESTER	1 Jan 74	27 Dec 69–17 Feb 74
Capt.	D OF ST ALBANS	22 Dec 68	M of Huntley
Yeomen			21 Jul 70–1 Mar 73
of Guard			E of Kenmare
Master of	E OF CORK	12 Dec 68	25 Feb 72–17 Feb 74
Buckhounds			E of Breadalbane
Mistress	DUCH OF ARGYLL	17 Dec 68	1 Mar 73–17 Feb 74
of Robes	DUCH OF SUTHERLAND		
		22 Jan 70	

CONSERVATIVE GOVERNMENT, 1874–1880

MINISTERS IN CABINET			JUNIOR MINISTERS ATTACHED
P.M.	**B. Disraeli**		*P.S. to Treasury:*
	20 Feb 74–21 Apr 80		W. H. Dyke	21 Feb 74
	(*1st E of Beaconsfield* 1876)		
Ld Chanc.	**Ld Cairns (E)**	21 Feb 74	
Ld Pres.	**D of Richmond**	21 Feb 74	
Privy S.	**E of Malmesbury**	21 Feb 74	
	B. Disraeli	12 Aug 76	
	(*1st E of Beaconsfield* 1876)		
	D of Northumberland		
		4 Feb 78	

CONSERVATIVE GOVERNMENT, 1874–1880 (contd.)

MINISTERS IN CABINET			JUNIOR MINISTERS ATTACHED		
Home O.	**R. A. Cross**	21 Feb 74	*U.-S.*	Sir H. Selwin-Ibbetson	
					25 Feb 74
				Sir M. White Ridley	6 Apr 78
For. O.	**E of Derby**	21 Feb 74	*U.-S.*	R. Bourke	23 Feb 74
	M of Salisbury	2 Apr 78			
War O.	**G. Hardy**	21 Feb 74	*U.-S.*	E of Pembroke	2 Mar 74
	F. A. Stanley	2 Apr 78		Earl Cadogan	24 May 75
				Vt Bury	4 Mar 78
			F.-S.	F. A. Stanley	26 Feb 74
				R. J. Loyd-Lindsay	13 Aug 77
			Surveyor-Gen. Ordnance	Ld E. Cecil	26 Feb 74
Col. O.	**E of Carnarvon**	21 Feb 74	*U.-S.*	J. Lowther	25 Feb 74
	Sir M. Hicks Beach	4 Feb 78		Earl Cadogan	2 Mar 78
India O.	**M of Salisbury**	21 Feb 74	*U.-S.*	Ld G. Hamilton	22 Feb 74
	Vt Cranbrook	2 Apr 78		E. Stanhope	6 Apr 78
Exch.	**Sir S. Northcote**	21 Feb 74	*F.S. to Treasury:*		
				W. H. Smith	21 Feb 74
				F. A. Stanley	14 Aug 77
				Sir H. Selwin-Ibbetson	
					2 Apr 78
Admir.	**G. W. Hunt**	21 Feb 74	*P.S.*	A. Egerton	21 Feb 74
	W. H. Smith	14 Aug 77	*Civil Ld*	Sir M. Lopes	4 Mar 74
Chief Sec. Ireland	(*office not in cabinet*)				
	Sir M. Hicks Beach				
		12 Aug 76			
	(*J. Lowther* 15 *Feb* 78)				
	(*office not in cabinet*)				
Postm.-Gen.	**Ld J. Manners**	21 Feb 74			
B.o.T.	(*office not in cabinet*)				
	Vt Sandon	4 Apr 78	*P.S.*	G. Bentinck	2 Mar 74
				E. Stanhope	18 Nov 75
				J. G. Talbot	4 Apr 78

MINISTERS NOT IN CABINET		
Educ.	Vt Sandon	2 Mar 74
	Ld G. Hamilton	4 Apr 78
Chief Sec. Ireland	Sir M. Hicks Beach	
		27 Feb 74
	(*office in cabinet* 12 *Aug* 76)	
	J. Lowther	15 Feb 78
Ld Lieut. Ireland	D of Abercorn	2 Mar 74
	D of Marlborough	
		11 Dec 76
D. Lanc.	T. E. Taylor	2 Mar 74

CONSERVATIVE GOVERNMENT, 1874–1880 *(contd.)*

MINISTERS NOT IN CABINET

Loc. Govt Bd	G. SCLATER-BOOTH	21 Feb 74
Paym.-Gen.	S. CAVE	20 Apr 74
	D. R. PLUNKET	24 Nov 75
B.o.T.	SIR C. B. ADDERLEY	21 Feb 74

(*Vt Sandon* 4 *Apr* 78)
(*office in cabinet*)

1st C. Works	LD H. GORDON-LENNOX	21 Mar 74
	G. J. NOEL	14 Aug 76

Law Officers:

Att.-Gen.	SIR J. KARSLAKE	27 Feb 74
	SIR R. BAGGALLAY	20 Apr 74
	SIR J. HOLKER	25 Nov 75
Sol.-Gen.	SIR R. BAGGALLAY	27 Feb 74
	SIR J. HOLKER	20 Apr 74
	SIR H. GIFFARD	25 Nov 75
Judge Advoc. Gen.	S. CAVE	7 Mar 74
	G. BENTINCK	24 Nov 75
	E. GORDON	26 Feb 74
	W. WATSON	13 Oct 76
Sol.-Gen. Scotland	J. MILLAR	4 Mar 74
	W. WATSON	21 Jul 74
	J. H. MACDONALD	5 Dec 76
Att.-Gen. Ireland	J. BALL	12 Mar 74
	H. ORMSBY	21 Jan 75
	C. MAY	27 Nov 75
	E. GIBSON	15 Feb 77
Sol.-Gen. Ireland	H. ORMSBY	12 Mar 74
	D. PLUNKETT	29 Jan 75
	G. FITZGIBBON	3 Mar 77
	H. HOLMES	14 Dec 78

H.M. Household:

Ld Steward	EARL BEAUCHAMP	21 Feb 74
Ld Chamb.	M OF HERTFORD	21 Feb 74
	E OF MT EDGCUMBE	7 May 79
V. Chamb.	VT BARRINGTON	2 Mar 74
Master of Horse	E OF BRADFORD	7 Mar 74
Treas.	EARL PERCY	2 Mar 74
	LD H. THYNNE	14 Dec 75
Comptr.	LD H. SOMERSET	2 Mar 74
	E OF YARMOUTH	4 Feb 79
Capt. Gents at Arms	M OF EXETER	2 Mar 74
	E OF SHREWSBURY	4 Feb 75
	E OF COVENTRY	28 May 77

JUNIOR MINISTERS ATTACHED

P.S.	C. S. Read	21 Feb 74
	T. Salt	Jan 76

(*for Junior Ministers see above*)

Junior Lds of Treasury:

Vt Mahon
    4 Mar 74–16 Feb 76
R. Winn   4 Mar 74–21 Apr 80
Sir J. Elphinstone
    4 Mar 74–21 Apr 80
Vt Crichton
    16 Feb 76–21 Apr 80

Lds in Waiting:

E of Dunmore
    2 Mar 74–21 Apr 80
E of Roden
    2 Mar 74–6 Jan 80
Vt Hawarden
    2 Mar 74–21 Apr 80
Ld Bagot
    2 Mar 74–21 Apr 80
Ld de Ros
    2 Mar 74–21 Apr 80
Ld Elphinstone
    2 Mar 74–21 Apr 80
Ld Walsingham
    2 Mar 74–29 May 75

CONSERVATIVE GOVERNMENT, 1874–1880 (contd.)

MINISTERS NOT IN CABINET			

Capt. LD SKELMERSDALE 2 Mar 74
Yeomen
of Guard

Master of E OF HARDWICKE 2 Mar 74
Buckhounds

Mistress DUCH OF WELLINGTON
of Robes 2 Mar 74

Lds in Waiting (contd.):
E of Jersey
       29 May 75–4 Jul 77
Ld Henniker
       4 Jul 77–21 Apr 80
E of Onslow
       17 Feb 80–21 Apr 80
Extra Ld in Waiting:
Ld Sackville
       1 Oct 76–1 Oct 88

LIBERAL GOVERNMENT, 1880–1885

MINISTERS IN CABINET

P.M. **W. E. Gladstone**
       23 Apr 80–9 Jun 85
Ld Chanc. **Ld Selborne (E)** 28 Apr 80
Ld Pres. **Earl Spencer** 28 Apr 80
      Ld Carlingford 19 Mar 83
Privy S. **D of Argyll** 28 Apr 80
      Ld Carlingford 2 May 81
      E of Rosebery 5 Mar 85
Home O. **Sir W. V. Harcourt**
      28 Apr 80

For. O. **Earl Granville** 28 Apr 80

War O. **H. C. E. Childers** 28 Apr 80
      M of Hartington 16 Dec 82

Col. O. **E of Kimberley** 28 Apr 80
      E of Derby 16 Dec 82

India O. **M of Hartington** 28 Apr 80
      E of Kimberley 16 Dec 82

Exch. **W. E. Gladstone** 28 Apr 80
      H. C. E. Childers 16 Dec 82

JUNIOR MINISTERS ATTACHED

P.S. to Treasury:
    Ld R. Grosvenor 28 Apr 80

U-S. A. Peel 28 Apr 80
    L. H. Courtney 1 Jan 81
    E. of Rosebery 8 Aug 81
    J. T. Hibbert 7 Jun 83
    H. H. Fowler 12 Dec 84

U-S. Sir C. Dilke 28 Apr 80
    Ld E. Fitzmaurice 1 Jan 83

U-S. Earl Morley 1 May 80
F.S. H. Campbell-Bannerman
             28 Apr 80
    Sir A. D. Hayter 13 May 82
Surveyor- Sir J. Adye 1 Jun 80
Gen. H. Brand 17 Jan 83
Ordnance

U-S. M. E. Grant Duff 29 Apr 80
    L. H. Courtney 6 Aug 81
    A. Ashley 12 May 82

U-S. M of Lansdowne 29 Apr 80
    Vt Enfield 1 Sep 80
    J. K. Cross 16 Jan 83

F.S. to Treasury:
    Ld F. Cavendish 28 Apr 80
    L. H. Courtney 8 May 82
    J. T. Hibbert 12 Dec 84

LIBERAL GOVERNMENT, 1880–1885 *(contd.)*

MINISTERS IN CABINET			JUNIOR MINISTERS ATTACHED		
Admir.	**E of Northbrook**	28 Apr 80	*P.S.*	G. J. Shaw-Lefevre	28 Apr 80
				G. O. Trevelyan	29 Nov 80
				H. Campbell-Bannerman	
					10 May 82
				T. Brassey	23 Oct 84
			Civil Ld	T. Brassey	12 May 80
				G. W. Rendel	22 Jul 82
Chief Sec.	**W. E. Forster**	30 Apr 80			
Ireland	(*Ld F. Cavendish* 6 *May* 82)				
	(*office not in cabinet*)				
Ld Lieut.	(*office not in cabinet*)				
Ireland	**Earl Spencer**	4 May 82			
D. Lanc.	**J. Bright**	28 Apr 80			
	E of Kimberley	25 Jul 82			
	J. G. Dodson	28 Dec 82			
	G. O. Trevelyan	29 Oct 84			
Loc. Govt	**J. G. Dodson**	3 May 80	*P.S.*	J. T. Hibbert	3 May 80
Bd	**Sir C. Dilke**	28 Dec 82		G. W. E. Russell	7 Jun 83
Postm.-Gen.	(*office not in cabinet*)				
	G. J. Shaw-Lefevre	7 Nov 84			
B.o.T.	**J. Chamberlain**	3 May 80	*P.S.*	A. Ashley	29 Apr 80
				J. Holms	15 May 82
1st C.	(*office not in cabinet*)				
Works	**E of Rosebery**	13 Feb 85			

MINISTERS NOT IN CABINET			JUNIOR MINISTERS ATTACHED
Educ.	A. J. MUNDELLA	3 May 80	
Chief Sec.	(*office in cabinet*)		
Ireland	LD F. CAVENDISH	6 May 82	
	G. O. TREVELYAN	9 May 82	
	H. CAMPBELL-BANNERMAN		
		23 Oct 84	
Ld Lieut.	EARL COWPER	4 May 80	
Ireland	(*Earl Spencer* 4 *May* 82)		
	(*office in cabinet*)		
Paym.-Gen.	LD WOLVERTON	24 May 80	
Postm.-Gen.	H. FAWCETT	3 May 80	
	(*G. J. Shaw-Lefevre* 7 *Nov* 84)		
	(*office in cabinet*)		
1st C.	W. P. ADAM	3 May 80	
Works	G. J. SHAW-LEFEVRE		
		29 Nov 81	
	(*E of Rosebery* 13 *Feb* 85)		
	(*office in cabinet*)		

Law Officers:			*Junior Lds of Treasury.*
Att.-Gen.	SIR H. JAMES	3 May 80	Sir A. D. Hayter
Sol.-Gen.	SIR F. HERSCHELL	3 May 80	5 May 80–26 Jun 82

LIBERAL GOVERNMENT, 1880–1885 (*contd.*)

MINISTERS NOT IN CABINET

Judge Advoc. Gen.	G. O. MORGAN	7 May 80
Ld Advoc.	J. MCLAREN	5 May 80
	J. B. BALFOUR	19 Aug 81

Sol.-Gen. Scotland	J. B. BALFOUR	6 May 80
	A. ASHER	19 Aug 81
Att.-Gen. Ireland	H. LAW	10 May 80
	W. M. JOHNSON	17 Nov 81
	A. M. PORTER	3 Jan 83
	J. NAISH	19 Dec 83
	S. WALKER	1885
Sol.-Gen. Ireland	W. M JOHNSON	24 May 80
	A. M. PORTER	18 Nov 81
	J. NAISH	9 Jan 83
	S. WALKER	19 Dec 83
	THE MACDERMOT	1885

H.M. Household:

Ld Steward	EARL SYDNEY	3 May 80
Ld Chamb.	E OF KENMARE	3 May 80
V. Chamb.	LD E. BRUCE	3 May 80
Master of Horse	D OF WESTMINSTER	3 May 80
Treas.	E OF BREADALBANE	3 May 80
Comptr.	LD KENSINGTON	3 May 80
Capt. Gents at Arms	E OF FIFE	3 May 80
	M OF HUNTLEY	21 Jan 81
	LD CARRINGTON	27 Jun 81
Capt. Yeomen of Guard	LD MONSON	3 May 80
Master of Buckhounds	E OF CORK	3 May 80
Mistress of Robes	DUCH OF BEDFORD	3 May 80
	DUCH OF ROXBURGH	11 Jan 83

JUNIOR MINISTERS ATTACHED

J. Holms   5 May 80–26 Jun 82
C. C. Cotes
            5 May 80–9 Jun 85
H. J. Gladstone
            24 Aug 81–9 Jun 85
R. W. Duff
            26 Jun 82–9 Jun 85

Lds in Waiting:

Ld Methuen
            10 May 80–9 Jun 85
E of Zetland
            10 May 80–14 Sep 80
E of Listowel
            10 May 80–14 Sep 80
Ld Ribblesdale
            10 May 80–9 Jun 85
Ld Sudeley
            10 May 80–9 Jun 85
Ld Wrottesley
            10 May 80–9 Jun 85
Vt Enfield
            20 May 80–1 Sep 80
Vt Torrington
            23 Jun 59–27 Apr 84
            (*perm.*)
E of Dalhousie
            14 Sep 80–9 Jun 85
Ld Sandhurst
            14 Sep 80–9 Jun 85
Ld Thurlow
            14 Sep 80–9 Jun 85
Vt Bridport
            30 Jun 84–18 Feb 01
            (*perm.*)

Extra Ld in Waiting:

Ld Sackville
            1 Oct 76–1 Oct 88

CONSERVATIVE GOVERNMENT, 1885–1886

MINISTERS IN CABINET			JUNIOR MINISTERS ATTACHED		
P.M.	**M of Salisbury**				
	23 Jun 85–28 Jan 86				
1st Ld of Treasury	**E of Iddesleigh**	24 Jun 85	*P.S. to Treasury:*		
				A. Akers-Douglas	24 Jun 85
Ld Chanc.	**Ld Halsbury**	24 Jun 85			
Ld Pres.	**Vt Cranbrook**	24 Jun 85			
Privy S.	**E of Harrowby**	24 Jun 85			
Home O.	**Sir R. A. Cross**	24 Jun 85	*U-S.*	C. Stuart-Wortley	30 Jun 85
For. O.	**M of Salisbury**	24 Jun 85	*U-S.*	R. Bourke	25 Jun 85
War O.	**W. H. Smith**	24 Jun 85	*U-S.*	Vt Bury	26 Jun 85
			F.S.	H. S. Northcote	26 Jun 85
			Surveyor-Gen. Ordnance	G. C. Dawnay	27 Jun 85
Col. O.	**F. A. Stanley**	24 Jun 85	*U-S.*	E of Dunraven	24 Jun 85
India O.	**Ld R. Churchill**	24 Jun 85	*U-S.*	Ld Harris	25 Jun 85
Exch.	**Sir M. Hicks Beach**		*F.S. to Treasury:*		
		24 Jun 85		Sir H. T. Holland	24 Jun 85
				Sir M. White Ridley	
				W. L. Jackson	
Admir.	**Ld G. Hamilton**	24 Jun 85	*P.S.*	C. T. Ritchie	1 Jul 85
			Civil Ld	E. Ashmead Bartlett	1 Jul 85
Educ.	**E. Stanhope**	24 Jun 85			
	(*Sir H. T. Holland* 17 *Sep* 85)				
	(*office not in cabinet*)				
Chief Sec. Ireland	(*office not in cabinet*)				
	W. H. Smith	23 Jan 86			
Ld Lieut. Ireland	**E. of Carnarvon**	27 Jun 85			
Ld Chanc. Ireland	**Ld Ashbourne**	27 Jun 85			
Postm.-Gen.	**Ld J. Manners**	24 Jun 85			
Sec. for Scotland	**D of Richmond**	17 Aug 85			
B.o.T.	**D of Richmond**	24 Jun 85	*P.S.*	Baron H. de Worms	
	E. Stanhope	19 Aug 85			24 Jun 85

MINISTERS NOT IN CABINET		JUNIOR MINISTERS ATTACHED
Educ.	(*office in cabinet*)	
	SIR H. T. HOLLAND	
	17 Sep 85	
Chief Sec. Ireland	SIR W. HART DYKE	
	25 Jun 85	
	(*W. H. Smith* 23 *Jan* 86)	
	(*office in cabinet*)	

CONSERVATIVE GOVERNMENT, 1885–1886 (*contd.*)

MINISTERS NOT IN CABINET			JUNIOR MINISTERS ATTACHED		
D. Lanc.	H. CHAPLIN	24 Jun 85			
Loc. Govt Bd	A. J. BALFOUR	24 Jun 85	*P.S.*	Earl Brownlow	24 Jun 85
Paym.-Gen.	EARL BEAUCHAMP	24 Jun 85			
1st C. Works	D. R. PLUNKET	24 Jun 85			

Law Officers:

			Junior Lds of Treasury:
Att.-Gen.	SIR R. WEBSTER	27 Jun 85	C. Dalrymple
Sol.-Gen.	J. E. GORST	2 Jul 85	29 Jun 85–28 Jan 86
Judge Advoc. Gen.	W. T. MARRIOTT	13 Jul 85	S. Herbert
			29 Jun 85–28 Jan 86
Ld Advoc.	J. H. MACDONALD	2 Jul 85	W. H. Walrond
Sol.-Gen. Scotland	J. P. ROBERTSON	2 Jul 85	29 Jun 85–28 Jan 86
Att.-Gen. Ireland	H. HOLMES	3 Jul 85	
Sol.-Gen. Ireland	J. MUNROE	3 Jul 85	
	J. G. GIBSON	1885	

H.M. Household:

			Lds in Waiting:
Ld Steward	E OF MT EDGCUMBE	27 Jun 85	Ld de Ros
			27 Jun 85–28 Jan 86
Ld Chamb.	E OF LATHOM	27 Jun 85	E of Kintore
V. Chamb.	VT LEWISHAM	27 Jun 85	27 Jun 85–28 Jan 86
Master of Horse	E OF BRADFORD	1 Jul 85	Vt Hawarden
			27 Jun 85–28 Jan 86
Treas.	VT FOLKESTONE	27 Jun 85	Ld Henniker
Comptr.	LD A. HILL	27 Jun 85	27 Jun 85–28 Jan 86
Capt. Gents at Arms	E OF COVENTRY	6 Jul 85	E of Hopetoun
			27 Jun 85–28 Jan 86
Capt. Yeomen of Guard	VT BARRINGTON	27 Jun 85	Ld Elphinstone
			27 Jun 85–28 Jan 86
			Ld Boston
Master of Buckhounds	M OF WATERFORD	27 Jun 85	6 Jul 85–28 Jan 86

Extra Ld in Waiting:
Ld Sackville
   1 Oct 76–1 Oct 88

Mistress of Robes	DUCH OF BUCCLEUCH	27 Jun 85

LIBERAL GOVERNMENT, 1886

MINISTERS IN CABINET			JUNIOR MINISTERS ATTACHED		
P.M.	**W. E. Gladstone**		*P.S. to Treasury:*		
		1 Feb 86–20 Jul 86		A. Morley	6 Feb 86
Ld Chanc.	**Sir F. Herschell**	6 Feb 86			
	(*1st Ld Herschell* 1886)				

LIBERAL GOVERNMENT, 1886 (contd.)

MINISTERS IN CABINET			JUNIOR MINISTERS ATTACHED		
Ld Pres.	**Earl Spencer**	6 Feb 86			
Privy S.	**W. E. Gladstone**	17 Feb 86			
Home O.	**H. C. E. Childers**	6 Feb 86	U-S.	H. Broadhurst	6 Feb 86
For. O.	**E of Rosebery**	6 Feb 86	U-S.	J. Bryce	7 Feb 86
War O.	**H. Campbell-Bannerman**		U-S.	Ld Sandhurst	6 Feb 86
		6 Feb 86	F.S.	H. J. Gladstone	6 Feb 86
			Surveyor-Gen. Ordnance	W. Woodall	6 Feb 86
Col. O.	**Earl Granville**	6 Feb 86	U-S.	G. O. Morgan	6 Feb 86
India O.	**E of Kimberley**	6 Feb 86	U-S.	Sir U. Kay-Shuttleworth	7 Feb 86
				E. S. Howard	12 Apr 86
Exch.	**Sir W. V. Harcourt**	6 Feb 86	F.S. to Treasury:		
				H. H. Fowler	6 Feb 86
Admir.	**M of Ripon**	9 Feb 86	P.&F.S.	J. T. Hibbert	9 Feb 86
			Civil Ld	R. W. Duff	15 Feb 86
Chief Sec. Ireland	**J. Morley**	6 Feb 86			
Loc. Govt Bd	**J. Chamberlain** **J. Stansfeld**	6 Feb 86 3 Apr 86	P.S.	J. Collings W. Borlase	6 Feb 86 3 Apr 86
Sec. for Scotland	**G. O. Trevelyan** (E of Dalhousie 5 Apr 86) (office not in cabinet)	8 Feb 86			
B.o.T.	**A. J. Mundella**	17 Feb 86	P.S.	C. T. D. Acland	6 Feb 86

MINISTERS NOT IN CABINET			JUNIOR MINISTERS ATTACHED
Educ.	Sir L. Playfair	13 Feb 86	
Ld Lieut. Ireland	E of Aberdeen	8 Feb 86	
D. Lanc.	E. Heneage Sir U. Kay-Shuttleworth	6 Feb 86 16 Apr 86	
Paym.-Gen.	Ld Thurlow	3 Apr 86	
Postm.-Gen.	Ld Wolverton	17 Feb 86	
Sec. for Scotland	(office in cabinet) E of Dalhousie	5 Apr 86	
1st C. Works	E of Morley E of Elgin	17 Feb 86 16 Apr 86	

Law Officers:

Att.-Gen.	Sir C. Russell	9 Feb 86
Sol.-Gen.	Sir H. Davey	16 Feb 86
Judge Advoc. Gen.	J. W. Mellor	22 Feb 86
Ld Advoc.	J. B. Balfour	13 Feb 86

Junior Lds of Treasury:
Sir E. Reed
13 Feb 86–20 Jul 86
C. Flower
13 Feb 86–20 Jul 86
G. G. Leveson-Gower
13 Feb 86–20 Jul 86

LIBERAL GOVERNMENT, 1886 (contd.)

MINISTERS NOT IN CABINET			JUNIOR MINISTERS ATTACHED
Sol.-Gen. *Scotland*	A. ASHER	13 Feb 86	
Att.-Gen. *Ireland*	S. WALKER	Feb 86	
Sol.-Gen. *Ireland*	THE MACDERMOT	Feb 86	

H.M. Household:			*Lds in Waiting:*
Ld Steward	EARL SYDNEY	10 Feb 86	Ld Methuen
Ld Chamb.	E OF KENMARE	10 Feb 86	16 Feb 86–20 Jul 86
V. Chamb.	VT KILCOURSIE	19 Feb 86	Ld Thurlow
Master of *Horse*	E OF CORK	10 Feb 86	16 Feb 86–20 Jul 86 Ld Camoys
Treas.	E OF ELGIN	17 Feb 86	16 Feb 86–20 Jul 86
Comptr.	E MARJORIBANKS	10 Feb 86	Ld Houghton
Capt. Gents *at Arms*	LD SUDELEY	10 Feb 86	16 Feb 86–20 Jul 86 Ld Kensington
Capt. *Yeomen* *of Guard*	LD MONSON	10 Feb 86	1 Mar 86–20 Jul 86 Ld Hothfield 1 Mar 86–20 Jul 86 Ld Ribblesdale
Master of *Buckhounds*	LD SUFFIELD	17 Feb 86	1 Mar 86–27 Mar 86 *Extra Ld in Waiting:* Ld Sackville
Mistress *of Robes*	DUCH OF BEDFORD		1 Oct 76–1 Oct 88

CONSERVATIVE GOVERNMENT, 1886–1892

MINISTERS IN CABINET			JUNIOR MINISTERS ATTACHED		
P.M.	**M of Salisbury**				
	25 Jul 86–11 Aug 92				
1st Ld of *Treasury*	**M of Salisbury** **W. H. Smith** **A. J. Balfour**		*P.S. to Treasury:* 	A. Akers-Douglas	3 Aug 86
Ld Chanc.	**Ld Halsbury**	3 Aug 86			
Ld Pres.	**Vt Cranbrook**	3 Aug 86			
Privy S.	(*office not in cabinet*)				
	E of Cadogan	Apr 87			
Home O.	**H. Matthews**	3 Aug 86	*U-S.*	C. Stuart-Wortley	4 Aug 86
For. O.	**E of Iddesleigh**	3 Aug 86	*U-S.*	Sir J. Fergusson	4 Aug 86
	M of Salisbury	14 Jan 87		J. W. Lowther	22 Sep 91
War O.	**W. H. Smith**	3 Aug 86	*U-S.*	Ld Harris	4 Aug 86
	E. Stanhope	14 Jan 87		Earl Brownlow	1 Jan 90
			F.S.	W. StJ. Brodrick	4 Aug 86
			Surveyor- *Gen.* *Ordnance*	Sir H. S. Northcote (*office abolished* 1888)	4 Aug 86

CONSERVATIVE GOVERNMENT, 1886–1892 (*contd.*)

MINISTERS IN CABINET			JUNIOR MINISTERS ATTACHED		
Col. O.	**E. Stanhope**	3 Aug 86	*U-S.*	E of Dunraven	3 Aug 86
	Sir H. T. Holland	14 Jan 87		E of Onslow	16 Feb 87
	(*1st Ld Knutsford* 1888)			Baron H. de Worms	20 Feb 88
India O.	**Vt Cross**	3 Aug 86	*U-S.*	Sir J. E. Gorst	4 Aug 86
				G. N. Curzon	9 Nov 91
Exch.	**Ld R. Churchill**	3 Aug 86	*F.S. to Treasury:*		
	G. J. Goschen	14 Jan 87		W. L. Jackson	3 Aug 86
				Sir J. E. Gorst	9 Nov 91
Admir.	**Ld G. Hamilton**	9 Aug 86	*P.&F.S.*	A. B. Forwood	9 Aug 86
			Civil Ld	E. Ashmead Bartlett	9 Aug 86
Bd Ag.	**H. Chaplin**	9 Sep 89			
Chief Sec. Ireland	**Sir M. Hicks Beach**	5 Aug 86			
	A. J. Balfour	7 Mar 87			
	(*W. L. Jackson* 9 *Nov* 91)				
	(*office not in cabinet*)				
Ld Chanc. Ireland	**Ld Ashbourne**	3 Aug 86			
D. Lanc.	**Vt Cranbrook**	3 Aug 86			
	Ld J. Manners	16 Aug 86			
	(*7th D of Rutland* 1888)				
Loc. Govt Bd	(*office not in cabinet*)				
	C. T. Ritchie	Apr 87			
Min. without Portfolio	**Sir M. Hicks Beach**	7 Mar 87–20 Feb 88			
Sec. for Scotland	(*office not in cabinet*)				
	A. J. Balfour	Nov 86			
	(*M of Lothian* 11 *Mar* 87)				
	(*office not in cabinet*)				
B.o.T.	**Sir F. A. Stanley**	3 Aug 86	*P.S.*	Baron H. de Worms	4 Aug 86
	(*1st Ld Stanley of Preston* 1886)			E of Onslow	21 Feb 88
	Sir M. Hicks Beach			Ld Balfour of Burleigh	
		21 Feb 88			1 Jan 89

MINISTERS NOT IN CABINET			JUNIOR MINISTERS ATTACHED		
Educ.	SIR H. T. HOLLAND	3 Aug 86			
	SIR W. HART DYKE	25 Jan 87			
Chief Sec. Ireland	(*office in cabinet*)				
	W. L. JACKSON	9 Nov 91			
Ld Lieut. Ireland	M OF LONDONDERRY	3 Aug 86			
	E OF ZETLAND	30 Jul 89			
Loc. Govt Bd	C. T. RITCHIE	3 Aug 86	*P.S.*	W. Long	3 Aug 86
	(*office in cabinet Apr* 87)				

CONSERVATIVE GOVERNMENT, 1886–1892 *(contd.)*

MINISTERS NOT IN CABINET			JUNIOR MINISTERS ATTACHED
Paym.-Gen.	EARL BEAUCHAMP	19 Aug 86	
	EARL BROWNLOW	Mar 87	
	E OF JERSEY	1889	
	LD WINDSOR	Dec 90	
Postm.-Gen.	H. C. RAIKES	19 Aug 86	
	SIR J. FERGUSSON	21 Sep 91	
Privy S.	E OF CADOGAN	3 Aug 86	
	(office in cabinet Apr 87)		
Sec. for	A. J. BALFOUR	5 Aug 86	
Scotland	*(office in cabinet Nov 86)*		
	M OF LOTHIAN	11 Mar 87	
1st C.	D. R. PLUNKET	5 Aug 86	
Works			

Law Officers:

			Junior Lds of Treasury:
Att.-Gen.	SIR R. WEBSTER	5 Aug 86	S. Herbert
Sol.-Gen.	SIR E. CLARKE	6 Aug 86	9 Aug 86–11 Aug 92
Judge	W. T. MARRIOTT	9 Aug 86	(Sir) W. H. Walrond
Advoc. Gen.			9 Aug 86–11 Aug 92
Ld Advoc.	J. H. MACDONALD	6 Aug 86	Sir H. Maxwell
	J. P. ROBERTSON	27 Oct 88	9 Aug 86–11 Aug 92
	(vacant 20 Aug 91)		
	SIR C. PEARSON	1 Oct 91	
Sol.-Gen.	J. P. ROBERTSON	6 Aug 86	
Scotland	M. T. S. DARLING	27 Oct 88	
	SIR C. PEARSON	31 Oct 90	
	A. G. MURRAY	1 Oct 91	
Att.-Gen.	H. HOLMES	Aug 86	
Ireland	J. G. GIBSON	1887	
	P. O'BRIEN	1888	
	D. H. MADDEN	1890	
Sol.-Gen.	J. G. GIBSON	Aug 86	
Ireland	D. H. MADDEN	1888	
	J. ATKINSON	1890	
	E. CARSON	Jun 92	

H.M. Household:

			Lds in Waiting:
Ld Steward	E OF MT EDGCUMBE		E of Onslow
		16 Aug 86	5 Aug 86–21 Feb 87
Ld Chamb.	E OF LATHOM	5 Aug 86	E of Limerick
V. Chamb.	VT LEWISHAM	5 Aug 86	5 Aug 86–29 Jan 89
	LD BURGHLEY	24 Nov 91	Ld Henniker
Master of	D OF PORTLAND	9 Aug 86	5 Aug 86–11 Aug 92
Horse			E of Hopetoun
Treas.	VT FOLKESTONE	5 Aug 86	5 Aug 86–12 Aug 89
	(E of Radnor 1889)		Ld Elphinstone
	LD W. GORDON-LENNOX		5 Aug 86–11 Aug 92
		20 Nov 91	Ld de Ros
			5 Aug 86–11 Aug 92

CONSERVATIVE GOVERNMENT, 1886–1892 *(contd.)*

MINISTERS NOT IN CABINET

Comptr.	LD A. HILL	5 Aug 86
Capt. Gents	VT BARRINGTON	5 Aug 86
at Arms	E OF ROSSLYN	24 Nov 86
	E OF YARBOROUGH	
		11 Aug 90
Capt.	E OF KINTORE	5 Aug 86
Yeomen	E OF LIMERICK	29 Jan 89
of Guard		
Master of	E OF COVENTRY	16 Aug 86
Buckhounds		
Mistress	DUCH OF BUCCLEUCH	
of Robes		5 Aug 86

Lds in Waiting (contd.):
> Earl Waldegrave
>> 5 Aug 86–11 Aug 92
> Ld Balfour of Burleigh
>> 21 Feb 87–18 Mar 89
> E of Romney
>> 5 Feb 89–11 Aug 92
> Vt Torrington
>> 18 Mar 89–20 Oct 89
> Ld Churchill
>> 12 Aug 89–11 Aug 92
> Ld de Ramsey
>> 10 Mar 90–11 Aug 92

Extra Ld in Waiting:
> Ld Sackville
>> 1 Oct 76–1 Oct 88

LIBERAL GOVERNMENT, 1892–1895

MINISTERS IN CABINET

P.M.	**W. E. Gladstone**	
		15 Aug 92–2 Mar 94
	E of Rosebery	
		5 Mar 94–21 Jun 95
Ld Chanc.	**Ld Herschell**	18 Aug 92
Ld Pres.	**E of Kimberley**	18 Aug 92
	E of Rosebery	10 Mar 94
Privy S.	**W. E. Gladstone**	20 Aug 92
	Ld Tweedmouth	10 Mar 94
Home O.	**H. H. Asquith**	18 Aug 92
For. O.	**E of Rosebery**	18 Aug 92
	E of Kimberley	11 Mar 94
War O.	**H. Campbell-Bannerman**	
		18 Aug 92
Col. O.	**M of Ripon**	18 Aug 92
India O.	**E of Kimberley**	18 Aug 92
	H. H. Fowler	10 Mar 94
Exch.	**Sir W. V. Harcourt**	
		18 Aug 92
Admir.	**Earl Spencer**	19 Aug 92
Educ.	**A. H. D. Acland**	25 Aug 92
Chief Sec.	**J. Morley**	22 Aug 92
Ireland		

JUNIOR MINISTERS ATTACHED

P.S. to Treasury:

	E. Marjoribanks	18 Aug 92
	T. Ellis	10 Mar 94
U.-S.	H. J. Gladstone	19 Aug 92
	G. W. E. Russell	12 Mar 94
U.-S.	Sir E. Grey	19 Aug 92
U.-S.	Ld Sandhurst	22 Aug 92
	Ld Monkswell	5 Jan 95
F.S.	W. Woodall	22 Aug 92
U.-S.	S. Buxton	18 Aug 92
U.-S.	G. W. E. Russell	19 Aug 92
	Ld Reay	11 Mar 94

F.S. to Treasury:

	Sir J. T. Hibbert	18 Aug 92
P. & F.S.	Sir U. Kay-Shuttleworth	
		19 Aug 92
Civil Ld	E. Robinson	25 Aug 92

LIBERAL GOVERNMENT, 1892–1895 *(contd.)*

MINISTERS IN CABINET			JUNIOR MINISTERS ATTACHED	
D. Lanc.	**J. Bryce**	18 Aug 92		
	Ld Tweedmouth	28 May 94		
Loc. Govt	**H. H. Fowler**	18 Aug 92		
Bd	**G. J. Shaw-Lefevre**			
		10 Mar 94		
Postm.-Gen.	**A. Morley**	18 Aug 92		
Sec. for	**G. O. Trevelyan**	18 Aug 92		
Scotland				
B.o.T.	**A. J. Mundella**	18 Aug 92	P. S. T. Burt	18 Aug 92
	J. Bryce	28 May 94		
1st C.	**G. J. Shaw-Lefevre**			
Works		18 Aug 92		
	(*H. J. Gladstone* 10 Mar 94)			
	(*office not in cabinet*)			

MINISTERS NOT IN CABINET			JUNIOR MINISTERS ATTACHED
Bd Ag.	H. GARDNER	25 Aug 92	
Ld Lieut.	LD HOUGHTON	18 Aug 92	
Ireland			
Paym.-Gen.	C. SEALE-HAYNE	18 Aug 92	
1st C.	(*office in cabinet*)		
Works	H. J. GLADSTONE	10 Mar 94	

Law Officers:

			Junior Lds of Treasury:
Att.-Gen.	SIR C. RUSSELL	20 Aug 92	T. E. Ellis
	SIR J. RIGBY	3 May 94	22 Aug 92–21 Jun 95
	SIR R. T. REID	24 Oct 94	R. K. Causton
Sol.-Gen.	SIR J. RIGBY	20 Aug 92	22 Aug 92–21 Jun 95
	SIR R. T. REID	3 May 94	W. A. Macarthur
	SIR F. LOCKWOOD	28 Oct 94	22 Aug 92–21 Jun 95
Judge	SIR F. H. JEUNE	31 Dec 92	
Advoc. Gen.			
Ld Advoc.	J. B. BALFOUR	20 Aug 92	
Sol.-Gen.	A. ASHER	20 Aug 92	
Scotland	T. SHAW	22 Mar 94	
Att.-Gen.	THE MACDERMOT	Aug 92	
Ireland			
Sol.-Gen.	C. H. HEMPHILL	Aug 92	
Ireland			

H.M. Household:

			Lds in Waiting:
Ld Steward	M OF BREADALBANE		Ld Acton
		25 Aug 92	19 Sep 92–21 Jun 95
Ld Chamb.	LD CARRINGTON	25 Aug 92	Ld Camoys
V. Chamb.	C. R. SPENCER	25 Aug 92	19 Sep 92–21 Jun 95
Master of	VT OXENBRIDGE	25 Aug 92	Ld Hamilton of Dalzell
Horse	E OF CORK	19 Mar 94	19 Sep 92–1 May 94
Treas.	E OF CHESTERFIELD		Ld Monkswell
		25 Aug 92	19 Sep 92–4 Feb 95
	A. G. BRAND	13 Mar 94	Ld Wolverton
			19 Sep 92–14 Jun 93

LIBERAL GOVERNMENT, 1892–1895 (contd.)

MINISTERS NOT IN CABINET

Comptr.	G. G. Leveson-Gower	
		25 Aug 92
Capt. Gents	Ld Vernon	25 Aug 92
at Arms	E of Chesterfield	
		13 Mar 94
Capt. Yeomen of Guard	Ld Kensington	25 Aug 92
Master of Buckhounds	Ld Ribblesdale	25 Aug 92

Lds in Waiting (contd.):

Ld Playfair
26 Nov 92–21 Jun 95
Ld Brassey
14 Jun 93–21 Jun 95
Vt Drumlanrig
1 Jul 93–18 Oct 94
Ld Hawkesbury
1 May 94–21 Jun 95
E of Buckinghamshire
17 Jan 95–21 Jun 95
Earl Granville
4 Feb 95–21 Jun 95

CONSERVATIVE GOVERNMENT, 1895–1905

MINISTERS IN CABINET   JUNIOR MINISTERS ATTACHED

P.M.	**M. of Salisbury (3rd)**	
	25 Jun 95–11 Jul 02	
	A. J. Balfour	
	12 Jul 02–4 Dec 05	

1st Ld of Treasury	**A. J. Balfour** 29 Jun 95	P.S. to Treasury:
	(office combined with P.M. when Balfour succeeded Salisbury)	Sir W. H. Walrond 29 Jun 95
		Sir A. Acland Hood 8 Aug 02

Ld Chanc.	**Ld Halsbury (E)** 29 Jun 95
Ld Pres.	**D of Devonshire** 29 Jun 95
	M of Londonderry 19 Oct 03
Privy S.	**Vt Cross** 29 Jun 95
	M of Salisbury (3rd)
	12 Nov 00
	A. J. Balfour 14 Jul 02
	M of Salisbury (4th)
	17 Oct 03

Home O.	**Sir M. White Ridley** 29 Jun 95	U-S.	J. Collings 3 Jul 95
			T. Cochrane 11 Aug 02
	C. T. Ritchie 12 Nov 00		
	A. Akers-Douglas 11 Aug 02		
For. O.	**M of Salisbury (3rd)** 29 Jun 95	U-S.	G. N. Curzon 30 Jun 95
	M of Lansdowne 12 Nov 00		W. StJ. Brodrick 15 Oct 98
			Vt Cranborne 12 Nov 00
			(4th M of Salisbury 1902)
			Earl Percy 9 Oct 03
War O.	**M of Lansdowne** 4 Jul 95	U-S.	W. StJ. Brodrick 4 Jul 95
	W. StJ. Brodrick 12 Nov 00		G. Wyndham 10 Oct 98
	H. Arnold-Forster 12 Oct 03		Ld Raglan 13 Nov 00
			E of Hardwicke 8 Aug 02
			E of Donoughmore 12 Oct 03
		F.S.	J. Powell Williams 3 Jul 95
			Ld Stanley 1 Jan 01
			W. Bromley-Davenport 12 Oct 03

CONSERVATIVE GOVERNMENT, 1895–1905 (contd.)

MINISTERS IN CABINET

Col. O.	**J. Chamberlain**	29 Jun 95
	A. Lyttelton	9 Oct 03
India O.	**Ld G. Hamilton**	4 Jul 95
	W. StJ. Brodrick	9 Oct 03
Exch.	**Sir M. Hicks Beach**	
		29 Jun 95
	C. T. Ritchie	11 Aug 02
	J. A. Chamberlain	9 Oct 03
Admir.	**G. J. Goschen**	29 Jun 95
	E of Selborne	12 Nov 00
	Earl Cawdor	27 Mar 05
Bd Ag.	**W. Long**	4 Jul 95
	R. W. Hanbury	16 Nov 00
	E of Onslow	20 May 03
	A. E. Fellowes	14 Mar 05
Bd Educ.	**D of Devonshire**	3 Mar 00
	M of Londonderry	
		11 Aug 02

Chief Sec.	(*office not in cabinet*)	
Ireland	**G. Wyndham**	9 Nov 00
	W. Long	12 Mar 05
Ld Lieut.	**Earl Cadogan**	29 Jun 95
Ireland	(*E of Dudley* 11 *Aug* 02)	
	(*office not in cabinet*)	
Ld Chanc.	**Ld Ashbourne**	29 Jun 95
Ireland		
D. Lanc.	**Vt Cross**	29 Jun 95
	Ld James of Hereford	
		4 Jul 95
	(*Sir W. H. Walrond*	
	11 *Aug* 02)	
	(*office not in cabinet*)	
Loc. Govt	**H. Chaplin**	29 Jun 95
Bd	**W. Long**	12 Nov 00
	G. W. Balfour	14 Mar 05
Postm.-Gen.	(*office not in cabinet*)	
	M of Londonderry 7 Nov 00	

JUNIOR MINISTERS ATTACHED

U-S.	E of Selborne	28 Jun 95
	E of Onslow	26 Nov 00
	D of Marlborough	22 Jul 03
U-S.	E of Onslow	5 Jul 95
	E of Hardwicke	17 Jan 01
	Earl Percy	18 Aug 02
	E of Hardwicke	12 Oct 03
	(*vacant* 29 *Nov* 04)	
	M of Bath	20 Jan 05
F.S. to Treasury:		
	R. W. Hanbury	29 Jun 95
	J. A. Chamberlain	7 Nov 00
	W. Hayes Fisher	8 Aug 02
	A. Elliott	10 Apr 03
	V. Cavendish	9 Oct 03
P.&F.S.	W. G. Macartney	29 Jun 95
	H. Arnold-Forster	7 Nov 00
	E. Pretyman	11 Oct 03
Civil Ld	J. A. Chamberlain	6 Jul 95
	E. Pretyman	7 Nov 00
	A. H. Lee	11 Oct 03
Sec.	(*office not established*)	
	Sir W. Anson	11 Aug 02
	(*previously Vice-President of*	
	Committee of Council on	
	Education–Sir J. E. Gorst	
	4 *Jul* 95–8 *Aug* 02)	

P.S.	T. Russell	30 Jun 95
	Sir J. Lawson	12 Nov 00
	A. Jeffreys	27 Jun 05

CONSERVATIVE GOVERNMENT, 1895–1905 *(contd.)*

MINISTERS IN CABINET			JUNIOR MINISTERS ATTACHED		
	J. A. Chamberlain				
		11 Aug 02			
	Ld Stanley	9 Oct 03			
Sec. for	**Ld Balfour of Burleigh**				
Scotland		29 Jun 95			
	A. G. Murray	9 Oct 03			
	M of Linlithgow	2 Feb 05			
B.o.T.	**C. T. Ritchie**	29 Jun 95	*P.S.*	E of Dudley	29 Jun 95
	G. W. Balfour	12 Nov 00		A. Bonar Law	8 Aug 02
	M of Salisbury (4th)				
		14 Mar 05			
1st C.	**A. Akers-Douglas**	4 Jul 95			
Works	(*Ld Windsor* 11 *Aug* 02)				
	(*office not in cabinet*)				

MINISTERS NOT IN CABINET			JUNIOR MINISTERS ATTACHED
Committee	Sir J. E. Gorst	4 Jul 95	
on Educ.			
Chief Sec.	G. W. Balfour	4 Jul 95	
Ireland	(*G. Wyndham* 9 *Nov* 00)		
	(*office in cabinet*)		
D. Lanc.	(*office in cabinet*)		
	Sir W. H. Walrond		
		11 Aug 02	
Paym.-Gen.	E of Hopetoun	16 Jul 95	
	D of Marlborough	1899	
	Sir S. Crossley	11 Mar 02	
Postm.-Gen.	D of Norfolk	6 Jul 95	
	M of Londonderry	1899	
		10 Apr 00	
	(*office in cabinet* 7 *Nov* 00)		
1st C.	(*office in cabinet*)		
Works	Ld Windsor	11 Aug 02	

Law Officers: *Junior Lds of Treasury:*

Att.-Gen.	Sir R. Webster	8 Jul 95	H. T. Anstruther
	Sir R. Finlay	11 May 00	6 Jul 95–11 Oct 03
Sol.-Gen.	Sir R. Finlay	30 Aug 95	W. H. Fisher
	Sir E. Carson	11 May 00	6 Jul 95–8 Aug 02
Ld Advoc.	Sir C. J. Pearson	11 Jul 95	Ld Stanley
	A. G. Murray	14 May 96	6 Jul 95–7 Nov 00
	C. S. Dickson	17 Oct 03	A. E. Fellowes
Sol.-Gen.	A. G. Murray	11 Jul 95	7 Nov 00–15 Mar 05
Scotland	C. S. Dickson	14 May 96	H. W. Forster
	D. Dundas	17 Oct 03	8 Aug 02–4 Dec 05
	E. Salvesen	2 Feb 05	Ld Balcarres
	J. Clyde	17 Oct 05	11 Oct 03–4 Dec 05
Att.-Gen.	J. Atkinson	8 Jul 95	Ld E. Talbot
Ireland			16 Jun 05–4 Dec 05

CONSERVATIVE GOVERNMENT, 1895–1905 *(contd.)*

MINISTERS NOT IN CABINET			JUNIOR MINISTERS ATTACHED	

Sol.-Gen. W. KENNY 28 Aug 95
Ireland D. BARTON
         G. WRIGHT 30 Jan 00
         J. CAMPBELL 8 Jul 03

H.M. Household:

Ld Steward E OF PEMBROKE &
         MONTGOMERY 16 Jul 95

Ld Chamb. E OF LATHOM 16 Jul 95
         E OF HOPETOUN 7 Dec 98
         E OF CLARENDON 21 Sep 00

V. Chamb. A. E. FELLOWES 10 Jul 95
         SIR A. ACLAND HOOD
                  3 Dec 00
         LD WOLVERTON 17 Nov 02

Master of D OF PORTLAND 16 Jul 95
Horse

Treas. M OF CARMARTHEN
                  10 Jul 95
         VT CURZON 11 Feb 96
         V. CAVENDISH 4 Dec 00
         M OF HAMILTON 13 Oct 03

Comptr. LD A. HILL 10 Jul 95
         VT VALENTIA 19 Oct 98

Capt. Gents LD BELPER 16 Jul 95
at Arms

Capt. E OF LIMERICK 16 Jul 95
Yeomen EARL WALDEGRAVE
of Guard   26 Aug 96

Master of E OF COVENTRY 16 Jul 95
Buckhounds LD CHESHAM 1 Nov 00
         (*office abolished* 1901)

Mistress DUCH OF BUCCLEUCH
of Robes   16 Jul 95

Lds in Waiting:

Ld Churchill
        16 Jul 95–4 Dec 05
Ld Harris 16 Jul 95–4 Dec 00
Ld Henniker
        16 Jul 95–1 Nov 95
Ld Lawrence
        16 Jul 95–4 Dec 05
E of Ranfurley
        16 Jul 95–21 Apr 97
Earl Waldegrave
        16 Jul 95–9 Sep 96
E of Clarendon
        17 Jul 95–30 Oct 00
Vt Bridport
        30 Jun 84–18 Feb 01
E of Kintore
        1 Nov 95–4 Dec 05
Ld Bagot 9 Sep 96–2 Jul 01
E of Denbigh
        22 Apr 97–4 Dec 05
Earl Howe
        30 Oct 00–1 Oct 03
Ld Kenyon
        4 Dec 00–4 Dec 05
E of Erroll
        19 Oct 03–4 Dec 05

Ministerial Offices, 1830–1900

Admiralty. First Lord of the Admiralty, 1830–

Agriculture. President of the Board of Agriculture, 1889–1903 (there was a Committee of the Privy Council on Agriculture, 1883–89)

Attorney-General, 1830–

Attorney-General for Ireland, 1830–

Control, Board of. President of the Board of Control, 1830–58

Colonies. Secretary of State, 1854–

Education. Vice-President of the Committee of the Privy Council on Education in England and Wales, 1857–1902; President of the Board of Education, 1900–

Foreign Affairs. Secretary of State, 1830–

Health. President of the General Board of Health, 1854–58

Home Affairs. Secretary of State, 1830–

India. President of the Board of Control, 1830–58; Secretary of State, 1858–

Ireland. Chief Secretary to the Lord Lieutenant of Ireland, 1830–

Judge Advocate General. 1830– (political appointments ceased, 1892)

Local Government. President of the Local Government Board, 1871–

Lord Advocate, 1830–

Lord Chancellor, 1830–

Lord President of the Council, 1830–

Lord Privy Seal, 1830–

Mint. Master of the Mint, 1830– (from 1850 appointments non-political; from 1870 title held by Chancellor of Exchequer and duties by a permanent deputy Master)

Navy. Treasurer of the Navy, 1830–36 (abolished 1836 and duties given to Paymaster-General)

Ordnance, Board of. Master-General of the Ordnance, 1830–55 (the Board and the political appointments were abolished 1855, and duties given to Secretary of State for War)

Paymaster-General of the Forces, 1830–36

Paymaster-General, 1836– (1848–68 office held jointly with Vice-President of Board of Trade)

Poor Law. President of the Poor Law Board, 1847–71

Portfolio. Minister without portfolio, 1830–34, 1841–46, 1852–58, 1853–54, 1867–68, 1887–88

Post Office. Postmaster-General, 1830– (until 1866 Postmaster-General could not sit in House of Commons)

Prime Minister, 1830– (also known as Head of H.M. Government, First Lord of the Treasury)

Scotland. Secretary for Scotland, 1885–

Solicitor-General, 1830–

Solicitor-General for Ireland, 1830–

Solicitor-General for Scotland, 1830–

Trade. President of the Board of Trade, 1830– ; Vice-President of the Board of Trade, 1830–68

Treasury. Chancellor of the Exchequer, 1830–

War. Secretary of State for War, 1854– ; Secretary at War, 1830–63 (Secretary at War held jointly with Secretary of State for War, 1855–63, and abolished 1863)

War and Colonies. Secretary of State, 1830–54 (duties separated 1854)

Woods and Forests. First Commissioner of Woods, Forests and Land Revenue, 1830–51

Works. First Commissioner of Works and Public Building, 1851–

Holders of Ministerial Office

Prime Minister

22 Nov 30	Earl Grey (2nd)
16 Jul 34	Vt Melbourne
17 Nov 34	D of Wellington
10 Dec 34	Sir R. Peel
18 Apr 35	Vt Melbourne
30 Aug 41	Sir R. Peel
30 Jun 46	Ld J. Russell (E)
23 Feb 52	E of Derby (14th)
19 Dec 52	E of Aberdeen
6 Feb 55	Vt Palmerston
21 Feb 58	E of Derby (14th)
12 Jun 59	Vt Palmerston
29 Oct 65	Earl Russell
28 Jun 66	E of Derby (14th)
27 Feb 68	B. Disraeli
3 Dec 68	W. E. Gladstone
20 Feb 74	B. Disraeli (1st E of Beaconsfield 1876)
23 Apr 80	W. E. Gladstone
23 Jun 85	M of Salisbury (3rd)
1 Feb 86	W. E. Gladstone
25 Jul 86	M of Salisbury (3rd)
15 Aug 92	W. E. Gladstone
5 Mar 94	E of Rosebery
25 Jun 95	M of Salisbury (3rd)
12 Jul 02	A. J. Balfour

Lord President of the Council

22 Nov 30	M of Lansdowne (3rd)
15 Dec 34	E of Rosslyn
18 Apr 35	M of Lansdowne (3rd)
3 Sep 41	Ld Wharncliffe
21 Jan 46	D of Buccleuch
6 Jul 46	M of Lansdowne (3rd)
27 Feb 52	E of Lonsdale
28 Dec 52	Earl Granville
12 Jun 54	Ld J. Russell
8 Feb 55	Earl Granville
26 Feb 58	M of Salisbury (2nd)
18 Jun 59	Earl Granville
6 Jul 66	D of Buckingham
8 Mar 67	D of Marlborough
9 Dec 68	E of Ripon (M)
9 Aug 73	Ld Aberdare
21 Feb 74	D of Richmond
28 Apr 80	Earl Spencer
19 Mar 83	Ld Carlingford
24 Jun 85	Vt Cranbrook
6 Feb 86	Earl Spencer
3 Aug 86	Vt Cranbrook

18 Aug 92	E of Kimberley
10 Mar 94	E of Rosebery
29 Jun 95	D of Devonshire
19 Oct 03	M of Londonderry

Lord Chancellor

22 Nov 30	Ld Brougham & Vaux
21 Nov 34	Ld Lyndhurst
23 Apr 35	in Commission
16 Jan 36	Ld Cottenham
3 Sep 41	Ld Lyndhurst
6 Jul 46	Ld Cottenham
19 Jun 50	in Commission
15 Jul 50	Ld Truro
27 Feb 52	Ld St Leonards
28 Dec 52	Ld Cranworth
26 Feb 58	Ld Chelmsford
18 Jun 59	Ld Campbell
26 Jun 61	Ld Westbury
7 Jul 65	Ld Cranworth
6 Jul 66	Ld Chelmsford
29 Feb 68	Ld Cairns
9 Dec 68	Ld Hatherley
15 Oct 72	Ld Selborne
21 Feb 74	Ld Cairns (E)
28 Apr 80	Ld Selborne (E)
24 Jun 85	Ld Halsbury
6 Feb 86	Ld Herschell
3 Aug 86	Ld Halsbury
18 Aug 92	Ld Herschell
29 Jun 95	Ld Halsbury (E)

Lord Privy Seal

22 Nov 30	Ld Durham (E)
3 Apr 33	E of Ripon (1st)
5 Jun 34	E of Carlisle (6th)
30 Jul 34	E of Mulgrave
15 Dec 34	Ld Wharncliffe
23 Apr 35	Vt Duncannon
15 Jan 40	E of Clarendon
3 Sep 41	D of Buckingham
2 Feb 42	D of Buccleuch
21 Jan 46	E of Haddington
6 Jul 46	E of Minto
27 Feb 52	M of Salisbury (2nd)
4 Jan 53	D of Argyll
7 Dec 55	E of Harrowby
3 Feb 58	M of Clanricarde
26 Feb 58	E of Hardwicke
18 Jun 59	D of Argyll
6 Jul 66	E of Malmesbury
9 Dec 68	E of Kimberley

6 Jul 70	Vt Halifax
21 Feb 74	E of Malmesbury
12 Aug 76	E of Beaconsfield
4 Feb 78	D of Northumberland
28 Apr 80	D of Argyll
2 May 81	Ld Carlingford
5 Mar 85	E of Rosebery
24 Jun 85	E of Harrowby
17 Feb 86	W. E. Gladstone
3 Aug 86	E of Cadogan
20 Aug 92	W. E. Gladstone
10 Mar 94	Ld Tweedmouth
29 Jun 95	Vt Cross
12 Nov 00	M of Salisbury (3rd)
14 Jul 02	A. J. Balfour
19 Oct 03	M of Salisbury (4th)

Secretary of State for the Home Department

22 Nov 30	Vt Melbourne
19 Jul 34	Vt Duncannon
15 Dec 34	H. Goulburn
18 Apr 35	Ld J. Russell
30 Aug 39	M of Normanby
3 Sep 41	Sir J. Graham
6 Jul 46	Sir G. Grey
27 Feb 52	S. Walpole
28 Dec 52	Vt Palmerston
8 Feb 55	Sir G. Grey
26 Feb 58	S. Walpole
3 Mar 59	T. H. S. Sotheron Estcourt
18 Jun 59	Sir G. C. Lewis
25 Jul 61	Sir G. Grey
6 Jul 66	S. Walpole
17 May 67	G. Hardy
9 Dec 68	H. A. Bruce
9 Aug 73	R. Lowe
21 Feb 74	R. A. Cross
28 Apr 80	Sir W. V. Harcourt
24 Jun 85	Sir R. A. Cross
6 Feb 86	H. C. E. Childers
3 Aug 86	H. Matthews
18 Aug 92	H. H. Asquith
29 Jun 95	Sir M. White Ridley
12 Nov 00	C. T. Ritchie
11 Aug 02	A. Akers-Douglas

Secretary of State for Foreign Affairs

22 Nov 30	Vt Palmerston
17 Nov 34	D of Wellington
18 Apr 35	Vt Palmerston
3 Sep 41	E of Aberdeen
6 Jul 46	Vt Palmerston
26 Dec 51	Earl Granville
27 Feb 52	E of Malmesbury

28 Dec 52	Ld J. Russell
21 Feb 53	E of Clarendon
26 Feb 58	E of Malmesbury
18 Jun 59	Ld J. Russell (E)
3 Nov 65	E of Clarendon
6 Jul 66	Ld Stanley
9 Dec 68	E of Clarendon
6 Jul 70	Earl Granville
21 Feb 74	E of Derby (15th)
2 Apr 78	M of Salisbury (3rd)
28 Apr 80	Earl Granville
24 Jun 85	M of Salisbury (3rd)
6 Feb 86	E of Rosebery
3 Aug 86	E of Iddesleigh
14 Jan 87	M of Salisbury (3rd)
18 Aug 92	E of Rosebery
11 Mar 94	E of Kimberley
29 Jun 95	M of Salisbury (3rd)
12 Nov 00	M of Lansdowne (5th)

Secretary of State for War and the Colonies

22 Nov 30	Vt Goderich
3 Apr 33	E. G. Stanley
5 Jun 34	T. Spring-Rice
20 Dec 34	E of Aberdeen
18 Apr 35	Ld Glenelg
20 Feb 39	M of Normanby
30 Aug 39	Ld J. Russell
3 Sep 41	Ld Stanley
23 Dec 45	W. E. Gladstone
6 Jul 46	Earl Grey (3rd)
27 Feb 52	Sir J. Pakington
28 Dec 52	D of Newcastle

Secretary of State for the Colonies

12 Jun 54	Sir G. Grey
8 Feb 55	S. Herbert
23 Feb 55	Ld J. Russell
21 Jul 55	Sir W. Molesworth
21 Nov 55	H. Labouchere
26 Feb 58	Ld Stanley
5 Jun 58	Sir E. Bulwer-Lytton
18 Jun 59	D of Newcastle
7 Apr 64	E. Cardwell
6 Jul 66	E of Carnarvon
8 Mar 67	D of Buckingham
9 Dec 68	Earl Granville
6 Jul 70	E of Kimberley
21 Feb 74	E of Carnarvon
4 Feb 78	Sir M. Hicks Beach
28 Apr 80	E of Kimberley
16 Dec 82	E of Derby (15th)
24 Jun 85	F. A. Stanley
6 Feb 86	Earl Granville

3 Aug 86	E. Stanhope
14 Jan 87	Sir H. T. Holland (1st Ld Knutsford 1888)
18 Aug 92	M of Ripon
29 Jun 95	J. Chamberlain
9 Oct 03	A. Lyttelton

Secretary of State for War

12 Jun 54	D of Newcastle
8 Feb 55	Ld Panmure
26 Feb 58	J. Peel
18 Jun 59	S. Herbert (Ld)
22 Jul 61	Sir G. C. Lewis
28 Apr 63	Earl de Grey & Ripon
16 Feb 66	M of Hartington
6 Jul 66	J. Peel
8 Mar 67	Sir J. Pakington
9 Dec 68	E. Cardwell
21 Feb 74	G. Hardy
2 Apr 78	F. A. Stanley
28 Apr 80	H. C. E. Childers
16 Dec 82	M of Hartington
24 Jun 85	W. H. Smith
6 Feb 86	H. Campbell-Bannerman
3 Aug 86	W. H. Smith
14 Jan 87	E. Stanhope
18 Aug 92	H. Campbell-Bannerman
4 Jul 95	M of Lansdowne (5th)
12 Nov 00	W. StJ. Brodrick
12 Oct 03	H. Arnold-Forster

Secretary of State for India

2 Sep 58	Ld Stanley
18 Jun 59	Sir C. Wood
16 Feb 66	Earl de Grey & Ripon
6 Jul 66	Vt Cranborne
8 Mar 67	Sir S. Northcote
9 Dec 68	D of Argyll
21 Feb 74	M of Salisbury (3rd)
2 Apr 78	Vt Cranbrook
28 Apr 80	M of Hartington
16 Dec 82	E of Kimberley
24 Jun 85	Ld R. Churchill
6 Feb 86	E of Kimberley
3 Aug 86	Vt Cross
18 Aug 92	E of Kimberley
10 Mar 94	H. H. Fowler
4 Jul 95	Ld G. Hamilton
9 Oct 03	W. StJ. Brodrick

Chancellor of the Exchequer

22 Nov 30	Vt Althorp
10 Dec 34	Sir R. Peel
18 Apr 35	T. Spring-Rice
26 Aug 39	F. T. Baring
4 Sep 41	H. Goulburn
6 Jul 46	Sir C. Wood
27 Feb 52	B. Disraeli
30 Dec 52	W. E. Gladstone
5 Mar 55	Sir G. C. Lewis
26 Feb 58	B. Disraeli
18 Jun 59	W. E. Gladstone
6 Jul 66	B. Disraeli
29 Feb 68	G. W. Hunt
9 Dec 68	R. Lowe
11 Aug 73	W. E. Gladstone
21 Feb 74	Sir S. Northcote
28 Apr 80	W. E. Gladstone
16 Dec 82	H. C. E. Childers
24 Jun 85	Sir M. Hicks Beach
6 Feb 86	Sir W. V. Harcourt
3 Aug 86	Ld R. Churchill
14 Jan 87	G. J. Goschen
18 Aug 92	Sir W. V. Harcourt
29 Jun 95	Sir M. Hicks Beach
11 Aug 02	C. T. Ritchie
9 Oct 03	J. A. Chamberlain

First Lord of the Admiralty

22 Nov 30	Sir J. Graham
7 Jun 34	Ld Auckland
22 Dec 34	Earl de Grey
22 Apr 35	Ld Auckland
15 Sep 35	E of Minto
6 Sep 41	E of Haddington
8 Jan 46	E of Ellenborough
7 Jul 46	E of Auckland
15 Jan 49	Sir F. T. Baring
28 Feb 52	D of Northumberland
30 Dec 52	Sir J. Graham
13 Mar 55	Sir C. Wood
8 Mar 58	Sir J. Pakington
27 Jun 59	D of Somerset
12 Jul 66	Sir J. Pakington
8 Mar 67	H. T. L. Corry
9 Dec 68	H. C. E. Childers
24 Mar 71	G. J. Goschen
21 Feb 74	G. W. Hunt
14 Aug 77	W. H. Smith
28 Apr 80	E of Northbrook
24 Jun 85	Ld G. Hamilton
9 Feb 86	M of Ripon
9 Aug 86	Ld G. Hamilton
19 Aug 92	Earl Spencer
29 Jun 95	G. J. Goschen
12 Nov 00	E of Selborne
27 Mar 05	Earl Cawdor

President of the Board of Agriculture

9 Sep 89	H. Chaplin
25 Aug 92	H. Gardner
4 Jul 95	W. Long
16 Nov 00	R. W. Hanbury
20 May 03	E of Onslow
14 Mar 05	A. E. Fellowes

Attorney-General

24 Nov 30	Sir T. Denman
26 Nov 32	Sir W. Horne
1 Mar 34	Sir J. Campbell
17 Dec 34	Sir F. Pollock
30 Apr 35	Sir J. Campbell
3 Jul 41	Sir T. Wilde
6 Sep 41	Sir F. Pollock
15 Apr 44	Sir W. W. Follett
29 Jun 45	Sir F. Thesiger
7 Jul 46	Sir T. Wilde
17 Jul 46	Sir J. Jervis
11 Jul 50	Sir J. Romilly
28 Mar 51	Sir A. Cockburn
27 Feb 52	Sir F. Thesiger
28 Dec 52	Sir A. Cockburn
15 Nov 56	Sir R. Bethell
26 Feb 58	Sir F. Kelly
18 Jun 59	Sir R. Bethell
4 Jul 61	Sir W. Atherton
2 Oct 63	Sir R. Palmer
10 Jul 66	Sir H. Cairns
29 Oct 66	Sir J. Rolt
18 Jul 67	Sir J. Karslake
12 Dec 68	Sir R. Collier
10 Nov 71	Sir J. Coleridge
20 Nov 73	Sir H. James
27 Feb 74	Sir J. Karslake
20 Apr 74	Sir R. Baggallay
25 Nov 75	Sir J. Holker
3 May 80	Sir H. James
27 Jun 85	Sir R. Webster
9 Feb 86	Sir C. Russell
5 Aug 86	Sir R. Webster
20 Aug 92	Sir C. Russell
3 May 94	Sir J. Rigby
24 Oct 94	Sir R. T. Reid
8 Jul 95	Sir R. Webster
11 May 00	Sir R. Finlay

President of the Board of Control

1 Dec 30	C. Grant
18 Dec 34	Ld Ellenborough
23 Apr 35	Sir J. C. Hobhouse
4 Sep 41	Ld Ellenborough (E)
23 Oct 41	Ld Fitzgerald
17 May 43	E of Ripon (1st)
8 Jul 46	Sir J. C. Hobhouse
5 Feb 52	F. Maule
28 Feb 52	J. C. Herries
30 Dec 52	Sir C. Wood
3 Mar 55	R. V. Smith
6 Mar 58	E of Ellenborough
5 Jun 58	Ld Stanley

Vice-President of the Committee of the Privy Council on Education in England and Wales

5 Feb 57	W. F. Cowper
12 Mar 58	C. B. Adderley
24 Jun 59	R. Lowe
26 Apr 64	H. A. Bruce
12 Jul 66	H. T. L. Corry
19 Mar 67	Ld R. Montagu
9 Dec 68	W. E. Forster
2 Mar 74	Vt Sandon
4 Apr 78	Ld G. Hamilton
3 May 80	A. J. Mundella
24 Jun 85	E. Stanhope
17 Sep 85	Sir H. T. Holland
13 Feb 86	Sir L. Playfair
3 Aug 86	Sir H. T. Holland
25 Jan 87	Sir W. Hart Dyke
25 Aug 92	A. H. D. Acland
4 Jul 95	Sir J. E. Gorst

President of the Board of Education

3 Mar 00	D of Devonshire
11 Aug 02	M of Londonderry

President of the General Board Health

14 Aug 54	Sir B. Hall
13 Aug 55	W. F. Cowper
9 Feb 57	W. Monsell
24 Sep 57	W. F. Cowper
8 Mar 58	C. B. Adderley

Chief Secretary for Ireland

29 Nov 30	E. G. Stanley
29 Mar 33	Sir J. C. Hobhouse
17 May 33	E. J. Littleton
16 Dec 34	Sir H. Hardinge
22 Apr 35	Vt Morpeth
6 Sep 41	Ld Eliot
1 Feb 45	Sir T. F. Fremantle
14 Feb 46	E of Lincoln
6 Jul 46	H. Labouchere
22 Jul 47	Sir W. Somerville
1 Mar 52	Ld Naas
6 Jan 53	Sir J. Young
1 Mar 55	E. Horsman

27 May 57	H. A. Herbert
4 Mar 58	Ld Naas
24 Jun 59	E. Cardwell
29 Jul 61	Sir R. Peel
7 Dec 65	C. S. Fortescue
10 Jul 66	Ld Naas
29 Sep 68	J. Wilson-Patten
16 Dec 68	C. S. Fortescue
12 Jan 71	M of Hartington
27 Feb 74	Sir M. Hicks Beach
15 Feb 78	J. Lowther
30 Apr 80	W. E. Forster
6 May 82	Ld F. Cavendish
9 May 82	G. O. Trevelyan
23 Oct 84	H. Campbell-Bannerman
25 Jun 85	Sir W. Hart Dyke
23 Jan 86	W. H. Smith
6 Feb 86	J. Morley
5 Aug 86	Sir M. Hicks Beach
7 Mar 87	A. J. Balfour
9 Nov 91	W. L. Jackson
22 Aug 92	J. Morley
4 Jul 95	G. W. Balfour
9 Nov 00	G. Wyndham
12 Mar 05	W. Long

Chancellor of the Duchy of Lancaster

25 Nov 30	Ld Holland
26 Dec 34	C. W. Williams Wynn
23 Apr 35	Ld Holland
31 Oct 40	E of Clarendon
23 Jun 41	Sir G. Grey
3 Sep 41	Ld G. Somerset
6 Jul 46	Ld Campbell
6 Mar 50	E of Carlisle (7th)
1 Mar 52	R. A. Christopher
3 Jan 53	E. Strutt
21 Jun 54	Earl Granville
31 Mar 55	E of Harrowby
7 Dec 55	M. T. Baines
26 Feb 58	D of Montrose
22 Jun 59	Sir G. Grey
25 Jul 61	E. Cardwell
7 Apr 64	E of Clarendon
26 Jan 66	G. J. Goschen
10 Jul 66	E of Devon
26 Jun 67	J. Wilson-Patten
7 Nov 68	T. E. Taylor
12 Dec 68	Ld Dufferin (E)
9 Aug 72	H. C. E. Childers
30 Sep 73	J. Bright
2 Mar 74	T. E. Taylor
28 Apr 80	J. Bright

25 Jul 82	E of Kimberley
28 Dec 82	J. G. Dodson
29 Oct 84	G. O. Trevelyan
24 Jun 85	H. Chaplin
6 Feb 86	E. Heneage
16 Apr 86	Sir U. Kay-Shuttleworth
3 Aug 86	Vt Cranbrook
16 Aug 86	Ld J. Manners (7th D of Rutland 1888)
18 Aug 92	J. Bryce
28 May 94	Ld Tweedmouth
29 Jun 95	Vt Cross
4 Jul 95	Ld James of Hereford
11 Aug 02	Sir W. H. Walrond

President of the Local Government Board

19 Aug 71	J. Stansfeld
21 Feb 74	G. Sclater-Booth
3 May 80	J. G. Dodson
28 Dec 82	Sir C. Dilke
24 Jun 85	A. J. Balfour
6 Feb 86	J. Chamberlain
3 Apr 86	J. Stansfeld
3 Aug 86	C. T. Ritchie
18 Aug 92	H. H. Fowler
10 Mar 94	G. J. Shaw-Lefevre
29 Jun 95	H. Chaplin
12 Nov 00	W. Long
14 Mar 05	G. W. Balfour

Paymaster-General

16 Dec 30	Ld J. Russell
23 Dec 34	Sir E. Knatchbull
27 Apr 35	Sir H. Parnell
19 Jun 41	E. J. Stanley
8 Sep 41	Sir E. Knatchbull
1 Mar 45	W. B. Baring
7 Jul 46	T. B. Macaulay
8 May 48	Earl Granville
12 Feb 52	Ld Stanley of Alderley
28 Feb 52	Ld Colchester
5 Jan 53	Ld Stanley of Alderley
31 Mar 55	E. P. Bouverie
28 Aug 55	R. Lowe
6 Apr 58	E of Donoughmore
3 Mar 59	Ld Lovaine
18 Jun 59	J. Wilson
12 Aug 59	W. F. Cowper
22 Feb 60	(Sir) W. Hutt
29 Nov 65	G. J. Goschen
12 Mar 66	W. Monsell
10 Jul 66	S. Cave
12 Dec 68	Ld Dufferin
9 Aug 72	H. C. E. Childers

11 Aug 73	W. P. Adam
20 Apr 74	S. Cave
24 Nov 75	D. R. Plunket
24 May 80	Ld Wolverton
24 Jun 85	Earl Beauchamp
3 Apr 86	Ld Thurlow
19 Aug 86	Earl Beauchamp
Jul 87	Earl Brownlow
1889	E of Jersey
Dec 90	Ld Windsor
24 Aug 92	C. Seale-Hayne
16 Jul 95	E of Hopetoun
1899	D of Marlborough
11 Mar 02	Sir S. Crossley

President of the Poor Law Board

23 Jul 47	C. Buller
1 Jan 49	M. T. Baines
1 Mar 52	Sir J. Trollope
30 Dec 52	M. T. Baines
13 Aug 55	E. P. Bouverie
6 Mar 58	T. H. S. Sotheron Estcourt
7 Mar 59	E of March
24 Jun 59	T. M. Gibson
9 Jul 59	C. P. Villiers
12 Jul 66	G. Hardy
21 May 67	E of Devon
9 Dec 68	G. J. Goschen
24 Mar 71	J. Stansfeld

Minister without Portfolio

22 Nov 30–5 Jun 34	E of Carlisle (6th)
3 Sep 41–27 Jun 46	D of Wellington
28 Dec 52–21 Feb 58	M of Lansdowne (3rd)
26 Feb 53–8 Jun 54	Ld J. Russell
17 May 67–1 Dec 68	S. Walpole
7 Mar 87–20 Feb 88	Sir M. Hicks Beach

Postmaster-General

14 Dec 30	D of Richmond
5 Jul 34	M of Conyngham
23 Dec 34	Ld Maryborough
30 Apr 35	M of Conyngham
22 May 35	E of Lichfield
9 Sep 41	Vt Lowther (2nd E of Lonsdale 1844)
30 Dec 45	E of St Germans
7 Jul 46	M of Clanricarde
1 Mar 52	E of Hardwicke

5 Jan 53	Vt Canning
30 Nov 55	D of Argyll
13 Mar 58	Ld Colchester
24 Jun 59	E of Elgin
11 May 60	D of Argyll
17 Aug 60	Ld Stanley of Alderley
19 Jul 66	D of Montrose
9 Dec 68	M of Hartington
14 Jan 71	W. Monsell
18 Nov 73	L. Playfair
21 Feb 74	Ld J. Manners
3 May 80	H. Fawcett
7 Nov 84	G. J. Shaw-Lefevre
24 Jun 85	Ld J. Manners
17 Feb 86	Ld Wolverton
19 Aug 86	H. C. Raikes
21 Sep 91	Sir J. Fergusson
18 Aug 92	A. Morley
6 Jul 95	D of Norfolk
10 Apr 00	M of Londonderry
11 Aug 02	J. A. Chamberlain
9 Oct 03	Ld Stanley

Secretary for Scotland

17 Aug 85	D of Richmond
8 Feb 86	G. O. Trevelyan
5 Apr 86	D of Dalhousie
5 Aug 86	A. J. Balfour
11 Mar 87	M of Lothian
18 Aug 92	G. O. Trevelyan
29 Jun 95	Ld Balfour of Burleigh
9 Oct 03	A. G. Murray
2 Feb 05	M of Linlithgow

President of the Board of Trade

22 Nov 30	Ld Auckland
5 Jun 34	C. P. Thomson
15 Dec 34	A. Baring
18 Apr 35	C. P. Thomson
29 Aug 39	H. Labouchere
3 Sep 41	E of Ripon
15 May 43	W. E. Gladstone
5 Feb 45	E of Dalhousie
6 Jul 46	E of Clarendon
22 Jul 47	H. Labouchere
27 Feb 52	J. W. Henley
28 Dec 52	E. Cardwell
31 Mar 55	Ld Stanley of Alderley
26 Feb 58	J. W. Henley
3 Mar 59	E of Donoughmore
6 Jul 59	T. M. Gibson
6 Jul 66	Sir S. Northcote
8 Mar 67	D of Richmond
9 Dec 68	J. Bright

14 Jan 71	C. S. Fortescue
21 Feb 74	Sir C. B. Adderley
4 Apr 78	Vt Sandon
3 May 80	J. Chamberlain
24 Jun 85	D of Richmond
19 Aug 85	E. Stanhope
17 Feb 86	A. J. Mundella
3 Aug 86	Ld Stanley of Preston
21 Feb 88	Sir M. Hicks Beach
18 Aug 92	A. J. Mundella
28 May 94	J. Bryce
29 Jun 95	C. T. Ritchie
12 Nov 00	G. W. Balfour
14 Mar 05	M of Salisbury (4th)

Secretary at War

30 Nov 30	C. W. Williams Wynn
4 Apr 31	Sir H. Parnell
1 Feb 32	Sir J. C. Hobhouse
6 Apr 33	E. Ellice
16 Dec 34	J. C. Herries
18 Apr 35	Vt Howick
27 Sep 39	T. B. Macaulay
4 Sep 41	Sir H. Hardinge
17 May 44	Sir T. F. Fremantle
4 Feb 45	S. Herbert
6 Jul 46	F. Maule
6 Feb 52	R. V. Smith
28 Feb 52	W. Beresford
30 Dec 52	S. Herbert

(*office merged with Secretary of State for War* 1855, *and abolished* 1863)

First Commissioner of Woods, Forests and Land Revenue

2 Dec 30	G. J. W. A. Ellis
7 Feb 31	Vt Duncannon

22 Jul 34	Sir J. C. Hobhouse
23 Dec 34	Ld G. Somerset
28 Apr 35	Vt Duncannon
16 Sep 41	E of Lincoln
2 Mar 46	Vt Canning
7 Jul 46	Vt Morpeth (7th E of Carlisle 1848)
17 Apr 49–1 Aug 51	Ld Seymour

First Commissioner of Works

1 Aug 51	Ld Seymour (12th D of Somerset, 1855)
4 Mar 52	Ld J. Manners
5 Jan 53	Sir W. Molesworth
21 Jul 55	Sir B. Hall
26 Feb 58	Ld J. Manners
18 Jun 59	H. Fitzroy
9 Feb 60	W. F. Cowper
6 Jul 66	Ld J. Manners
9 Dec 68	A. H. Layard
26 Oct 69	A. S. Ayrton
11 Aug 73	W. P. Adam
21 Mar 74	Ld H. Gordon-Lennox
14 Aug 76	G. J. Noel
3 May 80	W. P. Adam
29 Nov 81	G. J. Shaw-Lefevre
13 Feb 85	E of Rosebery
24 Jun 85	D. R. Plunket
17 Feb 86	E of Morley
16 Apr 86	E of Elgin
5 Aug 86	D. R. Plunket
18 Aug 92	G. J. Shaw-Lefevre
10 Mar 94	H. Gladstone
4 Jul 95	A. Akers-Douglas
11 Aug 02	Ld Windsor

Biographical Notes

Prime Ministers, Foreign Secretaries and Chancellors of the Exchequer:

Aberdeen, 4th E of (1801). George Hamilton-Gordon
b. 1784. *Educ.* Harrow; St. John's Coll., Camb. A Scottish representative peer, 1806–14. Ambassador Extraordinary at Vienna, 1813. British representative at Treaty of Paris, 1814. Created a peer of U.K., 1814. Chanc. of D. of Lanc., Jan–Jun 1828. For. Sec., 1828–30. Sec. for War and Cols., 1834–35. For. Sec., 1841–46. Peelite leader in Lords after 1846. P.M., 1852–55. Resigned after the carrying of Roebuck's motion for a committee of inquiry into the conduct of the Crimean War, 1855. d. 1860.

Balfour, Arthur James. 1st E of Balfour (1922)

b. 1848. *Educ.* Eton; Trinity Coll., Camb. M.P. (Con.) for Hertford, 1874–85. M.P. for Manchester E., 1885–1906. M.P. for City of London, 1906–22. P.P.S. to Ld. Salisbury, 1878–80. Pres. of Loc. Govt. Bd., 1885. Sec. for Scotland, 1886 (member of cabinet, Nov 1886). Ch. Sec. for Ireland, 1887–91. Leader of Commons and 1st Ld. of Treas., 1891–92 and 1895–1902. P.M., 1902–05. Leader of Con. party, 1902–11. Member of Committee of Imperial Defence, 1914. Attended meetings of War Cabinet, 1914–15. 1st Ld. of Admir., 1915–16. For. Sec., 1916–19. Ld. Pres. of Council, 1919–22 and 1925–29. d. 1930.

Baring, Sir Francis Thornhill. 3rd Bt (1848), 1st Ld Northbrook (1866)

b. 1796. *Educ.* Winchester; Ch. Ch. Oxf. M.P. (Whig) for Portsmouth, 1826–65. Junior Ld. of Treas., 1830–34. Jt. Sec. to Treas., 1834 and 1835–39. Chanc. of Exch., 1839–41. 1st Ld. of Admir., 1849–52. d. 1866.

Bright, John

b. 1811. *Educ.* Elementary. Worked in his father's mill in Rochdale. Treasurer, Rochdale branch of Anti-Corn Law League, 1840. M.P. (Rad.) for Durham, 1843–47. M.P. for Manchester, 1847–57. M.P. for Birmingham, 1857–85. M.P. for Birmingham C., 1885–89. Pres. of Bd. of Trade, 1868–70. Chanc. of D. of Lanc., 1873–74 and 1880–82. Resigned in protest at bombardment of Alexandria, 1882. Opposed Home Rule. d. 1889.

Cardwell, Edward. 1st Vt Cardwell (1874)

b. 1813. *Educ.* Winchester; Balliol Coll., Oxf. Barrister, 1838. M.P. (Con.) for Clitheroe, 1842–47. M.P. (Peelite) for Liverpool, 1847–52. M.P. for Oxford City, 1852–74. Jt. Sec. to Treas., 1845–46. Pres. of Bd. of Trade, 1852–55. Ch. Sec. for Ireland, 1859–61. Chanc. of D. of Lanc., 1861–64. Col. Sec., 1864–66. Sec. for War, 1868–74. d. 1886.

Chamberlain, Joseph

b. 1836. *Educ.* University College School. Family business. Mayor of Birmingham, 1873–75. M.P. (Lib.) for Birmingham, 1876–85. M.P. for Birmingham W., 1885–86. M.P. (Lib. U.) for Birmingham W., 1886–1914. Pres. of Bd. of Trade, 1880–85. Pres. of Loc. Govt. Bd., 1886. Col. Sec., 1895–1903. Resigned over imperial preference, 1903. d. 1914.

Childers, Hugh Culling Eardley

b. 1827. *Educ.* Cheam School; Wadham Coll., Oxf.; Trinity Coll., Camb. M.P. (Lib.) for Pontefract, 1860–85. M.P. for Edinburgh S., 1886–92. Civil Ld. of Admir., 1864–66. F.S. to Treas., 1865–66. 1st Ld. of Admir., 1868–71. Chanc. of D. of Lanc.,

1872–73. Sec. for War, 1880–82. Chanc. of Exch., 1882–85. Home Sec., 1886. d. 1896.

Churchill, Lord Randolph Henry Spencer
b. 1849. *Educ.* Eton; Merton Coll., Oxf. M.P. (Con.) for Woodstock, 1874–85. M.P. for Paddington S., 1885–95. Leader of 'Fourth Party' in Commons, 1880–85. Sec. for India, 1885–86. Chanc. of Exch. and Leader of Commons, 1886. Resigned over Estimates, 1886. d. 1895.

Clarendon, 4th E of (1838). George William Frederick Villiers
b. 1800. *Educ.* St. John's Coll., Camb. Succeeded his uncle as 4th E, 1838. Ld. Privy S., 1840–41. Chanc. of D. of Lanc., 1840–41. Pres. of Bd. of Trade, 1846–47. Ld. Lieut. of Ireland, 1847–52. For. Sec., 1853–58. Chanc. of D. of Lanc., 1864–65. For. Sec., 1865–66 and 1868–70. d. 1870.

Derby, 14th E of (1851). Edward George Geoffrey Smith Stanley
b. 1799. *Educ.* Eton; Ch. Ch. Oxf. M.P. (Whig) for Stockbridge, 1820–26. M.P. for Preston, 1826–30. M.P. for Windsor, 1831–32. M.P. for Lancs. N., 1832–44. Called to Lords as Ld. Stanley of Bickerstaffe, 1844. U.-S. Col. O., 1827–28. Ch. Sec. for Ireland, 1830–33. Col. Sec., 1833–34. Resigned in protest at proposed lay appropriation of surplus Irish Church revenue, 1834. Col. Sec. (Con.), 1841–45. Resigned in defence of Corn Laws, 1845. P.M., 1852, 1858–59 and 1866–68. d. 1869.

Derby, 15th E of (1869). Edward Henry Stanley
b. 1826. *Educ.* Rugby; Trinity Coll., Camb. Styled Ld. Stanley, 1851–69. M.P. (Con.) for Lynn Regis, 1848–69. U.-S. For. O., 1852. Col. Sec., 1858. Pres. of Bd. of Control, 1858. Sec. for India, 1858–59. Declined crown of Greece, 1863. For. Sec., 1866–68 and 1874–78. Resigned over Eastern Question, 1878. Left Con. party, 1879. Col. Sec. (Lib.), 1882–85. Leader of Lib. Unionists in Lords, 1886–91. d. 1893.

Devonshire, 8th D of (1891). Spencer Compton Cavendish, M of Hartington, 1858–91
b. 1833. *Educ.* Trinity Coll., Camb. M.P. (Lib.) for Lancs. N., 1857–68. M.P. for Radnor Boroughs, 1869–80. M.P. for Lancs. N.E., 1880–85. M.P. for Rossendale, 1885–91. U.-S. War O., 1863–66. Sec. for War, 1866. Postm.-Gen., 1868–70. Ch. Sec. for Ireland, 1870–74. Leader of Liberals in Commons, 1875–80. Sec. for India, 1880–82. Sec. for War, 1882–85. Leader of Lib. Unionists in Commons, 1886–91, and in Lords, 1891–95. Ld. Pres. of Council, 1895–1903. Resigned in defence of free trade, 1903. d. 1908.

Disraeli, Benjamin. 1st E of Beaconsfield (1876)
b. 1805. *Educ.* Privately. M.P. (Con.) for Maidstone, 1837–41.

M.P. for Shrewsbury, 1841–47. M.P. for Bucks., 1847–76. Leader of Commons and Chanc. of Exch., 1852, 1858–59, 1866–68. P.M., 1868, 1874–80. Ld. Privy Seal, 1876–78. d. 1881.

Forster, William Edward

b. 1818. *Educ.* Friends' School, Tottenham. Woollen manufacturer at Bradford. M.P. (Lib.) for Bradford, 1861–85. M.P. for Bradford C., 1885–86. U.-S. Col. O., 1865–66. V. Pres. of Privy Council Committee on Educ., 1868–74 (with a seat in cabinet, 1870–74). Ch. Sec. for Ireland, 1880–82. Resigned in protest at weak Irish policy, 1882. Opposed Home Rule, 1886. d. 1886.

Gladstone, William Ewart

b. 1809. *Educ.* Eton; Ch. Ch. Oxf. M.P. (Con.) for Newark, 1832–46. M.P. (Peelite) for Oxford Univ., 1847–65. M.P. (Lib.) for Lancs. S., 1865–68. M.P. for Greenwich, 1868–80. M.P. for Midlothian, 1880–95. Junior Ld. of Treas., 1834–35. U.-S. Col. O., 1835. V. Pres. of Bd. of Trade, 1841–43. Pres. of Bd. of Trade, 1843–45. Master of Mint, 1841–45. Resigned over Maynooth Grant, 1845. Col. Sec., 1845–46. Chanc. of Exch., 1852–55, 1859–66, 1873–74 and 1880–82. Leader of Commons, 1865–66. P.M., 1868–74, 1880–85, 1886 and 1892–94. Ld. Privy S., 1886, 1892–94. Resigned over Estimates, 1894. d. 1898.

Goschen, George Joachim.   1st Vt Goschen (1900)

b. 1831. *Educ.* Rugby; Oriel Coll., Oxf. M.P. (Lib.) for City of London, 1863–80. M.P. for Ripon, 1880–85. M.P. for Edinburgh S., 1885–87. M.P. (Con.) for St. George's, Hanover Square, 1887–1900. V. Pres. of Bd. of Trade and Paym.-Gen., 1865–66. Chanc. of D. of Lanc., 1866. Pres. of Poor Law Bd., 1868–71. 1st Ld. of Admir., 1871–74. A Liberal Unionist, 1886. Chanc. of Exch., 1887–92. 1st Ld. of Admir., 1895–1900. d. 1907.

Goulburn, Henry

b. 1784. *Educ.* Trinity Coll., Camb. M.P. (Tory) for Horsham, 1808–12. M.P. for St Germains, 1812–18. M.P. for Looe W., 1818–26. M.P. for Armagh, 1826–31. M.P. for Cambridge Univ., 1831–56. U.-S. Home O., 1810–12. U.-S. Col. O., 1812–21. Ch. Sec. for Ireland, 1821–27. Chanc. of Exch., 1828–30. Home Sec., 1834–35. Defeated for Speakership by C. S. Lefevre, 1839. Chanc. of Exch., 1841–46. d. 1856.

Graham, Sir James.   2nd Bt (1824)

b. 1792. *Educ.* Westminster; Ch. Ch. Oxf. M.P. (Whig) for Hull, 1818. M.P. for St. Ives, 1820–21. M.P. for Carlisle, 1826–29. M.P. for Cumberland, 1829–32. M.P. for Cumberland E., 1832–37. M.P. for Pembroke, 1838–41. M.P. (Con.) for Dorchester, 1841–47. M.P. (Peelite) for Ripon, 1847–52. M.P. for Carlisle, 1852–61. 1st Ld. of Admir., 1830–34. Resigned over proposed lay appropriation of surplus Irish Church revenues, 1834.

Home Sec. (Con.), 1841–46. 1st Ld. of Admir., 1852–55. Resigned, 1855. d. 1861.

Granville, 2nd E (1846). Granville George Leveson-Gower b. 1815. *Educ.* Eton; Ch. Ch. Oxf. Styled Ld. Leveson, 1833–46. M.P. (Whig) for Morpeth, 1837–40. M.P. for Lichfield, 1841–46. Master of Buckhounds, 1846–48. V. Pres. of Bd. of Trade and Paym.-Gen., 1848–51. V. Pres. of Royal Commission on Great Exhibition, 1850. For. Sec., 1851–52. Ld. Pres. of Council, 1852–54. Chanc. of D. of Lanc., 1854–55. Ld. Pres. of Council, 1855–58 and 1859–66. Col. Sec., 1868–70. For. Sec., 1870–74 and 1880–85. Col. Sec., 1886. Liberal leader in Lords from 1855. d. 1891.

Grey, 2nd Earl (1807). Charles Grey
b. 1764. *Educ.* Eton; King's Coll., Camb. M.P. (Whig) for Northumberland, 1786–1807. M.P. for Appleby, 1807. 1st Ld. of Admir., 1806. For. Sec., 1806–07. P.M., 1830–34. d. 1845.

Harcourt, (Sir) William Vernon
b. 1827. *Educ.* Trinity Coll., Camb. Barrister, 1854. Q.C., 1866. M.P. (Lib.) for Oxford City, 1868–80. M.P. for Derby, 1880–95. M.P. for Monmouth W., 1895–1904. Sol.-Gen., 1873–74. Knighted, 1873. Home Sec., 1880–85. Chanc. of Exch., 1886 and 1892–95. Leader of Commons, 1894–95. Leader of Lib. party, 1896–98. d. 1904.

Hicks Beach, Sir Michael Edward. 9th Bt (1854), 1st Vt St Aldwyn (1906), 1st E (1915)
b. 1837. *Educ.* Eton; Ch. Ch. Oxf. M.P. (Con.) for Gloucs. E., 1864–85. M.P. for Bristol W., 1885–1906. Sec. of Poor Law Bd., 1868. U.-S. Home O., 1868. Ch. Sec. for Ireland, 1874–78 (seat in cabinet, 1876). Col. Sec., 1878–80. Chanc. of Exch. and Leader of Commons, 1885–86. Leader of Opposition in Commons, 1886. Ch. Sec. for Ireland, 1886–87. Resigned, 1887, but remained in cabinet without portfolio. Pres. of Bd. of Trade, 1888–92. Chanc. of Exch., 1895–1902. Resigned, 1902. d. 1916.

Hunt, George Ward
b. 1825. *Educ.* Eton; Ch. Ch. Oxf. Barrister; 1851. M.P. (Con.) for Northants. N., 1857–77. F.S. to Treas., 1866–68. Chanc. of Exch., 1868. 1st Ld. of Admir., 1874–77. d. 1877.

Lewis, Sir George Cornwall. 5th Bt (1855)
b. 1806. *Educ.* Eton; Ch. Ch. Oxf. Barrister, 1831. Poor Law Commissioner, 1839–47. M.P. (Whig) for Herefordshire, 1847–52. M.P. for Radnor Boroughs, 1855–63. Jt. Sec. of Bd. of Control, 1847–48. U.-S. Home O., 1848–50. F.S. to Treas., 1850–52. Editor of *Edinburgh Review*, 1852–55. Chanc. of Exch., 1855–58. Home Sec., 1859–61. Sec. for War, 1861–63. d. 1863.

Lowe, Robert. 1st Vt Sherbrooke (1880)

    b. 1811. *Educ.* Winchester; Univ. Coll., Oxf. Barrister, practised in Australia. *Times* leader writer from 1850. M.P. (Lib.) for Kidderminster, 1852–59. M.P. for Calne, 1859–68. M.P. for London Univ., 1868–80. Jt. Sec. of Bd. of Control, 1853–55. V. Pres. of Bd. of Trade and Paym.-Gen., 1855–58. V. Pres. of Privy Council Committee on Educ., 1859–64. Leader of Adullamites against Reform Bill, 1866. Chanc. of Exch., 1868–73. Home Sec., 1873–74. d. 1892.

Malmesbury, 3rd E (1841). James Howard Harris

    b. 1807. *Educ.* Eton; Oriel Coll., Oxf. Styled Vt Fitz-Harris, 1820–41. M.P. (Tory) for Wilton, 1841. For. Sec., 1852 and 1858–59. Ld. Privy S., 1866–68 and 1874–76. Con. leader in Lords, Feb–Dec 1868. d. 1889.

Melbourne, 2nd Vt (1829). William Lamb

    b. 1779. *Educ.* Eton; Trinity Coll., Camb. M.P. (Whig) for Leominster, 1806. M.P. for Portarlington, 1807–12. M.P. for Northampton, 1816–19. M.P. for Hertfordshire, 1819–29. Ch. Sec. for Ireland, 1827–28. Home Sec., 1830–34. P.M., 1834 and 1835–41. d. 1848.

Morley, John. 1st Vt Morley (1908)

    b. 1838. *Educ.* Cheltenham Coll.; Lincoln Coll., Oxf. Barrister, 1878. Editor of *Fortnightly Review*, 1867–82. Editor of *Pall Mall Gazette*, 1880–83. M.P. (Lib.) for Newcastle-upon-Tyne, 1883–95. M.P. for Montrose Burghs, 1896–1908. Ch. Sec. for Ireland, 1886, 1892–95. Sec. for India, 1905–10. Ld. Pres. of Council, 1910–14. Resigned in protest at declaration of war, 1914. d. 1923.

Northcote, Sir Stafford Henry. 8th Bt (1851), 1st E of Iddesleigh (1885)

    b. 1818. *Educ.* Eton; Balliol Coll., Oxf. Private Sec. to Gladstone at Bd. of Trade, 1842–45. M.P. (Con.) for Dudley, 1855–57. M.P. for Stamford, 1858–66. M.P. for Devon N., 1866–85. F.S. to Treas., 1859. Pres. of Bd. of Trade, 1866–67. Chairman, Hudson's Bay Co., 1869–74. Chanc. of Exch., 1874–80. Leader of Commons, 1877–80. 1st Ld. of Treas., 1885–86. For. Sec., 1886–87. d. 1887.

Palmerston, 3rd Vt (1802). Henry John Temple

    b. 1784. *Educ.* Harrow; Edinburgh Univ.; St. John's Coll., Camb. M.P. (Tory) for Newport, 1807–11. M.P. for Cambridge Univ., 1811–31. M.P. (Whig) for Bletchingly, 1831–32. M.P. for Hants. S., 1832–34. M.P. for Tiverton, 1835–65. A Lord of the Admir., 1807–09. Declined Chanc. of Exch., 1809. Sec. at War, 1809–28. For. Sec., 1830–34, 1835–41, 1846–51. Home Sec., 1852–55. P.M., 1855–58, 1859–65. d. 1865.

Peel, Sir Robert. 2nd Bt (1830)

b. 1788. *Educ.* Harrow; Ch. Ch. Oxf. M.P. (Tory) for Cashel, 1809–17. M.P. for Oxford Univ., 1817–28. M.P. for Westbury, 1829. M.P. for Tamworth, 1830–50. U.-S. Col. O., 1810–12. Ch. Sec. for Ireland 1812–18. Home Sec., 1822–27, 1828–30. Leader of Commons, 1828–30. P.M. and Chanc. of Exch., 1834–35. P.M., 1841–46. Resigned, 1845, but resumed when Whigs were unable to form a Govt. d. 1850.

Rosebery, 5th E of (1868). Archibald Philip Primrose

b. 1847. *Educ.* Eton; Ch. Ch. Oxf. U.-S. Home O., 1881–83. 1st Comm. Works, 1885. Ld. Privy S., 1885. For. Sec., 1886 and 1892–94. P.M. and Ld. Privy S., 1894–95. Chairman of L.C.C., 1889–90, 1892. Resigned Lib. leadership, 1896. d. 1929.

Russell, Lord John. 1st Earl Russell (1861)

b. 1792. *Educ.* Westminster School; Edinburgh Univ. M.P. (Whig) for Tavistock, 1813–19. M.P. for Hunts., 1820–26. M.P. for Bandon Bridge, 1826–30. M.P. for Tavistock, 1831. M.P. for Devon, 1831–32. M.P. for Devon S., 1832–35. M.P. for Stroud, 1835–41. M.P. for City of London, 1841–61. Paym.-Gen., 1830–34 (with a seat in cabinet from 1831). Home Sec., 1835–39. Col. Sec., 1839–41. P.M., 1846–52. For. Sec., 1852–53. Remained in cabinet without portfolio, 1853–54. Ld. Pres. of Council, 1854–55. Col. Sec., 1855. For. Sec., 1859–65. P.M., 1865–66. d. 1878.

Salisbury, 3rd M of (1868). Robert Arthur Talbot Gascoyne-Cecil, Vt Cranborne (1865–68)

b. 1830. *Educ.* Eton; Ch. Ch. Oxf. M.P. (Con.) for Stamford, 1853–68. Sec. for India, 1866. Resigned, 1867. Sec. for India, 1874–76. For. Sec., 1878–80. Leader of Opposition in Lords, 1881–85. Leader of Con. party, 1885–1902. P.M. and For. Sec., 1885–86. P.M., 1886. P.M. and For. Sec., 1887–92 and 1895–1900. P.M. and Ld. Privy S., 1900–02. d. 1903.

Smith, William Henry

b. 1825. *Educ.* Elementary. Entered his father's newsagency business, 1841. M.P. (Con.) for Westminster, 1868–85. M.P. for Westminster-Strand, 1885–91. F.S. to Treas., 1874–77. 1st Ld. of Admir., 1877–80. Sec. for War, 1885–86 and 1886–87. Ch. Sec. for Ireland, 1886. 1st Ld. of Treas. and Leader of Commons, 1887–91. d. 1891.

Spencer, 3rd E (1834). John Charles Spencer

b. 1782. *Educ.* Harrow; Trinity Coll., Camb. Styled Ld. Althorp until 1834. M.P. (Whig) for Okehampton, 1804–06. M.P. for St. Albans, 1806. M.P. for Northants., 1806–34. Junior Ld. of Treas., 1806–07. Chanc. of Exch. and Leader of Commons, 1830–34. d. 1845.

Spring-Rice, Thomas. 1st Baron Monteagle (1839)
> b. 1790. *Educ.* Trinity Coll., Camb. M.P. (Whig) for Limerick, 1820–32. M.P. for Cambridge, 1832–39. U.-S. Home O., 1827–28. Jt. Sec. to Treas., 1830–34. Col. Sec., 1834. Chanc. of Exch., 1835–39. Comptroller-Gen. of Exch., 1839–65. d. 1866.

Wellington, 1st D of (1814). Arthur Wellesley, Vt (1809), E (1812), M (1812)
> b. 1769. *Educ.* Eton; Angers Military Academy. M.P. for Trim in Irish Parl., 1790–97. Gov. of Seringapatam and of Mysore, 1799–1805. Numerous military commands, 1805–18. Field-Marshal, 1813. Master-Gen. of Ordnance, with a seat in cabinet, 1818–27. Commander-in-Chief, 1827–28 and 1842–52. P.M., 1828–30. Sec. of State for all depts., Nov 1834. For. Sec., 1834–35. Cabinet Minister without portfolio, 1841–46. d. 1852.

Wood, Sir Charles. 3rd Bt (1846), 1st Vt Halifax (1866)
> b. 1800. *Educ.* Eton; Oriel Coll., Oxf. M.P. (Whig) for Great Grimsby, 1826–31. M.P. for Wareham, 1831. M.P. for Halifax, 1832–65. M.P. for Ripon, 1865–66. Jt. Sec. to Treas., 1832–34. Sec. to Admir., 1835–39. Chanc. of Exch., 1846–52. Pres. of Bd. of Control, 1852–55. 1st Ld. of Admir., 1855–58. Sec. for India, 1859–66. Ld. Privy S., 1870–74. d. 1885.

Index of Ministers

This index provides basic information on all holders of Ministerial office. When an individual held office under different names, he is entered in the index under each of the names. Educational details are as complete as the sources permit, that is to say, not always very full. Where information is not available, this is indicated by *n.a.*.

Name	Born	Education	Died	Page references
Acland Hood, Sir A.				44, 47
Acton, 1st Ld (1869). Sir J. E. Dalberg (8th Bt 1835)	1834	Oscott Coll., B'ham; Edin. Univ.; Munich Univ.	1902	43
Adam, W. P.	1823	Rugby; Trinity Coll., Camb.	1881	24, 29, 34, 54, 55
Adderley, C. B. 1st Ld Norton (1878)	1814	Privately; Ch. Ch. Oxf.	1905	21, 26, 31, 52, 55
Adye, Sir J.	1819	Woolwich Military Academy	1900	33
Ailesbury, 2nd M of (1856). G. W. F. Brudenell-Bruce	1804	Ch. Ch. Oxf.	1878	25, 30
Ailesbury, 3rd M of (1878). E. C. A. Brudenell-Bruce, styled Ld E. Bruce (1821–78)	1811	Eton; Trinity Coll., Camb.	1886	10, 17, 20, 35
Akers-Douglas, A. 1st Vt Chilston (1911)	1851	Eton; Univ. Coll., Oxf.	1926	36, 39, 44, 46, 50, 55
Albemarle, 7th E of (1891). W. Coutts-Keppel, styled Vt Bury (1851–91)	1832	Eton	1894	3, 8
Althorp, Vt (styled 1783–1834). J. C. Spencer, 3rd Earl Spencer (1834)	1782	Harrow; Trinity Coll., Camb.	1845	7, 51
Anderson, A.	1797	Edin. Univ.	1853	10, 15
Anglesey, 1st M of (1815). H. W. Paget, 2nd E of Uxbridge (1812)	1768	Westminster Sch; Ch. Ch. Oxf.	1854	2, 12
Anglesey, 2nd M of (1854). H. Paget, 1st Ld Paget (1833), styled E of Uxbridge (to 1853)	1797	Privately	1869	7, 8
Anson, G.	1797	Entered Army	1857	3, 7, 12
Anson, Sir W (3rd Bt 1873)	1843	Eton; Balliol Coll., Oxf.	1914	45
Anstruther, H. T.	1860	Eton; Edin. Univ.	1926	46
Arabin, W. St J.				7
Argyll, 8th D of (1847). G. J. D. Campbell, 1st U.K. Duke (1892)	1823	Privately	1900	3, 8, 16, 18, 23, 24, 28, 33, 49, 50, 51, 54
Arnold-Forster, H. O.	1855	Rugby; Univ. Coll., Oxf.	1909	44, 45, 51
Ashbourne, 1st Ld (1885). E. Gibson	1837	Trinity Coll., Dublin	1913	36, 40, 45
Asher, A.	1835	Edin. Univ.	1905	35, 39, 43
Ashley, Ld (styled 1811–51). A. Ashley-Cooper, 7th E of Shaftesbury (1851)	1801	Harrow; Ch. Ch. Oxf.	1885	4
Ashley (A.) E.	1836	Harrow; Trinity Coll., Camb.	1907	33, 34
Ashmead Bartlett, Sir E. (Kt 1892)	1849	Torquay Sch.; Ch. Ch. Oxf.	1902	36, 40
Asquith, H. H. 1st E of Oxford & Asquith (1925)	1852	City of London Sch; Balliol Coll., Oxf.	1928	42, 50
Atherton, Sir W. (Kt 1860)	1806	n.a.	1864	24, 52
Auckland, 2nd Ld (1814), 1st E (1839). G. Eden	1784	Ch. Ch. Oxf.	1849	1, 2, 6, 12, 51, 54

Name	Born	Education	Died	Page references
Ayrton, A. S.	1816	Ealing Sch.	1886	28, 29, 55
Baggallay, Sir R. (Kt 1868)	1816	Gonville & Caius Coll., Camb.	1888	27, 31, 52
Bagot, 3rd Ld (1856). W. Bagot	1811	Charterhouse; Eton; Magdalene Coll., Camb.	1887	27
Bagot, 4th Ld (1887). W. Bagot	1857	Eton	1932	32, 47
Bagwell, J.	1811	Winchester	1883	24
Baillie, C. Ld Jerviswood (Life Peer 1859)	1804	Privately	1879	22
Baillie, H. J.	1804	Eton; Ch. Ch. Oxf.	1885	14, 21
Baines, M. T.	1799	Richmond G.S.; Trinity Coll., Camb.	1860	13, 17, 18, 19, 53, 54
Balcarres Ld. D. A. E. Lindsay, 27th E of Crawford (1913)	1871	Eton; Magdalen Coll., Oxf.	1940	46
Balfour, A. J. 1st E of Balfour (1922)	1848	Eton; Trinity Coll., Camb.	1930	37, 39, 40, 41, 44, 49, 50, 53, 54, 56
Balfour, G. W. 2nd E of Balfour (1930)	1853	Eton;	1945	45, 46, 53, 55
Balfour, J. B. 1st Ld Kinross (1902)	1837	Edin. Academy; Edin. Univ.	1905	35, 38, 43
Balfour of Burleigh, 6th Ld (1869). A. H. Bruce	1849	Eton; Oriel Coll., Oxf.	1921	40, 42, 46, 54
Ball, J. T.	1815	Trinity Coll., Dublin	1898	18, 27, 32
Ball, N.	1791	Stonyhurst; Trinity Coll., Dublin	1865	7
Bankes, G.	1788	Westminster; Trinity Hall, Camb.	1856	15
Baring, A. 1st Ld Ashburton (1835)	1774	Privately	1848	4, 5, 54
Baring, Sir F. T. (3rd Bt 1848). 1st Ld Northbrook (1866)	1796	Winchester; Ch. Ch. Oxf.	1866	1, 3, 6, 12, 51, 56
Baring, H. B.	1804	Ch. Ch. Oxf.	1869	10
Baring, T. G. 2nd Ld Northbrook (1866), 1st E of (1876)	1826	Ch. Ch. Oxf.	1904	18, 23
Baring, W. B. 2nd Ld Ashburton (1848)	1799	Oriel Coll., Oxf.	1864	9, 53
Barrington, 7th Vt (1867) G. W. Barrington, 1st Ld Shute (U.K. 1880)	1824	Ch. Ch. Oxf.	1886	32, 37, 42
Barry, C. R.	1825	Trinity Coll., Dublin	1897	30
Bateman, 2nd Ld (1845). W. Bateman-Hanbury	1826	Eton; Trinity Coll., Camb.	1901	22
Bateson, T.	1819	n.a.	n.a.	15
Bath, 5th M of (1896). T. H. Thynne, styled Vt Weymouth (to 1896)	1862	Eton; Balliol Coll., Oxf.	1946	45
Baxter, W. E.	1825	Dundee H.S.; Edin. Univ.	1890	28
Beaconsfield 1st E (1876). B. Disraeli	1804	Privately	1881	14, 21, 25, 26, 30, 50
Beauchamp, 6th E of (1866). F. Lygon	1830	Eton; Ch. Ch. Oxf.	1891	32, 37, 41, 54
Beaufort, 8th D of (1853). H. C. F. Somerset	1824	Eton	1899	22, 27

Name	Born	Education	Died	Page references
Beckett, Sir J.	n.a.	n.a.	n.a.	4, 5
Belfast, E of (styled 1799–1844). G. Hamilton Chichester, 3rd M of Donegall (1844), U.K. Peer (1841)	1797	Eton; Ch. Ch. Oxf.	1883	3, 8
Bellew, R. M.	1803	n.a.	1880	13
Belmore, 4th E of (1845). Sir S. R. Lowry-Corry	1835	Eton; Trinity Coll., Camb.	1913	25
Belper, 1st Ld (1856). E. Strutt	1801	Trinity Coll., Camb.	1880	47
Bentinck, G. A.	1821	Westminster; Trinity Coll., Camb.	1891	31, 32
Beresford, W.	1797	Eton; St Mary's Hall, Oxf.	1883	15, 55
Berkeley, Sir G. H. F. (K.C.B. 1815)	1785	Entered Army	1857	15, 17, 19
Bessborough, 4th E of (1844). J. W. Ponsonby, 1st Ld Duncannon (1834)	1781	Ch. Ch. Oxf.	1847	12, 14, 17, 20, 25, 30
Bethell, Sir R. (Kt 1853). 1st Ld Westbury (1861)	1800	Wadham Coll., Oxf.	1873	17, 19, 20, 24, 52
Beverly, 2nd E of (1830). G. Percy, 5th D of Northumberland (1865)	1778	Eton; St John's Coll., Camb.	1867	11
Blackburn, P.	1811	Eton	1870	22
Blackburne, F.	1782	Trinity Coll., Dublin	1867	3, 10
Boldero, H. G.	1797	Entered Army	1873	10
Bonham, F. R.				
Borlase, W.	1848	Winchester; Trinity Coll., Oxf.	1899	38
Boston, 6th Ld (1877). G. F. Irby	1860	Eton; Ch. Ch. Oxf.	1944	37
Bouverie, E. P.	1818	Trinity Coll., Camb.	1889	11, 19, 53, 54
Bovill, Sir W. (Kt 1866)	1814	Articled solicitor	1873	27
Bradford, 3rd E of (1865). O. G. C. Bridgeman, styled Vt Newport (1825–65)	1819	Harrow; Trinity Coll., Camb.	1898	27, 32, 37
Brady, Sir M. (1st Bt 1869)	1796	Trinity Coll., Dublin	1871	7
Brand, A. G.	1853	Rugby	1917	43
Brand, H. B. W. 1st Vt Hampden (1884), 23rd Ld Dacre (1890)	1814	Eton	1892	20
Brand, H. R. 2nd Vt Hampden (1892), 24th Ld Dacre	1841	Rugby	1906	33
Brassey, Sir T. (K.C.B. 1881). 1st Ld Brassey (1886)	1836	Rugby; Univ. Coll., Oxf.	1918	34, 44
Breadalbane, 2nd M of (1834). J. Campbell (U.K. title extinct on his death)	1796	Glasgow Coll.; Eton	1862	14, 17, 20
Breadalbane, 1st Ld (1873), 1st M of (1885). G. Campbell	1851	St Andrews Univ.	1922	30, 35, 43
Brett, W. B. 1st Ld Esher (1885), 1st Vt (1897)	1815	Westminster; Gonville & Caius Coll., Camb.	1899	27
Brewster, A.	1796	Kilkenny College; Univ. of Dublin	1874	10, 17, 20
Bridport, 1st Vt (1868). A. N. Hood	1814	n.a.	1904	35, 47

Name	Born	Education	Died	Page references
Coleridge, Sir J. T. (Kt 1835)	1790	Eton; C. C. C. Oxf.	1876	29, 52
Collier, Sir R. P. (Kt 1863). 1st Ld Monkswell (1885)	1817	Plymouth G.S.; Trinity Coll., Camb.	1886	24, 29, 52
Collings, J.	1831	Church Hse Sch., Plymouth	1920	38, 44
Colville of Culross, 10th Ld (1849), 1st U.K. Baron (1885), 1st Vt (1902). C. J. Colville	1818	Harrow	1903	16, 22, 27
Conyngham, 2nd M of (1832). F. N. Conyngham	1797	Privately	1876	2, 7, 8, 54
Cork & Orrery 9th E of (1856). R. E. St J. Boyle	1829	Eton; Ch. Ch. Oxf.	1904	25, 30, 35, 39, 43
Corry, H. T. L.	1803	Eton; Ch. Ch. Oxf.	1873	5, 9, 21, 26, 51, 52
Cotes, C. C.	1846	Eton; Ch. Ch. Oxf.	1898	35
Cottenham, 1st Ld (1836), 1st E of (1850). Sir C. C. Pepys (3rd Bt 1845)	1781	Harrow; Trinity Coll., Camb.	1851	6, 11, 49
Courtney, L. H. 1st Ld Courtney (1900)	1832	St John's Coll., Camb.	1918	33
Courtown, 3rd E of (1810)	1765		1835	5
Coventry, 9th E of (1843). G. W. Coventry	1838	Eton; Ch. Ch. Oxf.	1930	32, 37, 42, 47
Cowan, J.	1798	Ayr Academy; Edin. Univ.	1878	13
Cowper, 6th E (1837). G. A. F. Cowper, styled Vt Fordwich (to 1837)	1806	Privately	1856	1
Cowper, 7th E (1856). F. T. de G. Cowper	1834	Eton; Ch. Ch. Oxf.	1905	30, 34
Cowper, W. F. (afterwards Cowper-Temple). 1st Ld Mount-Temple (1880)	1811	Eton	1888	7, 12, 16, 18, 19, 24, 52, 53, 55
Craig, Sir W. G. (2nd Bt 1850)	1797	n.a.	1878	13
Crampton, P. C.	1782	Trinity Coll., Dublin	1862	3
Cranborne, Vt (styled 1865–68). R. A. T. Gascoyne-Cecil, 3rd M of Salisbury (1868)	1830	Eton; Ch. Ch. Oxf.	1903	26, 51
Cranborne, Vt (1868). J. E. H. Gascoyne-Cecil, 4th M of Salisbury (1903)	1861	Eton; Ch. Ch. Oxf.	1947	44
Cranbrook, 1st Vt (1878), 1st E of (1892). G. Gathorne-Hardy	1814	Shrewsbury Sch.; Oriel Coll., Oxf.	1906	31, 36, 39, 40, 49, 51, 53
Cranworth, 1st Ld (1850). R. M. Rolfe	1790	Winchester Sch.; Trinity Coll., Camb.	1868	16, 18, 23, 49
Craufurd, J. A. A.	1805	Edin. Univ.; Glasgow Univ.	1876	17
Cremorne, 3rd Ld (1827). R. Dawson, 1st Ld Dartrey (1847), 1st E of (1866)	1817	Privately	1897	20, 25
Crichton, Vt Sir J. H. Crichton	1839	Eton; Ch. Ch. Oxf.	1914	32
Cripps, W.	n.a.	n.a.	n.a.	10

Name	Born	Education	Died	Page references
Crofton, 2nd Ld (1817). E. Crofton	1806	Privately	1869	15, 22, 27
Cross, J. K.	1832	n.a.	1887	33
Cross, 1st Vt (1886). R. A. Cross	1823	Rugby; Trinity Coll., Camb.	1914	31, 36, 40, 44, 45, 50, 51, 53
Crossley, Sir S. 1st Ld Somerleyton (1916)	1857	Eton; Balliol Coll.	1935	46, 54
Cunningham, J.	n.a.	n.a.	n.a.	7
Curzon, G. N. 1st Ld Curzon (1898), 1st E (1911), 1st M (1921), K.G. (1916)	1859	Eton; Balliol Coll., Oxf.	1925	40, 44
Curzon, Vt, 5th E of Howe (1900)	1861	Eton; Ch. Ch. Oxf.	1929	47
Dalhousie, 10th E of (1838), 1st M (1849). J. A. Brown-Ramsey	1812	Harrow; Ch. Ch. Oxf.	1860	9, 54
Dalhousie, 11th E of (1860). F. Maule-Ramsey, 2nd Ld Panmure (1852)	1801	Charterhouse	1874	18, 51
Dalhousie, 13th E of (1880). J. W. Ramsay	1847	Privately	1887	35, 38, 54
Dalmeny, Ld	n.a.	n.a.	n.a.	6
Dalrymple, C.	n.a.	n.a.	n.a.	37
Darling, M. T. S.	n.a.	n.a.	n.a.	41
Davey, H. (Life Peer 1894)	1833	Rugby; Univ. Coll., Oxf.	1907	38
Davison, J. R.	1826	Houghton G.S.; Durham G.S.; C. C. C. Oxf.	1871	29
Dawnay, G. C.	1848	Eton; Ch. Ch. Oxf.	1889	36
Dawson, G. R.	1790	Harrow; Ch. Ch. Oxf.	1856	4, 11
Deas, Sir G. (Kt 1858). Life Peer (1853)	1804	Edin. Univ.	1887	13
Deasy, R.	1812	Trinity Coll., Dublin	1883	24
de la Warr, 5th E of (1795). G. J. Sackville-West	1791	Harrow; Brasenose Coll., Oxf.	1869	10, 22
Denbigh, 8th E of (1865). R. W. B. Fielding	1823	Eton; Trinity Coll., Camb.	1892	47
Denman, T. (Kt 1830). 1st Ld Denman (1834)	1779	Eton; St John's Coll., Camb.	1854	3, 52
Derby, 14th E of (1851). E. G. S. Stanley, 1st Ld Stanley of Bickerstaffe (1844)	1779	Eton; Ch. Ch. Oxf.	1869	14, 21, 49, 57
Derby, 15th E of (1869). E. H. Stanley, styled Ld Stanley (1851–69)	1826	Rugby; Trinity Coll., Camb.	1893	25, 31, 33, 50, 57
Desart, 3rd E (1820). J. O. O'C. Cuffe	1818	Ch. Ch. Oxf.	1865	14
Devon, 11th E of (1859). W. R. Courtenay	1807	Westminster Sch.; Ch. Ch. Oxf.	1888	26, 53, 54
Devonshire, 6th D of (1811). W. G. Spencer Cavendish	1790	Harrow; Trinity Coll., Camb.	1858	3, 44
Devonshire, 8th D of (1891). S. C. Cavendish, M. of Hartington (1858), K.G. (1902)	1833	Trinity Coll., Camb.	1908	45, 49, 52, 57

Name	Born	Education	Died	Page references
Gibson, T. M.	1806	Charterhouse; Trinity Coll., Camb.	1884	12, 24, 54
Giffard, Sir H. S. 1st Ld Halsbury (1885), 1st E (1898)	1823	Merton Coll., Oxf.	1921	32
Gilpin, C.	1815	n.a.	1874	24
Gladstone, H. J. 1st Vt Gladstone (1910)	1854	Eton; Univ. Coll., Oxf.	1930	35, 38, 42, 43, 55
Gladstone, W. E.	1809	Eton; Ch. Ch. Oxf.	1898	4, 5, 8, 9, 16, 18, 23, 28, 29, 33, 37, 38, 42, 49, 50, 51, 54, 56
Glenelg, 1st Ld (1835). C. Grant	1778	Magdalene Coll., Camb.	1866	50
Glenlyon, 2nd Ld (1837). G. A. F. J. Murray, 6th D of Atholl (1846)	1814	Privately	1864	11
Glyn, G. G. 2nd Ld Wolverton (1873)	1824	Rugby; Univ. Coll., Oxf.	1887	28
Goderich, 1st Vt (1827). F. J. Robinson, 1st E of Ripon (1833)	1782	Harrow; St John's Coll., Camb.	1859	7, 50
Gordon, E. S.	1814	Glasgow Univ; Edin. Univ.	1879	27, 32
Gordon, R.	1786	Ch. Ch. Oxf.	1864	1, 6
Gordon-Lennox, Ld H.	1821	n.a.	1886	15, 22, 26, 32, 55
Gorst, Sir J. E. (Kt 1885)	1835	Preston G.S.; St John's Coll., Camb.	1911	37, 40, 46, 52
Goschen, G. J. 1st Vt Goschen (1900)	1831	Rugby; Oriel Coll., Oxf.	1907	23, 24, 28, 29, 40, 45, 51, 53, 54, 56
Gosford, 2nd E of (1807). A. Acheson	1776	Ch. Ch. Oxf.	1849	3, 8
Goulburn, H.	1784	Trinity Coll., Camb.	1856	4, 9, 50, 51, 56
Graham, Sir J. R. G. (2nd Bt 1824)	1792	Westminster Sch.; Ch. Ch. Oxf.	1861	7, 8, 16, 18, 50, 51, 56
Graham, R.	n.a.	n.a.	n.a.	3
Grant, C. 1st Ld Glenelg (1835)	1778	Magdalene Coll., Camb.	1866	7, 6, 52
Grant, Sir R. (Kt 1834)	1779	Magdalene Coll., Camb.	1838	3
Grant Duff, M. E.	1829	n.a.	1906	28, 33
Granville, 5th E (1846). G. G. Leveson-Gower	1815	Eton; Ch. Ch. Oxf.	1891	11, 12, 13, 14, 16, 18, 23, 28, 33, 38, 44, 49, 50, 53, 56
Greene, R. W.	1792	Trinity Coll., Dublin	1861	10
Gregson, W.	1790	Brasenose Coll., Oxf.	1863	4
Greville, A. F.	1798	Entered Navy 1814	1864	29
Grey, 2nd E (1807). C. Grey	1764	Eton; King's Coll., Camb.	1845	1, 18, 49, 56
Grey, 3rd E (1845). H. Grey, styled Vt Howick (1807–45)	1802	Trinity Coll., Camb.	1894	11, 50
de Grey and Ripon, 2nd E de Grey (1859), 1st M of Ripon (1871). G. F. S. Robinson	1827	Privately	1909	23, 28, 51
Grey, Sir E. (3rd Bt 1882). 1st Vt Grey of Fallodon (1916)	1862	Winchester Sch; Balliol Coll., Oxf.	1933	42

Name	Born	Education	Died	Page references
Hawarden, 3rd Vt (1807)	1780	Privately	1856	11, 15, 27, 32, 37
Hawes, Sir B (K.C.B. 1856)	1797	*n.a.*	1862	11
Hawkesbury, 1st Ld (1893). G. C. S. Foljambe, 1st E of Liverpool (1905)	1846	Eton; Royal Navy	1907	44
Hay, Sir A. L. (Kt 1834)	1785	*n.a.*	1862	2, 7
Hay, Ld J.	1793	Entered Navy 1804	1851	23
Hayes, E.	1804	Trinity Coll., Dublin	1867	22
Hayes Fisher, W. 1st Ld Downham (1919)	1853	Haileybury; Univ. Coll., Oxf.	1920	45, 46
Hayter, Sir A. D. 2nd Bt (1878)	1835	Eton; Balliol Coll., Oxf.; B.N.C. Oxf.	*n.a.*	34
Hayter, Sir W. G. (1st Bt 1858)	1792	Winchester Sch.; Trinity Coll., Oxf.	1878	11, 13, 16, 18
Headfort, 2nd M of (1829). T. Taylour (U.K. Peer 1831)	1787	Harrow; Trinity Coll., Camb.	1870	7
Headlam, T. E.	1813	Shrewsbury; Trinity Coll., Camb.	1875	24
Hemphill, C. H. 1st Ld Hemphill (1906)	1822	Trinity Coll., Dublin	1908	43
Henley, J. W.	1793	Fulham Sch.; Magdalen Coll., Oxf.	1884	15, 21, 54
Henniker, 5th Ld (1870). J. M. Henniker	1842	Eton; Trinity Coll., Camb.	1893	32, 37, 41, 47
Herbert, Sir P. (K.C.B. 1869)	1822	Eton; Sandhurst	1876	27
Herbert, S. 1st Ld Herbert of Lea (1860)	1810	Harrow; Oriel Coll., Oxf.	1861	4, 9, 10, 16, 18, 23, 37, 41, 50, 51, 55
Hereford, 14th Vt (1804). H. F. L. Devereux	1777	Winchester Sch.; Trinity Coll., Oxf.	1843	5
Herries, J. C.	1778	Cheam Sch.; Univ. of Leipzig	1855	4, 14, 52, 55
Herschell, 1st Ld (1886). Sir F. Herschell (Kt 1880)	1837	Univ. Coll., London; Bonn Univ.	1899	12, 34, 37, 42, 49
Hertford, 5th M of (1870). F. H. G. Seymour	1812	Harrow; Entered Army 1827	1884	32
Hervey, Ld A.	1816	Eton; Trinity Coll., Camb.	1875	17, 19
Heytesbury, 1st Ld (1828). Sir W. A. Court (2nd Bt 1817)	1779	Eton	1860	9
Hibbert, J. T.	1824	St John's Coll., Camb.	1908	29, 33, 34, 38, 42
Hicks Beach, Sir M. E. (9th Bt 1854). 1st Vt St Aldwyn (1906), 1st E (1915)	1837	Eton.; Ch. Ch. Oxf.	1916	25, 26, 31, 36, 40, 45, 50, 51, 53, 54, 55, 56
Hill, Ld A. M.	*n.a.*	*n.a.*	*n.a.*	8, 14, 37, 42, 47
Hobhouse, Sir J. C. (2nd Bt 1831). 1st Ld Broughton (1851)	1786	Westminster Sch.; Trinity Coll., Camb.	1869	1, 2, 3, 6, 11, 52, 55
Holker, J.	1828	Bury G.S.	1882	32, 52
Holland, 3rd Ld (1774). H. Fox	1773	Eton; Ch. Ch. Oxf.	1840	1, 6

Name	Born	Education	Died	Page references
Holland, 1st Ld (1888). H. T. Holland, 1st Vt Knutsford (1895)	1825	Harrow; Durham Univ.; Trinity Coll., Camb.	1914	36, 40, 51, 52, 53
Holms, J.	1830	n.a.	1891	34, 35
Hope, G.	1808	Ch. Ch. Oxf.	1863	8
Hopetoun, 7th E of (1873). J. A. L. Hope, 1st M of Linlithgow (U.K. Peer 1902)	1860	Eton	1908	37, 41, 46, 47, 54
Horne, W.	1774	n.a.	1860	3, 52
Horsman, E.	1807	Rugby; Trinity Coll., Camb.	1876	7, 19, 52
Hothfield, 1st Ld (1881). Sir H. J. Tufton (2nd Bt 1871)	1844	Eton; Ch. Ch. Oxf.	1926	39
Houghton, 2nd Ld (1885). R. O. A. Crewe Milnes, 1st E of Crewe (1895), 1st M (1911)	1858	Harrow; Trinity Coll., Camb.	1945	39, 43
Howard of Glossop, 1st Ld (1869). E. G. Fitzalan-Howard	1818	Trinity Coll., Camb.	1883	14
Howe, 4th E (1900). R. G. P. Curzon-Howe	1861	Eton; Ch. Ch. Oxf.	1929	47
Howick, Vt (styled 1807–45). H. Grey, 3rd Earl Grey (1845)	1802	Trinity Coll., Camb.	1894	7, 6, 55
Hughes, H. G.	1810	Trinity Coll., Dublin	1872	13, 20
Hunt, G. W.	1825	Eton; Ch. Ch. Oxf.	1877	26, 31, 51, 56
Huntley, 11th M of (1863). C. Gordon, styled E of Aboyne (1853–63)	1847	Eton; Trinity Coll., Camb.	1937	30, 35
Hutt, Sir W. (K.C.B. 1865)	1801	St Mary's Hall, Oxf.; Trinity Coll., Camb.	1882	24, 53
Iddesleigh, 1st E of (1885). Sir S. H. Northcote (8th Bt 1851)	1818	Eton; Balliol Coll., Oxf.	1887	36, 39, 50
Ilchester, 3rd E of (1802). H. S. Fox-Strangways	1787	Ch. Ch. Oxf.	1858	8
Ilchester, 5th E of (1865). H. E. Fox-Strangways	1847	Eton; Ch. Ch. Oxf.	1905	30
Inglis, J.	1810	Glasgow Univ.; Balliol Coll., Oxf.	1891	15, 22
Ivory, J.	1792	Edin. Univ.	1866	7
Jackson, W. L. 1st Ld Allerton (1902)	1840	Moravian Sch. at Fulneck	1917	36, 40, 53
James of Hereford, 1st Ld (1895). H. James	1828	Cheltenham Coll.	1911	29, 34, 45, 52, 53
Jeffrey, F.	1773	Edin. H.S.; Glasgow Univ.; Edin. Univ.; Queen's Coll., Oxf.	1850	3
Jermyn, E of (styled 1826–59). F. W. Hervey, 2nd M of Bristol (1859)	1800	Eton; Trinity Coll., Camb.	1864	11
Jersey, 7th E of (1859). V. A. G. C. Villiers	1845	Eton; Balliol Coll., Oxf.	1915	5, 10, 15, 32, 41, 54

Name	Born	Education	Died	Page references
Jervis, J.	1802	Westminster Sch.; Trinity Coll., Camb.	1856	13, 52
Jessel, G.	1824	Univ. Coll., London	1883	29
Jeune, F. H. 1st Ld St Helier (1905)	1843	Harrow; Balliol Coll., Oxf.	1905	43
Jocelyn, Vt (styled 1820–54). R. Jocelyn	1816	n.a.	1880	9
Jolliffe, Sir W. (1st Bt 1821). 1st Ld Hylton (1866)	1800	Entered Army 1817	1876	14, 21
Karslake, J. B.	1821	Harrow	1881	26, 27, 31, 52
Kay-Shuttleworth, Sir U. (2nd Bt 1877) 1st Ld Shuttleworth (1902)	1844	Harrow; London Univ.	1939	38, 42, 53
Keating, Sir H. S. (Kt 1857)	1804	Trinity Coll., Dublin	1888	20, 24
Kelly, Sir F. (Kt 1845)	1796	n.a	1880	10, 15, 22, 52
Kempt, Sir J. (K.C.B. 1815)	1765	Entered Army	1854	2
Kenmare, 4th E of (1871). V. A. Browne, styled Vt Castlerosse (1853–71)	1825	Privately	1905	30, 35, 39
Kennedy, T. F.	1788	Harrow; Edin. Univ.	1879	2, 3
Kensington, 4th Ld (1872). W. Edwardes (U.K. Peer 1886)	1835	Eton	1896	35, 39, 44
Kenyon, 4th Ld (1869). L. Kenyon	1864	Eton; Ch. Ch. Oxf.	1927	47
Keogh, W. N.	1817	Trinity Coll., Dublin	1878	17, 20
Kilcoursie, Vt (styled to 1887). F. E. G. Lambert, 9th E of Cavan (1887)	1839	Harrow	1900	39
Kimberley, 1st E of (1866). J. Wodehouse, 3rd Ld Wodehouse (1846)	1826	Eton; Ch. Ch. Oxf.	1902	28, 33, 34, 38, 42, 49, 50, 51, 53
Kinnaird, 9th Ld (1826). C. W. F. Kinnaird, 1st U.K. Ld (1860)	1807	Eton	1878	8
Kintore, 9th E of (1880). A. H. J. Keith-Falconer		Eton; Trinity Coll., Camb.		37, 42, 47
Knatchbull, Sir E. 9th Bt (1819), Knatchbull Huggessen	1781	n.a.	1849	4, 9, 23, 24, 28, 53
Knight, Sir F. W. (K.C.B. 1886)	1812	Charterhouse	1897	15, 21
Knutsford, 1st Ld (1888), 1st Vt (1895). H. T. Holland	1825	Harrow; Durham Univ.; Trinity Coll., Camb.	1914	36, 40, 51, 52, 53
Labouchere, H. 1st Ld Taunton (1859)	1798	Winchester Sch.; Ch. Ch. Oxf.	1869	1, 2, 6, 7, 12, 18, 50, 52, 54
Laing, S.	1812	Houghton-le-Spring G.S.; St John's Coll., Camb.	1897	23
Lamb, G.	1784	n.a.	1834	1
Lansdowne, 3rd M of (1809). H. Petty-Fitzmaurice	1780	Westminster Sch.; Edin. Univ.; Trinity Coll., Camb.	1863	1, 6, 16, 18, 49, 54
Lansdowne, 4th M of (1863). H. Petty-Fitzmaurice, styled E of Shelburne (1836–63)	1816	Westminster Sch.; Trinity Coll., Camb.	1866	11, 44

Name	Born	Education	Died	Page references
Lansdowne, 5th M of (1866). H. C. K. Petty-Fitzmaurice	1845	Eton; Balliol Coll., Oxf.	1927	28, 29, 33, 50, 51
Lascelles, W. S.				14
Lathom, 1st E of (1880). E. Bootle-Wilbraham, 2nd Ld Skelmersdale (1853)	1837	Eton; Ch. Ch. Oxf.	1898	37, 41, 47
Law, A. B.	1858	Glasgow H.S.	1923	46
Law, H.	1818	Royal Sch., Dungannon	1883	30, 35
Lawrence, 2nd Ld (1879). J. H. Lawrence	1846	Trinity Coll., Camb.	1913	47
Lawson, J. A.	1817	Waterford Sch.; Trinity Coll., Dublin	1887	24, 45
Layard, Sir A. H. (G.C.B. 1878)	1817	Solicitor's office	1894	11, 23, 29, 55
Lee, A. H. 1st Ld Lee of Fareham (1918)	1868	Woolwich RMA	1947	45
Lefevre, G. J. Shaw-. 1st Ld Eversley (1906)	1831	Trinity Coll., Camb.	1928	23, 26, 29, 34, 43, 53, 54, 55
Lefevre, Sir J. G. Shaw- (K.C.B. 1857)	1797	Eton; Trinity Coll., Camb.	1879	1
Le Marchant, Sir D. (1st Bt 1841)	1795	Eton; Trinity Coll., Camb.	1874	6, 11
Lennox, Ld A.	1806	Army career	1864	10
Leveson-Gower, G. G. 5th Earl Granville (1846), styled Ld Leveson (1833–46)	1815	Eton; Ch. Ch. Oxf.	1891	6, 38, 44
Lewis, Sir G. C. (2nd Bt 1855)	1806	Eton; Ch. Ch. Oxf.	1863	11, 18, 23, 50, 51, 56
Lewisham, Vt (styled 1853–91). W. H. Legge, 6th E of Dartmouth(1891)	1851	Eton; Ch. Ch. Oxf.	1936	37, 41
Lichfield, 1st E of (1831). T. W. Anson, 2nd Vt Anson (1818)	1795	Eton; Ch. Ch. Oxf.	1854	7, 54
Lilford, 3rd Ld (1825). T. A. Powys	1801	Eton; Ch. Ch. Oxf.	1861	7
Limerick, 3rd E of (1866). W. H. J. C. Pery	1840	n.a.	1896	41, 42, 47
Lincoln, E of (styled to 1851). H. P. Pelham-Clinton, 5th D of Newcastle (1851)	1811	Eton; Ch. Ch. Oxf.	1864	5, 9, 10, 52, 55
Linlithgow, 1st M of (U.K. Peer) 1902). J. A. Hope, 7th E of Hopetoun (1873)	1860	Eton	1908	46, 54
Listowel, 2nd E of (1837). W. Hare	1801	Eton	1856	8, 14, 17, 20
Littleton, E. J. 1st Ld Hatherton (1835)	1791	Rugby; Brasenose Coll., Oxf.	1863	2, 52
Liverpool, 3rd E of (1828). C. C. C. Jenkinson	1784	Ch. Ch. Oxf.	1851	10
Lockwood, Sir F. (Kt 1894)	1846	Manchester G.S.; Caius Coll., Camb.	1897	43
Londonderry, 4th M of (1854). F. W. R. Stewart, styled Vt Castlereagh (1822–54)	1805	Eton	1872	44

Name	Born	Education	Died	Page references
Northcote, Sir H. S. (8th Bt 1851). 1st E of Iddesleigh (1885)	1818	Eton; Balliol Coll., Oxf.	1887	36, 39
Northumberland, 4th D of (1847). A. Percy, 1st Ld Prudhoe (1816)	1792	Eton; Entered Navy 1805	1865	14
Northumberland, 5th D of (1865). G. Percy, 2nd E of Beverly (1830)	1778	Eton; St John's Coll., Camb.	1867	11
Northumberland, 6th D of (1867). A. G. Percy, styled Ld Lovaine (1830–65), Earl Percy (1865–7)	1810	Eton; St John's Coll., Camb.	1899	30, 50
Nugent, 2nd Ld (1812). G. Nugent-Grenville	1789	Brasenose Coll., Oxf.	1850	3
O'Brien, Sir P. (1st Bt 1891). 1st Ld O'Brien (1900)	1842	Trinity Coll., Dublin	1914	41
O'Ferrall, R. M.	1797	n.a.	1880	6, 7
O'Hagan, T. 1st Ld O'Hagan (1870)	1812	Belfast Acad. Inst.	1885	24
O'Loghlen, Sir C. M. (2nd Bt 1842)	1819	Trinity Coll., Dublin	1877	29
O'Loghlen, Sir M. (1st Bt 1838)	1789	Trinity Coll., Dublin	1842	3, 7
Onslow, 4th E of (1870). W. H. Onslow	1853	Eton; Exeter Coll., Oxf.	1911	32, 40, 41, 45, 52
Ord, W. H.				7
Ormonde, 2nd M of (1838). J. Butler	1808	Harrow	1854	10, 14, 17
Osborne, R. Bernal	1808	Charterhouse; Trinity Coll., Camb.	1882	16, 18
Otway, A. J.	1822	Sandhurst	1912	28
Owen, Sir E. C. R. (K.C.B. 1815)	1771	n.a.	1849	4
Oxenbridge, 1st Vt (1886). W. J. Monson, 7th Ld Monson (1862)	1829	Eton; Ch. Ch. Oxf.	1898	43
Page Wood, Sir W. 1st Ld Hatherley (1868)	1801	n.a.	1881	13
Paget, 1st Ld (1833). H. Paget, 2nd M of Anglesey (1854)	1797	Privately	1869	7, 8
Paget, Ld A.	1816	Westminster Sch.	1888	14, 18, 20, 25, 27
Paget, Ld C. E.	1811	Westminster Sch.	1895	23
Pakington, Sir J. (1st Bt 1846). 1st Ld Hampton (1874)	1799	Eton; Oriel Coll., Oxf.	1880	14, 21, 25, 26, 50, 51
Palles, C.	1831	Trinity Coll., Dublin	1920	30
Palmer, Sir R. (Kt 1861). 1st Ld Selborne (1872), 1st E (1882)	1812	Rugby; Winchester; Ch. Ch. Oxf.	1895	24, 52
Palmerston, 3rd Vt (1802). H. Temple	1784	Harrow; Edin. Univ.; St John's Coll., Camb.	1865	1, 6, 11, 16, 18, 22, 49, 50
Panmure, 2nd Ld (1852). F. Maule, 11th E of Dalhousie (1860)	1801	Charterhouse Sch.	1874	18, 51
Parker, J.	1799	Repton Sch.; Brasenose Coll., Oxf.	1881	6, 7, 11, 12
Parnell, Sir H. B. (4th Bt 1812). 1st Ld Congleton (1841)	1776	Eton; Winchester Sch.; Trinity Coll., Camb.	1842	2, 7, 53, 55
Patton, G.	1803	Edin.; Trinity Coll., Camb.	1869	22, 27
Pearson, Sir C. J. (Kt 1887)	1843	C. C. C. Oxf.	1910	41, 46

Name	Born	Education	Died	Page references
Wellesley, Ld C.				
Wellesley, 1st Ld (1797). R. C. Wellesley	1760	Eton; Ch. Ch. Oxf.	1842	2, 3, 8, 11
Wellington, 1st D of (1814). A. Wellesley (spelt Wesley until 1798)	1769	Eton; Brussels; Angers Military Academy	1852	4, 9, 17, 20, 49, 50, 54
Westbury, 1st Ld (1861). R. Bethell	1800	Wadham Coll., Oxf.	1873	23, 49
Westminster, 2nd M of (1845). R. Grosvenor	1795	Westminster Sch.; Ch. Ch. Oxf.	1869	13
Westminster, 3rd M of (1869), 1st D of (1874). H. L. Grosvenor	1825	Eton; Balliol Coll., Oxf.	1899	35
Wharncliffe, 1st Ld (1826). J. A. Stuart-Wortley-Mackenzie	1776	Charterhouse	1845	4, 8, 49
White, L.	n.a.	n.a.	n.a.	24
White Ridley, Sir M. (5th Bt 1877). 1st Vt Ridley (1900)	1842	Harrow; Balliol Coll., Oxf.	1904	31, 36, 44, 50
Whiteside, J.	1804	Trinity Coll., Dublin	1876	15, 22
Whitmore, H.	n.a.	n.a.	n.a.	22, 27
Wilde, Sir T. (Kt 1840). 1st Ld Truro (1850)	1782	Great Ealing Sch.	1885	7, 13, 52
Wilson, J.	1805	Quaker schools	1860	11, 16, 18, 24, 53
Wilson-Patten, J. 1st Ld Winmarleigh (1874)	1802	Eton; Magdalen Coll., Oxf.	1892	26, 53
Wilton, 2nd E of (1814). T. Grosvenor (later Egerton)	1799	Westminster Sch.; Ch. Ch. Oxf.	1882	5
Windsor, 14th Ld (1869). R. G. Windsor-Clive, 1st E of Plymouth (1905), 1st Vt Windsor (1905)	1857	Eton; St John's Coll., Camb.	1923	41, 46, 54, 55
Winn, R.				32
Winterbotham, H.	1837	Univ. Coll., London	1873	28
Wodehouse, 3rd Ld (1846). J. Wodehouse, 1st E of Kimberley (1866)	1826	Eton; Ch. Ch. Oxf.	1902	16, 18, 23, 24
Wolverton, 2nd Ld (1873). G. G. Glyn	1824	Rugby; Univ. Coll., Oxf.	1887	34, 38, 43, 47, 54
Wood, Sir C. (G.C.B. 1856). 1st Vt Halifax (1866)	1800	Eton; Oriel Coll., Oxf.	1885	1, 6, 11, 16, 18, 23, 51, 52
Woodall, W.	1832	Liverpool	1901	38, 42
Wortley, T. S.				4, 20
Woulfe, S.	1787	Stonyhurst; Trinity Coll., Dublin	1840	7
Wrottesley, 3rd Ld (1867). A. Wrottesley	1824	Rugby; Ch. Ch. Oxf.	1910	30, 35
Wyndham, G.	1863	Eton; Sandhurst	1913	44, 45, 46, 53
Wynn, C. W. W.	1775	Westminster Sch.; Ch. Ch. Oxf.	1850	25, 53, 55
Wyse, Sir T. (K.C.B. 1857)	1791	Stonyhurst Coll.; Trinity Coll., Dublin	1862	7, 11
Yarborough, 4th E of (1875). C. A. W. Anderson-Pelham	1859	Eton; Trinity Coll., Camb.	1936	42

2 Political Parties

Leaders of the Conservative Party

House of Lords		House of Commons	
D of Wellington	Jan 1828–Jul 1846	Sir R. Peel	1834–Jul 1846
Ld Stanley (14th	Mar 1846–Feb 1868	Ld G. Bentinck	Jul 1846–Dec 1847
E of Derby,		Ld Granby	Feb 1848–Mar 1848
1851)		no formal leaders	Mar 1848–Feb 1849
E of Malmesbury	Feb 1868–Feb 1869	Triumvirate:	
Ld Cairns	Feb 1869–Feb 1870	B. Disraeli	
E of Derby (15th)	elected leader 19	Ld Granby	Feb 1849–Feb 1852
	Feb 70 but declined	J. C. Herries	
	to serve	B. Disraeli	Feb 1852–Aug 1876
D of Richmond	Feb 1870–Aug 1876	Sir S. Northcote	Aug 1876–Jun 1885
E of Beaconsfield	Aug 1876–Apr 1881	Sir M. Hicks Beach	Jun 1885–Aug 1886
M of Salisbury	May 1881–Jul 1902	Ld R. Churchill	Aug 1886–Dec 1886
(3rd)		W. H. Smith	Dec 1886–Oct 1891
		A. J. Balfour	Oct 1891–Jul 1902

Leaders of the Liberal Party

House of Lords		House of Commons	
Earl Grey	Nov 1830–Jul 1834	Vt Althorp	Mar 1830–Nov 1834
Vt Melbourne	Jul 1834–Oct 1842	Ld J. Russell	Nov 1834–Feb 1855
M of Lansdowne	Oct 1842–Dec 1852	Ld Palmerston	Feb 1855–Oct 1865
(3rd)		W. E. Gladstone	Oct 1865–Feb 1875
E of Aberdeen	Dec 1852–Feb 1855	Ld Hartington	Feb 1875–Apr 1880
Earl Granville	Feb 1855–Oct 1865	W. E. Gladstone	Apr 1880–Mar 1894
Earl Russell	Oct 1865–Dec 1868	Sir W. Harcourt	Mar 1894–Dec 1898
Earl Granville	Dec 1868–Mar 1891	Sir H. Campbell-	Feb 1899–Apr 1908
E of Kimberley	Apr 1891–Mar 1894	Bannerman	
E of Rosebery	Mar 1894–Nov 1896		
E of Kimberley	Jan 1897–Apr 1902		

SOURCES: *D.N.B.*; Boase; H of Lords Record Office, Memo No. 31.

Conservative Chief Whips

House of Lords		House of Commons	
Earl Nelson	–Feb 1852	W. Holmes	c. 1802–1832[1]
Ld Colville of	Feb 1852–c. 1870	Sir G. Clerk	1835–1837
Culross		Sir T. F. Fremantle	1837–1844
Ld Skelmersdale	c. 1870–Jul 1885	Sir J. Young	1844–1846
1st E of Lathom,		W. Beresford	1846–1850
1880)		F. Mackenzie	1850–1853
E of Kintore	Jul 1885–Feb 1889	Sir W. H. Jolliffe	1853–1859

[1]He lost his seat in 1832, and there is no evidence of whipping activities until 1835.

92

E of Limerick	Feb 1889–Aug 1896		Col. T. E. Taylor	1859–1868
Earl Waldegrave	Aug 1896–Nov 1911		G. Noel	1868–1873
			Col. T. E. Taylor	1873–1874
			Sir W. Hart Dyke	1874–1880
			R. Winn	1880–1885
			A. Akers-Douglas	1885–1895
			Sir W. H. Walrond	1895–1902

Liberal Chief Whips

House of Lords		**House of Commons**	
Vt Falkland	1837–1840	E. Ellice	1830–1832
	1846–1848	C. Wood	1832–1834
E of Bessborough	May 1848–Jan 1880	F. T. Baring	1834–1835
Ld Monson (1st Vt	Jan 1880–Aug 1892	E. J. Stanley	1835–1841
Oxenbridge,		R. M. O'Ferrall	1841–1846
1886)		H. Tufnell	1846–1850
Ld Kensington	Aug 1892–Oct 1896	W. G. Hayter	1850–1858
Ld Ribblesdale	Oct 1896–May 1907	H. B. W. Brand	1859–1866[1]
		G. G. Glyn	1866–1873
		A. W. Peel	1873–1874
		W. P. Adam	1874–1880
		Ld R. Grosvenor	1880–1885
		A. Morley	1885–1892
		E. Marjoribanks	1892–1894
		T. E. Ellis	1894–1899

SOURCES: *D.N.B.*; *Hansard*; Boase; H of Lords Record Office, Memo No. 31.

Annual Conferences of the Conservative and Unionist Party, 1867–1900

Date	Place		President
12 Nov 1867	London	(InauguralMeeting)	J. E. Gorst
29 Dec 1868	Birmingham	E of Dartmouth	Vt Holmesdale
11 Jun 1869	Liverpool	Ld Skelmersdale	H. C. Raikes
20 Apr 1870	York	E of Feversham	,,
2 Jun 1871	Bristol	,,	,,
24 Jun 1872	London	D of Abercorn	,,
16 Apr 1873	Leeds	E of Wharncliffe	,,
1 Jul 1874	London	Ld Hampton	,,
19 Jun 1875	Brighton	Ld Colchester	Vt Mahon
25 Oct 1876	Manchester	M of Abergavenny	Ld C. Hamilton
30 Jun 1877	Portsmouth	Ld Winmarleigh	,,
17 Jul 1878	Nottingham	E of Cadogan	,,
25 Oct 1879	Birmingham	Earl Manvers	Earl Percy
23 Jul 1880	London	M of Hertford	,,
11 Oct 1881	Newcastle	M of Salisbury	,,
14 Nov 1882	Bristol	D of Northumberland	,,
2 Oct 1883	Birmingham	D of Beaufort	,,
23 Jul 1884	Sheffield	E of Dartmouth	{ Ld R. Churchill { Sir M. Hicks Beach

[1]Brand continued to assist, however, until the 1868 General Election.

Date	Place		President
6 Oct 1885	Newport, Mon.	D of Norfolk	Ld C. Hamilton
26 Oct 1886	Bradford	Ld Tredegar	E. Ashmead Bartlett
22 Nov 1887	Oxford	E of Londesborough	,,
2–3 Nov 1888	Wolverhampton	E of Jenty	,,
26 Nov 1889	Nottingham	E of Dartmouth	Sir A. K. Rollit
18–18 Nov 1890	Liverpool	D of Portland	F. Dixon-Hartland
24 Nov 1891	Birmingham	E of Lathom	H. Byron-Reed
13–14 Dec 1892	Sheffield	Ld Windsor	C. B. Stuart-Wortley
1893	Cardiff	E of Scarborough	Sir S. Northcote
13 Nov 1894	Newcastle	E of Dunraven	J. Rankin
19 Nov 1895	Brighton	M of Londonderry	Sir C. E. H. Vincent
17 Nov 1896	Rochdale	D of Norfolk	M of Granby
16 Nov 1897	London	E of Derby	A. H. Smith-Barry
29 Nov 1898	Bristol	E of Cadogan	Sir B. Stone
28–29 Nov 1899	Dewsbury	D of Beaufort	G. W. E. Loder
·18 Dec 1900	London	M of Zetland	Ld Windsor

SOURCE: Minutes of the Annual Conferences of the National Union of Conservative and Constitutional Associations.

The National Liberal Federation: Annual Meetings, 1877–1900

Date	Place	President
31 May 1877	Birmingham	J. Chamberlain
22 Jan 1879	Leeds	,,
3 Feb 1880	Darlington	,,
26–27 Jan 1881	Birmingham	J. Collings
25 Oct 1881	Liverpool	H. Fell Pease
19 Dec 1882	Ashton-under-Lyne	,,
26 Nov 1883	Bristol	J. Kitson, Jr
7 Oct 1884	Stoke-on-Trent	,,
1 Oct 1885	Bradford	,,
3 Nov 1886	Leeds	Sir J. Kitson
18–19 Oct 188	Nottingham	,,
6–7 Nov 1888	Birmingham	,,
3–4 Dec 1889	Manchester	,,
20–21 Nov 1890	Sheffield	R. Spence Watson
1–2 Oct 1891	Newcastle	,,
1892	no meeting	
19–20 Jan 1893	Liverpool	,,
12–14 Feb 1894	Portsmouth	,,
16–18 Jan 1895	Cardiff	,,
26–27 Mar 1896	Huddersfield	,,
17–18 Mar 1897	Norwich	,,
22–23 Mar 1898	Leicester	,,
7–8 Mar 1899	Hull	,,
27–28 Mar 1900	Nottingham	,,

SOURCE: R. Spence Watson, *The National Liberal Federation, 1877–1906.*

Liberal Party Agents

J. Parkes	−1847
J. Coppock	−1857
W. R. Drake	1857–1865
J. Travers. Smith	1865 only
1865–1886	Work undertaken by Chief Whips. Legal business done by firm of Wyatt, Hoskins & Hooker.
F. Schnadhorst	1886–1892

Conservative Party Agents

F. R. Bonham	1832–1846
P. Rose	1853–1859
M. Spofforth	1859–1870
Sir J. Gorst	1870–1877
W. B. Skene	1877–1880
Sir J. Gorst	1880–1882
G. C. T. Bartley	1882–Dec 1884
R. W. E. Middleton	1885–1903

MINOR PARTIES

Peelites

112 Tories voted for the repeal of the Corn Laws in 1846. But 242 of Peel's former supporters voted on the side of Bentinck and Protection. Not all who followed Peel were convinced of the actual merits of his Free Trade policy. A substantial number voted for Peel solely from personal loyalty and the desire to keep him in office. However, Peel carried with him all the important elements in the party. He was followed by every member of the Government in and out of the Cabinet except three; by the Chief Whip, Sir J. Young; and by the party's election manager, F. R. Bonham. In the election of 1847 the party fund was used to support only Peelite candidates. 89 were elected, but in Parliament Peel refused to organise them in any way, to the frustration of younger men like Gladstone, Lincoln and Herbert.

The Peelites represented the brains of the old Conservative Party, the administrators and men of business. They also represented that broad range of centre opinion which overlapped with the moderate Liberals. Peel died in 1850, but only in Dec 1852 were parliamentary circumstances favourable enough to permit the Peelites to join a coalition under a Peelite Prime Minister (Aberdeen) and virtually on their own terms (they held half the Cabinet offices).'

Seats won by Peelites

	Eng.	Wales	Scot.	Ire.	Total
1847	62	7	11	9	89
1852	28	6	8	3	45
1857	13	3	7	3	26

SOURCE: R. Blake, *The Conservative Party from Peel to Churchill* (1970) p. 96.

Irish Home Rule Party

In Nov 1873 the Home Rule League was founded in Dublin with the object of winning self-government for Ireland. The League put forward candidates at the General Election of 1874, and 59 Home Rulers were returned for Irish constituencies. But only two of these seats were in Ulster. Almost immediately after the election the Home Rule members met in Dublin, and adopted resolutions constituting themselves 'a separate and distinct party in the House of Commons', appointed an Executive Council, secretaries and whips, and agreed upon motions to be introduced. Thus, there was at Westminster after 1874 an Irish party stronger in numbers and in organisation, and with a clearer and more comprehensive policy, than any Irish party which had preceded it there. I. Butt was party leader, but the most active members were J. G. Biggar (who initiated in 1875 the policy of 'obstruction') and C. S. Parnell.

When Butt died in 1879 W. Shaw was elected Chairman of the party. In the General Election of 1880, 61 Home Rule candidates were returned, many of whom owed their success to Parnell's backing. And when the newly elected Members met to elect a party chairman, Parnell defeated the rather colourless Shaw by 23 votes to 18. The result led to a split in the party: most of those who had voted against Parnell refused to serve under him. The dissidents did not, however, form a new party of their own; and the only effective Home Rule party was that led by Parnell. The strength of the Parnellites rose during the life of the Parliament to about 40. In 1885 the Home Rulers won 86 seats, and 85 in the following year. Parnell's divorce case in 1890 split the party. 45 Nationalists demanded his resignation as party leader. 26 continued to support him. Parnell's death in 1891 did not reunite the party. At the General Election of 1892 only 9 Parnellites were returned, and 71 anti-Parnellites. The former were led by J. Redmond, the anti-Parnellites by J. McCarthy. In 1895 there were 12 Parnellites and 70 anti-Parnellites. Only in 1900 did the Irish Nationalists reunite, under the leadership of Redmond.

SOURCE: J. C. Beckett, *The Making of Modern Ireland* (1966).

Scottish 'Crofters' Party'

The Scottish 'Crofters' Party' was essentially the protest of small-holders in the Highlands against the neglect of their grievances by the Liberal Party in Scotland. The Reform Act of 1884 enabled the Crofters to make an effective electoral challenge in the Highlands. At the General Election of 1885 the Crofters possessed their own organisation, in close alliance with the Highland Land League. Six Crofter candidates stood, three closely associated with the League.

Five were elected, for Ross-shire, Caithness-shire, Argyllshire, Wick Burghs and Inverness Burghs. In 1886 Crofters also won Suther-landshire and N.W. Lanarkshire. At the election of 1892, however, Crofters' candidates no longer described themselves as such, but stood as Gladstonians or Home Rule Liberals.

SOURCE: D. W. Crowley, 'The "Crofters' Party", 1885–1892,' *Scottish Historical Review*, XXXV (1956) 110.

Liberal Unionist Party

The Liberal Unionist Party was based on those Liberals who, under Joseph Chamberlain and the M of Hartington, broke with the party over Irish Home Rule in 1886. 93 Liberals voted against the Second Reading of the Home Rule Bill, 46 of them followers of Chamberlain, the rest Whigs. Both groups of Liberal Unionists set up organisations to contest the General Election of 1886: Hartington founded the Liberal Unionist Association, Chamberlain the Na-tional Radical Union. Election pacts with the Conservatives secured the return of 79 Liberal Unionists, most of them followers of Hartington. In 1889 Chamberlain renamed his organisation the National Liberal Union and there followed a virtual amalgamation of his supporters and those of Hartington. Chamberlain became leader of the Liberal Unionists in the House of Commons in 1891, when Hartington went to the Lords as 8th D of Devonshire. After the two leaders accepted office in Ld Salisbury's 1895 Government, the Liberal Unionists became increasingly fused with the Conserva-tive Party, although they preserved a separate organisation with separate funds. The final merger took place in 1912.

Liberal Unionist M.P.s

1886	79	1906	23
1892	47	Jan 1910	31
1895	70	Dec 1910	35
1900	68		

Independent Labour Party

In spite of the revival of socialism and the extension and increased militancy of trade unionism in the 1880s, the idea of an independent party of labour was slow to gain acceptance. One of its main advocates was J. K. Hardie who, along with three others, was returned as an Independent Labour Member in the General Elec-tion of 1892. This success led to the setting-up of a national organisation, the Independent Labour Party, at Bradford in Jan 1893. The main strength of the party lay in the North of England and in Scotland; it attracted some support from trade unions and socialist societies, though nationally the S.D.F. did not co-operate. In the 1895 election the party fielded 28 candidates who, together with 4 S.D.F. candidates, polled 44,000 votes, but did not elect a single

Member. Hardie lost his seat at West Ham. Despite this set-back, the idea of an independent party gradually gained further ground in the labour movement, under the impact of a deteriorating legal position for the unions and the reluctance of local Liberal parties to adopt working-class candidates. The I.L.P. joined with other organisations in setting up the Labour Representation Committee in Feb 1900.

SOURCES: Henry Pelling, *The Origins of the Labour Party*, 2nd ed. (1965); R. E. Dowse, *Left in the Centre* (1966).

3 Parliament

House of Commons

Speaker

10 Feb 1802	Charles Abbott (1757–1829) (Ld Colchester, 1817) (T)	30 Apr 1857	John Evelyn Denison (1800–1873) (Vt Ossington, 1872) (L)
2 Jun 1817	Charles Manners-Sutton (1780–1845) (Vt Canterbury, 1835) (T)	9 Feb 1872	Henry Bouverie Brand (1814–1892) (Vt Hampden, 1884) (L)
19 Feb 1835	James Abercromby (1776–1858) (Ld Dunfermline, 1839)(W)	26 Feb 1884	Arthur Wellesley Peel (1829–1912) (Vt Peel, 1895) (L)
27 May 1839	Charles Shaw-Lefevre (1794–1888) (Vt Eversley 1857) (W)	10 Apr 1895	William Court Gully (1835–1909) (Vt Selby, 1905) (L)

Contested Elections for the Speakership

1817	312:152
1833	241:310
1835	316:306
1839	317:299
1895	285:274

Only twice after the Reform Act, 1832, was the Speaker opposed in his constituency–1885 and 1895. On both occasions he was re-elected.

SOURCES: Commons Journals; P. Laundy (1964).

Officers of the House of Commons

Clerk of the House	Librarian	Serjeant at Arms
1768 J. Hatsell	1831 T. Vardon	1812 H. Seymour
1820 J. H. Ley	1867 G. Howard	1835 Sir W. Gosset
1850 Sir D. Le Marchant	1887 R. Walpole	1848 Ld C. Russell
1871 Sir T. E. May	1908 A. Smyth	1875 (Sir) R. A. Gosset
1886 R. F. D. Palgrave		1885 (Sir) H. D. Erskine
1900 (Sir) A. Milman		1915 Sir C. Keppel
1902 Sir C. Ilbert		

SOURCES: Commons Journals; Boase; Br. Imp. Cal.

99

Parliamentary Hours of Sitting

In 1831 the House usually met at 4 p.m., the usual hour since about 1760. In 1833 and 1834 the House met at noon, and adjourned between 3 p.m. and 5 p.m., when it met again. The early sitting was mostly devoted to Petitions, which then occupied much time.

Between 1835 and 1888 the House usually met at 4 p.m., except on Wednesdays after 9 Aug 1843 when it met occasionally at noon, a practice established by Resolution on 26 Jan 1846, and by Standing Order, 25 Jun 1852. Between 1867 and 1888, on Tuesdays and Fridays before and after Whitsuntide, the House often met at 2 p.m., the sitting being suspended between 7 p.m. and 9 p.m., at which hour it was resumed; these sittings were termed Morning and Evening Sittings respectively. From 27 Feb 1888 until 2 May 1902 the House usually met at 3 p.m.

The Palace of Westminster

The Old Houses of Parliament were destroyed by fire on 16 Oct 1834, except for Westminster Hall. Sir C. Barry was the architect of the new Houses, work on which began in 1840. Improvements to the Embankment had begun three years earlier. The new House of Lords was first used on 13 Apr 1847 and the new House of Commons on 30 May 1850. An explosion of dynamite on 24 Jan 1885 extensively damaged the Commons' Chamber, but the necessary repairs were completed before the House re-assembled on 19 Feb.

Parliamentary Sessions

Parliament Met	Parliament Prorogued	Total No. of Days on which the House Sat	Average Time of Daily Sitting Hrs. Mins.
26 Oct 30	24 Dec 30		
3 Feb 31	22 Apr 31		

Date of Dissolution: 23 Apr 31   Duration of Parliament   Y. M. D.   – 7 8

14 Jun 31	20 Oct 31 ⎫		
6 Dec 31	18 Dec 31 ⎬ 140		8 28
17 Jan 32	16 Aug 32 ⎭		

Date of Dissolution: 3 Dec 32   Duration of Parliament   Y. M. D.   1 5 19

| 29 Jan 33 | 29 Aug 33 | 144 | 9 33 |

Date of Dissolution: 29 Dec 34   Duration of Parliament   Y. M. D.   1 11 0

Parliament Met	Parliament Prorogued	Total No. of Days on which the House Sat	Average Time of Daily Sitting Hrs. Mins.
19 Feb 35	10 Sep 35	128	7 53
4 Feb 36	20 Aug 36	131	7 42
31 Jan 37	17 Jul 37	115	6 24

| | | Y. M. D. |
Date of Dissolution: 17 Jul 37   Duration of Parliament   2 4 26

15 Nov 37 16 Jan 38	23 Dec 37⎱ 16 Aug 38⎰	176	6 24
5 Feb 39	27 Aug 39	128	6 59
16 Jan 40	11 Aug 40	141	6 38
26 Jan 41	22 Jun 41	93	6 05

Y. M. D.
Date of Dissolution: 23 Jun 41   Duration of Parliament   3 9 12

19 Aug 41	7 Oct 41		
3 Feb 42	12 Aug 42	117	8 06
2 Feb 43	24 Aug 43	122	8 11
1 Feb 44	5 Sep 44	123	7 26
4 Feb 45	9 Aug 45	119	8 37
22 Jan 46	28 Aug 46	139	6 51
19 Jan 47	23 Jul 47	121	7 34

Y. M. D.
Date of Dissolution: 23 Jul 47   Duration of Parliament   5 11 4

18 Nov 47 3 Feb 48	20 Dec 47⎱ 5 Sep 48⎰	170	8 16
1 Feb 49	1 Aug 49	121	7 55
31 Jan 50	15 Aug 50	129	8 33
4 Feb 51	8 Aug 51	120	7 40
3 Feb 52	1 Jul 52	82	7 31

Y. M. D.
Date of Dissolution: 1 Jul 52   Duration of Parliament   4 9 10

4 Nov 52 10 Feb 53	31 Dec 52⎱ 20 Aug 53⎰	160	7 27
31 Jan 54	12 Aug 54	127	7 51
12 Dec 54 23 Jan 55	23 Dec 54⎱ 14 Aug 55⎰	136	7 39
31 Jan 56	29 Jul 56	110	7 53
3 Feb 57	21 Mar 57	116	7 47

Y. M. D.
Date of Dissolution: 21 Mar 57   Duration of Parliament   4 7 1

20 Apr 57	28 Aug 57		
3 Dec 57 4 Feb 58	12 Dec 57⎱ 2 Aug 58⎰	111	8 02
3 Feb 59	19 Apr 59	100	6 29

Y. M. D.
Date of Dissolution: 23 Apr 59   Duration of Parliament   1 11 23

Parliament Met	Parliament Prorogued	Total No. of Days on which the House Sat	Average Time of Daily Sitting Hrs. Mins.
31 May 59	13 Aug 59		8 34
24 Jan 60	28 Aug 60	145	8 34
5 Feb 61	6 Aug 61	116	7 56
6 Feb 62	7 Aug 62	113	7 50
5 Feb 63	28 Jul 63	107	7 54
4 Feb 64	29 Jul 64	111	7 46
7 Feb 65	6 Jul 65	94	6 47

Y. M. D.

Date of Dissolution: 6 Jul 65   Duration of parliament   6 1 6

1 Feb 66	10 Aug 66	114	7 03
5 Feb 67	21 Aug 67	128	8 08
19 Nov 67	7 Dec 67 ⎱	118	7 08
13 Feb 68	31 Jul 68 ⎰		

Y. M. D.

Date of Dissolution: 11 Nov 68   Duration of Parliament   3 2 27

10 Dec 68	29 Dec 68 ⎱	119	7 50
16 Feb 69	11 Aug 69 ⎰		
8 Feb 70	10 Aug 70	120	8 13
9 Feb 71	21 Aug 71	129	8 33
6 Feb 72	10 Aug 72	120	8 33
6 Feb 73	5 Aug 73	112	7 50

Y. M. D.

Date of Dissolution: 26 Jan 74   Duration of Parliament   5 1 16

5 Mar 74	7 Aug 74	97	7 22
5 Feb 75	13 Aug 75	121	8 16
8 Feb 76	15 Aug 76	126	8 11
8 Feb 77	14 Aug 77	122	8 31
17 Jan 78	16 Aug 78	136	8 23
5 Dec 78	17 Dec 78 ⎱	130	8 49
13 Feb 79	15 Aug 79 ⎰		
5 Feb 80	24 Mar 80	121	8 36

Y. M. D.

Date of Dissolution: 24 Mar 80   Duration of Parliament   6 0 19

29 Apr 80	7 Sep 80		
6 Jan 81	27 Aug 81	154	9 05
7 Feb 82	18 Aug 82 ⎱	162	8 51
24 Oct 82	2 Dec 82 ⎰		
15 Feb 83	25 Aug 83	129	9 01
5 Feb 84	14 Aug 84	126	8 49
23 Oct 84	6 Dec 84 ⎱	129	7 58
19 Feb 85	14 Aug 85 ⎰		

Y. M. D.

Date of Dissolution: 18 Nov 85   Duration of Parliament   5 6 20

Parliament Met	Parliament Prorogued	Total No. of Days on which the House Sat	Average Time of Daily Sitting Hrs. Mins.
12 Jan 86	25 Jun 86	89	7 46

			Y. M. D.
Date of Dissolution:	26 Jun 86	Duration of Parliament	– 5 14

5 Aug 86	25 Sep 86	31	7 46
27 Jan 87	16 Sep 87	160	9 05
9 Feb 88	13 Aug 88 }	160	8 40
6 Nov 88	24 Dec 88 }		
21 Feb 89	30 Aug 89	122	8 53
11 Feb 90	18 Aug 90	125	8 42
25 Nov 90	9 Dec 90 }	141	8 23
22 Jan 91	5 Aug 91 }		
9 Feb 92	28 Jun 92	89	8 02

			Y. M. D.
Date of Dissolution:	28 Jun 92	Duration of Parliament	5 10 23

4 Aug 92	18 Aug 92	7	5 17
31 Jan 93	5 Mar 94	226	8 27
12 Mar 94	25 Aug 94	113	8 25
5 Feb 95	6 Jul 95	97	7 48

			Y. M. D.
Date of Dissolution:	8 Jul 95	Duration of Parliament	2 11 4

12 Aug 95	5 Sep 95	20	7 48
11 Feb 96	14 Aug 96	124	9 02
19 Jan 97	6 Aug 97	127	8 08
8 Feb 98	12 Aug 98	119	8 22
7 Feb 99	9 Aug 99	117	8 22
17 Oct 99	27 Oct 99	9	5 33
30 Jan 00	8 Aug 00	113	8 24

			Y. M. D.
Date of Dissolution:	25 Sep 00	Duration of Parliament	5 1 13

The duration of Parliament is reckoned from the day appointed by the Writ of Summons for the new Parliament to meet, in accordance with the provisions of the Septennial Act, 1715.

Composition of the House of Commons

Period	England	Wales	Scotland	Ireland	County	Borough	Univ	Total
1707–1800	489	24	45	–	122	432	4	558
1801–26	489	24	45	100	186	467	5	658
1826–32	489	24	45	100	188	465	5	658
1832–67	471	29	53	105	253	399	6	658
1868–85	463	30	60	105	283	366	9	658
1885–1918	465	30	72	103	377	284	9	670
1918–22	498	30	74	105	372	320	15	707
1922	492	36	74	13	300	303	12	615

SOURCES: Public General Acts; Acland and Ransome, *Handbook*; Constit. Year Book.

House of Lords

Lord Chairmen of Committees

(*Deputy Speaker of H of Lords ; the Ld Chancellor is the Speaker*)

10 Nov 1814	E of Shaftesbury.
4 Feb 1851	Ld Redesdale
19 Aug 1886	D of Buckingham and Chandos
11 Feb 1890	E of Morley
16 Feb 1905	E of Onslow

Officers of the House of Lords

Clerk of the Parliaments

24 Feb 1788	G. Rose
27 Jan 1818	H. Cowper (acting)
2 Mar 1818	(Sir) G. H. Rose
25 Jun 1855	Sir J. G. Shaw-Lefevre
27 Apr 1875	Sir W. Rose
22 Dec 1885	(Sir) H. Graham
27 Apr 1917	Sir A. T. Thring

Gentleman Usher of the Black Rod

1812	Sir T. Tyrwhitt
1832	Sir A. Clifford
1877	Sir T. W. Knollys
1883	Sir J. R. Drummond
1895	Sir M. Biddulph
1904	Sir H. F. Stephenson

Serjeant at Arms

1818	G. F. Seymour
1841	A. Perceval
1858	Sir W. P. M. C. Talbot
1899	Sir A. Ellis
1901	Sir F. Edwards

Librarian

1826	J. F. Leary
1861	J. H. Pulman
1897	S. A. Strong
1904	E. Gosse

SOURCES: Lords Journals; Br. Imp. Cal.; Boase; H of Lords Record Office, Memo No. 31.

Composition of the House of Lords

Year	Peers of Royal Blood	Dukes	Marquesses	Earls	Viscounts	Barons	Archbps. & Bishops	Irish Reprs Prelates	Irish Reprs Peers	Scottish Reprs Peers	Total entitled to vote
1830	4	19	18	103(1)	22	160	26	4	28	16	399
1837	3	21	19(1)	112(2)	19	193(11)	26	4	28	16	421
1840	3	21	20(1)	114(3)	20	211(7)	26	16	28	16	448
1845	3(1)	20	20(2)	115(3)	21	200(10)	26	4	28	16	434
1850	3(1)	20(1)	21(3)	116(2)	22(1)	199(5)	26	4	28	16	441
1855	3(1)	20(1)	21(2)	112(3)	22(1)	196(6)	26	4	28	16	433
1860	3(1)	20(2)	21(2)	110(5)	22(1)	210(5)	26	4	28	16	443
1865	3	20(2)	19(1)	109(8)	21	207(8)	26	4	28	16	434
1870	4	20	18	110(4)	23	230(9)	26	–	28	16	462
1875	5	21	18(1)	111(2)	24	244(12)	26	–	28	16	478
1880	4	22(1)	19(1)	118(3)	25(1)	254(6)	26	–	28	16	500
1885	5(1)	22	20(1)	119(7)	28	277(5)	26	–	28	16	526
1890	6(1)	22	21(1)	119(3)	28(1)	288(6)	26	–	28	16	539
1895	6(1)	22(1)	22	121(3)	29(2)	308(8)	26	–	28	16	561
1900	5(1)	22	22(1)	123(1)	30(4)	321(7)	26	–	28	16	577

Figures in brackets indicate minors.

SOURCES: Oliver & Boyd's *Edinburgh Almanac* for 1837 etc.; Royal Calendar, 1831 (for 1830 figures).

4 Monarchy

William IV

Born 21 Aug 1765, 3rd son of George III and Queen Charlotte; entered Navy as midshipman upon *Prince George* in 1779; thereafter pursued a naval career and held various commands; retired from active service as rear-admiral, 1791; created D of Clarence, 1789, and provided with parliamentary annuity of £12,000, raised to £18,000 on marriage in 1818; 1791–1811 lived with Mrs Dorothy Jordan (1762–1816) by whom he had ten children of family name Fitzclarence; promoted Admiral of the Fleet, 1811; married 18 Jul 1818 Adelaide of Saxe-Coburg-Meiningen; Lord High Admiral, 1827–8; succeeded to throne 26 Jun 1830; crowned 8 Sep 1831; died 20 Jun 1837; no legitimate heirs.

(Alexandrina) Victoria

Born 24 May 1819 at Kensington Palace, only daughter of Edward, D of Kent (1767–1820) and Princess Victoria of Saxe-Saalfeld-Coburg (1786–1861), married 11 Jul 1818; succeeded to throne 20 Jun 1837 on death of her uncle, William IV; crowned at Westminster Abbey 28 Jun 1838; married 10 Feb 1840, at Chapel Royal, St James's, Albert of Saxe-Coburg-Gotha, by whom she had nine children; widowed 14 Dec 1861; declared Empress of India 1 May 1876; died at Osborne 22 Jan 1901; buried at Frogmore.

H. R. H. Prince Albert

Born 26 Aug 1819, 2nd son of Ernest, D of Saxe-Coburg-Gotha and Louise (divorced 1826); educated privately, at Brussels (1836) and at University of Bonn (1837–8); married 10 Feb 1840; proposed parliamentary annuity of £50,000, reduced to £30,000; Privy Councillor, 1840; naturalised Englishman, 1840; Regent, in event of Queen's death, 1840; Chairman, Royal Commission on Fine Arts, 1841–61; President, Royal Society of Arts, 1843; elected Chancellor of Cambridge University, 1847; purchased Osborne (1845) and Balmoral (1848); President, Royal Commission on Great Exhibition, 1849–51; rejected post of Commander-in-Chief, 1850; Master of the Trinity House, 1852; President of British Association for Advancement of Science, 1859; President of Statistical Congress, 1860; created Prince Consort by Letters Patent 25 Jun 1857; died at

Windsor 14 Dec 1861; buried finally at Frogmore. 'The dates are few, and the career is, above all, remarkable for its calmness' (*Times*, 24 Dec 1861).

The Children and Grandchildren of Queen Victoria

1. H.R.H. Princess Victoria (Princess Royal); born 21 Nov 1840; married 25 Jan 1858 Prince Frederick of Prussia, afterwards Kaiser Frederick III (died 1888); died 5 Aug 1901. Children: (1) Kaiser William II (1859–1941); (2) Charlotte (1860–1919); (3) Henry (1862–1929); (4) Sigismund (1864–6); (5) Victoria (1866–1929); (6) Waldemar (1868–79); (7) Sophia (1870–1932), Queen of Hellenes (1889); (8) Margarete (1872–1954).

2. H.R.H. Prince Albert Edward, D of Cornwall (1841), Prince of Wales (1841), King Edward VII (1901); born 9 Nov 1841; married 10 Mar 1863 Princess Alexandra, eldest daughter of Christian IX of Denmark; succeeded to throne 22 Jan 1901; crowned 9 Aug 1902; died 6 May 1910. Children: (1) Albert (1864–92), D of Clarence and Avondale (1891); (2) George (1865–1936), D of York (1893), Prince of Wales (1901–10), King George V (1910–36); (3) Louise (Princess Royal) (1867–1931); (4) Victoria (1868–1935); (5) Maud (1869–1938), married King of Norway, 1896.

3. H.R.H. Princess Alice, born 25 Apr 1843; married Grand Duke Ludwig of Hesse (1862); died 14 Dec 1878. Children: (1) Victoria (1863–1950); (2) Elizabeth (1864–1918); (3) Irene (1866–1953); (4) Ernest-Ludwig (1868–1937), Grand Duke of Hesse; (5) Frederick (1870–3); (6) Alix (1872–1918), married Tsar Nicholas II of Russia, 1894, assassinated 1918; (7) Mary (1874–8).

4. H.R.H. Prince Alfred, D of Edinburgh (1866), D of Saxe-Coburg-Gotha (1893); born 6 Aug 1844; married Grand Duchess Maria Alexandrovna of Russia, 1874, only d. of Tsar Alexander II; died 30 July 1900. Children: (1) Alfred (1874–99); (2) Marie (1875–1938), Queen of Roumania (1893); (3) Victoria (1876–1936); (4) Alexandra (1878–1942); (5) Beatrice (1884–1966).

5. H.R.H. Princess Helena, born 25 May 1846; married Prince Christian of Schleswig-Holstein, 1866; died 9 Jun 1923. Children: (1) Christian (1867–1900); (2) Albert (1869–1931); (3) Helena Victoria (1870–1948); (4) Louise (1872–1956); (5) Harold (12–20 May 1876).

6. H.R.H. Prince Louise, born 18 Mar 1848; married, 1871, M of Lorne, 9th D of Argyll (1900), no children, died 3 Dec 1939.

7. H.R.H. Prince Arthur, D of Connaught and Strathearn (1874), born 1 May 1850; married Princess Louisa of Prussia, 1879; died 16 Jan 1942. Children: (1) Margaret (1882–1920); (2) Arthur (1883–1938); (3) Victoria Patricia (Lady Patricia Ramsey) (1886–   ).

8. H.R.H. Prince Leopold, D of Albany (1881), born 7 Apr 1853,

married Princess Helena of Waldeck, 1882; died 28 Mar 1884. Children: (1) Alice (1883–1957), Countess of Athlone (1904); (2) Charles Edward (1884–1954), D of Saxe-Coburg-Gotha (1900–18).

9. H.R.H. Princess Beatrice, born 14 Apr 1857; married Prince Henry of Battenberg, 1885; died 26 Oct 1944. Children: (1) Alexander (1886–1960), M of Carisbrooke, (2) Victoria Eugenie (1887–1969), married Alfonso XIII of Spain, 1906; (3) Leopold (1889–1922); (4) Maurice (1891–1914).

SOURCES: *D.N.B.*: *Whitaker*; *Statesman's Year Book.*

Royal Secretaries

1830	Sir Herbert Taylor
1837	Ld Melbourne
1840	Prince Albert
1861–6	Sir Charles Phipps
1861–70	Gen Charles Grey
1870	Sir Henry Ponsonby
1895	Sir Arthur Bigge
	(Ld Stamfordham)
1901	Sir Frederick Knollys

Coronation Expenses

George IV	£243,390 6s. 2d.
William IV	£43,159 11s. 6d.
Victoria	£69,421 1s. 10d.

Dates on which Sovereign Opened Parliament in Person

2 Nov 1830	1 Feb 1844	3 Feb 1859
21 Jun 1831	4 Feb 1845	7 Jun 1859
3 Dec 1831	22 Jan 1846	24 Jan 1860
5 Feb 1833	19 Jan 1847	5 Feb 1861
4 Feb 1834	1 Feb 1849	6 Feb 1866
24 Feb 1835	4 Feb 1851	5 Feb 1867
4 Feb 1836	3 Feb 1852	9 Feb 1871
20 Nov 1837	11 Nov 1852	6 Feb 1873
5 Feb 1839	31 Jan 1854	8 Feb 1876
16 Jan 1840	12 Dec 1854	8 Feb 1877
26 Jan 1841	31 Jan 1856	5 Feb 1880
3 Feb 1842	3 Dec 1857	21 Jan 1886

Royal Grants and Civil List

William IV   £510,000

1. For Privy Purse	£60,000	4. Expenses of Household	£171,500
2. Queen Adelaide's Privy		5. Special and Secret Service	£23,500
Purse	£50,000	6. Pensions	£75,000
3. Salaries of Household	£130,000	Total	£510,000

Victoria	£385,000		
1. For Privy Purse	£60,000	4. Royal Bounty and Alms	£13,200
2. Salaries, etc., of		5. Unappropriated Money	£8,040
Household	£131,260	Total	£385,000
3. Expenses of Household	£172,500		

In addition, Queen Victoria had the right to issue new pensions to the amount of £1,200 per annum. Also, the revenues of the Duchy of Lancaster, which went to the Sovereign, rose from £5,000 (1838) to £50,000 (1888).

Grants to the Family of Queen Victoria

Annually out of Consolidated Fund		Grants in One Sum, from Supply	
Prince Albert	£30,000	£40,000	on marriage
Princess Royal	£8,000		
Prince of Wales*	£40,000	£23,455	on coming of age and marriage
Princess of Wales	£10,000		
Children of			
Prince of Wales (from 1889)	£36,000		
Princess Alice	£6,000	£30,000	on marriage
D of Edinburgh	£15,000	£5,883	,,
raised to	£25,000		
Princess Helena	£6,000	£30,000	,,
Princess Louise	£6,000	£30,000	,,
D of Connaught	£25,000		
Princess Beatrice	£6,000	£30,000	,,
Duch of Albany	£6,000		

*Plus revenues from Duchy of Cornwall, which increased from £20,000 to £67,000 during reign.

Total Annuities to Royal Family at Various Times

Year	Amount	No. of Persons in Receipt
1830	£213,788	15
1836	209,788	14
1837	311,788	12
1840	341,788	13
1850	173,788	10
1860	142,000	8
1870	111,000	10
1880	146,000	11
1889	152,000	12
1900	168,000	16*

*Includes 4 children of Prince of Wales.
SOURCE: P.P. (1889) XI.

5 Parliamentary Reform

The Impact of the Reform Acts; 1832–1885

Changes in the distribution of seats by the 1832 Reform Act:

England

Seats disfranchised:

55 boroughs returning 2 members	− 110
Higham Ferrers	− 1
30 double-member seats deprived of one member	− 30
Weymouth and Melcombe Regis to return 2 members conjointly instead of 4	− 2
	− 143

Seats enfranchised:

22 cities and boroughs to return 2 members each	+ 44
19 boroughs to return one member each	+ 19
26 counties divided, each division to return 2 members	+ 52
Yorkshire to have 3 divisions returning 2 members, instead of 4 members for the whole county	+ 2
Isle of Wight made a county and given one seat	+ 1
7 other counties to return 3 members instead of 2	+ 7
	+ 125
Net reduction in English seats:	18

This reduction for England was accompanied by the following increased representation elsewhere:

Wales

3 counties given an additional member	+3
2 new boroughs enfranchised	+2

Scotland

Additional members to Edinburgh and Glasgow	+2
Perth, Aberdeen and Dundee to return one member each (instead of being grouped with other burghs).	+3
Paisley, Greenock and the Leith burghs to return one member each	+3

Ireland

Additional members to Belfast, Dublin University, Galway, Limerick and Waterford	+ 5
Net increase	18

The Changes in Detail

A. English boroughs totally disfranchised (56):

Bucks. (− 2)
Amersham
Wendover

Cornwall (− 13)
Bossiney
Callington
Camelford
East Looe
Fowey
Lostwithiel
Newport
St Germains
St Mawes
St Michael's
Saltash
Tregony
West Looe

Devonshire (− 3)
Beeralston
Okehampton
Plympton

Dorset (− 1)
Corfe Castle

Hampshire (− 4)
Stockbridge
Whitchurch
Newtown (I.o.W.)
Yarmouth (I.of.W.)

Herefordshire (− 1)
Weobley

Kent (− 2)
Queenborough
Romney

Lancs (− 1)
Newton

Norfolk (− 1)
Castle Rising

Northants (− 2)
Brackley
Higham Ferrers

Shropshire (− 1)
Bishop's Castle

Somerset (− 3)
Ilchester
Milborne Port
Minehead

Suffolk (− 3)
Aldeburgh
Dunwich
Orford

Surrey (− 3)
Bletchingley

Gatton
Haslemere

Sussex (− 5)
Bramber
East Grinstead
Seaford
Steyning
Winchelsea

Westmorland (− 1)
Appleby

Wiltshire (− 7)
Downton
Great Bedwin
Heytesbury
Hindon
Ludgershall
Old Sarum
Wootton Bassett

Yorkshire (− 3)
Aldbrough
Boroughbridge
Hedon

N.B. Each of the above boroughs had returned 2 members, except Higham Ferrers which returned only one.

B. English boroughs deprived of one member (30 in all): Arundel; Ashburton; Calne; Christchurch; Clitheroe; Dartmouth; Droitwich; Eye; Grimsby; Helston; Horsham; Hythe; Launceston; Liskeard; Lyme Regis; Malmesbury; Midhurst; Morpeth; Northallerton; Petersfield; Reigate; Rye; St Ives; Shaftesbury; Thirsk; Wallingford; Wareham; Westbury; Wilton; Woodstock.

N.B. In addition, the representation of Weymouth and Melcombe Regis was reduced from 4 to 2.

C. The 26 counties to be divided into 2 divisions returning 2 members each (+ 52):

Cheshire	Kent	Somerset
Cornwall	Lancs.	Staffs.
Cumberland	Leics.	Suffolk
Derbyshire	Lincs.	Surrey
Devon	Norfolk	Sussex
Durham	Northants.	Warwicks.
Essex	Northumberland	Wilts.
Gloucs.	Notts.	Worcs.
Hants	Shropshire	

D. Additional county changes (+ 10):
7 counties to return 3 members instead of 2: Berkshire; Bucks.; Cambridgeshire; Dorset; Hereford; Herts.; Oxon.
One new county enfranchised: Isle of Wight.
Yorkshire to be divided into 3 divisions returning 2 members each instead of 4 members for whole county.

E. The 22 new boroughs returning 2 members each (+ 44): Birmingham; Blackburn; Bolton; Bradford; Brighton; Devonport; Finsbury; Greenwich; Halifax; Lambeth; Leeds; Macclesfield; Manchester; Marylebone; Oldham; Sheffield; Stockport; Stoke-on-Trent; Stroud; Sunderland; Tower Hamlets; Wolverhampton.

F. The 19 new boroughs returning one member each (+ 19): Ashton-under-Lyne; Bury; Chatham; Cheltenham; Dudley; Frome; Gateshead; Huddersfield; Kendal; Kidderminster; Rochdale; Salford; South Shields; Tynemouth; Wakefield; Walsall; Warrington; Whitby; Whitehaven.

G. Additional representation to Wales, Ireland and Scotland:
(a) Additions to Wales (5):
   Carmarthenshire, Glamorganshire and Denbighshire to return 2 members each instead of one.
   Swansea and Merthyr Tydfil created new boroughs returning one member each.
(b) Additions to Ireland (5):
   One additional member each to Dublin University, Belfast, Galway, Limerick and Waterford.
(c) Additions to Scotland (8):
   Clackmannan and Kinross shires, previously represented in alternate Parliaments, to be united to each other. Bute and Caithness shires, previously represented in alternate Parliaments, to return one member each. Cromarty and Nairn shires, previously represented in alternate Parliaments, to be united— the former to Ross, the latter to Elgin.
   Additional member for Edinburgh.
   Paisley, Leith Burghs and Greenock to return one member each.

In addition, the following groups of burghs were represented after 1832:

Before 1832		After 1832	
Aberdeen	} 1	Aberdeen	1
Montrose			
Brechin		Montrose	} 1
Inverbervie		Brechin	
Aberbrothick		Inverbervie	
		Aberbrothick	
Crail		Forfar	
Anstruther E.	} 1		
Anstruther W.		Perth	1
Kilrenny			
Pittenweem		Dundee	1
Forfar		St Andrews	
St Andrews		Cupar	
Cupar	} 1	Crail	
Perth		Anstruther E.	} 1
Dundee		Anstruther W.	
		Kilrenny	
Glasgow		Pittenweem	
Dumbarton	} 1		
Renfrew		Glasgow	2
Rutherglen			
		Kilmarnock	
		Renfrew	
		Dumbarton	} 1
		Rutherglen	
		Port Glasgow	

Changes under the Reform Acts of 1867 and 1868

England

A. Disfranchisement:

6 boroughs returning 2 members } totally disfranchised 5 boroughs returning 1 member	− 17
35 boroughs returning 2 members deprived of one member	− 35
	− 52

B. Enfranchisement:

(a) Boroughs:

London University to return one member	+ 1
Salford to return 2 members in place of one	+ 1
Leeds, Liverpool, Birmingham and Manchester each to return 3 members instead of 2	+ 4
Chelsea and Hackney each to return 2 members	+ 4
9 new boroughs to return one each	+ 9
	+ 19

(b) Counties:

Yorkshire (West Riding) to be divided into 3 divisions instead of 2, each returning 2 members	+ 2

Lancashire to be divided into 4 divisions, each returning 2 members   +3
10 counties to be divided into 3 instead of 2 divisions, each
   returning 2 members   +20
                                                                          ——
                                                                         +25

Thus:
     Total new enfranchisement   +4
     Net loss of seats   −8

Apportionment of these 8 seats was as follows:
One additional member for Merthyr Tydfil   +1
2 new Scottish University constituencies, each returning one
   member   +2
Additional members for Glasgow and Dundee   +2
3 counties (Aberdeen, Ayr and Lanark) divided into 2 divisions,
   each returning one member   +3
Peeblesshire and Selkirkshire to return one member conjointly
   instead of one each   −1
One member for the 'Border Burghs'   +1
                                                                          ——
                                                                          +8

The Changes in Detail

Boroughs totally disfranchised:
(a) Returning 2 members: Honiton, Lancaster, Thetford, Totnes, Wells and Yarmouth.
(b) Returning one member each: Arundel, Ashburton, Dartmouth, Lyme Regis and Reigate.
Boroughs deprived of one member (35):
Andover; Bodmin; Bridgnorth; Bridport; Buckingham; Chichester; Chippenham; Cirencester; Cockermouth; Devizes; Dorchester; Evesham; Guildford; Harwich; Hertford; Huntingdon; Knaresborough; Leominster; Lewes; Lichfield; Ludlow; Lymington; Maldon; Malton, Marlborough; Marlow; Newport (I.o.W.); Poole; Richmond (Yorks.); Ripon; Stamford; Tavistock; Tewkesbury; Windsor; Chipping Wycombe.
New constituencies (each returning one member):
London University; Burnley; Darlington; Dewsbury; Gravesend; Middlesbrough; Stalybridge; Stockton; The Hartlepools; Wednesbury.
   N.B. The Tower Hamlets were divided into two, the boroughs of Hackney and Tower Hamlets, each with two members.
The following counties were divided into 3 divisions instead of 2 (10):
Cheshire; Derbyshire; Devonshire; Essex; Kent; Lincolnshire; Norfolk; Somerset; Staffordshire; Surrey.

Changes under the 1885 Reform Act

England and Wales
Disfranchisement:

13 boroughs returning 2 members merged in the counties	− 26
66 boroughs returning one member merged in the counties	− 66
36 boroughs returning 2 members deprived of one member	− 36
2 boroughs (Macclesfield and Sandwich), each returning 2 members, disfranchised	− 4
	− 132

New seats added to House of Commons	6
Thus: total seats to be redistributed	138

Enfranchisement:

London (including Croydon) to return 62 members instead of 22	+ 40
Additional members allocated to provincial boroughs	+ 26
New provincial boroughs created	+ 6
Additional members allocated to counties	+ 66
	+ 138

Scotland
Disfranchisement and new seats:

2 boroughs returning one member each merged in counties	− 2
12 new seats allocated to Scotland	12
Total seats to be redistributed	14

Enfranchisement:

7 new seats to be allocated to counties	+ 7
7 seats added to Aberdeen, Edinburgh and Glasgow	+ 7
	+ 14

Ireland
Disfranchisement:

22 boroughs returning one member each	− 22
3 boroughs returning 2 members each deprived of one member	− 3
	− 25

Enfranchisement:

21 seats allocated to counties	+ 21
4 seats allocated to Belfast and Dublin	+ 4
	+ 25

After 1885 the following towns returned more than one member each. All other towns returned a single member each.

England
Four or more members:
London (61); Liverpool (9); Birmingham (7); Manchester (6); Sheffield (5); Leeds (5); Bristol (4).
Three members:
Bradford; Hull; Nottingham; Salford; Wolverhampton.
Two members:
Bath; Blackburn; Bolton; Brighton; Devonport; Derby; Halifax; Ipswich; Leicester; Newcastle; Northampton; Norwich; Oldham; Plymouth; Portsmouth; Preston; Southampton; Stockport; Sunderland; York.

Ireland
Belfast (4); Cork (2); Dublin (4).

Scotland
Aberdeen (2); Dundee (2); Edinburgh (4); Glasgow (7).

Wales
Merthyr Tydfil (2).

Boroughs Disfranchised for Bribery

1821	Grampound	1869	Beverley
1844	Sudbury		Bridgwater
1852	St Albans		Cashel
1867	Lancaster		Sligo
	Reigate	1885	Macclesfield
	Totnes		Sandwich
	Yarmouth		

The Electors

Estimates of the size of the electorate during the nineteenth century vary considerably. All such estimates are, of course, only approximate. The first published set of figures, and that which provides the basis of most later estimates, was produced by Sir John Lambert in 1889:

No. of Voters in Each of the Following Years

England & Wales (excluding University electors)

Year	Counties	Boroughs	Total	Increase
1831*	247,000	188,391	435,391	
1833	370,379	285,958	656,337	220,946
1866	540,271	514,026	1,054,297	
1869	764,876	1,195,360	1,960,236	905,939
1883	966,721	1,651,732	2,618,453	
1886	2,538,142	1,842,191	4,380,333	1,761,880

Scotland

1831	3,276	1,303	4,579	
1833	33,115	31,332	64,447	59,868
1866	49,979	55,515	105,494	
1869	76,791	158,918	235,709	130,215
1883	99,652	210,789	310,441	
1886	315,267	235,564	550,831	240,390

Ireland

1831	52,162	23,798	75,960	
1833	60,607	31,545	92,152	16,192
1866	172,010	32,655	204,665	
1869	176,825	45,625	222,450	17,785
1883	165,997	58,021	224,018	
1886	631,651	106,314	737,965	513,947

*Estimated.

SOURCE: J. Lambert, 'Parliamentary Franchises Past and Present', *The Nineteenth Century* (Dec. 1889) p. 958.

Lambert had been Permanent Secretary to the Local Government Board, and was therefore well placed to collect authoritative statistics on the size of the electorate. Charles Seymour, however, in his *Electoral Reform in England and Wales: The Development and Operation of the Parliamentary Franchise, 1832–1885* (1915), found much to criticise in Lambert's figures. He wrote that they were 'marred by inaccuracies and misprints', and he produced a revised estimate for England and Wales:

The Electorate and the Reforms in England and Wales

	County Electorate	Borough Electorate	Total Electorate	Increase	% Increase
1831	247,000	188,391	435,391		
1833	370,379	282,398	652,777	217,386	49
1866	542,633	514,026	1,056,659		
1869	791,916	1,203,170	1,995,086	938,427	88
1883	966,721	1,651,732	2,618,453		
1886	2,538,349	1,842,191	4,380,540	1,762,087	67

SOURCE: Seymour (1915) p. 533.

Such variations in the figures make it convenient to express the number of voters as a proportion of the adult male population:

	England and Wales	Scotland	Ireland
1833	1 in 5	1 in 8	1 in 20
1869	1 in 3	1 in 3	1 in 6
1886	2 in 3	3 in 5	1 in 2

A comprehensive summary for the nineteenth century has been compiled by David Butler and James Cornford, based on the estimates of Lambert and of Seymour:

The Effects of the Reform Acts of 1832, 1867–8 and 1885 on the Growth of the Electorate*

	England and Wales	Scotland	Ireland	United Kingdom
Estimated electorate in 1831	435,391	4,579	75,950	515,920
Percentage increase 1831–3 { counties	49	915	16	53
boroughs	49	2,320	32	62
total	49	1,310	21	57
Electorate in 1833	652,777	64,447	92,152	809,376
Proportion of electorate to adult males	1/5	1/8	1/20	–
Percentage increase 1833–66	62	64	122	69

*Excluding University Electors.

		England and Wales	Scotland	Ireland	United Kingdom
Percentage	counties	45	54	3	37
increase	boroughs	134	178	31	134
1866–9	total	88	119	8	80
Electorate in 1869		1,995,086	230,606	220,155	2,445,847
Proportion of electorate to adult males		1/3	1/3	1/6	–
Percentage increase 1869–83		31	36	1	29
Percentage	counties	162	226	282	183
increase	boroughs	11	12	83	14
1883–6	total	67	80	229	80
Electorate in 1886		4,376,624	560,580	737,760	5,674,964
Proportion of electorate to adult males		2/3	3/5	1/2	–

SOURCE: *International Guide to Electoral Statistics* (1968) p. 333.

Qualifications for Voting

There was great variety in the qualifications for voting both before 1832 and after. Full details are listed below. For England and Wales two fundamental changes were made: (1) the creation of a basic qualification for the borough franchise–the £10 householder qualification; (2) the supplementing of the ancient 40s. freeholder qualification in the counties by a variety of new franchises.

Persons Entitled to Vote under the Reform Act of 1832

In English Counties. 1. Forty shilling freeholders, being seised or possessed of inheritance; or being lifeholders who came into possession before June 1832, whether in actual possession or only in receipt of rents, or who, coming subsequently into possession, were in *bona fide* occupation, or had acquired their holdings by marriage, marriage settlement, devise, or promotion to any benefice or office. 2. £10 freeholders. 3. £10 copyholders. 4. Tenants at a yearly rent of £50. 5. Leaseholders for 60 years at clear yearly value of £10. 6. Leaseholders for 20 years paying £50 clear yearly value. 7. Mortgagees in possession of freeholds, if after payment of interest there remained a clear yearly value of £10; or in actual possession and receipt of rents of the yearly value of 40s. 8. Leasehold mortgagees in possession of yearly values of £10. 9. Trustees in receipt of requisite rents. 10. Beneficed clergymen. 11. Annuitants from freehold or copyhold, the latter claim being registered 12 months prior to election. 12. Holders of life-offices with emoluments (not less than 40s.) arising out of lands. 13. Purchasers of redeemed land tax (40s.). 14. Irremovable schoolmasters, parish clerks, and sextons. 15. Proprietors of tithes and rent charges (40s.). 16. Joint tenants whose separate interests amounted to 40s. freehold or £10 leasehold. 17. Owners of shares in mines, rivers, canals, fairs, markets, &c., if amounting to an interest in the soil of sufficient annual value. *Note.* No person could vote in a county in respect of property that would confer on him a qualification to vote for a borough; but a freehold in a borough of the annual value of 40s., under £10, entitled the owner to a vote for the county, and above £10 if in the occupation of the tenant. If he occupied it himself he had no county vote.

In English Boroughs. 1. The ancient franchise holders in boroughs not disfranchised if their qualifications existed on the last day of July in the year for which they claimed, and if they had resided for six months in the borough or within 7 miles, and their names were on the register. 2. Occupiers either as owners or tenants of any house, warehouse, or counting-house, shop, or other building, *either with or without land,* of the clear yearly value of £10 within the borough, provided they had been in possession 12 calendar months prior to the last day of July in the year of the claim and had paid before 20th July all the poor-rates and assessed taxes payable from them in respect of the premises previous to the April preceding. 3. Lodgers if sharing with other lodgers and the value divided by number of lodgers came to £10 a year for each. If the landlord occupied any part of the house he, and not his lodgers, was in occupation.

In Scotch Counties. The persons possessed of the suffrage before March 1831, or who would have been entitled to it, that is to say, tenants in chief of the Crown with lands of 40 shillings (old extent), or of £400 Scotch valued rent, together with owners of land £10 annual value; 57 years leaseholders and life-holders with a clear £10 yearly interest, 19 years leaseholders with do., yearly tenants at a £50 rent, and all tenants whose interest had cost them £300.

In Scotch Cities, Burghs, and Contributory Districts. The occupiers of houses of £10 clear yearly value, whether as proprietor, tenant, life-renter, or joint-occupier, with the non-resident true owners of similar premises, and husbands *jure uxoris* after the death of their wives holding by the courtesy of Scotland.

In Irish Counties. £10 freeholders; leaseholders for lives and copyholders of estates of £10; 60 years leaseholders and their assignees of estates of the same value; 14 years leaseholders of £20 estates.

In Irish Cities and Boroughs. £10 occupiers and resident freemen if by birth or servitude, or admitted before March 1831.

SOURCE: A. Paul, *The History of Reform*, 3rd ed. (1884) pp. 172–4.

1867–8

The Representation of the People Act, 1867, extended the borough franchise in England and Wales to householders, subject to a one-year residential qualification and to the payment of rates; and to lodgers who had occupied lodgings worth £10 a year, subject to the one-year residential qualification. Also, it created an occupation franchise in the counties for those occupying lands worth £12 a year and a property franchise for those with lands worth £5 a year.

The Representation of the People (Scotland) Act, 1868, introduced similar changes in Scotland but fixed the property qualification for county occupiers at £14 instead of £12 a year.

1884

The Representation of the People Act, 1884, created a uniform householder and lodger franchise in every borough and county in the United Kingdom, based on the franchise created for the English boroughs in 1867. It also provided for an occupation franchise for those with lands or tenements worth £10 a year.

SOURCE: H. J. Hanham, *The Reformed Electoral System in Great Britain*, 1832–1914 (1968) p. 35.

The Constituencies

Welsh Counties

Constituency	M.P.s	Population				Registered Electorate			
		1831	1851	1861	1881	1832	1852	1864	1884
Anglesey	1	48,325	44,575	41,334	36,722	1,187	2,577	3,495	2,791
Brecknockshire	1	47,763	53,167	53,531	48,800	1,668	2,779	3,600	3,802
Cardiganshire	1	64,780	60,954	62,354	58,956	1,184	2,235	5,115	5,026
Carmarthenshire	2	100,740	90,315	89,439	93,389	3,887	4,791	8,025	8,565
Carnarvonshire	1	66,448	65,660	72,787	90,500	1,688	1,913	4,852	7,073
Denbighshire	2	83,629	75,969	82,890	86,100	3,401	3,901	7,623	7,319
Flintshire	1	60,012	49,342	50,892	55,153	1,271	2,912	4,150	4,915
Glamorganshire	2	126,612	105,459	143,305	234,115	3,680	6,424	?	13,104
Merionethshire	1	35,815	38,843	38,963	54,793	580	1,006	3,185	3,986
Montgomeryshire	1	66,482	49,448	48,883	45,756	2,523	2,986	4,803	5,227
Pembrokeshire	1	81,425	66,876	63,847	55,019	3,700	3,132	4,690	5,181
Radnorshire	1	24,651	18,112	18,305	16,888	1,046	1,802	2,216	2,286

SOURCES: Population: 1831 (incl. Parliamentary Boroughs) P.P. (1833) vol. 37.
1851 (excl. Parliamentary Boroughs) P.P. (1852–3) vol. 85.
1861 (excl. Parliamentary Boroughs) P.P. (1862) vol. 50.
1881 (excl. Parliamentary Boroughs) P.P. (1881) vol. 96.
Electorates: 1832 and 1852, Dod, *Electoral Facts*, 2nd ed. (1853).
1868 and 1884, McCalmont, *Parliamentary Pollbook*, 7th ed. (1910).

Welsh Boroughs

Constituency	M.P.s	Population				Registered Electorate			
		1831	1851	1861	1881	1832	1852	1868	1884
Beaumaris (Dist.)	1	10,817	12,752	13,275	14,242	329	459	1,944	2,538
Brecknock	1	5,026	6,070	5,639	6,623	242	336	794	845
Cardiff (Dist.)	1	14,034	20,424	35,541	82,573	687	968	5,388	10,384
Cardigan (Dist.)	1	8,230	11,760	11,646	14,517	1,030	849	1,561	2,097
Carmarthen (Dist.)	1	17,641	19,234	21,439	30,529	684	849	3,190	4,942
Carnarvon (Dist.)	1	7,642	22,210	22,907	28,695	855	861	3,376	4,145
Denbigh (Dist.)	1	14,245	16,614	17,888	22,831	1,131	858	2,785	3,054
Flint (Dist.)	1	31,327	18,814	18,845	24,234	1,279	817	3,280	3,686

Constituency	M.P.s	1831	1851	1861	1881	1832	1852	1868	1884
Haverfordwest (Dist.)	1	10,832	9,729	9,821	9,176	723	682	1,528	1,440
Merthyr Tydfil	1(2)	22,083	63,080	83,875	91,347	502	938	14,500	13,044
Montgomery (Dist.)	1	18,680	17,887	18,036	20,042	723	1,003	2,559	2,760
Pembroke (Dist.)	1	12,366	16,700	21,773	25,309	1,308	951	3,022	3,630
Radnor (Dist.)	1	8,410	6,653	7,106	6,700	529	484	800	886
Swansea (Dist.)	1	18,833	45,123	57,488	105,949	1,307	1,694	11,203	15,832

Figures in brackets indicate changes due to the 1867 Reform Act, unless otherwise stated.
SOURCES: Population: 1831, Dod, op. cit.
1851 and 1861, P.P. (1862) vol. 50.
1881, P.P. (1881) vol. 96.
Electorates: as for Welsh Counties.

Scottish Counties

Constituency	M.P.s	Population				Registered Electorate			
		1831	1851	1861	1881	1832	1852	1868	1884
Aberdeenshire	1(0)	177,657	130,021	137,135	–	2,450	4,022†	–	–
Aberdeenshire (E)	(1)	–	–	–	83,295	–	–	4,297	4,915
Aberdeenshire (W)	(1)	–	–	–	66,834	–	–	4,081	4,298
Argyllshire	1	101,973	79,612	70,779	63,506	985	2,156†	2,870	3,595
Ayrshire	1(0)	145,055	143,257	150,629	–	3,197	3,823†	–	–
Ayrshire (N)	(1)	–	–	–	73,608	–	–	3,219	3,848
Ayrshire (S)	(1)	–	–	–	89,256	–	–	3,370	4,074
Banffshire	1	48,604	46,474	50,616	50,875	560	813†	2,241	2,777
Berwickshire	1	34,048	35,192	35,476	34,415	1,060	1,073†	1,580	1,834
Buteshire	1	14,151	16,608	16,188	17,489	294	491†	1,270	1,493
Caithness	1	34,529	31,987	33,636	30,763	270	642†	1,005	1,238
Clackmannan & Kinross	1	23,801	31,875	29,427	42,057	878	1,658	1,151	2,134
Dumbartonshire	1	33,211	39,658	43,781	61,394	924	1,314	2,156	3,224
Dumfriesshire	1	73,770	61,871	55,434	57,575	1,170	2,520	2,989	3,547
Edinburghshire (Midlothian)	1	219,345	57,625	60,459	86,576	1,294	2,017†	2,489	4,195
Elgin & Nairn	1	43,585	36,133	38,274	38,605	662	683†	1,338	2,041
Fifeshire	1	128,839	98,172	99,204	103,089	2,186	3,211†	4,206	4,865
Forfarshire	1	139,606	64,161	65,421	67,479	1,340	2,873†	3,380	3,702

121

Constituency	M.P.s	Population				Registered Electorate			
		1831	1851	1861	1881	1832	1852	1868	1884
Haddingtonshire	1	36,145	28,602	25,125	29,077	617	716†	895	1,079
Inverness-shire	1	94,797	83,707	76,379	72,755	546	908†	1,661	1,994
Kincardinshire	1	31,431	33,664	33,514	33,349	890	951†	1,731	1,918
Kirkcudbrightshire	1	40,590	36,174	39,481	34,632	1,045	1,326†	1,940	2,294
Lanarkshire	1(0)	316,819	167,506	199,983	-	2,705	3,471†	-	-
Lanarkshire (N)	(1)	-	-	-	301,655	-	-	4,458	11,349
Lanarkshire (S)	(1)	-	-	-	85,800	-	-	2,871	3,644
Linlithgowshire	1	23,291	24,727	33,572	37,567	730	502†	1,226	1,343
Orkney & Shetland	1	58,239	59,082	60,546	57,492	270	418†	1,361	1,824
Peeblesshire	1(0)	10,578	10,738	11,408	-	360	542†	-	-
Peebles & Selkirk	(1)	-	-	-	20,861	-	-	1,049	1,282
Perthshire	1	142,894	114,220	107,733	95,044	3,134	4,938†	4,847	6,032
Renfrewshire	1	133,443	64,466	77,615	111,914	1,132	2,450†	3,571	7,036
Ross & Cromarty	1	74,820	75,532	75,124	72,483	516	832†	2,000	1,729
Roxburghshire	1	43,663	48,027	50,691	33,856	1,313	2,033†	2,101	1,999
Selkirkshire	1(0)	6,833	9,809	10,449	-	280	497	-	-
Stirlingshire	1	72,621	64,648	68,559	78,000	1,787	2,431†	2,751	3,455
Sutherlandshire	1	25,518	25,194	24,599	22,805	104	207†	358	350
Wigtownshire	1	36,258	33,878	32,172	28,735	863	1,272†	1,530	1,687

1831 population figures include Parliamentary Borough constituents; 1851, 1861 and 1881 figures exclude them.
†1851 returns.

SOURCES: Population: 1831, P.P. (1833) vol. 37.
1851, P.P. (1852–3) vol. 85.
1861, P.P. (1862) vol. 50.
1881, P.P. (1882) vol. 76.
Electorates: 1832 and 1852, Dod, op. cit.
1868 and 1884, McCalmont, op. cit.

Scottish Boroughs

Constituency	M.P.s	Population				Registered Electorate			
		1831	1851	1861	1881	1832	1852	1868	1884
Aberdeen	1	58,019	71,973	73,805	105,003	2,160	4,547†	8,312	14,776
Ayr (Dist.)	1	22,626	34,844	34,578	41,723	623	1,039†	2,558	4,793
Dumfries (Dist.)	1	c.20,000	22,752	22,996	25,584	980	881	2,379	2,982
Dundee	1(2)	45,355	78,931	90,417	140,063	1,622	3,190†	14,748	16,420

Constituency	M.P.s	Population				Qualified Electors			
		1831	1851	1861	1881	1832	1852	1868	1884
Edinburgh	2	162,156	160,302	168,121	228,357	6,048	6,230	20,799	28,876
Elgin (Dist.)	1	20,732	24,072	26,771	31,804	777	988	3,080	4,038
Falkirk (Dist.)	1	39,112	42,038	41,530	49,351	969	1,905	4,444	5,728
Glasgow	2(3)	202,426	329,097	394,864	487,985	6,994	15,502†	47,854	68,025
Greenock	1	25,571	36,689	42,098	63,902	985	1,164†	6,223	7,641
Haddington (Dist.)	1	17,755	12,504	13,142	13,764	539	642†	1,477	1,685
Hawick (Dist.)	(1)	–	–	–	34,709	–	–	3,400	5,210
Inverness (Dist.)	1	19,674	20,386	20,380	26,425	715	825†	1,115	3,234
Kilmarnock (Dist.)	1	34,382	43,365	49,376	65,652	1,200	1,380†	3,304	9,543
Kirkcaldy (Dist.)	1	17,083	22,808	23,476	30,086	700	786†	3,975	4,654
Leith (Dist.)	1	38,086	41,508	45,417	72,856	1,640	2,027	5,037	11,000
Montrose (Dist.)	1	32,857	49,106	49,545	59,674	1,494	1,586†	5,300	8,397
Paisley	1	31,460	47,952	47,406	55,627	1,242	1,342†	3,264	5,608
Perth	1	25,571	23,835	25,250	28,949	780	1,034	2,801	4,126
St Andrews (Dist.)	1	17,697	16,878	16,777	19,396	600	680†	411	2,075
Stirling (Dist.)	1	37,769	30,325	30,777	36,780	1,182	1,097†	4,336	4,938
Wick (Dist.)	1	21,522	16,799	16,995	17,461	681	699	913	1,834
Wigtown (Dist.)	1	8,675	9,958	10,385	10,139	320	400†	980	1,254

†Based on 1851 returns in Dod.

University Seats

University(ies)	M.P.s	Qualified Electors			
		1832	1852	1868	1884
Cambridge	2	2,269	4,063	5,936	6,458
Dublin	2	2,058	1,780	2,151	4,074
Edinburgh & St Andrews	(1)	–	–	4,858	6,583
Glasgow & Aberdeen	(1)	–	–	4,500	6,438
London	(1)	–	–	186	2,390
Oxford	2	2,522	3,474	4,214	5,382

SOURCES: Population: 1831, Dod, op. cit.
1851, P.P. (1852-3) vol. 85.
1861, P.P. (1862) vol. 50.
1881, P.P. (1882) vol. 76.

Electorates: 1832 and 1852, Dod, op. cit.
1868 and 1884 McCalmont, op. cit.

Irish Boroughs

Constituency	M.P.s	Population				Registered Electorate			
		1831	1851	1861	1881	1832	1851	1868	1884
Armagh	1	9,189	8,856	8,933	8,797	442	318	603	616
Athlone	1	6,161	8,014	6,170	6,901	243	181	318	365
Bandon	1	9,820	7,942	6,322	6,045	266	209	295	404
Belfast	2	49,338	78,354	76,491	207,671	1,659	2,697	12,168	21,422
Carlow	1	9,012	11,587	8,967	7,036	278	237	317	308
Carrickfergus	1	8,700	8,520	9,398	10,009	1,024	720	1,116	1,337
Cashel	1	6,971	9,069	5,596	—	277	111	203	Disfran-chised 1869
Clonmel	1	12,256	15,204	11,190	10,519	521	379†	439	434
Coleraine	1	5,752	6,517	6,208	6,684	207	222	346	443
Cork	2	107,000	114,232	101,534	97,526	4,322	3,039	3,777	5,045
Downpatrick	1	4,779	4,854	4,310	3,902	507	236	246	307
Drogheda	1	17,365	19,829	18,094	14,662	560	501	729	763
Dublin	2	250,000	265,252	258,328	273,064	7,008	11,290	12,560	14,928
Dundalk	1	10,750	10,253	10,404	12,294	318	267	446	617
Dungannon	1	3,758	3,854	3,886	4,081	154	158	245	300
Dungarvan	1	6,519	11,582	8,614	7,377	677	314	311	310
Ennis	1	9,727	10,519	7,127	6,302	222	143	231	242
Enniskillen	1	6,796	6,094	5,701	5,842	212	172	344	439
Galway	2	33,120	34,146	24,990	18,906	2,062	1,038	1,525	1,124
Kilkenny	1	6,897	5,565	4,624	5,560	206	139	172	183
Limerick	2	66,375	69,561	55,234	48,246	2,868	1,144	2,033	1,977
Lisburn	1	6,201	7,673	9,653	10,834	91	188	468	875
Londonderry	1	14,020	19,973	20,493	28,947	611	724	1,488	2,133
Mallow	1	7,688	5,683	4,824	4,437	458	143	211	382
New Ross	1	6,284	10,145	7,115	6,626	130	171	258	225
Newry	1	13,369	14,734	12,334	15,085	1,017	517	796	1,199
Portarlington	1	3,091	2,964	2,679	2,426	137	71	134	140

Constituency	M.P.s	1831	1851	1861	1881	1832	1852	1868	Disfranchised 1870
Sligo	1	12,762	14,393	13,361	—	418	336	521	
Tralee	1	9,562	13,759	10,921	9,664	180	228	263	308
Waterford	2	28,821	32,604	29,160	28,952	1,241	1,135†	1,300	1,369
Wexford	1	10,670	12,863	12,015	12,055	269	348	520	556
Youghal	1	9,600	9,653	6,749	6,040	297	261	280	277

†Based on 1852 returns.
SOURCES: Population: 1831, Dod, op. cit.
1851 and 1861, P.P. (1861) vol. 50.
1881, P.P. (1881) vol. 96.
Electorates: 1832 and 1852, Dod, op. cit.
1868 and 1884, McCalmont, op. cit.

Irish Counties

Constituency	M.P.s	Population					Registered Electorate		
		1831	1851	1861	1881	1832	1852	1868	1884
Antrim	2	314,608	251,383	324,741	218,123	3,487	8,207	11,715	12,157
Armagh	2	220,651	196,084	189,382	148,078	3,342	4,341	7,443	N.A.
Carlow	2	81,549	68,078	57,232	40,640	1,246	2,090	2,090	2,200
Cavan	2	228,050	174,064	153,972	129,008	2,248	3,850	6,415	6,055
Clare	2	258,262	212,440	166,275	134,908	2,518	2,581	5,649	5,085
Cork	2	700,366	563,576	458,604	373,202	3,834	13,192	17,500	14,631
Donegal	2	298,104	255,158	236,859	205,443	1,448	3,748	4,595	4,379
Down	2	352,571	320,817	299,866	269,927	3,130	10,028	11,646	12,412
Dublin	2	175,987	146,778	106,658	145,088	2,025	4,864	4,464	5,605
Fermanagh	2	149,552	116,047	105,372	78,791	1,429	3,497	5,175	4,651
Galway	2	694,287	297,897	254,256	222,756	3,057	3,491	5,387	4,599
Kerry	2	219,989	238,254	201,988	190,784	1,161	5,222	5,506	4,880
Kildare	2	108,400	95,723	84,930	76,102	1,122	2,774	2,999	2,702
Kilkenny	2	169,691	138,773	109,476	83,810	1,246	5,036	5,137	4,746
King's	2	144,096	112,076	88,491	71,867	1,310	2,397	3,387	3,102
Leitrim	2	141,303	111,897	104,615	95,561	1,318	1,265	2,673	2,383
Limerick	2	233,505	208,684	170,983	128,957	2,565	5,079	6,291	5,481
Londonderry	2	222,416	192,022	184,137	129,083	2,172	4,305	5,582	5,798

125

Constituency	M.P.s	Population				Registered Electorate			
		1831	1851	1861	1881	1832	1852	1868	1884
Longford	2	112,391	82,348	71,592	60,790	1,294	2,321	2,815	2,390
Louth	2	108,171	908,815	75,140	51,272	863	2,078	2,443	2,061
Mayo	2	366,576	274,499	254,449	243,030	1,350	1,395	3,783	2,999
Meath	2	176,326	140,748	110,609	86,301	1,520	4,218	4,018	3,660
Monaghan	2	195,532	141,823	126,340	102,590	2,139	4,119	5,591	5,320
Queen's	2	145,843	111,664	90,750		1,471	2,727	5,152	3,190
Roscommon	2	239,903	173,436	156,154	128,064	1,664	2,236	3,816	3,128
Sligo	2	171,508	128,515	125,079	110,955	695	2,105	3,233	3,147
Tipperary	2	482,908	331,567	247,496	188,537	2,369	6,760	9,498	8,829
Tyrone	2	302,493	255,661	238,426	193,152	1,151	5,692	8,879	8,758
Waterford	2	148,077	138,738	111,116	76,854	1,448	3,248	3,445	3,060
Westmeath	2	148,161	111,407	90,856	68,303	1,395	3,132	3,614	3,397
Wexford	2	182,991	180,158	143,594	105,196	2,907	5,917	6,110	5,547
Wicklow	2	122,301	98,979	86,093	73,679	1,566	3,330	3,613	3,188

N.B. Only 1881 figures exclude represented boroughs and cities.
SOURCES: Population: 1831,
1851 and 1861, Dod, op cit. P.P. (1861) vol. 50.
1881, McCalmont, op. cit.
Electorates: 1832 and 1852, Dod, op. cit.
1868 and 1884, McCalmont, op. cit.

English Counties

Constituency	M.P.s	Population				Registered Electorate			
		1831	1851	1861	1881	1832	1852	1868	1884
Bedfordshire	2	95,483	112,785	121,874	129,929	3,966	4,513	6,680	7,381
Berkshire	3	145,389	125,443	128,590	145,260	5,582	5,129	7,647	7,805
Buckinghamshire	3	146,529	115,901	119,073	117,823	5,306	5,659	7,894	8,311
Cambridgeshire	3	143,955	157,590	149,655	144,593	6,500	6,989	9,502	9,951
Cheshire (N)	2(0) }	334,391 }	169,756	182,347	–	5,103	7,494	–	–
Cheshire (S)	2(0) }		178,959	160,481	–	5,130	8,117	–	–
Cheshire (E)	(2)	–	–	–	104,953	–	–	3,277	7,168
Cheshire (Mid)	(2)	–	–	–	135,365	–	–	7,158	10,421
Cheshire (W)	(2)	–	–	–	161,104	–	–	8,894	13,835
Cornwall (E)	2 }	302,440 }	130,256	136,998	125,546	4,462	5,694	8,107	9,629
Cornwall (W)	2 }		165,167	169,614	140,959	3,353	4,649	8,168	7,717

County		1	2	3	4	5	6	7	8
Cumberland (E)	2	169,681	76,699	75,972	72,698	4,035	5,352	6,672	8,123
Cumberland (W)	2		66,292	73,988	115,168	3,848	4,144	5,395	7,941
Derbyshire (E)	(2)	–	–	–	139,910	–	–	4,550	6,313
Derbyshire (N)	2	237,170	130,067	159,044	97,582	4,370	5,315	6,231	7,516
Derbyshire (S)	2		125,408	137,192	146,013	5,541	7,099	7,873	9,137
Devonshire (E)	(2)	–	–	–	165,372	–	–	2,933	11,149
Devonshire (N)	2	494,478	159,759	150,178	122,460	5,368	8,064	9,260	9,520
Devonshire (S)	2		217,884	220,209	98,331	7,453	9,569	8,047	8,532
Dorset	3	159,252	133,017	135,695	137,294	5,632	5,690	7,443	8,072
Durham (N)	2	253,910	136,986	169,543	298111	4,267	6,631	10,576	13,228
Durham (S)	2		118,907	170,412	181,304	4,336	5,616	9,352	11,616
Essex (E)	(2)	–	–	–	123,067	–	–	6,379	6,509
Essex (W)	(2)	–	–	–	113,240	–	–	5,479	5,847
Essex (N)	2(0)	317,507	165,541	162,441	296,290	5,163	5,715	7,127	17,859
Essex (S)	2		173,995	207,270	88,631	4,488	5,819	8,852	8,798
Gloucestershire (E)	2	387,019	99,784	103,804	177,509	6,457	7,986	11,463	12,802
Gloucestershire (W)	2		138,159	143,410	141,042	6,521	8,635	5,774	5,819
Hampshire (N)	2	314,280	111,304	131,634	126,720	2,424	3,596	8,135	10,296
Hampshire (S)	2		98,935	112,652	95,083	3,143	5,694	9,528	8,679
Herefordshire	3	111,211	98,035	102,321	194,434	4,970	6,972	9,424	10,638
Hertfordshire	3	143,341	153,693	166,511	50,926	4,245	5,268	3,748	3,658
Huntingdonshire	2	53,192	57,964	57,996	209,249	2,653+	2,852	–	–
Kent (E)	2	479,155	151,666	165,261	208,260	7,026	7,119	12,956	13,691
Kent (W)	2		231,711	277,058	137,637	6,678	9,379	8,828	18,183
Kent (Mid)	(2)	–	–	–	273,417	–	–	–	9,939
Lancashire (N)	2	1,336,854	316,804	374,489	–	6,593	12,297	14,292	18,905
Lancashire (S*)	2		500,711	627,656	–	10,039	21,196	–	–
Lancashire (NE)	(2)	–	–	–	238,544	–	–	8,650	13,839
Lancashire (SE)	(2)	–	–	–	534,963	–	–	19,340	28,728
Lancashire (SW)	(2)	–	–	–	482,148	–	–	19,218	30,624
Leicestershire (N)	2	197,003	91,308	92,078	109,250	3,658	4,097	6,438	6,872
Leicestershire (S)	2		78,416	77,278	89,417	4,125	5,131	8,306	8,984
Lincolnshire (N)	2	317,465	192,074	193,757	122,472	9,134	11,677	9,436	10,435
Lincolnshire (S)	2		78,416	146,602	121,332	7,956	8,554	10,493	11,232

127

Constituency	M.P.s	Population				Registered Electorate			
		1831	1851	1861	1881	1832	1852	1868	1884
Lincolnshire (Mid)	(2)	-	-	-	99,689	-	-	8,694	9,699
Middlesex	2	1,358,330	282,256	368,424	393,948	6,939	14,610	23,085	41,299
Monmouthshire	2	98,130	130,906	144,056	166,441	3,738	4,973	7,971	8,688
Norfolk (E)	2(0)	390,054	{155,230	148,798	-	7,041	8,216	-	-
Norfolk (W)	2	-	168,979	161,218	108,702	4,396	7,827	7,062	6,489
Norfolk (N)	(2)	-	-	-	116,714	-	-	6,432	6,459
Norfolk (S)	(2)	-	-	-	113,091	-	-	7,770	7,380
Northamptonshire (N)	2	179,336	{86,528	91,294	108,702	4,396	7,827	7,062	6,489
Northamptonshire (S)	2	-	88,413	89,553	82,091	4,425	4,568	6,338	6,253
Oxfordshire	3	152,156	125,216	125,379	122,054	4,721	5,198	7,668	6,784
Rutland	2	19,385	22,983	21,861	21,434	1,296	1,876	2,200	1,725
Shropshire (N)	2	222,938	{108,481	114,247	119,119	4,682	4,685	7,611	8,020
Shropshire (S)	2	-	67,688	69,346	68,420	2,791	3,571	5,847	5,785
Somerset (E)	2	404,200	{172,189	172,712	118,863	8,996	10,140	8,795	10,232
Somerset (W)	2	-	160,512	159,551	116,960	7,884	8,210	7,669	9,431
Somerset (Mid)	(2)	-	-	-	115,319	-	-	8,364	8,789
Staffordshire (E)	(2)	-	-	-	138,824	-	-	9,557	11,878
Staffordshire (N)	2	410,512	{139,038	162,986	132,634	8,756	9,546	10,258	11,815
Staffordshire (S)	2(0)	-	206,305	260,262	-	3,107	10,116	-	-
Staffordshire (W)	(2)	-	-	-	85,740	-	-	9,942	11,820
Suffolk (E)	2	296,317	{148,480	146,833	161,869	4,265	6,343	9,700	9,851
Suffolk (W)	2	-	130,391	126,634	121,818	3,326	4,379	5,583	5,360
Surrey (E)	2	486,326	{147,017	209,345	227,208	3,150	6,618	9,986	25,216
Surrey (W)	2	-	96,116	109,546	151,408	2,912	3,897	6,708	8,752
Surrey (Mid)	(2)	-	-	-	308,134	-	-	10,565	26,776
Sussex (E)	2	272,340	{120,629	126,234	163,364	3,437	5,298	9,380	10,917
Sussex (W)	2	-	56,526	53,025	62,279	2,365	3,257	3,672	3,855
Warwickshire (N)	2	336,610	{101,464	117,127	169,270	3,740	7,002	10,265	11,993
Warwickshire (S)	2	-	88,776	90,938	99,470	2,550	3,980	6,205	6,590
Westmorland	2	55,041	46,458	48,788	50,488	4,392	4,062	5,700	5,767
Wight, Isle of	1	-	42,277	47,428	64,542	1,167	1,877	3,807	5,320
Wiltshire (N)	2	240,156	{86,024	79,362	80,313	3,614	4,955	6,857	7,434
Wiltshire (S)	2	-	73,615	73,932	64,760	2,540	3,256	3,810	3,427

128

Constituency	M.P.s	Population				Registered Electorate			
		1831	1851	1861	1881	1832	1852	1868	1884
Worcestershire (E)	2 }	211,563	{ 112,845	129,690	208,348	5,161	6,515	10,313	12,455
Worcestershire (W)	2 }		{ 61,110	67,256	67,081	3,122	4,135	6,311	6,557
Yorkshire (ER)	2	168,891	123,920	127,053	141,451	5,559	7,538	10,818	11,599
Yorkshire (NR†)	2	226,434	176,224	201,004	221,937	9,539	11,319	19,192	21,774
Yorkshire (WR*)	2(0)	976,350	794,888	880,994	–	18,056	37,319	–	–
Yorkshire (WRN)	(2)	–	–	–	301,048	–	–	16,918	22,950
Yorkshire (WRS)	(2)	–	–	–	497,568	–	–	19,908	27,625
Yorkshire (WRE)	(2)	–	–	–	303,713	–	–	18,491	22,526

†Based on 1836 return.
*A third seat was given to S. Lancs before the division was split in 1867.
†Including the City and Ainsty of the City of York.
*West Riding given two extra seats in 1865, before the division was re-split in 1867.

Sources: Population: 1831, P.P. (1833) vol. 37.
1851, P.P. (1852–3) vol. 85.
1861, P.P. (1862) vol. 50.
1881, P.P. (1881) vol. 96.
Electorates: 1832 and 1852, Dod, op. cit.
1868 and 1884, McCalmont, op. cit.

English Boroughs

Constituency	M.P.s	Population				Registered Electorate			
		1831	1851	1861	1881	1832	1852	1868	1884
Abingdon	1	5,259	5,954	5,680	6,608	300	312	795	935
Andover	2(1)	5,259	5,395	5,430	5,871	246	241	774	876
Arundel	1(0)	2,803	2,748	2,498	–	351	208	Disfranchised	1868
Ashburton	1(0)	4,165	3,432	3,062	–	198	236	„	1868
Ashton-under-Lyne	1	14,673	29,791	33,917	43,389	433	937	4,822	6,112
Aylesbury	2	4,907	26,794	27,090	28,899	1,654	1,417	3,602	4,473
Banbury	1	5,906	8,715	10,216	12,072	329	491	1,529	1,881
Barnstable	2	6,840	11,371	10,743	12,494	720	771	1,593	1,934
Bath	2	38,063	54,240	52,528	53,761	2,853	3,278	5,024	5,965
Bedford	2	6,959	11,693	13,413	19,532	1,572	910	2,144	2,820
Berwick-on-Tweed	2	8,920	15,094	13,265	13,955	705	781	1,415	2,080
Beverley	2(0)	8,302	10,058	10,868	–	1,011	1,405	2,672	Dis.1869
Bewdley	1	7,384	7,318	7,084	8,677	377	390	1,043	1,317

129

Constituency	M.P.s	Population				Registered Electorate			
		1831	1851	1861	1881	1832	1852	1868	1884
Birkenhead	(1)	–	–	51,649	83,324	Seat given 1861	–	5,892	9,802
Birmingham	2(3)	146,986	232,841	296,076	400,757	4,309	7,936	42,840	63,483
Blackburn	2	27,091	46,536	63,126	100,618	626	1,258	9,714	15,208
Bodmin	2(1)	5,228	6,337	6,381	6,866	252	367	886	879
Bolton	2	43,396	61,171	70,395	105,973	1,040	1,671	12,653	15,080
Boston	2	12,818	17,518	17,893	18,867	1,257	987	2,537	2,941
Bradford	2	43,527	103,778	106,218	180,459	1,139	2,683	21,518	27,689
Bridgnorth	2(1)	6,284	7,610	7,699	7,216	746	717	1,140	1,207
Bridgwater	2(0)	7,807	10,317	11,320	–	484	688	1,484	Dis. 1869
Bridport	2(1)	4,242	7,566	7,719	6,790	433	524	1,013	1,077
Brighton	2	41,994	69,673	87,317	128,407	1,649	3,675	8,661	13,340
Bristol	2	104,338	137,328	154,093	206,503	10,309	12,548	21,158	26,502
Buckingham	2(1)	3,610	8,069	7,626	6,859	300	349	943	1,097
Burnley	(1)	–	–	–	63,502	–	–	5,860	9,123
Bury	1	15,086	31,262	37,563	49,746	539	959	5,583	7,463
Bury St Edmunds	2	11,436	13,900	13,318	16,211	580	741	1,493	2,181
Calne	1	4,973	5,195	5,179	5,272	191	160	258	900
Cambridge	2	20,917	27,815	26,361	40,882	1,499	1,984	4,076	5,324
Canterbury	2	15,316	18,398	21,324	21,701	1,511	1,874	3,001	3,508
Carlisle	2	20,006	26,310	29,417	35,866	977	1,134	4,537	5,251
Chatham	1	19,000	28,424	36,177	46,806	677	1,371	4,518	6,228
Chelsea	(2)	–	–	–	366,516	–	–	17,408	36,151
Cheltenham	1	29,420	35,051	39,693	46,844	919	2,400	3,536	5,577
Chester	2	21,363	27,766	31,110	40,372	2,028	2,524	6,994	6,313
Chichester	2(1)	8,270	8,662	8,059	9,652	852	757	1,224	1,285
Chippenham	2(1)	5,270	6,283	7,075	6,776	208	300	906	1,045
Christchurch	1	6,077	7,475	9,368	28,537	206	313	1,329	3,570
Cirencester	2(1)	5,420	6,096	6,336	8,431	604	434	1,076	1,138
Clitheroe	1	8,915	11,480	10,864	14,463	306	448	1,595	2,204
Cockermouth	2(1)	6,022	7,275	7,057	7,189	305	355	1,095	1,069
Colchester	2	16,167	19,443	23,809	28,395	1,099	1,258	3,145	3,749
Coventry	2	27,076	36,812	41,647	47,366	3,285	4,502	7,925	9,028

Cricklade	2	11,661	35,503	36,893	51,956	1,534	1,647	5,825	8,101
Darlington	(1)	–	–	–	33,426	–	–	3,057	5,323
Dartmouth	1(0)	4,597	4,508	4,444	–	243	302	284	Dis.1868
Derby	2	23,607	40,609	43,091	77,636	1,384	2,448	9,240	14,054
Devizes	2(1)	6,367	6,554	6,638	6,645	315	373	858	977
Devonport	2	44,454	50,159	64,783	63,870	1,777	2,407	3,274	5,573
Dewsbury	(1)	–	–	–	69,531	–	–	7,072	10,806
Dorchester	2(1)	3,063	6,394	6,823	7,568	322	432	638	911
Dover	2	11,924	22,244	25,325	28,486	1,651	2,064	3,403	4,537
Droitwich	1	2,487	7,096	7,086	9,858	243	367	1,532	1,407
Dudley	1	23,043	37,962	44,975	87,407	670	912	11,847	14,401
Durham	2	10,125	13,188	14,088	15,372	806	1,157	1,756	2,236
Evesham	2(1)	3,991	4,605	4,689	5,112	359	349	750	825
Exeter	2	28,201	40,688	41,749	47,098	2,952	2,501	6,501	7,518
Eye	1	7,206	7,531	7,038	6,293	253	356	1,206	983
Finsbury	2	224,839	323,772	387,278	524,480	10,309	20,025	31,759	47,560
Frome	1	12,240	10,148	9,522	9,376	322	383	1,249	1,375
Gateshead	1	15,177	25,568	33,587	65,873	454	711	5,542	12,553
Gloucester	2	11,933	17,572	16,512	36,552	1,527	1,621	4,437	5,721
Grantham	2	7,427	10,873	11,121	17,345	698	774	1,800	2,635
Gravesend	(1)	–	–	–	31,355	–	–	2,720	2,635
Greenwich	2	65,917	105,784	139,436	206,651	2,714	6,308	15,509	22,863
Grimsby, Great	1	6,836	12,263	15,060	45,373	656	861	3,880	7,428
Guildford	2(1)	3,916	6,740	8,020	11,593	342	648	1,150	1,574
Hackney	(2)	–	–	–	417,191	–	–	40,613	48,076
Halifax	2	31,317	33,582	37,014	73,633	531	1,200	9,328	11,998
Hartlepool	(1)	–	–	–	46,998	–	–	3,922	7,807
Harwich	2(1)	4,297	4,451	5,070	7,810	204	272	603	924
Hastings	2	10,097	17,011	22,910	47,735	574	1,090	2,832	5,076
Helston	1	3,293	7,328	8,497	7,919	341	317	1,029	1,028
Hereford	2(1)	10,180	12,108	15,585	19,822	920	1,013	2,380	2,788
Hertford	2(1)	5,247	6,605	6,769	8,556	700	685	842	1,093
Honiton		3,509	3,427	3,301	–	511	273	Dis.1868	
Horsham	1(0)	5,105	5,947	6,747	9,552	257	350	880	1,390

Constituency	M.P.s	Population				Registered Electorate			
		1831	1851	1861	1881	1832	1852	1868	1884
Huddersfield	1	19,095	30,880	34,877	87,146	608	1,364	10,026	14,335
Hull	2	46,426	84,690	97,661	161,519	3,863	5,221	17,146	29,102
Huntingdon	2(1)	3,267	6,219	6,254	6,417	384	390	928	1,016
Hythe	1	6,903	13,164	21,367	28,066	469	856	2,275	3,468
Ipswich	2	20,454	32,914	37,950	50,762	1,219	1,838	5,352	8,287
Kendal	1	11,577	11,829	12,029	13,696	327	382	1,884	1,976
Kidderminster	1	20,165	18,462	15,399	25,634	390	495	2,465	3,915
Knaresborough	2(1)	6,253	5,536	5,402	5,000	278	242	767	651
Lambeth	2	154,613	251,345	294,883	498,967	4,768	18,131	33,377	55,558
Lancaster	2(0)	12,613	16,168	16,005	–	1,109	1,393	Dis.1867	
Launceston	1	5,394	6,005	5,140	5,675	243	361	749	853
Leeds	2(3)	123,393	172,270	207,165	309,126	4,172	6,406	37,510	51,228
Leicester	2	40,512	60,584	68,056	122,351	1,769	3,853	15,161	20,685
Leominster	2(1)	5,249	5,214	5,658	6,042	779	551	744	817
Lewes	2(1)	6,353	9,533	9,716	11,199	872	713	1,276	1,510
Lichfield	2(1)	6,499	7,012	6,893	8,360	861	836	1,115	1,237
Lincoln	2(1)	11,892	17,536	20,999	37,312	1,043	1,363	4,157	6,797
Liskeard	1	4,042	6,204	6,585	5,591	218	343	881	760
Liverpool	2(3)	165,175	375,955	443,938	552,425	11,283	17,433	39,637	61,326
London, City of	4	122,799	127,869	112,063	50,526	18,584	20,728	20,185	26,783
Ludlow	2(1)	5,253	5,376	6,033	6,663	359	450	742	992
Lyme Regis	1(0)	3,345	3,516	3,215	–	212	309	Dis.1868	
Lymington	2(1)	5,472	5,282	5,179	5,462	249	338	680	822
Lynn Regis (King's Lynn)	1(0)	13,370	19,355	16,170	18,475	836	1,176	2,4444	2,967
Macclesfield	2	23,129	39,048	36,101	37,620	718	1,058	5,100	5,221
Maidstone	2	15,387	20,801	23,058	39,662	1,108	1,751	3,420	3,916
Maldon	2(1)	4,895	5,888	6,261	7,128	716	845	1,397	1,481
Malmesbury	1	6,185	6,998	6,881	6,866	291	309	785	963
Malton, New	2(1)	6,802	7,661	8,072	8,750	667	539	605	1,341
Manchester	2(3)	164,378	316,213	357,979	393,676	6,726	13,921	48,256	51,150
Marlborough	2(1)	4,186	5,135	4,893	5,180	263	271	616	620

Marlow, Great	2(1)	6,162	6,523	6,496	6,779	457	354	714	953
Marylebone	2	240,294	370,957	436,252	498,311	8,901	19,710	35,575	41,023
Middlesbrough	(1)	–	–	–	54,965	–	–	5,352	13,044
Midhur	1	5,627	7,021	6,405	7,277	252	279	995	1,116
Monmouth (Dist.)	1	11,163	26,512	30,577	44,933	899	1,676	3,771	5,560
Morpeth	1	6,678	10,012	13,704	33,402	321	415	1,698	5,967
Newark-on-Trent	2	9,557	11,330	11,515	14,019	1,575	867	1,803	2,293
Newcastle-under-Lyme	2	8,192	10,569	12,938	17,506	973	1,090	3,038	2,732
Newcastle-on-Tyne	2	53,613	87,784	109,108	145,228	3,905	5,269	17,870	26,267
Newport (I.o.W.)	2(1)	6,780	8,047	7,934	9,110	420	707	967	1,347
Northallerton	1	4,839	4,995	4,755	5,445	232	281	808	862
Northampton	2	15,351	26,657	32,813	57,553	2,497	2,263	5,690	8,885
Norwich	2	61,110	68,713	74,891	87,843	4,238	5,390	13,000	14,479
Nottingham	2	50,680	57,407	74,693	111,631	5,220	5,260	14,168	20,013
Oldham	2	32,381	72,357	94,344	152,511	1,131	1,890	13,454	23,057
Oxford	2	18,800	27,843	27,560	40,862	2,312	2,818	5,000	6,495
Penryn & Falmouth	2	11,805	13,656	14,485	17,561	875	907	882	2,392
Peterborough	2	5,563	8,672	11,735	22,394	773	518	2,461	3,790
Petersfield	1	4,922	5,550	5,655	6,546	234	353	782	853
Plymouth	2	31,080	52,221	62,599	77,401	1,491	2,482	4,846	10,058
Pontefract	2	9,857	11,515	11,736	15,329	956	684	1,907	2,341
Poole	2(1)	6,959	9,255	9,759	12,303	412	508	1,418	1,983
Portsmouth	2	50,389	72,096	94,799	127,953	1,295	3,332	11,590	18,532
Preston	2	33,871	69,542	82,985	93,707	6,352	2,854	11,314	13,579
Reading	2	15,595	21,456	25,045	42,050	1,001	1,399	3,228	6,020
Reigate	1(0)	3,397	4,927	9,975	–	152	228	Dis.1867	8,392
Retford, East	2	37,245	46,054	47,330	50,031	2,312	2,710	7,510	711
Richmond (Yorks.)	2(1)	4,722	4,969	5,134	5,542	273	243	650	1,113
Ripon	2(1)	5,735	6,080	6,172	7,390	341	353	1,132	10,796
Rochdale	1	20,156	29,195	38,184	68,865	687	1,160	9,280	3,000
Rochester	2	12,058	14,938	16,862	21,590	973	1,269	2,571	1,437
Rye	1	3,361	8,541	8,202	8,409	422	562	1,153	
St Albans	2	5,771	7,000	–	–	657	511	Dis.1852	

133

Constituency	M.P.s	Population				Registered Electorate			
		1831	1851	1861	1881	1832	1852	1868	1884
St Ives	1	4,476	9,872	10,353	8,705	584	578	1,514	1,075
Salford	1(2)	40,786	85,108	102,449	176,233	1,497	2,950	14,827	22,876
Salisbury	2	11,673	11,657	12,278	15,659	576	680	1,516	2,161
Sandwich	2	12,183	12,710	13,750	15,566	916	960	1,906	2,225
Scarborough	2	8,760	12,915	18,377	30,484	432	895	3,371	4,167
Shaftesbury	1	8,518	9,404	8,983	8,479	634	509	1,311	1,347
Sheffield	2	91,692	135,310	185,172	284,410	3,508	5,322	29,955	43,297
Shoreham, New	2	25,008	30,553	32,622	42,442	1,925	1,865	4,554	5,770
Shrewsbury	2	16,055	19,681	22,163	26,478	1,714	1,666	3,381	3,779
Southampton	2	19,324	35,305	49,960	60,235	1,403	2,419	5,437	7,594
South Shields	1	18,576	28,974	35,239	56,922	475	925	7,037	11,161
Southwark	2	134,117	172,863	193,593	221,866	4,775	9,458	17,703	24,817
Stafford	2	6,956	11,829	12,532	19,901	1,176	1,246	3,152	3,112
Stalybridge	(1)	-	-	-	39,671	-	-	5,388	5,714
Stamford	2(1)	7,062	8,933	8,047	8,995	851	566	1,096	1,294
Stockport	2	41,000	53,835	54,681	59,544	1,012	1,341	5,702	8,977
Stockton	(1)	-	-	-	55,446	-	-	4,024	9,179
Stoke-on-Trent	2	52,946	84,027	101,207	152,457	1,349	1,778	16,190	21,909
Stroud	2	41,205	36,535	35,517	40,573	1,247	1,328	5,614	6,368
Sudbury	2	5,503	-	-	-	509	-	Dis.1844	
Sunderland	2	40,735	67,394	85,797	124,960	1,378	1,973	11,464	17,458
Tamworth	2	7,182	8,655	10,192	14,098	586	382	1,748	2,310
Taunton	2	12,148	14,176	14,667	16,611	941	790	1,902	2,357
Tavistock	2(1)	5,602	8,086	8,857	6,909	247	349	4 857	950
Tewkesbury	2(1)	5,780	5,878	5,876	5,100	386	370	745	746
Thetford	2(0)	3,462	4,075	4,208	-	146	200	223	Dis.1868
Thirsk	1	2,835	5,319	5,350	6,306	254	357	860	955
Tiverton	2	9,766	11,144	10,447	10,462	462	461	1,155	1,440
Totnes	2(0)	3,442	4,419	4,001	-	217	371	Dis.1868	
Tower Hamlets	2	359,864	539,111	647,845	438,910	9,906	23,534		
Truro	2	8,252	10,733	11,337	10,663	405	607	1,435	1,586

Constituency	Seats	Population 1831	Population 1851	Population 1861	Population 1881	Electorate 1832	Electorate 1852	Electorate 1868	Electorate 1884
Tynemouth & North Shields	1	23,206	29,170	34,021	43,863	760	883	2,601	6,207
Wakefield	1	21,139	22,057	23,150	30,573	722	850	3,615	4,026
Wallingford	1	7,000	8,064	7,794	8,194	453	428	927	1,226
Walsall	1	15,066	25,680	37,760	59,415	597	1,026	6,047	10,042
Wareham	1	2,566	7,218	6,694	6,192	387	418	783	1,112
Warrington	1	18,184	23,363	26,947	45,257	456	701	4,471	6,977
Warwick	2	9,109	10,973	10570	11,802	1,340	723	1,688	1,734
Wednesbury	(1)	-	-	-	124,438	-	-	15,612	19,113
Wells	2(0)	6,649	4,736	4,648	-	358	325	Dis. 1868	
Wenlock	2	17,435	20,588	21,590	20,143	691	905	3,445	3,312
Westbury	1	7,324	7,029	6,495	6,014	185	314	1,046	999
Westminster	2	202,460	241,611	254,623	228,932	11,576	14,883	18,879	24,990
Weymouth & Melcombe Regis	2	8,095	9,458	11,383	13,704	431	679	1,378	1,816
Whitby	1	10,399	10,989	12,051	14,554	442	454	2,058	2,285
Whitehaven	1	15,716	18,916	18,842	19,717	458	512	2,495	2,767
Wigan	2	20,774	31,941	37,658	48,196	483	718	4,385	6,408
Wilton	1	7,000	8,607	8,657	8,639	214	219	913	1,381
Winchester	2	9,212	13,704	14,776	17,469	537	788	1,557	2,034
Windsor	2(1)	7,071	9,596	9,520	19,080	507	712	1,775	2,296
Wolverhampton	2	67,514	119,748	147,670	164,303	1,700	3,587	15,772	23,422
Woodstock	1	7,055	7,983	7,827	7,027	317	347	1,127	1,884
Worcester	2	27,313	27,528	31,227	40,421	2,366	2,290	5,642	6,323
Wycombe, Chipping	2(1)	6,299	7,179	8,373	13,154	298	346	1,338	2,092
Yarmouth, Great	2(0)	21,448	30,879	34,810	-	1,683	1,249	1,606	Dis. 1868
York	2	34,461	40,359	45,385	59,596	2,873	4,133	9,088	11,610

SOURCES: Population: 1831, Dod, op. cit.
1851 and 1861, P.P. (1862) vol. 50.
1881 and P.P. (1881) vol. 96.

Electorates: 1832 and 1852, Dod, op. cit.
1868 and 1884, McCalmont, op. cit.

6   Elections

The Conduct of Elections

1832

Under the Reform Acts of this year the time allowed for polling in each constituency was reduced from 15 days to 2 days (and after the General Election of 1835 to one day in the boroughs), although General Elections still took place over a fortnight.

For the first time an electoral register was introduced, and a fee had to be paid for registration. In the boroughs the elector paid 1s. at the time of registration and 1s. a year thereafter. In the counties every elector had to pay 1s. at the time of claiming his vote.

1854

The Corrupt Practices Prevention Act, sponsored by Lord John Russell as Leader of the House, was passed in 1854. The Act contained comprehensive definitions of bribery, treating, and (for the first time) of undue influence and intimidation. The penalties for candidates guilty of bribery were expulsion from the House during the lifetime of the existing Parliament and a fine of £50; for candidates guilty of treating and undue influence, a fine of £50 and risk of prosecution for misdemeanour, but not loss of the seat; for voters guilty of bribery, a fine of £10 and prosecution for a misdemeanour; for voters guilty of the other offences, the striking-off of the vote. The Act also contained another innovation: the election accounts. In future every candidate was to publish itemised accounts of his expenditure which an election auditor might inspect. However, the auditors possessed no powers of investigation, and they were unable therefore to prevent evasion of these terms of the Act. In 1863 the office of auditor was abolished and his duties transferred to the Returning Officer, without any noticeable improvement in results.

1868

The Parliamentary Elections Act, 1868, transferred jurisdiction over disputed elections from the election committees of the House of Commons to the judges of the High Court. The new special election court was to be composed of three judges, one from each of the three superior Courts of Common Law. The Act also introduced stiffer penalties for bribery.

1872

The Ballot Act, 1872, introduced voting by secret ballot, increased the number of polling places and abolished public nominations.

1878

The registration system in the English boroughs was reformed to improve the work of the overseers in compiling the original register, to minimise objections, and to assimilate the parliamentary and municipal electoral rolls. In some boroughs this reform did more to increase the electorate than the extension of the franchise had done in 1867.

1883

The Corrupt and Illegal Practices Act, 1883, was the first really effective measure against electoral corruption. The Act had two main objects: to lessen election expenditure and to make the penalties for corrupt practices much more severe. The first object was achieved by a list of maximum election expenses for various types of constituency; and the number of clerks, messengers and committee rooms that might be employed was regulated on the same principle. More severe penalties were also introduced: all those found guilty by an election court of corrupt practices faced one year's imprisonment (with the option of hard labour) and a fine of £200; candidates found guilty of corrupt practices were to suffer perpetual exclusion from the constituency concerned, withdrawal of voting rights, and exclusion from the House of Commons and from all public and judicial offices for seven years; illegal (as distinct from corrupt) practices were punished by penalties slightly less severe.

The impact of the Act can be judged from the following tables:

Expenses Incurred by Candidates at the General Elections, Including the Returning Officer's Charges	
1880	£1,786,781
1885	£1,026,645
1886	£624,086
1892	£958,532
1895	£773,333
1900	£777,429

Number of Petitions Succeeding on the Ground of Bribery, etc., 1832–1900

Year of General Election	Number of Petitions Presented	Number Successful
1832	23	6
1835	16	2
1837	47	4
1841	26	10
1847	24	14
1852	49	25
1857	19	5
1859	30	12
1865	61	13
1868	51	22
1874	22	10
1880	28	16
1885	8	3
1886	3	0
1892	12	5
1895	7	1

SOURCE: C. O'Leary, *The Elimination of Corrupt Practices in British Elections*, 1868–1911 (Oxford, 1962) App. 1.

General Election Results, 1832–1900

1832

Overall result[1]

Lib.	Con.
479	179

Seats won by area

	Lib.	Con.
England:		
Counties	104	40
Boroughs & Univ.	244	83
Wales:		
Counties	6	9
Boroughs	10	4
Scotland:		
Counties	21	9
Burghs & Univ.	22	1
Ireland:		
Counties	45	19
Boroughs & Univ.	27	14
Totals:		
England	348	123
Wales	16	13
Scotland	43	10
Ireland	72	33
Total	479	179

1835

Overall result

Lib.	Con.
383	275

Seats won by area

	Lib.	Con.
England:		
Counties	74	70
Boroughs & Univ.	192	135
Wales:		
Counties	6	9
Boroughs	6	8
Scotland:		
Counties	16	14
Burghs & Univ.	22	1
Ireland:		
Counties	41	23
Boroughs & Univ.	26	15
Totals:		
England	266	205
Wales	12	17
Scotland	38	15
Ireland	67	38
Total	383	275

[1]The Reform Act of 1832 left the total number of Members unaltered at 658.

1837

Overall result

Lib.	Con.
349	309

Seats won by area

	Lib.	Con.
England:		
Counties	47	97
Boroughs & Univ.	185	142
Wales:		
Counties	3	12
Boroughs	8	6
Scotland:		
Counties	11	19
Burghs & Univ.	22	1
Ireland:		
Counties	44	20
Boroughs & Univ.	29	12
Totals:		
England	232	239
Wales	11	18
Scotland	33	20
Ireland	73	32
Total	349	309

1847

Overall result[1]

Lib.	Con.[2]
329	327

Seats won by area

	Lib.	Con.
England:		
Counties	36	108
Boroughs & Univ.	186	139
Wales:		
Counties	3	12
Boroughs	7	7
Scotland:		
Counties	12	18
Burghs & Univ.	22	1
Ireland:		
Counties	37	27
Boroughs	26	15
Totals:		
England	222	247
Wales	10	19
Scotland	34	19
Ireland	63	42
Total	329	327

1841

Overall result

Lib.	Con.
290	368

Seats won by area

	Lib.	Con.
England:		
Counties	20	124
Boroughs & Univ.	167	160
Wales:		
Counties	3	12
Boroughs	7	7
Scotland:		
Counties	10	20
Burghs & Univ.	21	2
Ireland:		
Counties	39	25
Boroughs & Univ.	23	18
Totals:		
England	187	284
Wales	10	19
Scotland	31	22
Ireland	62	43
Total	290	368

1852

Overall result[3]

Lib.	Con.
323	331

Seats won by area

	Lib.	Con.
England:		
Counties	29	115
Boroughs & Univ.	187	136
Wales:		
Counties	4	11
Boroughs	7	7
Scotland:		
Counties	11	19
Burghs & Univ.	22	1
Ireland:		
Counties	39	25
Boroughs & Univ.	24	17
Totals:		
England	216	251
Wales	11	18
Scotland	33	20
Ireland	63	42
Total	323	331

[1] In 1844 Sudbury was disfranchised for corruption, and thus the total number of Members reduced from 658 to 656.

[2] Of the Conservatives about 225 were Protectionists and 100 were Peelites.

[3] In 1852 St Albans was disfranchised and thus the total number of Members reduced from 656 to 654.

1857

Overall result

Lib	Con.
373	281

Seats won by area

	Lib.	Con.
England:		
Counties	50	94
Boroughs & Univ.	216	107
Wales:		
Counties	5	10
Boroughs	9	5
Scotland:		
Counties	15	15
Burghs & Univ.	23	0
Ireland:		
Counties	33	31
Boroughs & Univ.	22	19
Totals:		
England	266	201
Wales	14	15
Scotland	38	15
Ireland	55	50
Total	373	281

1865

Overall result[1]

Lib.	Con.
360	298

Seats won by area

	Lib.	Con.
England:		
Counties	48	99
Boroughs & Univ.	198	126
Wales:		
Counties	6	9
Boroughs	12	2
Scotland:		
Counties	18	12
Burghs & Univ.	23	0
Ireland:		
Counties	32	32
Boroughs & Univ.	23	18
Totals:		
England	246	225
Wales	18	11
Scotland	41	12
Ireland	55	50
Total	360	298

1859

Overall result

Lib.	Con.
347	307

Seats won by area

	Lib.	Con.
England:		
Counties	45	99
Boroughs & Univ.	202	121
Wales:		
Counties	5	10
Boroughs	9	5
Scotland:		
Counties	16	14
Burghs & Univ.	22	1
Ireland:		
Counties	28	36
Boroughs & Univ.	20	21
Totals:		
England	247	220
Wales	14	15
Scotland	38	15
Ireland	48	57
Total	347	307

1868

Overall result

Lib.	Con.
382	276

Seats won by area

	Lib.	Con.
England:		
Counties	45	127
Boroughs & Univ.	198	93
Wales:		
Counties	9	6
Boroughs	13	2
Scotland:		
Counties	24	8
Burghs & Univ.	28	0
Ireland:		
Counties	37	27
Boroughs & Univ.	28	13
Totals:		
England	243	220
Wales	22	8
Scotland	52	8
Ireland	65	40
Total	382	276

[1]In 1861 additional seats were allotted as follows: 1 to S. Lancs, 1 to Birkenhead and 2 to the West Riding of Yorks. The total number of Members was thus increased from 654 to 658.

1874

Overall result[1]

Lib.[2]	Con.
300	352

Seats won by area

	Lib.	Con.
England:		
Counties	27	145
Boroughs & Univ.	144	143
Wales:		
Counties	6	9
Boroughs	13	2
Scotland:		
Counties	17	15
Burghs & Univ.	23	5
Ireland:		
Counties	43	21
Boroughs & Univ.	27	12
Totals:		
England	171	288
Wales	19	11
Scotland	40	20
Ireland	70	33
Total	300	352

1880

Overall result

Lib.[3]	Con.
414	238

Seats won by area

	Lib.	Con.
England:		
Counties	54	118
Boroughs & Univ.	202	85
Wales:		
Counties	13	2
Boroughs	15	0
Scotland:		
Counties	26	6
Burghs & Univ.	27	1
Ireland:		
Counties	53	11
Boroughs & Univ.	24	15
Totals:		
England	256	203
Wales	28	2
Scotland	53	7
Ireland	77	26
Total	414	238

[1] The Reform Act of 1867 set the total number of Members at 658. But in 1870 Beverley (2 seats), Bridgwater (2 seats), Sligo (1 seat) and Cashel (1 seat) were disfranchised. The 6 seats were not allotted elsewhere, thus reducing the total of Members to 652.

[2] The Liberal total includes 58 Home Rulers.

[3] The Liberal total includes 60 Home Rulers.

1885

Overall result

Lib.	Con.	Irish Nat.
334	250	86

Seats won by area

	Lib.	Con.	Ind. Lib	Scottish Crofter	Lab.	Irish Nat.	Total
England	233	214	4	–	4	1	456
Wales	29	4	–	–	1	–	34
Scotland	58	8	–	4	–	–	70
Ireland		16	–	–	–	85	101
Univ.	1	8	–	–	–	–	9
Total	321	250	4	4	5	86	670

1886

Overall result

Lib.	Lib. U.	Con.	Irish Nat.
190	79	316	85

Seats won by area

	Lib.	Lib. U.	Con.	Irish. Nat	Total
England	123	55	277	1	456
Wales	24	4	6	–	34
Scotland	43	17	10	–	70
Ireland	–	2	15	84	101
Univ.	–	1	8	–	9
Total	190	79	316	85	670

1892

Overall result

Lib.	Lib. U.	Con.	Lab.	Irish Nat.
270	47	268	4	81

Seats won by area

	Lib.	Lib. U.	Con.	Lab.	Parnell Nat.	Nat.	Total
England	189	31	231	4	–	1	456
Wales	31	–	3	–	–	–	34
Scotland	50	11	9	–	–	–	70
Ireland	–	4	17	–	9	71	101
Univ.	–	1	8	–	–	–	9
Total	270	47	268	4	9	72	670

1895

Overall result

Lib.	Lib. U.	Con.	Irish Nat.
177	70	341	82

Seats won by area

	Lib.	Lib. U.	Con.	Lab.	Parnell Nat.	Nat.	Total
England	112	50	293	–	–	1	456
Wales	25	1	8	–	–	–	34
Scotland	39	14	17	–	–	–	70
Ireland	1	4	15	–	12	69	101
Univ.	–	1	8	–	–	–	9
Total	177	70	341	–	12	70	670

1900

Overall result

Lib.	Lib. U.	Con.	Nat.
186	68	334	82

Seats won by area

	Lib.	Lib. U.	Con.	Lib.-Lab.	Nat.	Total
England	123	45	287	–	1	456
Wales	26	–	6	2	–	34
Scotland	34	17	19	–	–	70
Ireland	1	3	16	–	81	101
Univ.	–	3	6	–	–	9
Total	184	68	334	2	82	670

SOURCE: election results 1832–80 are based upon figures in the *Constitutional Yearbook* (1886); results after 1885 are taken from figures in M. Kinnear, *The British Voter*, 1885–1966 (1968).

Uncontested Constituencies in the United Kingdom, 1832–1900

Year of Election	Number of Constituencies	Number Uncontested
1832	401	124
1835	401	174
1837	401	150
1841	401	213
1847	400	236
1852	399	170
1857	399	219
1859	399	240

Year of Election	Number of Constituencies	Number Uncontested
1865	401	194
1868	420	140
1874	416	122
1880	416	67
1885	643	39
1886	643	219
1892	643	60
1895	643	185
1900	643	236

SOURCE: Figures for elections before 1847 from N. Gash, *Politics in the Age of Peel* (1953) p. 441; figures for elections after 1852 from T. Lloyd, 'Uncontested Seats in British General Elections, 1852–1918', *Historical Journal*, VIII, 2 (1965) 260–5.

Number of Votes Recorded, 1874–1900.

The following return gives, approximately, the number of votes polled in contested constituencies from 1874 to 1900. Its value for purposes of comparison is very much neutralised by the large number of uncontested elections, especially in 1886, 1895 and 1900.

	1874		1880		1885			1886			
	Con.	Lib.	Con.	Lib.	Con.	Lib.	Nat.	Con.	Lib. U.	Lib.	Nat.
England	556,966	567,025	738,420	873,282	1,599,718	1,736,935	2,824	884,600	231,292	997,849	2,911
Wales	27,465	38,444	25,034	41,837	67,293	105,444	–	24,791	23,809	60,183	–
Scotland	50,872	84,666	62,936	127,023	156,589	283,879	–	53,295	106,077	183,325	–
Ireland	55,429	66,251	55,176	46,108	111,616	30,694	296,960	75,093	24,808	–	96,863
Total	690,732	756,386	881,566	1,088,250	1,935,216	2,156,952	299,784	1,037,779	385,986	1,241,357	99,774

	1892					1895					1900		
	Con. and Lib.	Lib.	Lab. and Ind.	Nat.	Par-nellite	Unionist	Lib.	Ind. Lab.	Nat.	Par-nellite	Unionist	Lib. and Lab.	Nat.
England	1,703,053	1,563,402	54,494	2,537	–	1,425,890	1,301,917	32,835	2,089	–	1,334,234	1,192,815	2,044
Wales	63,924	109,455	–	–	–	88,240	114,500	2,677	–	–	53,148	85,744	–
Scotland	207,636	248,757	5,446	–	–	209,783	228,839	4,877	–	–	228,774	238,857	–
Ireland	82,124	–	–	239,756	69,194	56,840	12,600	–	93,119	48,017	59,864	2,869	80,534
Total	2,056,737	1,921,614	59,940	242,293	69,194	1,780,753	1,657,856	40,389	95,208	48,017	1,676,020	1,520,285	82,578

SOURCE: *Constitutional Year book.*

Ministerial Gains and Losses at By-elections, 1868–1900

Gladstone, 1868–74

Losses, 30.

1869	Wareham	1872	Galway Co.
	Glasgow Univ.		Londonderry
	Stafford		N. Notts
	Dumfries Co.		Oldham
1870	Colchester		Tamworth
	Shrewsbury		N.W. Yorks
	Southwark		S.W. Yorks
	W. Surrey	1873	Dover
	Isle of Wight		Exeter
1871	Durham		Gloucester
	Hereford		Greenwich
	Newry		Hull
	Plymouth		Renfrewshire
	East Surrey		Shaftesbury
	Truro	1874	Stroud

Gains, 6.

1869	Horsham		Norwich
	Taunton		Nottingham
1870	Bridgnorth		Net loss (6 years) 24 seats.
	Dublin		

Ld Beaconsfield, 1874–80

Losses, 15.

1875	Norwich	1877	Oldham
	Manchester		Grimsby
	Leominster	1878	Tamworth
	Brecon Co.		Newcastle-under-
1876	Carmarthen		Lyme
	Cumberland E		Maldon
	Frome	1879	Glasgow
	Leitrim		Donegal

Gains, 10.

1874	Northampton	1878	Worcester
	Oxford		Co. Down
	Boston		New Ross
1875	Tipperary		Southwark
1876	Cork		Net loss (6 years) 5 seats.
1877	Wilton		

Gladstone, 1880–5

Losses, 25.

1880	Wigtown Dist.	1881	Coventry
	Sandwich		St. Ives
	Oxford City		Knaresborough
	Evesham		N. Durham
	Louth		N. Lincoln
	Buteshire		Stafford
	Berwick	1882	Salisbury
	Liverpool	1883	Southampton

	York		Athlone (Nat.)
	Mallow (Nat.)		S. Warwick
	Monaghan Co.	1885	W. Gloucester
1884	Brighton		Wakefield
	Cambridgeshire		

Gains, 6.

1880	Bandon		Hastings
1881	Cumberland, E	1885	Antrim
1882	Liverpool		Net loss (6 years) 19 seats.
1883	Ipswich		

Gladstone, 1886
1886   Ipswich (2)
Net loss   2 seats.

Ld Salisbury, 1886–92
Losses, 22.

1887	Lincs., Spalding		Bucks N.
	Chesh., Northwich	1890	St. Pancras N.
	Burnley		Carnarvon
	Coventry		Barrow
1888	Edinburgh W.		Lancs., Eccles
	Southampton	1891	Hartlepool
	Ayr District		Suffolk N.W.
1889	Lanark, Govan		Leicestershire S.
	Kennington		Cambs N.
	Rochester		Devon N.
	Peterborough	1892	Lancs., Rossendale

Gains, 2.

1888	Yorks, Doncaster		Net loss (6 years) 20 seats.
1890	Ayr District		

Gladstone–Rosebery Ministries, 1892–5.
Losses, 9.

1893	Huddersfield		Lincolnshire Brigg
	Linlithgow	1895	Norfolk, Mid
	Hereford		Walworth
	Great Grimsby		Inverness Co.
1894	Forfarshire		

Gains, 4.

Walsall		Hexham
Pontefract		Colchester
Northumberland,		Net loss (5 years) 5 seats.

Ld Salisbury, 1895–1900
Losses, 14.

1896	Southampton	1898	Durham, S.E.
	Somerset, Frome		Wilts, N
	Wick Dist.	1898	Tower Hamlets, Stepney
1897	Essex S.W.		Norfolk S.
	Lancs., Middleton		Reading

Lancs., Southport Oldham (2)
1900 Edinburgh S.

Gains, 3.

1898 York Grimsby
   Durham Net loss (5 years) 11 seats.

SOURCE: *Constitutional Year Book.*

7 Civil Service

Heads of Departments and Public Offices

Admiralty
(*2nd Sec. before* 1869;
Perm. Sec. after)

1804 ⎫
–6 ⎬ (Sir) J. Barrow
1807 ⎪
–45 ⎭

1845 W. A. B. Hamilton
1855 T. Phinn
1857 W. G. Romaine
1869 V. Lushington
1877 ⎱ (Sir) G. Tryon
–82 ⎰ (*acting for* R. G.
      C. Hamilton)
1884 (Sir) E. Mac-
      Gregor
1907 Sir I. Thomas

Agriculture
(*Perm. Sec.*)
1889 Sir G. Leach
1892 (Sir) T. H. Elliott
1913 Sir S. Olivier (Ld)

Charity Commission
(*Chief Commissioner*)
1853 P. Erle
1872 J. Hill
1875 W. R. S. Fitz-
      gerald
1885 H. Longley
1900 C. H. Alderson
1903 G. Young

Church Estates Commission
(*First Commissioner*)
1850 E of Chichester
1878 Earl Stanhope
1905 Sir L. Dibdin

Civil Service Commission
(*First Commissioner*)
1855 Sir E. Ryan ⎱ *joint*
      Sir J. G. Shaw- ⎰
      Lefevre
1862 Sir E. Ryan
1875 Ld Hampton
1880 Vt Enfield
      (3rd E of
      Strafford)
1888 Sir G. W. Dasent ⎱ *joint*
      W. J. Courthope ⎰
1892 W. J. Courthope
1907 Ld F. Hervey

Colonial Office
(*Perm. Under-Sec. of State*)
1854 H. Merivale
1859 Sir F. Rogers
      (Ld Blachford)
1871 (Sir) R. G. W.
      Herbert
1892 Sir R. H. Meade
1897 (Sir) E. Wingfield
1900 (Sir) M. Ommanney

Customs Establishment
(*Chairman*)
1805 W. Roe
1813 F. F. Luttrell
1819 R. B. Dean
1846 Sir T. F.
      Fremantle
1873 F. Goulburn
1878 Sir C. Du Cane
1890 H. H. Murray
1895 Sir R. G. C.
      Hamilton
1898 H. W. Primrose
1900 (Sir) G. Ryder
1903 (Sir) T. Pittar

Board of Excise
(*Chairman*)
1822 Ld G. Seymour
1833 Sir F. H. Doyle
1838 J. Wood
1849 (see *Inland Rev-
      enue*)

Education
(*Secretary to the
Committee of the Council
on Education*)
1839 (Sir) J. Kay-
      Shuttleworth
1849 (Sir) R. R. W.
      Lingen
1870 Sir F. R. Sand-
      ford
1884 P. Cumin
1890 (Sir) G. W.
      Kekewich
1903 Sir R. Morant

Exchequer
(*Comptroller-General*)
1834 Sir J. Newport
1839 Ld Monteagle
1865 Sir W. Dunbar

Exchequer and Audit Department
(*Comptroller and
Auditor-General*)
1867 Sir W. Dunbar
1888 Sir C. Ryan
1896 R. Mills
1900 D. Richmond

Foreign Office
(*Perm. Under-Sec. of
State*)
1817 J. Planta
1827 J. Backhouse

148

1842	H. U. Addington
1854	E. Hammond (Ld)
1873	Ld Tenterden
1882	Sir J. Pauncefote (Ld)
1889	Sir P. W. Currie (Ld)
1894	Sir T. H. Sanderson (Ld)
1906	Sir C. Hardinge (Ld)

Home Office
(*Perm. Under-Sec. of State*)

1817	H. Hobhouse
1827	S. M. Phillipps
1840	H. Waddington
1867	(Sir) A. O. Liddell
Jun 1885	Sir H. Maine
Jul 1885	Sir G. Lushington
1895	Sir K. E. Digby
1903	Sir M. Chalmers

India Office
(*Perm. Under-Sec. of State*)

1858	Sir G. R. Clerk
1860	H. Merivale
1874	Sir L. Mallet
1883	(Sir) A. Godley
1909	Sir R. Ritchie

Board of Inland Revenue
(*Chairman*)

1849	J. Wood
1856	C. Pressley
1862	Sir W. H. Stephenson
1877	Sir C. J. Herries
1881	Sir A. E. West
1892	A. Milner (Ld)
1897	G. H. Murray
1899	Sir H. W. Primrose
1907	(Sir) R. Chalmers

Irish Office
(*Under-Sec. at Dublin Castle*)

1831	Sir W. Gosset
1835	T. Drummond
1840	N. MacDonald
1841	E. Lucas
1845	R. Pennefather
1846	(Sir) T. N. Redington
1852	J. Wynne
1853	T. A. Larcom
1868	Sir E. R. Wetherall
1869	T. Burke
1882	(Sir) R. G. C. Hamilton
1886	Sir R. Buller
1887	Sir J. W. Ridgeway
1892	(Sir) D. Harrel
1902	Sir A. Macdonnell

Local Government Board
(*Perm. Sec.*)

1871 –6	H. Fleming
1871 –82	(Sir) J. Lambert
1882	Sir H. Owen
1898	(Sir) S. B. Provis
1910	Sir H. C. Monroe

Poor Law Board
(*Perm. Sec.*)

1847	Sir G. Nicholls
1850	Ld Courtenay (11th E of Devon)
1859	H. Fleming

Poor Law Commissioners (3)

18 Aug 34–30 Jan 39	Sir T. F. Lewis
18 Aug 34–25 Nov 41	J. G. Shaw-Lefevre
18 Aug 34–17 Dec 47	(Sir) G. Nicholls
30 Jan 39–2 Aug 47	Sir G. C. Lewis
25 Nov 41–17 Dec 47	Sir E. Head

5 Nov 45–23 Jul 47 E. T. B. Twistleton (additional)
(*office wound up 17 Dec 47*)

Secretary to the Poor Law Commission

1834–47	E. Chadwick

Post Office
(*Secretary*)

1797	Sir F. Freeling
1836	W. L. Maberley
1854	(Sir) R. Hill*
1864	(Sir) J. Tilley
1880	Sir S. A. Blackwood
1893	Sir S. Walpole
1899	Sir G. H. Murray
1903	Sir H. Babington-Smith
1909	A. F. King (*acting*)
1910	Sir M. Nathan

*1846–54 Secretary to Postm.-Gen.

Privy Council
(*Clerk of the Council*)

1821 –59	C. C. F. Greville
1827 –60	W. L. Bathurst
1860	(Sir) A. Helps
1875	Sir C. L. Peel
1899	Sir A. FitzRoy
1923	Sir M. Hankey

Public Building and Works
(*Perm. Sec.*)

1851	T. W. Philipps
1854	A. Austin
1868	G. Russell
1874	Sir A. Mitford (Ld Redesdale)
1886	H. W. Primrose
1895	(Sir) R. Brett (Vt Esher)
1902	Hon Sir S. McDonnell

General Register Office
(*Registrar-General for England and Wales*)

1837	T. H. Lister
1842	G. Graham
1880	Sir B. P. Henniker
1900	R. MacLeod
1902	(Sir) W. Dunbar

Scottish Office
(*Perm. Under-Sec. of State*)

1885	Sir F. Sandford (Ld)
1888	R. W. Cochran-Patrick
1892	Sir C. Scott-Montcrieff
1902	Sir R. MacLeod

Scottish Education Department
(*Secretary*)

1873	Sir F. Sandford (Ld)
1884	P. Cumin
1885	(Sir) H. Craik
1904	(Sir) J. Struthers

Board of Trade
(*Joint Sec. 1829–67; Perm. Sec. after 1867*)

1825–36	T. Lack
1829–40	J. D. Hume
1836–41	Sir D. Le Marchant
1840–7	J. MacGregor
1841–8	Sir J. G. Shaw-Lefevre
1847–52	G. R. Porter
1848–50	Sir D. Le Marchant
1850–65	J. Booth
1852–67	T. H. Farrer (Ld)
1867	T. H. Farrer (Ld)
1886	Sir H. G. Calcraft
1893	Sir C. E. Boyle
1901	Sir F. Hopwood (Ld Southborough)

Treasury
(*Asst. Sec. before 1867; Perm. Sec. after*)

1805	G. Harrison
1826	W. Hill
1828	Col. J. Stewart
1836	(Sir) A. Y. Spearman
1840	(Sir) C. E. Trevelyan

1859	G. A. Hamilton
1867	G. A. Hamilton
1870	(Sir) R. R. W. Lingen
1885	(Sir) R. E. Welby
1894	Sir F. Mowatt
1902	⎰ Sir F. Mowatt
	⎱ Sir E. Hamilton

War Office
(*Deputy Sec. at War*)

1775	M. Lewis
1803	F. Moore
1809	W. Merry
1826	L. Sulivan
1851	(Sir) B. Hawes
(office abolished 1854)	

War Office
(*Perm. Under-Sec. of State*)

1854	G. C. Mundy
1857	Sir B. Hawes
1862	Sir E. Lugard
1871	J. C. Vivian
1878	Sir R. W. Thomson
1895	Sir A. L. Haliburton
1897	Sir R. H. Knox
1901	Sir E. W. D. Ward

SOURCE: British Imperial Calendar; Royal Kalendar; Departmental Lists; Boase. For full details, see Essay on Bibliography.

The Size of The Civil Service

Year	Total Number	
1797	16,267	
1815	24,598	
1821	27,000	
1832	21,305	
1841	16,750	(excl. clerks, messengers, etc.)
1851	39,147	
1861	31,943	
1871	53,874	(incl. some workmen)
1881	50,859	(excl. the Telegraph and Telephone Service)
1891	79,241	
1901	116,413	(incl. the G.P.O.)
1914	280,000	(incl. Scotland and Ireland)

SOURCE: H. Finer, *The Theory and Practice of Modern Government* (1932), vol. II, pp. 1294–5.

8   Justice

Major Criminal Justice Legislation

The Abolition of Most Capital Offences, 1808–1841

In 1800 there were about 200 capital offences on the statute book.

Larceny Act, 1808 (48 Geo. 3, c. 129). Abolished the death sentence for larceny from the person, and broadened the definition of the offence. This was the first of the eighteenth-century capital statutes to be repealed, as a result of Romilly's campaign.

Stealing from Bleaching Grounds Act, 1811 (51 Geo. 3, c. 39), and *Stealing of Linen Act, 1811* (51 Geo. 3, c. 41). Two obsolete capital statutes repealed by Romilly.

Stealing in Shops Act, 1820 (1 Geo. 4, c. 117). Raised the minimum amount stolen in shops which would constitute a capital offence, from 5s. to £15.

Judgement of Death Act, 1823 (4 Geo. 4, c. 48). Gave discretion to the judge to abstain from pronouncing the death sentence on a person convicted of any crime except murder, if the judge felt the offender was fit to be recommended for the King's mercy.

Benefit of Clergy Act, 1823 (4 Geo. 4, c. 53). Abolished the death penalty for: (*a*) larceny of property to the value of 40s. on ships on navigable rivers; (*b*) larceny of property to the value of 40s. in shops.

'Peel's Acts.' Essentially consolidating statutes, codifying the statute law on a number of offences:

(1) *Criminal Statutes (Repeal) Act, 1827* (7&8 Geo. 4, c. 27). Consolidated about 90 statutes relating to larceny and allied offences, and repealed obsolete statutes on this subject.

(2) *Indemnity Act, 1827* (7&8 Geo. 4, c. 30). Consolidated about 50 statutes relating to malicious injuries to property.

(3) *Offences against the Person Act, 1828* (9 Geo. 4, c. 31). Consolidated 56 statutes relating to offences against the person.

Criminal Justice Act, 1827 (7&8 Geo. 4, c. 28). Reversed the previous position on the punishment of felonies. Previously, all felonies were automatically capital offences unless 'benefit of clergy' was allowed; by this Act, 'benefit of clergy' was abolished, and the death penalty restricted to those felonies from which 'benefit of clergy' had previously been excluded, or which new statutes would

151

expressly specify should be capital. The punishment for non-capital felonies was to be transportation or imprisonment.

Larceny Act, 1827 (7&8 Geo. 4, c. 29). Abolished the separate offence of grand larceny (theft of over 12d.) which had carried the death sentence for a second offence. Simple larceny was now to constitute a single offence, punishable by imprisonment or transportation. The only larcenies which remained capital were: (*a*) larceny in a dwellinghouse of property worth £5 or more; (*b*) stealing horses, sheep or cattle.

Forgery Act, 1830 (11 Geo. 4 & 1 Will. 4, c. 66). Consolidated the law relating to forgery. It abolished the death sentence for a number of offences, but retained it for 42 kinds of forgery. This Act was *repealed* by the *Forgery Act, 1832* (2&3 Will. 4, c. 123), which abolished the death sentence for all forgery offences, except forgery of wills, and of powers of attorney for the transfer of government stock.

Coinage Offences Act, 1832 (2&3 Will. 4, c. 34). Consolidated the statutes relating to coinage offences, and abolished the death penalty for all coinage offences.

Punishment of Death Act, 1832 (2&3 Will. 4, c. 62). Repealed the death penalty for the 2 remaining capital larcenies (see above); replaced it by a mandatory sentence of transportation for life.

Criminal Law Act, 1833 (3&4 Will. 4, c. 44). Abolished the death penalty for house-breaking.

Transportation Act, 1834 (4&5 Will. 4, c. 67). Abolished the death penalty for transported convicts returning to Britain before their term of transportation was over.

Forgery Act, 1837 (7 Will. 4 & 1 Vict. c. 84), *Offences against the Person Act, 1837* (7 Will. 4 & 1 Vict. c. 85), *Burglary Act, 1837* (7 Will. 4 & 1 Vict. c. 86), *Robbery from the Person Act, 1837* (7 Will. 4 & 1 Vict. c. 87), *Piracy Act, 1837* (7 Will. 4 & 1 Vict. c. 88), *Burning of Buildings, etc., Act, 1837* (7 Will. 4 & 1 Vict. c. 89), *Punishment of Offences Act, 1837* (7 Will. 4 & 1 Vict. c. 91). These 7 Acts together abolished the death penalty for: almost all cases of *burglary*; all acts involving *no violence to the person*, except high treason; most cases of *attempt at murder*; most cases of *piracy*; *arson*, except where it involved serious danger to life, or took place in H.M.'s dockyards; *robbery*, except when accompanied by serious violence; *forgery*. This left only 15 capital offences on the statute book, of which only 7 were offences of relatively regular occurrence.

Substitution of Punishments for Death Act, 1841 (4&5 Vict. c. 56). Abolished the death penalty for 4 of the above 15 offences: (1) rape; (2) carnal abuse of girls under the age of 10; (3) embezzlement by servants of the Bank of England; (4) riot and feloniously demolishing buildings.

Although 11 capital offences remained on the statute book, after 1836 *executions* were only carried out for *murder* and *attempted murder*; after 1841, for *murder* alone. For those found guilty of the other capital offences, the judge would record a sentence of death, but ensure, by a recommendation of mercy, that it was commuted to transportation or imprisonment.

1861 Acts (24&25 Vict. c. 96 and c. 100). Consolidated the criminal law, and left the death penalty for only murder, treason, piracy and arson in H.M.'s dockyard.

Capital Punishment Amendment Act, 1868 (31 Vict. c. 24). Put an end to public executions.

SOURCES: L. Radzinowicz, *A History of English Criminal Law*, vol. I (1948) and vol. IV (1968).

Other Penal Reforms and Changes in Criminal Law and Procedure

Peel's Gaol Act, 1823 (4 Geo. 4, c. 64). Laid down rules for the running of local gaols by Justices of the Peace; inmates to be classified and separated according to sex, age and type of offence.

Prisons Act, 1835 (5&6 Will. 4, c. 38). Gave Home Secretary power to appoint Inspectors of local prisons and control local prison rules; but they remained under the control of local authorities – Quarter Sessions or boroughs.

Prisoner's Counsel Act, 1836 (6&7 Will. 4, c. 114). Allowed counsel to defend men indicted for felony and to address the jury on their behalf.

1840. Transportation to New South Wales was stopped. But it continued to Tasmania.

December 1842. Pentonville model prison was opened. Many more prisons were built on this model in the 1840s and 1850s.

1842 Act (5&6 Vict. c. 38). Defined the limits of jurisdiction of the Quarter Sessions: they could try all misdemeanours, and all felonies except those for which death, or transportation for life for a first offence, could be imposed.

Summary Jurisdiction Act, 1848 (11&12 Vict. c. 43). Regularised the holding of Petty Sessions to try summary offences, by Justices of the Peace.

1849. Transportation to Western Australia began.

December 1853. Transportation to Tasmania was stopped, and it ceased to be a penal colony.

Penal Servitude Act, 1853 (16&17 Vict. c. 99). Substituted sentences of 4 years' penal servitude for the commonest transportation sentence, one of 7 years. Only the longest-term transportation sentences were retained.

Act for the Better Care and Reformation of Youthful Offenders, 1854 (17&18 Vict. c. 86). Enabled courts to send convicted offenders of under the age of 16 to Reformatories for 2–5 years. The Reformatories were privately run, but the Home Secretary was empowered to have them inspected and to issue certificates of efficiency; the Treasury could defray the whole cost of the maintenance of such offenders.

Penal Servitude Act, 1857 (20&21 Vict. c. 3). Abolished the sentence of transportation. But some long-term convicts were still to be sent to Western Australia for half their sentences.

Prisons Act, 1865 (28&29 Vict. c. 126). Consolidated prison legislation. It gave the Home Secretary greater powers to enforce uniform regulations for the running of local prisons.

October 1867. The last convict ship sailed for Western Australia.

Judicature Acts, 1873 (36&37 Vict. c. 66), *1875* and *1876.* Fused the Courts of Common Law, the Court of Chancery, and the Court of Admiralty, the Court of Probate, and the Divorce Court, into one Supreme Court of Judicature, divided into the High Court of Justice and the Court of Appeal.

The Appellate Jurisdiction Act, 1876 (39&40 Vict. c. 59), restored and reformed the final appellate jurisdiction of the House of Lords.

Prisons Act, 1877 (40&41 Vict. c. 21). Brought the control of all local prisons under the Home Office, and centralised the system under a Prison Commission.

Prosecution of Offenders Act, 1879 (42&43 Vict. c. 22). Established a Solicitor (later 'Director') of Public Prosecutions.

Summary Jurisdiction Act, 1879 (42&43 Vict. c. 49). Extended the power of magistrates' courts, providing an early form of probation and a general power to fine instead of imprisonment.

Criminal Law Amendment Act, 1885 (48&49 Vict. c. 69.). Made sexual acts between males an offence; made white slave trafficking an offence; raised the age of consent of women from 13 to 16.

Probation of First Offenders Act, 1887 (50&51 Vict. c. 25). Provided an early form of probation for use by the higher courts.

Prisons Act, 1898 (61&62 Vict. c. 41). Followed the recommendations of the *Gladstone Committee Report, 1895.* Gave Home Secretary power to make rules for prisons; the rules under the *Prisons Act, 1865,* were replaced by a comprehensive Prison Code and a set of Standing Orders. It strictly limited the imposition of flogging in local prisons. It extended remission of sentence for good conduct to short-term prisoners.

Sources: W. Holdsworth, *A History of English Law,* vol. i (1938); G. Rose, *The Struggle for Penal Reform* (1961); M. Grünhut, *Penal Reform* (1948); E. Ruggles-Brise, *The English Prison System* (1921); A. G. L. Shaw, *Convicts and the Colonies* (1966); S. and B. Webb, *English Prisons under Local Government* (1922); R. Ensor, *England 1870–1914* (1968); E. L. Woodward, *The Age of Reform 1815–1870*; F. W. Maitland, *Justice and Police* (1885); W. L. Burn, *The Age of Equipoise* (1964).

Principal Judges

Lord Chancellor

1830–1835	Ld Brougham	1865–1866	Ld Cranworth
1835	Ld Lyndhurst	1866–1868	Ld Chelmsford
1836–1841	Ld Cottenham	1868–1872	Ld Hatherley
1841–1846	Ld Lyndhurst	1872–1874	Ld Selborne
1846–1850	Ld Cottenham	1874–1880	Ld Cairns
1850–1852	Ld Truro	1880–1885	Ld Selborne
1852	Ld St Leonards	1885–1886	Ld Halsbury
1852–1858	Ld Cranworth	1886	Ld Herschell
1858–1859	Ld Chelmsford	1886–1892	Ld Halsbury
1859–1861	Ld Campbell	1892–1895	Ld Herschell
1861–1865	Ld Westbury	1895–1905	Ld Halsbury

Lords Chief Justice

(1) Until the Judicature Acts

Chief Justice of the Court of King's Bench
(Queen's Bench from 1837 to 1901)

1818–1832	Ld Tenterden	1851–1859	Ld Campbell
1832–1850	Ld Denman	1859–1873	Sir Alexander Cockburn

Chief Justice of the Court of Common Pleas

1830–1847	Sir Nicholas Conyngham Tindal
1847–1850	Sir Thomas Wilde
1851–1856	Sir John Jervis
1856–1859	Sir Alexander Cockburn
1859–1866	Sir William Erle
1866–1873	Sir William Bovill
1873–1880	Ld Coleridge

Chief Baron of the Court of Exchequer

1830–1834	Ld Lyndhurst	1844–1866	Sir F. J. Pollock
1834–1844	Ld Abinger	1866–1880	Sir Fitzroy Kelly

(2) After the Judicature Acts

Lord Chief Justice of England

1873–1880	Sir Alexander Cockburn
1880–1894	Ld Coleridge
1894–1900	Ld Russell of Killowen

Master of the Rolls

1827–1834	Sir John Leach	1873–1883	Sir George Jessel
1834–1836	Sir Charles Pepys	1883–1897	Sir William Brett
1836–1851	Ld Langdale		(Ld Esher, 1885)
1851–1873	Sir John Romilly	1897–1900	Sir Nathaniel Lindley
	(Ld Romilly, 1866)		(Ld Lindley, 1900)

Vice-Chancellor of England

1827–1850   Sir Launcelot Shadwell
(*office abolished* 1850)

Probate, Divorce and Admiralty

(1) Until the Judicature Acts

Judge of the High Court of Admiralty

1828–1833	Sir Christopher Robinson	1838–1867	Sir Stephen Lushington
1833–1838	Sir John Nicholl	1867–1876	Sir Robert Phillimore

Judge of the Probate, Matrimonial and Divorce Court
(established 1857)

1858–1863	Sir C. Cresswell	1872–1876	Sir James Hannen
1863–1872	Sir James Plaisted Wilde		
	(Ld Penzance, 1870)		

(2) After the Judicature Acts

President of the Probate, Divorce and Admiralty Division

1876–1891	Sir James Hannen	1893–1905	Sir Francis Jeune
1891–1893	Sir Charles Butt		

Lords of Appeal in Ordinary

1876–1887	Ld Blackburn	1889–1900	Ld Morris
1876–1879	Ld Gordon	1891–1893	Ld Hannen
1880–1889	Ld Watson	1893–1894	Ld Bowen
1882–1889	Ld Fitzgerald	1894–1907	Ld Davey
1887–1910	Ld Macnaghten	1899–1909	Ld Robertson

and such peers of Parliament as were holding, or had held, high judicial office.

Lords Justices of Appeal

1870–1881	Sir William Milbourne James	1882–1893	Sir C. S. C. Bowen
1870–1877	Sir George Mellish	1883–1892	Sir E. Fry
1875–1885	Sir Richard Baggallay	1885–1897	Sir H. C. Lopes
1876–1880	Sir G. W. W. Bramwell	1890–1897	Sir E. E. Kay
1876–1883	Sir W. B. Brett	1892–1900	Sir A. Levin Smith
1876–1877	Sir R. P. Amphlett	1893–1894	Sir H. Davey
1877–1890	Sir Henry Cotton	1894–1901	Sir J. Rigby
1877–1880	A. H. Thesiger	1897–1899	Sir J. W. Chitty
1880–1881	Sir R. Lush	1897–1901	Sir R. R. H. Collins
1881–1897	Sir N. Lindley	1897–1914	Sir R. Vaughan Williams
1882	Sir J. Holker	1899–1906	Sir R. Romer

and *ex officio* the Lord Chancellor, the Lord Chief Justice, the Master of the Rolls, and the President of the Probate, Divorce and Admiralty Division.

SOURCES: *Clarke's Law List* (1816); *Cockell's Law List* (1828 and 1829); *Clarke's New Law List* (1831, 1838, 1839, 1840); *The Law List* (Stevens & Sons Ltd., 1841–1900); *Dictionary of National Biography* (1897); W. Holdsworth, *A History of English Law*, vol. XV (1965) and vol. XVI (1966).

Establishment and Development of the Police Forces

Metropolitan Police Act, 1829 (10 Geo. 4, c. 44). Established the first paid, uniformed police force in Britain; it covered the 'Metropolitan Police District', a radius of about 7 miles from the centre of London, but excluding the City of London; it was controlled by 2 Justices (later renamed 'Commissioners') under the authority of the Home Secretary.

Municipal Corporations Act, 1835 (5&6 Will. 4, c. 76). This Act included police provisions: every corporate town was to elect a Borough Council, which was to choose from among its members a Watch Committee, which in turn was to appoint sufficient constables to keep the peace by day and night. The Watch Committees were to make their own regulations for their forces; they were to report quarterly to the Home Secretary, but did not fall directly under his authority.

County Police Act, 1839 (2&3 Vict. c. 93). Permitted, but did not compel, the Justices in Quarter Sessions for any county in England and Wales to establish a paid police force for all, or any part, of the county. Amended by the *County Police Act, 1840* (3&4 Vict. c. 88), which allowed the consolidation of county and borough forces by mutual agreement; it also allowed the Quarter Sessions to divide the county into separate police districts, on which different police rates could be imposed. Another *1839 Act* (2&3 Vict. c. 65) did the same for the Scottish counties, allowing them to utilise 'rogue money'–a fund levied in Scottish counties since 1724, to defray the cost of apprehending and prosecuting offenders–for the expense of county police forces as well.

Irish Constabulary Act, 1836 (6&7 Will. 4, c. 13.) Established a semi-military, armed police force for Ireland under the direct control of the Irish administration. This force, the Irish Constabulary (from 1867, the Royal Irish Constabulary), was a single force, replacing the Peace Preservation Force (established 1814 to cope with agrarian disturbances) and the Baronial Police Force (established 1822).

Dublin Metropolitan Police Act, 1836 (6&7 Will. 4, c. 29). Established a metropolitan force for Dublin on the model of the London Metropolitan Force, under 2 paid Justices (from 1841, known as 'Commissioners'). Like the Metropolitan Force, it was not armed.

Police Act, 1833 (3&4 Will. 4, c. 46). Permitted, but did not compel, the larger Scottish burghs to elect Commissioners, who were to appoint police officers and make rules for watching. *1847 Act* (10&11 Vict. c. 39) and *1850 Act* (13&14 Vict. c. 33) amended this to enable the smaller Scottish towns to do the same.

County and Borough Police Act, 1856 (19&20 Vict. c. 69), and *County and Burgh Police (Scotland) Act, 1857* (20&21 Vict. c. 72). Compelled all counties and boroughs to establish and maintain a police force. Three Inspectors of Constabulary were appointed, to assess the efficiency of all the forces, and make an annual report to Parliament; forces certified as efficient would qualify for an Exchequer grant of one-quarter (increased in 1874 to one-half) of the cost of the pay and clothing of the force; but boroughs with a population of under

5,000, which maintained separate forces of their own, were not to be eligible for this grant.

Municipal Corporations (New Charters) Act, 1877 (40&41 Vict. c. 69). No borough thereafter incorporated might set up its own police force, unless its population was over 20,000. Existing boroughs with populations under 20,000 and forces of their own, could keep their forces.

Local Government Act, 1888 (51&52 Vict. c. 41). Established elected County Councils to replace the Quarter Sessions as the organ of county government. Control of the county police forces was transferred to Standing Joint Committees, consisting of equal numbers of County Councillors, chosen by the Councils, and of Justices, chosen by the Quarter Sessions.

SOURCES: L. Radzinowicz, *A History of the Criminal Law*, vols. II (1956), III (1956) and IV (1968); C. Reith, *A New Study of Police History* (1956); T. A. Critchley, *A History of Police in England and Wales 900–1966* (1967); W. L. Melville Lee, *A History of Police in England* (1901); F. C. Mather, *Public Order in the Age of the Chartists* (1959); J. Hart, 'Reform of the Borough Police', *English Historical Review*, LXX (1955) 411–27, and 'The County and Borough Police Act, 1856', *Public Administration*, XXXIV (Winter 1956) 405; H. Parris, 'The Home Office and the Provincial Police in England and Wales 1856–1870', *Public Law* (1961) pp. 230–55; R. B. McDowell, *The Irish Administration 1801–1914* (1964).

Criminal Statistics: England and Wales

Years	Indictable Offences known to the Police		Total tried in all Courts for Indictable Offences		Non-indictable Offences			
					Criminal		Non-criminal	
Average for years	('000s)	Rate per 100,000 of Population	('000s)	Rate per 100,000 of Population	('000s)	Rate per 100,000 of Population	('000s)	Rate per 100,000 of Population
1857–1861	88	448	52	266	113	573	229	1,165
1862–1866	92	440	60	286	128	611	259	1,241
1867–1871	94	423	58	263	132	595	319	1,434
1872–1876	84	353	52	220	136	575	419	1,768
1877–1881	94	370	57	226	124	488	467	1,841
1882–1886	92	344	59	220	119	443	505	1,877
1887–1891	84	297	56	198	110	387	518	1,820
1892–1896	84	277	54	182	110	361	526	1,747
1897–1901	79	249	53	165	103	323	629	1,973

SOURCES: G. Rose, *The Struggle for Penal Reform* (1961) pp. 286–90; Annual Judicial and Criminal Statistics (Parliamentary Papers).

Number and Strength of Police Forces

Year	England and Wales								Scotland				Ireland			
	County		Borough		Metropolitan		City of London		County		Burgh		Constabulary (after 1867 the R.I.C.)		Dublin Metropolitan	
	No. of Forces	Strength	No. of Forces	Strength	No. of Forces	Strength	No. of Forces	Strength	No. of Forces	Strength	No. of Forces	Strength	No. of Forces	Strength	No. of Forces	Strength
1856	32	3,522	168	4,831	1	5,817	1	Not available	Not available				1	Not available	1	1,092
1857	59	7,301	172	5,251	1	6,083	1	552	32	839	57	1,625	1	12,067	1	1,063
1860	59	7,761	166	6,082	1	6,289	1	628	32	895	54	1,637	1	12,460	Not available	
1870	59	9,272	164	7,352	1	9,118	1	699	32	1,084	44	1,919	1	12,714	1	1,083
1880	59	10,751	167	8,955	1	10,952	1	830	32	1,331	39	2,371	1	11,199	1	1,101
1890	60	12,272	126	10,833	1	15,220	1	896	32	1,632	34	2,612	1	12,731	1	1,222
1900	58	13,785	127	13,338	1	15,654	1	1,277	31	1,861	33	3,290	1	11,174	1	1,151

SOURCES: Annual Criminal and Judicial Statistics; annual reports of H.M. Inspectors of Constabulary from 1857 (Parliamentary Papers); annual Miscellaneous Statistics (Parliamentary Papers); 'Return of the Number of Rural Police in each County in England and Wales, appointed under the Acts 2 & 3 Vict. c.93, and 3 & 4 Vict. c.88 etc.', P.P. (1856) vol. 186, p. 665; Reports (annual) of H.M. Inspector of Constabulary of Scotland (P.P. 1859 onwards).

9   Foreign Affairs

Secretaries of State for Foreign Affairs

2 Jun 1828	George Hamilton Gordon, 4th E of Aberdeen		Ld Stanley of Bickerstaffe (15th E of Derby, 1869)
22 Nov 1830	Henry John Temple, 3rd Vt Palmerston	9 Dec 1868	E of Clarendon
		6 Jul 1870	Earl Granville
15 Nov 1834	Arthur Wellesley, 1st D of Wellington	21 Feb 1874	E of Derby
		2 Apr 1878	Robert Arthur Talbot Gascoyne Cecil, 3rd M of Salisbury
18 Apr 1835	Vt Palmerston		
2 Sep 1841	E of Aberdeen		
6 Jul 1846	Vt Palmerston	28 Apr 1880	Earl Granville
26 Dec 1851	George Leveson-Gower, 2nd E Granville	24 Jun 1885	M of Salisbury
		6 Feb 1886	Archibald Philip Primrose, 5th E of Rosebery
26 Feb 1852	James Howard Harris, 3rd E of Malmesbury	3 Aug 1886	Stafford Henry Northcote, 1st E of Iddesleigh
28 Dec 1852	Ld John Russell, 1st Earl Russell	14 Jan 1887	M of Salisbury
21 Feb 1853	George William Frederick Villiers, 4th E of Clarendon	18 Aug 1892	E of Rosebery
		11 Mar 1894	John Wodehouse, 1st E of Kimberley
26 Feb 1858	E of Malmesbury	29 Jun 1895	M of Salisbury
18 Jun 1859	Earl Russell	12 Nov 1900	Henry Charles Keith Petty-Fitzmaurice, 5th M of Lansdowne
3 Nov 1865	E of Clarendon		
6 Jul 1866	Edward Henry Stanley,		

Permanent Under-Secretaries of State

23 Apr 1827	John Backhouse		Abbott, 3rd Ld Tenterden
4 Mar 1842	Henry Unwin Addington		
10 Apr 1854	Rt Hon. Edmund Hammond	23 Sep 1882	Sir Julian Pauncefote
		2 Apr 1889	Sir Philip W. Currie
10 Oct 1873	Charles Stuart Aubrey	1 Jan 1894	Sir Thomas H. Sanderson

Government, Political or Parliamentary Under-Secretaries of State*

9 Jun 1828	Cospatrick Alexander Home, Ld Dunglass, 11th E of Home	17 Dec 1834	Philip Henry Stanhope, Vt Mahon, 5th E of Stanhope
26 Nov 1830	Sir George Shee, Bt	15 Aug 1835	Hon. William Thomas Horner Fox Strangways, 4th E of Ilchester
13 Nov 1834	George Cowper, Vt Fordwich, afterwards 6th Earl Cowper		
		17 Mar 1840	George Leveson-Gower,

160

	2nd Earl Granville	12 Dec 1868	Arthur John Otway (Parl.)
4 Sep 1841	Charles John Canning, 1st Earl Canning	9 Jan 1871	George H. C. Byng, Vt Enfield (Parl.)
27 Jan 1846	Hon. George Augustus Frederick Percy Sydney Smythe, 7th Vt Strangford	23 Feb 1874·	Hon. Robert Bourke (Parl.)
6 Jul 1846	Rt Hon. Edward John Stanley, Ld Eddisbury, 2nd Ld Stanley of Alderley	28 Apr 1880	Sir Charles W. Dilke, Bt, M.P. (Parl.)
		1 Jan 1883	Lord Edmond George Petty-Fitzmaurice, M.P. (Parl.)
16 Feb 1852	Austen Henry Layard	25 Jun 1885	Rt Hon. Robert Bourke (Parl.)
22 May 1852	Edward Henry Stanley, Ld Stanley of Bickerstaffe	7 Feb 1886	James Bryce, M.P. (Parl.)
28 Dec 1852	John Wodehouse, 3rd Ld Wodehouse	4 Aug 1886	Rt Hon. Sir James Fergusson, Bt, M.P. (Parl.)
5 Jul 1855	Henry Petty-Fitzmaurice, E of Shelburne (4th M of Lansdowne)	22 Sep 1891	James W. Lowther, M.P. (Parl.)
26 Feb 1858	William R. S. V. Fitzgerald	19 Aug 1892	Sir Edward Grey, Bt, M.P. (Parl.)
19 Jun 1859	John Wodehouse, 1st E of Kimberley	30 Jun 1895	Rt Hon. George Nathaniel Curzon (Parl.)
15 Aug 1861	Austen Henry Layard, M.P. (Pol.)	15 Oct 1898	Rt Hon. William St John Fremantle Brodrick, M.P. (Parl.)
6 Jul 1866	Edward C. Egerton, M.P. (Parl.)	12 Nov 1900	Vt Cranborne, M.P. (Parl.)

*For difficulties in nomenclature and for an explanation of the source of confusion, see E. Jones-Parry, 'Under-Secretaries of State for Foreign Affairs, 1782–1855', *English Historical Review*, XLIX (1934) 308–20, esp. pp. 312–13.

Assistant Under-Secretaries of State

1 Oct 1858	James Murray	24 Oct 1882	Philip H. Wodehouse Currie
5 Jul 1869	Hon. Thomas C. W. Spring-Rice	2 Apr 1889	Sir Thomas H. Sanderson
10 Aug 1870	Odo W. L. Russell	1 Jan 1894	Sir H. Percy Anderson
16 Oct 1871	Charles Stuart Aubrey Abbott, Ld Tenterden	1 Jan 1894	Hon. Francis L. Bertie
10 Oct 1873	Thomas Villiers Lister	25 Jul 1896	Hon. Francis H. Villiers
14 Jul 1876	Sir Julian Pauncefote	25 Jul 1898	Sir Martin Le M. H. Gosselin

Chief Clerks at the Foreign Office

2 Feb 1824	Thomas Bidwell, Jr.	1 Dec 1866	Francis Beilby Alston
5 Apr 1841	George Lennox Conyngham	7 Feb 1896	Sir George E. Dallas, Bt

Major Ambassadors, Ministers Plenipotentiary, Ministers Resident, 1830–1900

Argentine Republic
Ministers Plenipotentiary

18 Apr 1828	Henry Stephen Fox
1 Jun 1834	H. C. J. Hamilton
2 Oct 1835	John H. Mandeville
13 Dec 1844	William Gore Ouseley
25 Jan 1847	J. H. Caradoc, Ld Howden
31 May 1848	Henry Southern
1851–1856	No Minister
15 Jan 1856	W. D. Christie
9 Sep 1859	Edward Thornton
10 Aug 1865	Hon. Richard Edwardes (*did not proceed*)
13 Apr 1866	G. B. Mathew
26 Sep 1867	William Lowther
11 Jan 1868	Hon. William Stuart
17 Sep 1872	Hon. L. S. Sackville-West
9 Feb 1878	F. C. Ford
15 Aug 1879	Sir H. Rumbold, Bt
1 Apr 1881	Sir G. G. Petre
16 Jan 1884	Hon. E. J. Monson
1 Feb 1885	Hon. F. J. Pakenham
1 Feb 1896	Hon. W. A. C. Barrington
9 Aug 1902	W. H. D. Haggard

Austria
(*Ambassadors and Ministers Plenipotentiary*)

7 Nov 1838	John R. Milbanke (*Minister Plenipotentiary ad int.*)
16 Oct 1841	Rt Hon. Sir Robert Gordon (*Ambassador*)
18 Jun 1845	Arthur C. Magenis (*Minister Plenipotentiary ad int.*)
10 Aug 1846	Vt Ponsonby (*Ambassador*)
20 Apr 1849	Arthur C. Magenis (*Minister Plenipotentiary ad int.*)
27 Jan 1851	E of Westmorland (*Minister Plenipotentiary*)
11 Feb 1855	Ld John Russell (*Special Ambassador*)
23 Nov 1855	Sir George H. Seymour (*Minister Plenipotentiary*)
31 Mar 1858	Ld A. W. F. S. Loftus (*Minister Plenipotentiary*)
23 Feb 1859	Earl Cowley (*Special Ambassador*)
22 Nov 1860	Rt Hon. Ld Bloomfield (*Ambassador*)
21 Jul 1867	M. of Bath (*Minister Plenipotentiary*)
16 Oct 1871	Sir Andrew Buchanan (*Ambassador*)
31 Dec 1877	Rt Hon. Sir H. G. Elliot (*Ambassador*)
1 Jan 1884	Rt Hon. Sir A. B. Paget (*Ambassador*)
1 Jul 1893	Rt Hon. Sir E. Monson (*Ambassador*)
15 Oct 1896	Sir H. Rumbold, Bt (*Ambassador*)
9 Sep 1900	Rt Hon. Sir F. R. Plunkett (*Ambassador*)
1 Nov 1900 –1903	Ralph Milbanke (*Minister Plenipotentiary ad int.*)

Bavaria
(*Ministers Plenipotentiary*)

4 Jan 1828	David Montague, Ld Erskine
24 Nov 1843	J. R. Milbanke
28 Oct 1862	Ld A. W. F. S. Loftus
19 Jan 1866	Sir H. F. Howard
1872	*Chargé d'Affaires only*
17 May 1890	V. A. W. Drummond (*Minister Resident to Bavaria and Württemberg*)
6 Jul 1903	Reginald T. Tower (*Minister Resident*)

Belgium
(*Ministers Plenipotentiary*)

27 Nov 1835	Sir G. H. Seymour
10 Dec 1846	Ld Howard de Walden & Seaford
19 Oct 1868	J. S. Lumley
29 Aug 1883	Sir E. B. Malet
15 Dec 1884	Hon. H. C. Vivian
26 Jan 1892	Hon. Sir. E. Monson
1 Jul 1893	Hon. Sir F. R. Plunkett
9 Sep 1900	E. C. H. Phipps

Brazil
(*Ministers Plenipotentiary*)

31 Jan 1828	John Ponsonby (Vt)
1 Jun 1832	H. S. Fox
23 Sep 1835	H. C. J. Hamilton
25 Jan 1847	J. H. Caradoc, Ld Howden

14 May 1850	Sir James Hudson
29 Aug 1851	Henry Southern
3 May 1853	H. F. Howard
31 Dec 1855	Hon. P. C. Scarlett
2 Sep 1859	W. D. Christie
May 1863	*Diplomatic relations suspended*
10 Aug 1865	Rt Hon. Sir Edward Thornton
19 Sep 1867	G. B. Mathew
14 Jun 1879	F. C. Ford
5 Mar 1881	Edwin Corbett
11 Feb 1885	Sidney Locock (*did not proceed*)
5 Nov 1885	Hugh G. Macdonell
1 Feb 1888	George H. Wyndham
3 Sep 1894	E. C. H. Phipps
9 Sep 1900	Sir H. Dering, Bt

Chile

(Ministers Resident and Consul-Generals)

24 Oct 1872	Rt Hon. Sir H. Rumbold
8 Mar 1878	Hon. F. J. Pakenham
17 Feb 1885	Hugh Fraser
1 Oct 1888	J. G. Kennedy
6 Aug 1897	Audley C. Gosling
(22 Feb 1899	*Envoy Extraordinary & Minister Plenipotentiary*)

China

(Ministers Plenipotentiary)

14 Jan 1859	Hon. F. W. A. Bruce
7 Apr 1865	Sir Rutherford Alcock
22 Jul 1871	Thomas Francis Wade
1 Jul 1883	Sir H. S. Parkes
2 May 1885	Sir R. Hart (*did not take up appointment*)
24 Nov 1885	Sir J. Walsham
1 Apr 1892	Rt Hon. Sir N. R. O'Conor
1 Jan 1896	Sir C. M. MacDonald
26 Oct 1900	Sir E. M. Satow

Colombia

(Ministers Resident and Consul-Generals)

12 Dec 1872	Robert Bunch
1 Jul 1878	Col. C. E. Mansfield
26 Apr 1881	A. H. Mounsey
10 May 1882	J. P. Harriss-Gastrell
25 Mar 1884	F. R. St John
11 Mar 1885	W. J. Dickson
21 Jul 1898	Sir C. B. Euan-Smith (*did not take up appointment*)
23 Nov 1898	George E. Welby

Corea

(Ministers Plenipotentiary)

27 Feb 1884	Sir H. S. Parkes
May 1885	Sir R. Hart (*did not take up appointment*)
24 Nov 1885	Sir J. Walsham
1 Apr 1892	Sir N. R. O'Conor
1 Jan 1896	Sir C. M. MacDonald
(1898	*Chargé d'Affaires only*)

Denmark

(Ministers Plenipotentiary)

10 Sep 1824	H. W. W. Wynn
9 Feb 1853	Sir Andrew Buchanan
31 Mar 1858	Hon. H. G. Elliott
4 Jul 1859	A. B. Paget
9 Jun 1866	Hon. Sir Charles A. Murray
16 Dec 1867	Sir C. L. Wyke
1 Jul 1881	Hon. H. C. Vivian
29 Dec 1884	Hon. E. J. Monson
1 Feb 1888	Hugh G. Macdonell
1 Jan 1893	Charles S. Scott
1 Jul 1898	Sir E. D. V. Fane
6 Apr 1900	W. E. Goschen

Ecuador

(Ministers Resident and Consul-Generals)

12 Dec 1872	Frederic Hamilton
28 Apr 1883	C. W. Lawrence
22 Nov 1890	W. H. D. Haggard
15 Jun 1895	Capt. H. M. Jones
8 Sep 1898	W. N. Beauclerk

France

(Ambassadors and Ministers Plenipotentiary)

1 Jul 1828	Ld Stuart de Rothesay (*Ambassador*)
1 Dec 1830	Vt Granville (*Ambassador*)
23 Mar 1832	H. C. J. Hamilton (*Minister Plenipotentiary*)
19 Apr 1833	Arthur Aston (*Minister Plenipotentiary*)
18 Mar 1835	Ld Cowley (*Ambassador*)
5 May 1835	Earl Granville (*Ambassador*)
9 May 1835	Sir Arthur Aston (*Minister Plenipotentiary*)
29 Jul 1839	H. L. Bulwer (*Minister Plenipotentiary*)
16 Oct 1841	Ld Cowley (*Ambassador*)
29 Jul 1845	Ld William Harvey (*Minister Plenipotentiary*)

18 Aug 1846	C. H. Phipps, M of Normanby (*Ambassador*)
3 Feb 1852	Ld Cowley (*Ambassador*)
1866	Hon. J. H. C. Fane (*Minister Plenipotentiary ad int.*)
6 Jul 1867	Ld Lyons (*Ambassador*)
1869	Hon. L. S. Sackville-West (*Minister Plenipotentiary ad int.*)
18 Feb 1871	Ld Lyons (*Ambassador*)
15 Sep 1871	Hon. Lionel S. Sackville-West (*Minister Plenipotentiary*)
10 Apr 1873	Ld Lytton (*Minister Plenipotentiary ad int.*)
23 Mar 1875	F. O. Adams (*Minister Plenipotentiary ad int.*)
11 Mar 1882	Hon. F. R. Plunkett (*Minister Plenipotentiary ad int.*)
30 Mar 1886	E. H. Egerton (*Minister Plenipotentiary ad int.*)
1 Nov 1887	Rt Hon. E of Lytton (*Ambassador*)
15 Dec 1891	M of Dufferin & Ava (*Ambassador*)
15 Feb 1892	E. C. H. Phipps (*Minister Plenipotentiary ad int.*)
3 Sep 1894	Henry Howard (*Minister Plenipotentiary ad int.*)
15 Oct 1896	Rt Hon. Sir E. Monson (*Ambassador*)
24 Oct 1896	M. le M. Gosselin (*Minister Plenipotentiary ad int.*)
4 Aug 1898 –1902	Hon. M. H. Herbert (*Minister Plenipotentiary ad int.*)

Germany
(Ministers Plenipotentiary)

30 Jul 1829	G. W. Chad (*Minister Plenipotentiary to Germanic Confederation and to Hesse-Cassel*)
3 Nov 1830	Thomas Cartwright (*Minister Plenipotentiary to Germanic Confederation*)
14 Jan 1831	Thomas Cartwright (*Minister Plenipotentiary to Hesse-Cassel*)
2 May 1838	Hon. H. E. Fox (*Minister Plenipotentiary to Germanic Confederation and Hesse-Cassel*)

2 Jan 1839	Hon. Ralph Abercromby (*Minister Plenipotentiary to Germanic Confederation*)
25 Jul 1839	Hon. Ralph Abercromby (*Minister Plenipotentiary to Hesse-Cassel*)
1840	Hon. W. T. H. Fox-Strangways (later E of Ilchester) *Minister Plenipotentiary to Germanic Confederation*)
1852	Sir A. Mallet (*Minister Plenipotentiary to Germanic Confederation*)
	(*On the annexation of Frankfurt to Prussia, 20 Sep 1866, the mission was abolished.*)

German Confederation (North)
(Ambassadors)

24 Feb 1868	Rt Hon. Ld A. W. F. S. Loftus

Germany
(Ambassadors)

16 Oct 1871	O. W. L. Russell
17 Mar 1884	Sir E. B. Mallet
24 Oct 1895	Rt Hon. Sir F. C. Lascelles
1908	Rt Hon. Sir E. Goschen

Greece
(Ministers Plenipotentiary)

1 Jan 1883	E. J. Dawkins
3 Jul 1835	Sir Edmund Lyons
9 Feb 1849	Rt Hon. J. Wyse
12 Jun 1862	Hon. P. C. Scarlett
7 May 1864	Hon. E. M. Erskine
29 Jul 1872	Hon. W. Stuart
7 Jan 1878	Edwin Corbett
5 Mar 1881	F. C. Ford
17 Dec 1884	Sir H. Rumbold, Bt
1 Feb 1888	Hon. Sir E. Monson
26 Jan 1892	Sir E. Egerton
8 Nov 1903	F. E. H. Elliott

Guatemala
(Ministers Plenipotentiary, Ministers Resident and Consul-Generals)

21 Aug 1861	G. B. B. Mathew (*Minister Plenipotentiary*)
12 Dec 1872	Edwin Corbett (*Minister Resident and Consul-General*)

23 May 1874	Sidney Locock (*Minister Resident and Consul-General*)
12 Feb 1881	F. R. St John (*Minister Resident and Consul-General*)
25 Mar 1884	J. P. Harris Gastrell (*Minister Resident and Consul-General*)
22 Nov 1890	Audley C. Gosling (*Minister Resident and Consul-General*)
6 Aug 1897	G. F. B. Jenner (*Minister Resident and Consul-General*)

Hanover
(*Ministers Plenipotentiary*)

2 May 1838	Hon. J. D. Bligh
2 Mar 1857	Sir J. F. T. Crampton, Bt
31 Mar 1858	George J. R. Gordon
11 Nov 1859	H. F. Howard
19 Jan 1866	Sir C. L. Wyke
20 Sep 1866	*Mission abolished*

Italy
(*Ambassadors, Ministers Plenipotentiary and Ministers Resident*)

1 Apr 1861	Sir James Hudson (*Minister Plenipotentiary*)
12 Sep 1863	Hon. H. G. Elliott (*Minister Resident*)
6 Jul 1867	Sir A. B. Paget (*Minister Resident*)
	(24 Mar 1876 *Ambassador*)
26 Aug 1883	Sir J. S. Lumley (*Ambassador*)
1 Dec 1888	M of Dufferin & Ava (*Ambassador*)
1 Jan 1892	Rt Hon. Ld Vivian (*Ambassador*)
26 Dec 1893	Rt Hon. Sir Clare Ford (*Ambassador*)
1 Jul 1898 –1903	Rt Hon. Sir P. W. Currie (*Ambassador*)

Japan
(*Ministers Plenipotentiary*)

30 Nov 1859	Rutherford Alcock
28 Mar 1865	Sir Harry Smith Parkes
1 Jul 1883	Hon. F. R. Plunkett
30 Apr 1888	Hugh Fraser
25 Jun 1894	Hon. P. le Poer Trench
1 Jun 1895	Sir E. M. Satow
26 Oct 1900	Sir C. M. MacDonald

Luxemburg
(*Ministers Plenipotentiary*)

27 Nov 1879	Hon. W. Stuart
1 Feb 1888	Sir H. Rumbold
15 Oct 1896	Henry Howard
1 May 1909	Sir G. W. Buchanan

Mexico
(*Ministers Plenipotentiary*)

1 Apr 1825	Henry George Ward
12 Mar 1835	Richard Pakenham
14 Dec 1843	Charles Bankhead
24 Dec 1851	P. W. Doyle
1 Sep–1 Dec 1856	*Diplomatic relations suspended*
19 Feb 1858	L. C. Otway
23 Jan 1860	C. L. Wyke
25 Jul 1861	*Diplomatic relations suspended*
9 Nov 1864	Hon. P. C. Scarlett
19 Jun 1867 –6 Aug 1884	*Diplomatic relations suspended*
28 Nov 1884	Sir S. St John
1 Jul 1893	Hon. P. le Poer Trench
8 Jul 1894	Sir Henry N. Dering, Bt
9 Sep 1900	George Greville

Morocco
(*Ministers Plenipotentiary and Ministers Resident*)

9 Jun 1860	Sir J. H. Drummond-Hay (*Minister Resident*)
	(1872 *Minister Plenipotentiary*)
1 Jul 1886	W. Kirby Green (*Minister Plenipotentiary*)
10 Mar 1891	Colonel Sir C. B. Euan-Smith (*Minister Plenipotentiary*)
1 Aug 1893	Ernest Mason Satow (*Minister Plenipotentiary*)
26 Jun 1895 –1905	Sir Arthur Nicholson, Bt (*Minister Plenipotentiary*)

Netherlands
(*Ministers Plenipotentiary*)

28 Jul 1829	Thomas Cartwright (*Minister Plenipotentiary ad int.*)
16 Jun 1832	Hon. J. D. Bligh (*Minister Plenipotentiary ad int.*)
28 Oct 1835	Sir E. C. Disbrowe
26 Nov 1851	Hon. R. Abercromby
15 Dec 1858	Francis Napier
11 Dec 1860	Sir A. Buchanan
28 Oct 1862	Sir J. R. Milbanke

22 Aug 1867	Vice-Admiral Hon. E. A. J. Harris
31 Oct 1877	Hon. W. Stuart
1 Feb 1888	Sir H. Rumbold, Bt
15 Oct 1896	Henry Howard
1 May 1909	Sir G. W. Buchanan

Paraguay
(Ministers Plenipotentiary)

30 Oct 1863	Edward Thornton
6 Dec 1866	G. B. Mathew
22 Jun 1868	Hon. W. Stuart (did not proceed)
2 Mar 1882	G. G. Petre
16 Jan 1884	Hon. E. J. Monson
1 Feb 1885	Hon. F. J. Pakenham
1 Feb 1896 –1902	Hon. W. A. C. Barrington

Persia
(Ambassadors, Ministers Plenipotentiary)

30 Jun 1835	Rt Hon. Sir H. Ellis (Ambassador)
9 Feb 1836	John McNeill (Minister Plenipotentiary)
17 Sep 1844	Lt-Col. J. Sheil (Minister Plenipotentiary)
3 Sep 1854	Hon. C. A. Murray (Minister Plenipotentiary)
5 Dec 1855 –4 Apr 1857	Diplomatic relations suspended
16 Apr 1859	Major-Gen. H. C. Rawlinson (Minister Plenipotentiary)
7 Apr 1860	Charles Alison (Minister Plenipotentiary)
15 Jul 1872	W. T. Thompson (Minister Plenipotentiary)
14 Jun 1879	R. F. Thompson (Minister Plenipotentiary)
3 Dec 1887	Rt Hon. Sir H. D. Wolffe (Minister Plenipotentiary)
24 Jul 1891	Sir F. C. Lascelles (Minister Plenipotentiary)
1 May 1894	Sir H. M. Durand (Minister Plenipotentiary)
21 Oct 1900	Sir A. H. Hardinge (Minister Plenipotentiary)

Peru
(Ministers Resident and Consul-Generals)

12 Dec 1872	Hon. W. G. S. Jermingham

14 Oct 1874	Sir S. St John
24 Dec 1884	Col. C. E. Mansfield
24 Oct 1894	Capt. H. M. Jones
8 Sep 1898	William N. Beauclerk
(15 Nov 1906–1908	Minister Plenipotentiary)

Portugal
(Ambassadors and Ministers Plenipotentiary)

28 Dec 1827	Rt Hon. Sir F. J. Lamb (Ambassador)
22 Nov 1833	C. A. Ellis, Ld Howard de Walden (Minister Plenipotentiary)
2 Feb 1847	Sir G. H. Seymour (Minister Plenipotentiary)
28 Apr 1851	Sir R. Pakenham (Minister Plenipotentiary)
10 Oct 1855	H. F. Howard (Minister Plenipotentiary)
11 Nov 1859	Sir A. C. Magenis (Minister Plenipotentiary)
9 Jun 1866	Sir A. B. Paget (Minister Plenipotentiary)
3 Sep 1867	Edward Thornton (Minister Plenipotentiary) (did not proceed)
13 Dec 1867	Hon. C. A. Murray (Minister Plenipotentiary)
26 Nov 1874	Ld Lytton (Minister Plenipotentiary)
1 Mar 1876	R. B. D. Morier (Minister Plenipotentiary)
22 Jun 1887	Sir C. L. Wyke (Minister Plenipotentiary)
16 Jan 1884	G. G. Petre (Minister Plenipotentiary)
1 Jan 1893	Sir H. G. Macdonell (Minister Plenipotentiary)
1 Aug 1902	Sir M. Gosselin

Prussia
(Ministers Plenipotentiary, later Ambassadors)

28 Dec 1827	Sir Brook Taylor
3 Nov 1830	G. W. Chad
18 Jul 1832	Gilbert Elliott, E of Minto
10 Oct 1834	Sir George Shee, Bt
30 Nov 1835	Ld G. W. Russell
16 Oct 1841	Ld Burghersh
28 Apr 1851	Ld Bloomfield
22 Nov 1860	Ld A. W. F. S. Loftus

28 Oct 1862	Sir Adrian Buchanan (*Ambassador*)
15 Sep 1864	Ld Napier (*Ambassador*)
19 Jan 1866	Ld A. W. F. S. Loftus (*Ambassador*)
1868	*see* German Confederation (North), Germany

Roumania
(*Ministers Plenipotentiary*)

3 Mar 1879	W. A. White
1 Jan 1887	Sir F. C. Lascelles
24 Jul 1891	Rt Hon. Sir H. O. Wolff
1 Apr 1892	Sir John Walsham
3 Sep 1894	Sir G. H. Wyndham
6 Aug 1897	John G. Kennedy
8 Dec 1905	Sir W. C. Greene

Russia
(*Ambassadors and Ministers Plenipotentiary*)

28 Dec 1827	Sir William A'Court (*Ambassador*)
4 Jan 1828	Hon. William Temple (*Minister Plenipotentiary ad int.*)
3 Sep 1832	Hon. J. D. Bligh (*Minister Plenipotentiary ad int.*)
30 Oct 1832	Sir Stratford Canning (afterwards Vt Stratford de Redcliffe) (*Ambassador*)
5 Jul 1835	J. G. Lambton, E of Durham (*Ambassador*)
29 Sep 1836	J. R. Milbanke (*Minister Plenipotentiary ad int.*)
6 Oct 1838	U. J. De Burgh (*Ambassador*)
28 Mar 1840	Hon. J. A. D. Bloomfield (*Minister Plenipotentiary ad int.*)
16 Oct 1841	Ld Stuart de Rothesay (*Ambassador*)
3 Apr 1844	Ld Bloomfield (*Minister Plenipotentiary*)
28 Apr 1851	Sir George Hamilton Seymour (*Minister Plenipotentiary*)
14 Feb 1854 – Jun 1856	*Diplomatic relations suspended*
4 May 1856	Ld Wodehouse (*Minister Plenipotentiary*)
31 Mar 1858	Sir John F. Crampton (*Minister Plenipotentiary*)

11 Dec 1860	Ld Napier (*Ambassador*)
15 Sep 1864	Sir Andrew Buchanan (*Ambassador*)
16 Oct 1871	Rt Hon. Ld A. W. F. S. Loftus (*Ambassador*)
8 Feb 1879	Rt Hon. E of Dufferin (*Ambassador*)
26 May 1881	Rt Hon. Sir E. Thornton (*Ambassador*)
1 Dec 1884	Sir R. B. D. Morier (*Ambassador*)
23 Dec 1893	Sir Henry Howard (*Minister Plenipotentiary ad int.*)
10 Mar 1894	Rt Hon. Sir F. C. Lascelles (*Ambassador*)
24 Oct 1895	Rt Hon. Sir N. R. O'Conor (*Ambassador*)
18 Aug 1897	W. E. Goschen (*Minister Plenipotentiary ad int.*)
1 Jul 1898	Rt Hon. Sir C. S. Scott (*Ambassador*)
28 Apr 1904	Rt Hon. Sir C. Hardinge (*Ambassador*)

Sardinia
(*Ministers Plenipotentiary*)

10 Sep 1824	Rt Hon. A. J. Foster (*Minister Plenipotentiary*)
30 May 1840	Hon. Ralph Abercromby (later Ld Dunfermline)
19 Jan 1852	James Hudson
1861	*see* Italy

Saxony
(*Ministers Plenipotentiary and Ministers Resident*)

12 Feb 1828	E. M. Ward (*Minister Plenipotentiary*)
18 Sep 1832	Hon. William Temple
9 Nov 1832	Hon. F. R. Forbes
2 May 1857	Hon. F. R. Forbes (*new credentials*)
13 Dec 1858	A. B. Paget
6 Jun 1859	Hon. C. A. Murray (*Minister Plenipotentiary*)
16 Jun 1866	J. S. Lumley (later Ld Savile)
1867–1890	*Chargés d'Affaires only*
1 Dec 1890	George Strachey (*Minister Resident*)
24 Jul 1897	Sir A. C. Stephen (*Minister Resident to Saxony and Saxe-Coburg-Gotha*)
15 Oct 1901	Vt Gough

Serbia

(*Ministers Plenipotentiary and Ministers Resident*)

3 Mar 1879	G. F. Gould (*Minister Resident*)
16 Apr 1881	Sidney Locock (*Minister Resident*)
25 Feb 1885	George H. Wyndham (*Minister Resident*)
(8 Sep 1886	*Minister Plenipotentiary*)
1 Feb 1888	F. R. St John (*Minister Plenipotentiary*)
1 Jan 1893	E. D. V. Fane (*Minister Plenipotentiary*)
1 Jul 1898	W. E. Goschen (*Minister Plenipotentiary*)
10 Apr 1900	Sir G. Bonham, Bt (*Minister Plenipotentiary*)

The Two Sicilies

(*Ministers Plenipotentiary*)

10 Sep 1824	Rt Hon. W. N. Hill
11 Nov 1830	Ld Burghersh (*not sent*)
25 May 1832	Ld Ponsonby
19 Nov 1832	Hon. William Temple
30 Oct 1856	*Diplomatic relations sus-*
– Jun 1859	*pended*
4 Jul 1859	Hon. H. G. Elliot
21 Nov 1860	*Mission withdrawn*

Spain

(*Ministers Resident, later Ambassadors*)

30 Jul 1829	H. U. Addington
16 Aug 1833	G. W. F. Villiers
13 Feb 1840	Arthur Aston
14 Nov 1843	H. L. Bulwer
May 1848	*Diplomatic relations sus-*
– Apr 1850	*pended*
9 May 1850	Ld Howden
31 Mar 1858	Andrew Buchanan
11 Dec 1860	Sir J. F. Crampton, Bt
23 Oct 1869	Rt Hon. A. H. Layard
11 Jan 1878	Hon. L. S. Sackville-West
22 Jun 1881	R. B. D. Morier
15 Dec 1884	F. C. Ford
9 Dec 1887	F. C. Ford, now Sir Clare Ford (*Ambassador*)
22 Jan 1892	Rt Hon. Sir H. D. Wolff (*Ambassador*)
21 Oct 1900	Sir H. M. Durand (*Ambassador*)

Sweden and Norway

(*Ministers Plenipotentiary*)

24 Apr 1823	Sir Benjamin Bloomfield
2 Oct 1832	Ld Howard de Walden
21 Nov 1833	Sir E. C. Disbrowe
28 Oct 1835	Hon. J. D. Bligh
6 Oct 1838	Sir T. Cartwright
27 Jan 1851	Sir Edmund Lyons
20 May 1854	A. C. Magenis
11 Nov 1859	Hon. G. S. S. Jermingham
24 Jul 1872	Hon. E. M. Erskine
1 Apr 1881	Sir H. Rumbold, Bt
24 Dec 1884	Edwin Corbett
30 Apr 1888	Hon. Sir F. R. Plunkett
1 Jul 1893	Sir S. St John
1 Feb 1896	Hon. F. J. Pakenham
21 Mar 1902	Hon. Sir W. Barrington

Switzerland

(*Ministers Plenipotentiary*)

10 Oct 1825	Hon. Algernon Percy
21 Jun 1832	D. R. Morier
29 Feb 1848	H. R. C. Wellesley, Ld Cowley
9 Feb 1849	Sir Edmund Lyons
27 Jan 1851	A. C. Magenis
12 Feb 1852	Andrew Buchanan
9 Feb 1853	Hon. C. A. Murray
19 Sep 1854	G. J. R. Gordon
31 Mar 1858	Hon. E. A. J. Harris
22 Aug 1867	J. S. Lumley
19 Oct 1868	A. G. G. Bonar
23 May 1874	Edwin Corbett (*Minister Resident*)
17 Jan 1878	Sir H. Rumbold, Bt (*Minister Resident*)
10 Oct 1879	Hon. H. C. Vivian (*Minister Resident*)
(1 Mar 1881	*Minister plenipotentiary*)
8 Jul 1881	F. O. Adams
1 May 1888	Charles S. Scott
1 Jan 1893	F. R. St John
1 May 1901	Sir W. C. Greene

Turkey

(*Ambassadors*)

8 Apr 1829	Rt Hon. Robert Gordon
31 Oct 1831	Rt Hon. Sir Stratford Canning
7 Nov 1831	J. H. Mandeville (*Minister Plenipotentiary ad int.*)
9 Nov 1832	Ld John Ponsonby
1 Mar 1837	Sir C. R. Vaughan

30 Mar 1841 Charles Bankhead (*Minister Plenipotentiary ad int.*)

16 Oct 1841 Rt Hon. Sir Stratford Canning (later Vt Stratford de Radcliffe)

14 Jun 1845 H. R. C. Wellesley (*Minister Plenipotentiary ad int.*)

10 May 1858 Rt Hon. Sir H. L. Bulwer

10 Aug 1865 Rt Hon. R. B. Pemell, Ld Lyons

6 July 1867 Rt Hon. H. G. Elliot

8 Nov 1876 Rt Hon. Robert Cecil, M of Salisbury (*Special Ambassador*)

31 Mar 1877 Rt Hon. A. H. Layard (*Special Ambassador ad int.*)

(31 Dec 1877 *Ambassador*)

18 Feb 1879 E. B. Mallet (*Minister Plenipotentiary ad int.*)

6 May 1880 Rt Hon. G. J. Goschen (*Special Ambassador*)

26 May 1881 Rt Hon. E of Dufferin

1 Dec 1884 Rt Hon. Sir E. Thornton

18 Apr 1885 Sir W. A. White (*Minister Plenipotentiary ad int.*)

(11 Oct 1886 *Special Ambassador*; 1 Jan 1887 *Ambassador*)

12 Jan 1892 Rt Hon. Sir Clare Ford

21 Jan 1892 E. D. V. Fane (*Minister Plenipotentiary ad int.*)

1 Jul 1898 Rt Hon. Sir N. R. O'Conor

1 Jul 1908 Rt Hon. Sir G. A. Lowther

United States of America
(*Ambassadors and Ministers Plenipotentiary*)

22 Mar 1825 Rt Hon. C. R. Vaughan (*Minister Plenipotentiary*)

23 Sep 1835 H. S. Fox (*Minister Plenipotentiary*)

14 Dec 1843 Rt Hon. R. Pakenham (*Minister Plenipotentiary*)

27 Apr 1849 Rt Hon. Sir H. L. Bulwer (*Minister Plenipotentiary*)

19 Jan 1852 J. F. Crampton (*Minister Plenipotentiary*)

(28 May 1856 *No official intercourse* – Jan 1857)

20 Jan 1857 Ld Napier (*Minister Plenipotentiary*)

13 Dec 1858 Ld Lyons (*Minister Plenipotentiary*)

1 Mar 1865 Hon. Sir F. W. A. Bruce (*Minister Plenipotentiary*)

6 Dec 1867 Edward Thornton (*Minister Plenipotentiary*)

22 Jun 1881 Hon. L. S. Sackville-West (later Ld Sackville) *Minister Plenipotentiary*)

2 Apr 1889 Sir Julian Pauncefote (*Minister Plenipotentiary*)

(25 Mar 1893 *Ambassador*)

4 Jun 1902 Hon. Michael H. Herbert (*Ambassador*)

Uruguay
(*Ministers Plenipotentiary and Ministers Resident*)

24 Feb 1879 F. C. Ford (*Minister Plenipotentiary*)

21 Jun 1879 Hon. E. J. Monson (*Minister Resident*)

16 Jan 1884 W. G. Palgrave (*Minister Resident*)

17 Dec 1888 E. M. Satow (*Minister Resident*)

1 Aug 1893 Walter Baring (*Minister Resident*)

11 May 1906 Robert J. Kennedy (*Minister Resident*)

Venezuela
(*Ministers Resident*)

12 Dec 1872 T. C. Middleton

1 Jul 1878 Robert Bunch

26 Apr 1881 Col. C. E. Mansfield

26 Apr 1884 F. R. St John

21 Mar 1887 *Diplomatic relations suspended*
– Jun 1897

1 Jul 1897 W. H. D. Haggard

1 Sep 1902 H. G. O. Bax-Ironside

Württemburg
(*Ministers Plenipotentiary and Ministers Resident*)

4 Jan 1828 E. C. Disbrowe (*Minister Plenipotentiary*)

22 Nov 1833 Ld William Russell (*Minister Plenipotentiary*)

20 Nov 1835 Sir George Shee, Bt (*Minister Plenipotentiary*)

29 Jun 1841	Sir George Shee, Bt (*also Minister Plenipotentiary to Baden*)
17 Sep 1844	Sir A. Mallet, Bt (*Minister Plenipotentiary, Württemburg and Baden*)
12 Feb 1852	A. C. Magenis (*Minister Plenipotentiary, Württemburg and Baden*)
20 May 1854	Hon. G. S. S. Jermingham (*Minister Plenipotentiary, Württemburg and Baden*)
11 Nov 1859	G. J. R. Gordon (*Minister Plenipotentiary, Württemburg and Baden*)
1871–1881	*Chargés d'Affaires only*
16 Apr 1881	G. F. Gould (*Minister Resident*)
1 Oct 1883	Sir H. Barron, Bt (*Minister Resident*)
17 May 1890	V. A. W. Drummond (*Minister Resident to Bavaria and Württemburg*)
6 Jul 1903	Reginald T. Tower (*Minister Resident*)

Treaties, 1830–1900

20 Jan 1831	Protocol of Conference. *The Separation of Belgium and Holland.* Parties: Great Britain, Austria, France, Prussia, Russia.
7 May 1832	Convention. *Sovereignty of Greece.* Parties: Great Britain, France, Russia and Bavaria.
22 Mar 1833	Supplementary Convention. *Traffic in Slaves.* Parties: Great Britain, France.
22 Apr 1834	Treaty of *Quadruple Alliance* with France, Spain and Portugal for the pacification of the peninsula.
5 Sep 1834	Agreement with Russia to respect the integrity and independence of *Persia.*
19 Apr 1839	Treaty between Great Britain, Austria, France, Prussia and Russia; and Belgium. Relative to the *Netherlands and Belgium.*
7 Feb 1840	Treaty with Saxe-Coburg-Gotha for the marriage of Queen Victoria with Prince Albert of Saxe-Coburg-Gotha.
15 Jul 1840	Convention between Great Britain, Austria, Prussia, Russia and Turkey for the *pacification of the Levant.*
13 Jul 1841	Convention with Austria, France, Prussia, Russia and Turkey respecting the *Straits of the Dardanelles and Bosphorus.*
20 Dec 1841	Treaty with Austria, France, Prussia and Russia for the suppression of the *African Slave Trade.*
9 Aug 1842	Treaty with the United States of America to settle and define the boundaries between the possessions of Great Britain in North America and the territories of the United States, for the final suppression of the slave trade, and for the giving-up of criminals.
29 Aug 1842	Treaty with China.
15 Jun 1846	Treaty with the United States of America for the *settlement of the Oregon boundary.*
5–6 Apr 1847	Agreement with China. *Entrance of British subjects into Canton;* the trade at Honan, and the erection of churches at the ports of trade.
2 Dec 1854	Treaty of *Alliance* with Austria and France, with Secret Article.
21 Nov 1855	Treaty with France and Sweden and Norway for

securing the integrity of the *United Kingdoms of Sweden and Norway.*

30 Mar 1856 General Treaty between Britain, Austria, France, Prussia, Russia, Sardinia and Turkey for the re-establishment of *Peace.*

30 Mar 1856 Convention between Great Britain, Austria, France, Prussia, Russia and Sardinia; and Turkey respecting the *Strait of the Dardanelles and of the Bosphorus.*

30 Mar 1856 Convention with France and Russia respecting the *Aaland Islands.*

15 Apr 1856 Treaty with Austria and France guaranteeing the independence and integrity of the *Ottoman Empire.*

16 Apr 1856 Declaration respecting *Maritime Law.* Signatories: Great Britain, Austria, France, Prussia, Russia, Sardinia, Turkey.

23 Jan 1860 Treaty of Commerce with France.

16 Jul 1863 Treaty for the redemption of the *Scheldt Toll.*

14 Nov 1863 Treaty between Great Britain, Austria, France, Prussia and Russia, relative to the *Ionian Islands.*

29 Mar 1864 Treaty respecting the union of the *Ionian Islands* to the Kingdom of Greece.

22 Aug 1864 Convention for the amelioration of the condition of the wounded in armies in the field.

21 Jul 1868 International Telegraph Convention.

17 Jan 1871 Declaration concerning the *binding force of treaties.* Parties: Great Britain, Austria–Hungary, Italy, North Germany, Russia, Turkey.

13 Mar 1871 Treaty concerning the *navigation of the Black Sea*

and the Danube. Parties: Great Britain, Austria, France, Germany, Italy, Russia and Turkey.

8 May 1871 Treaty between Great Britain and the United States of America for the amicable settlement of all causes of difference between the two countries.

9 Oct 1874 Treaty relative to the formation of a general (*Universal*) *Postal Union.*

20 May 1875 Metric Convention.

22 Jul 1875 Internal Telegraph Convention.

1 Jun 1878 Convention for the formation of a *Universal Postal Union.*

13 Jul 1878 Treaty between Great Britain, Austria–Hungary, France, Germany, Italy, Russia and Turkey for the settlement of affairs in the East.

14 Aug 1878 Agreement with Turkey giving Great Britain full powers for the government of *Cyprus.*

31 Mar 1880 Declaration between Great Britain, Austria–Hungary, France, Germany and Italy, respecting the appointment of a commission of liquidation of the *Egyptian Debt.*

18 Sep 1881 Final Act for the settlement of the *frontier between Greece and Turkey.* Parties: Great Britain, Austria – Hungary, France, Germany, Italy, Russia.

13 Feb 1883 Collective Declaration of the Conference respecting the *Navigation of the Danube.* Parties: Great Britain, Austria–Hungary, France, Germany, Italy, Russia, Turkey.

26 Feb 1885 General Act of the Conference at Berlin respecting (1) freedom of trade in the Basin of the

Congo; (2) the Slave Trade; (3) neutrality in the Territories of the Basin of the Congo; (4) navigation of the Congo; (5) navigation of the Niger; (6) rules for future occupation on the coasts of the African continent.

17 Mar 1885 Declaration respecting the finances of Egypt, and the *Free Navigation of the Suez Canal.* Parties: Great Britain, Austria–Hungary, France, Germany, Italy, Russia.

18 Mar 1885 Convention relative to the finances of Egypt.

21 Mar 1885 Additional Act to the Convention of 1 Jun 1878 establishing a *Universal Postal Union.*

29 Apr 1885 Agreement between Great Britain and Germany relative to their spheres of action in portions of *Africa.*

25 Jul 1885 Declaration relative to the payments of the *Egyptian Loan.* Parties: Great Britain, Austria–Hungary, France, Italy, Russia, Turkey.

10 Sep 1885 Protocol with Russia relative to the *Afghan frontier.*

29 Oct 1888 Convention respecting the *Free Navigation of the Suez Maritime Canal.*

14 Jun 1889 Final Act of the Conference on the affairs of *Samoa.*

29 Oct 1889 Commercial Convention with *Egypt.*

17 Mar 1890 Convention with China relating to *Sikkim and Tibet.*

14 Jun 1890 Agreement with Zanzibar placing *Zanzibar under the protection of Great Britain.*

1 Jul 1890 Agreement between Britain and Germany respecting *Zanzibar, Heligoland* and the spheres of influence of the two countries in Africa.

2 Jul 1890 General Act of the Brussels Conference relative to the *African Slave Trade.*

5 Aug 1890 Declarations exchanged with France respecting *territories in Africa.*

26 Jun 1891 Agreement with France for the demarcation of spheres of influence in Africa (Niger districts).

4 Jul 1891 *Universal Postal Convention,* with final Protocol and Regulations.

8 Jul 1893 Protocol with Germany respecting the delimitation of the Anglo-German boundary in East Equatorial Africa.

12 Jul 1893 Arrangements with France fixing the boundary between *British and French possessions on the Gold Coast.*

31 Jul 1893 Protocol with France respecting territories in the region of the *Upper Mekong.*

12 Nov 1893 Agreement with Afghanistan respecting the *frontier* between *India and Afghanistan.*

15 Nov 1893 Agreement with Germany respecting *boundaries in Africa.*

1 Mar 1894 Convention with China giving effect to Article III of the Convention of 24 Jul 1886 relative to *Burma and Tibet.*

3 Apr 1894 International *Sanitary* Convention.

5 May 1894 Protocol between Great Britain and Italy respecting the demarcation of their respective spheres of influence in *Eastern Africa.*

12 May 1894 Agreement with the *Congo* relating to the spheres of influence of Great Britain and the Congo in *East and Central Africa.*

15 Jun 1897 *Universal Postal Convention.*

18 Sep 1897 Convention with France relative to *Tunis*.

20 Apr 1898 Notes exchanged with Germany respecting the British occupation of *Weihaiwei*.

14 Jun 1898 Convention between the *United Kingdom and France* concerning their respective possessions and spheres of influence to the west and east of the *Niger*.

1 Jul 1898 Convention with China respecting *Weihaiwei*.

30 Aug 1898 Convention with Germany regarding *Portuguese Africa and Timor*.

21 Mar 1899 Declaration additional to the Convention of 14 Jun 1898 between *United Kingdom and France*.

29 Jul 1899 International Convention for the *Pacific Settlement of International Disputes*.

29 Jul 1899 International Convention for adapting to *Maritime Warfare* the principles of the Geneva Convention of 22 Aug 1864.

29 Jul 1899 International Convention with respect to the *Laws and Customs of War by Land*.

7 Nov 1899 Convention between the United Kingdom, Germany and the United States of America relating to the *settlement of certain claims in Samoa by arbitration*.

2 Dec 1899 Convention between the United Kingdom, Germany and the United States of America for the adjustment of questions relating to *Samoa*.

22–29 Sep/ 30 Nov/ 6 Dec 1899 Exchange of notes with the United States of America accepting the commercial policy of the 'open door' in *China*.

16 Oct 1900 Agreement with *Germany* relative to *China*.

10 Armed Forces

Secretaries of State for War, 1855–1903

1855	Ld Panmure	1878	Frederick Stanley
1858	Jonathan Peel	1880	Hugh Eardley Childers
1859	Sidney Herbert	1882	M of Hartington
1861	Sir George Lewis	1885	William Henry Smith
1863	E of Ripon	1887	Edward Stanhope
1866	Feb: M of Hartington	1892	Sir Henry Campbell-Bannerman
	Jul: Jonathan Peel	1895	M of Lansdowne
1867	Sir John Pakington	1900	William Brodrick
1868	Edward Cardwell	–03	
1874	Gathorne Gathorne-Hardy		

First Lords of the Admiralty, 1830–1905

1830	Sir James Graham	1867	Henry Corry
1834	Ld Auckland	1868	Hugh Eardley Childers
1835	E of Minto	1871	George Goschen
1841	E of Haddington	1874	George Hunt
1846	Jan: E of Ellenborough	1877	William Henry Smith
	Jul: E of Auckland	1880	E of Northbrook
1849	Sir Francis Baring	1885	Ld George Hamilton
1852	D of Northumberland	1886	Feb: M of Ripon
1853	Sir James Graham		Aug: Ld George Hamilton
1855	Sir Charles Wood	1892	E of Spencer
1858	Sir John Pakington	1895	George Goschen
1859	D of Somerset	1900	E of Selborne
1866	Sir John Pakington	–05	

Commanders-in-Chief, 1828–1904

1828	Vt Hill (1772–1842)	1895	Vt Wolseley (1833–1913)
1842	D of Wellington (1769–1852)	1900	Earl Roberts (1832–1914)
1852	Vt Hardinge (1785–1856)	–04	
1856	D of Cambridge (1819–1904)		

Principal Military Campaigns and Expeditions, 1830–1902

1. Europe

Crimean War, 1854–1855

Turkey declared war on Russia on 23 Sep 1853. The Turkish fleet was destroyed at Sinope on 30 Nov 1853, and British and French warships were sent into the Black Sea to prevent Russian landings. France and Great Britain declared war on Russia in May 1854.

14 Sep 1854	64,000 Allied troops began arriving in the Crimea
20 Sep 1854	Battle of Alma
25 Oct 1854	Battle of Balaclava
5 Nov 1854	Battle of Inkerman
8 Sep 1855	French stormed Malakoff and Russians evacuated Sebastopol
1 Feb 1856	Russians accepted preliminary peace under threat of an Austrian declaration of war

War ended by Treaty of Paris, Mar 1856.

2. Africa

(a) *Kaffir Wars*, 1834–1878

In Dec 1834 the Kaffirs invaded British territory. They were driven back, and in Apr 1835 a punitive expedition was mounted against them.

This was the sixth in a series of wars with the Kaffirs; the ninth and last took place 1877–8.

(b) *Abyssinian War*, 1867–1868

An expedition of 13,000 British and Indian troops, led by Sir Robert Napier, was sent to rescue diplomats and Europeans held by King Theodore of Abyssinia in his capital Magdala.

13 April 1868: Magdala was stormed and King Theodore committed suicide.

(c) *Ashanti Campaign*, 1873–1874

After initial fighting, Sir Garnet Wolseley, the Administrator and Commander-in-Chief on the Gold Coast, mounted an expedition against Kumasi, the capital of the Ashanti, who were threatening British settlements. Kumasi fell in Feb 1874 and peace was imposed.

Further expeditions took place against the Ashanti in 1896 and 1900, the latter leading to the annexation of the territory.

(d) *Żulu War*, 1878–1879

Ld Chelmsford planned to advance on the Zulu capital Ulundi, but part of his army was annihilated at Isandhlwana on 22 Jan 1879. The defence of Rorke's Drift saved Natal from being overrun.

The Zulus under their Chief Cetewayo were finally defeated at Ulundi on 4 Jul 1879.

Zululand was formally annexed in 1886.

(e) *First South African War*, 1880–1881

Great Britain had annexed the Transvaal Boer Republic in 1877. On 16 Dec 1880 the Boers proclaimed their independence. Major-

Gen. Colley leading troops from Natal was defeated and killed at Majuba Hill on 27 Feb 1881.

The British Government decided on withdrawal. An armistice was signed on 6 Mar 1881, and peace made by the Convention of Pretoria.

(f) *Egyptian War*, 1882

A nationalist uprising led by Col. Arabi against the growth of European influence in Egypt resulted in Jun 1882 in the deaths of many Europeans in riots in Alexandria.

As a result, British forces bombarded and occupied Alexandria and Col. Arabi's revolt was crushed at the battle of Tel-el-Kebir on 13 Sept 1882.

(g) *The Sudan*, 1884–1885, 1896–1899

In Oct 1883 an Egyptian army led by Col. Hicks was defeated at El Obeid by the Sudanese forces of the Mahdi.

In Jan 1884 Gen. Gordon was sent to Khartoum to bring back the Egyptian garrison, but he remained and was cut off there. A relief expedition under Sir Garnet Wolseley arrived on 28 Jan 1885, two days after Khartoum had fallen and Gordon been killed.

The British Government undertook the reconquest of the Sudan in 1896. The Sudanese were defeated on 2 Sep 1898 at the battle of Omdurman, and on 19 Jan 1899 an Anglo-Egyptian condominium was established over the Sudan.

(h) *Second South African War*, 1899–1902

War began on 12 Oct 1899 after rejection of a Boer ultimatum.

Oct 1899–Jan 1900: Initiative with the Boers. British defeats; Mafeking, Kimberley and Ladysmith besieged.

Feb–Aug 1900: British counter-offensive leading to relief of garrisons and occupation of Boer capital Pretoria on 5 Jun.

Sep 1900–May 1902: A period of guerrilla warfare, ended by the Peace of Vereeniging, 31 May 1902.

3. India

(a) *Afghan Wars*, 1838–1842, 1878–1880

1838: Invasion of Afghanistan by British forces to limit Russian influence by installing a puppet ruler.

Afghan uprising in Oct 1841 led Gen. Elphinstone, who had been left with the garrison in Kabul, to begin withdrawal. A single survivor reached Jellalabad on 13 Jan 1842.

15 Sep 1842: British army reoccupied and destroyed parts of Kabul but then evacuated. Dost Mahomet, who ruled prior to British invasion of 1838, returned to the throne.

The turning back of a British envoy after a Russian mission had been received at Kabul led to a further invasion of Afghanistan in Nov 1878. Treaty of Gandamak imposed May 1879.

Afghan uprising, but a fresh expedition reached Kabul in Oct 1879, and a new ruler was installed. A British brigade sent from Kandahar to assist him against his enemies was defeated at Maiwand. Sir Frederick Roberts marched an army 300 miles to relieve Kandahar.

Evacuation of Afghanistan completed by Apr 1881.

(b) *Sind Campaign*, 1843

War against the Baluchi Ameers of Sind, leading to the annexation of the country by Sir Charles Napier. Baluchis defeated at Miani 17 Feb 1843, and the capital Hyderabad occupied.

(c) *Sikh Wars*, 1845–1846, 1848–1849

11 Dec 1845: Sikh army crossed the Sutlej into British territory.

18 Dec 1845: British army under Sir Hugh Gough beat off an attack at Mudki.

Sikhs defeated in battle of Aliwal (29 Jan 1846) and battle of Sobraon (10 Feb 1846).

8 Mar 1846: Treaty of Kasure ended First Sikh War.

20 Apr 1848: Sikh garrison at Multan revolted.

22 Nov 1848: Sikhs defeated by Gough in cavalry action at Ramnuggur.

13 Jan 1849: Indecisive battle of Chillianwala.

22 Jan 1849: Multan stormed.

21 Feb 1849: Sikhs defeated at Gujerat.

14 Mar 1849: Sikh army surrendered.

7 Apr 1849: Annexation of the Punjab.

(d) *Indian Mutiny*, 1857–1858

10 May 1857: Indian troops at Meerut mutinied. From there the mutineers marched on Delhi and seized the city.

7 Jun: Siege of Cawnpore began; on 26 Jun the British surrendered to Nana Sahib who broke his word and murdered the prisoners.

30 Jun: Lucknow besieged by the mutineers.

14–20 Sep 1857: Delhi retaken by British troops.

25 Sep: Gen. Havelock relieved Lucknow, but was in turn besieged there. 17 Nov: Sir Colin Campbell relieved Lucknow a second time and evacuated it. Finally recaptured 11–19 Mar 1858.

3 Apr 1858: Sir Hugh Rose stormed Jhansi, and defeated Tantia Topi at Kalpi on 22 May 1858.

Peace proclaimed 8 Jul 1858.

4. Asia and New Zealand

(a) *Wars with China*, 1839–1900

    (i) '*Opium War*', 1839–1842. Originated in drastic action taken by the Chinese against British merchants in an attempt to curb the opium trade. An expedition under Sir Hugh

Gough captured Canton in May 1841. Peace was made by the Treaty of Nanking, 29 Aug 1842.

(ii) 1856–60. The removal of twelve Chinese seamen from a vessel, the *Arrow*, registered in Hong Kong, was regarded as cause for a British ultimatum which led to renewed war between China and Britain in 1856. Canton was taken, the Taku forts silenced and Tientsin occupied; the Treaty of Tientsin ending the war was signed on 26 Jun 1858.

However, in 1859 a naval force under Admiral James Hope was repulsed at the Taku forts on the way to obtain ratification of the Treaty of Tientsin. A British and French expedition led by Sir Hope Grant captured the Taku forts and occupied Peking on 9 Oct 1860.

24 Oct 1860: Treaty of Peking ended the war.

(*iii*) *Boxer Uprising*, 1900. British troops took part in the suppression of the Boxer Uprising in China by an international force, which rescued the Europeans in Peking on 15 Aug 1900.

(*b*) *Burma*, 1852–1853, 1885–1892

The first Burmese War (1824–6) had resulted in the defeat of the Burmese, but hostile treatment led to the withdrawal of our envoys and an appeal for protection by British merchants at Rangoon.

War was declared in Feb 1852, and in Apr 1852 an army sailed from India and captured Rangoon. Peace was made in Jun 1853.

The misrule of the Burmese King, Theebaw, led to a fresh expedition to Burma which captured the capital Mandalay in Nov 1885.

1 Jan 1886: Upper Burma became a province of India, though the country was not finally pacified until 1892.

(*c*) *Persian War*, 1856–1857

An army of 7,000 men was sent in Dec 1856 to compel the Persians to evacuate Herat. Sir James Outram arrived with reinforcements and the Persian army was defeated at Ahwaz. By the peace treaty of Mar 1857 the Shah agreed to evacuate Herat.

(*d*) *New Zealand*, 1845–1870

1845–7: Attacks by the Maoris on the settlement of Russell led to its evacuation in Mar 1845. British reinforcements arrived in May 1845, and after campaigns in which Maori fortresses (or 'pahs') were captured with some difficulty, the war ended in Jul 1847.

Three subsequent wars were fought against the Maoris–1860–1, 1863–6, 1868–70.

Principal Military Commanders

Brudenell, James Thomas, 7th E of Cardigan (1797–1868)
Entered Army 1824. Lieutenant-Colonel of the 15th Hussars, 1832.
Forced to resign this command, 1834. Purchased command of the
11th Light Dragoons, 1836. In 1854 he was appointed commander of
the Light Cavalry Brigade in the Crimea under his brother-in-law,
the E of Lucan. On 24 Oct 1854 he led the charge of the Light
Brigade at the battle of Balaclava. Inspector-General of Cavalry,
1855–60.

Buller, Sir Redvers Henry (1839–1908)
Entered Army 1858. Served in the Chinese War of 1860, the
expedition to put down the Red River rebellion in Canada (1870),
the Ashanti War of 1873, the Kaffir War of 1878, the Zulu War,
winning the V.C., the Egyptian War (1882) and the Sudan expedition
(1884–5). Commander at Aldershot, 1898, and Commander-in-Chief
in South Africa, 1899–1900. He returned to his command at Aldershot in Jan 1901, but was retired in the same year.

Campbell, Sir Colin, Ld Clyde (1792–1863)
Entered Army 1807. Served in the Walcheren expedition (1809), in
the Peninsula and in the war with the United States. Took part in
the Opium War with China, and was knighted for outstanding
service in the Second Sikh War. Commander of the Highland
Brigade in the Crimea, 1854. On the outbreak of the Indian Mutiny
he was appointed Commander-in-Chief in India. For his services
there he was raised to the peerage, 1858. Field-Marshal, 1862.

Colley, Sir George Pomeroy (1835–1881)
Entered Army 1852. Served in China in 1860, and managed the
transport services in the Ashanti War of 1873. Secretary to the
Viceroy of India, 1876. Chief of Staff in the Zulu War. Appointed
Governor and Commander-in-Chief of Natal in 1880. Commanded
in the first war against the Boers, and was killed at the battle of
Majuba Hill on 27 Feb 1881.

Gordon, Charles George (1833–1885)
Joined Royal Engineers, 1852. Fought in the Crimea. Went to China
in 1860 and took part in the capture of Peking. Commanded the
Chinese forces which crushed the Taiping rebellion, 1863–4, earning
the name 'Chinese Gordon'. Worked for Ismail Khedive of Egypt,
1873–6, opening up the Equatorial Nile. Governor-General of the
Sudan with the Equatorial Provinces, 1877–80. Sent by the British
Government in 1884 to extricate the Egyptian garrisons from the

Mahdi's revolt in the Sudan. Besieged at Khartoum, and killed there when the city fell on 26 Jan 1885.

Gough, Sir Hugh, 1st Vt Gough (1779–1869)
Entered Army 1793. By 1815 he had served at the Cape, the West Indies and in the Peninsula. Commanded the troops in China who captured the Canton forts in 1841. Commander-in-Chief in India, 1843. Successfully commanded in the First Sikh War, and was finally victorious in the Second Sikh War before the arrival of Sir Charles Napier, sent to replace him after the heavy losses of the initial battles. Field-Marshal, 1862.

Grant, Sir James Hope (1808–1875)
Entered Army 1826. Served in China, 1840–2, and distinguished himself in the First and Second Sikh Wars. Took part in the Indian Mutiny, and successfully commanded in China, 1860. Commander-in-Chief at Madras, 1862–3. Quartermaster-General at the Horse Guards, 1865. Commander at Aldershot, 1870.

Havelock, Sir Henry (1795–1857)
Entered Army 1815. Served in First Burmese War, First Afghan War, the Gwalior Campaign (1843) and the First Sikh War. Commanded a division in Persia in 1857. Distinguished service in the Indian Mutiny: in command of a mobile column he relieved Lucknow. Died of dysentery 24 Nov 1857.

Kitchener, Horatio Herbert, 1st Earl Kitchener (1850–1916)
Joined Royal Engineers, 1870. Served in the Sudan and Egypt, 1882–5; Governor-General of East Sudan, 1886–8. Appointed Commander of Egyptian Army, and set about the reconquest of the Sudan. Defeated the dervishes at Omdurman, 2 Sep 1898. Chief of Staff to Roberts in South Africa, and Commander-in-Chief there on Roberts's return to England. Commander-in-Chief in India, 1902–9. British Agent and Consul-General in Egypt, 1911–14. Joined Cabinet in 1914 as a serving Field-Marshal, and non-political Secretary for War. Drowned on a mission to Russia 5 Jun 1916, when the cruiser *Hampshire* struck a mine off the Orkney Islands.

Napier, Robert Cornelius, Ld Napier of Magdala (1810–1890)
Born in Ceylon. Joined Bengal Engineers, 1826. Served in the First and Second Sikh Wars, the Hazara expedition (1852) and the campaign against the Bori clan in Peshawar (1853). Went as second-in-command of the Central India force under Sir Hugh Rose, 1858. Commanded a division in the Chinese War of 1860. Returning to India in 1861, he was given command of the Bombay Army in 1865,

and of the expedition to Abyssinia in 1867, for which he was created
Baron Napier of Magdala. Commander-in-Chief in India, 1870–6.
Governor of Gibraltar, 1876–82. Constable of the Tower of London,
1887–90.

Outram, Sir James (1803–1863)
Joined the Bombay native infantry, 1819. In 1839 he attended Sir
John Keane as aide-de-camp into Afghanistan, and was then appointed political agent in Lower Sind. In 1854 he was made resident
at Lucknow, where in 1856 he carried out the annexation of Oudh.
Successfully commanded the expedition against Persia, 1857. Returned to India in 1857, and accompanied Sir Henry Havelock to the
relief of Lucknow. Created a baronet 1858, and appointed as the
military member of the Supreme Council of Calcutta. Returned to
England, 1860.

Roberts, Frederick Sleigh, 1st Earl Roberts (1832–1914)
Joined Bengal Artillery, 1851. Served in the Indian Mutiny and won
the v.c. in Jan 1858. Assistant Quartermaster-General in Abyssinian
expedition. Quartermaster-General of Army in India, 1875. As
commander of Punjab frontier force, he defeated the Afghans and
imposed the Treaty of Gandamak, May 1879. Relieved Kandahar
after the defeat of a British brigade at Maiwand, Jul 1880.
Commander-in-Chief of Madras Army, 1880. Commander-in-Chief
in India, 1885–93. Commander-in-Chief in Ireland, 1895–9. Appointed to supreme command in South Africa, 1899. Returned to
England in 1901 to be Commander-in-Chief (until 1904). President
of the National Service League, 1905. Died 14 Nov 1914, after
contracting pneumonia during a visit to Indian troops in France.

Rose, Hugh Henry, 1st Ld Strathnairn (1801–1885)
Born in Berlin. Entered Army 1820. Selected for special service in
Syria, 1840. Consul-General for Syria, 1841–8. Chargé d'Affaires at
Constantinople, 1852–4. Commissioner at the French headquarters
during the Crimean War. Commanded the Army of Central India
during the Mutiny. Commander-in-Chief of Bombay Army, Mar
1860. Commander-in-Chief in India, Jun 1860–1865. Commander-
in-Chief in Ireland, 1865–70. Field-Marshal, 1877.

Somerset, Ld Fitzroy James Henry, 1st Ld Raglan (1788–1855)
Served on Wellington's staff in the Copenhagen expedition (1807),
and as his aide-de-camp in the Peninsula. Lost his right arm in the
Waterloo campaign. Military Secretary to Wellington, 1811–14 and
again 1818–52. On Wellington's death in 1852 he was appointed
Master-General of the Ordnance. In 1854 he went to the Crimea as
Commander-in-Chief of the British expeditionary force. His leader-
ship was heavily criticised, and the failure of the Allied attack on

Sebastopol in Jun 1855 aggravated his dysentery; he died 28 Jun 1855.

Thesiger, Frederic Augustus, 2nd Ld Chelmsford (1827–1905)
Entered Rifle Brigade, 1844. Served in the Crimea and the Indian Mutiny. Deputy Adjutant-General in the Abyssinian expedition; Adjutant-General in the East Indies, 1869–74. Commanded troops in the Kaffir War of 1878, and in the Zulu War. After the initial disaster at Isandhlwana, he defeated Cetewayo at Ulundi in Jul 1879. Lieutenant of the Tower of London, 1884–9.

Wolseley, Garnet Joseph, 1st Vt Wolseley (1833–1913)
Entered Army 1852. Served in Second Burmese War, the Crimea, Indian Mutiny and expedition to China in 1860. Went to Canada as Assistant Quartermaster-General, 1861, and in 1870 put down the Red River Rebellion. Assistant Adjutant-General at the War Office, 1871, and worked with Cardwell to further Army reform. Commanded the punitive expedition into Ashanti, 1873–4. Promoted to Major-General and sent to Natal in a political post, 1875. High Commissioner in Cyprus, 1878. Supreme civil and military commander in Natal and the Transvaal, 1879. Returned to Britain 1880, and appointed Quartermaster-General. Adjutant-General responsible for training in the Army, 1882. Sent in Aug 1882 to Egypt to put down Arabi's revolt; defeated him at Tel-el-Kebir, 13 Sep 1882. In Jan 1885 the relieving force under Wolseley reached Khartoum two days after Gordon's death. Returned to War Office as Adjutant-General; Commander-in-Chief in Ireland, 1890–4. Commander-in-Chief of the forces, 1895–1900.

Wood, Sir Henry Evelyn (1838–1919)
Entered Royal Navy 1852, and served in the Crimea with the Naval Brigade. Transferred to the Army, and served as a cavalry officer in the Indian Mutiny. Served with Wolseley in the Ashanti War of 1873, and commanded a column in the Zulu War. Second-in-command to Sir George Colley in the First Boer War, and came to terms with the Boers in Mar 1881 on government orders. Commanded a brigade in Egypt, 1882, and was Commander of the Egyptian Army, 1882–6. Went to the War Office as Quartermaster-General, 1893. Adjutant-General to the forces, 1897, and responsible for mobilisation at the outbreak of the South African War. Field-Marshal, 1903.

Armed Forces: Administrative Changes

The nineteenth century saw slow changes in the composition, administration and higher direction of policy of the British armed forces, reflecting the effects of periods of military crisis, the role of the armed forces, and the attitude of government and society to them.

1832   Consolidation by Sir James Graham of all naval business under the Board of Admiralty.

1837   Lord Howick's Commission advocated the centralisation of the civil business of the Army in the hands of the Secretary at War.

1852   Militia Act. Reorganised the militia and transferred control from the Home Office to the Secretary at War.

1854   Jun: Secretary of State for War appointed to take over the military duties of the Secretary of State for War and the Colonies. Power over discipline and command of the Army were reserved to the Commander-in-Chief at the Horse Guards, though he was in theory responsible to the Secretary of State.

        Dec: The Commissariat Department was transferred from the Treasury to the War Department.

1855   Feb: Office of Secretary at War combined with Secretary of State for War. The former office was abolished in 1863.

        Mar: Control over the militia and yeomanry transferred to the War Department.

        May: Board of Ordnance abolished, and its duties divided between the Secretary of State and the Commander-in-Chief.

1858   India Act. Territories and Army of the East India Company transferred to the Crown.

1859   Fear of invasion from France led to the creation of a Volunteer Force, established at 150,000.

1860   Sir James Graham's Committee on Military Organisation declared that the Commander-in-Chief was subordinate to the Secretary of State, and recommended that the Horse Guards and the War Office should be under the same roof.

1862   March: House of Commons' resolution in favour of self-governing colonies undertaking their own defence. By 1870 colonial garrisons (excluding India) were under 24,000 men, as against nearly 50,000 in 1858.

1867   Reserve Forces Act and Militia Reserve Act.

1870   War Office Act. Following the recommendations of Lord Northbrook's Committee, the Horse Guards moved to the same building as the War Office, which was organised into three departments: Military under the Commander-in-Chief; Supply under the Surveyor-General; and Finance under the Financial Secretary. The Secretary of State was confirmed in his responsibility for Army business as a whole.

Army Enlistment Act. First term of engagement fixed at twelve years, part with the colours, part with the reserve.

1871   Jul: Purchase of commissions abolished by Royal Warrant.

1872   Feb: Edward Cardwell, Secretary of State for War, produces scheme to organise all regiments so as to have two battalions–one abroad, and one at home to act as a source of trained men for service overseas. The organisation of the regular infantry was to be localised, in order to encourage recruiting and to bring it into line with the militia, which was placed under the Commander-in-Chief instead of the Lords-Lieutenant.

1880   Lord Airey's Committee on Army Organisation reported that home battalions were not being allowed to train or form because the demand for men overseas was too great.

1881   Regulation of the Forces Act. On the recommendation of Colonel Stanley's Committee (1876), the Act amalgamated the line and militia battalions into territorial regiments with the same name and depot.

1885   Colonial Defence Committee established on a permanent basis.

1887   The Stephen Commission Report made a general indictment of civilian mismanagement of the Army.
        Dec: Office of Surveyor-General abolished, and all the principal departments of army business, except finance and manufacture, were united under the authority of the Commander-in-Chief.

1888   Jun: Lord Hartington's Commission on Naval and Military Administration appointed. Recommended the abolition of the post of Commander-in-Chief, the creation of a General Staff, and the establishment of a joint Naval and Military Council and a permanent War Office Council.

1895   Nov: The powers of the Commander-in-Chief, which had been increased in 1887, were curtailed by Order-in-Council. An Army Board was appointed to co-ordinate military opinion for the Secretary of State, and a War Office consultative council formed over which the Secretary of State presided.

1902   Committee of Imperial Defence created.

1903   Jul: Publication of the Report of the Royal Commission on the war in South Africa.

1904   On the recommendation of Lord Esher's Committee, the office of Commander-in-Chief was abolished, a General Staff was created, and an Army Council established; the War Office Council and the Army Board were abolished.

Parliamentary Provisions for the Finance and Manpower of the Armed Forces, 1830–1900

	Army		Navy	
	Total Cost (£)	Numbers of Men Voted	Total Supplies Granted (£)	Total Seamen and Marines Voted
1830	6,123,112	88,848	5,594,955	29,000
1835	5,898,833	81,271	4,434,783	26,500
				35,165 (2 months)
1840	6,254,953	93,471	6,182,247	37,165 (7 months)
				39,665 (3 months)
1845	5,979,272	100,011	7,344,363	40,000
1850	6,019,397	99,128	6,672,588	39,000
1855	32,006,603	223,224	19,590,833	70,000
1860	14,792,546	145,269	11,836,100	84,100
1865	14,348,447	142,477	10,392,224	69,000
1870	12,975,000	113,221	9,370,530	61,000
1875	14,677,700	129,281	10,825,194	60,000
1880	15,541,300	131,859	10,566,935	58,800
1885	17,820,700	142,194	12,694,900	58,334
1890	17,717,800	153,483	13,786,600	68,800
1895	17,983,800	155,403	18,701,000	88,850
1900	61,499,400	430,000	28,791,900	114,880

Effective Strength of the Army During the Boer War*

1899	231,851
1900	301,544
1901	421,173
1902	397,682

*SOURCE: General Annual Report on the British Army.

Size of the British Navy, 1830–1902

Number of Ships and Vessels in Commission, 1830–1880

	Line of Battle Ships	Frigates and Corvettes	Total Fleet and Coast Guard, including Tenders
1830	17	41	206
1840	23	28	269
1850	13	18	201
1860	27	50	361
1870	11	33	241
1880	14	28	243

The Naval Defence Act, 31 May 1889

The Act provided for the building in the next three years of eight first-class battleships, and two second-class battleships; nine large and twenty-nine smaller cruisers; four fast gunboats and eighteen torpedo-gunboats. The cost of this building programme would be £21·5 million.

Coincident with the Act, the 'Two-Power Standard' was established: the minimum standard of British naval strength was to be equality with the navies of the next two powers combined.

British Battleships Launched from 1889 to 1902

Class	Displacement (Tons)	Number of Battleships	Dates of Launch
Royal Sovereign	14,150	8	1891–2
Centurion	10,500	2	1892
Renown	12,350	1	1895
Majestic	14,900	9	1894–6
Canopus	12,950	6	1897–9
Formidable	15,000	6	1898–9
Duncan	14,000	6	1901
Improved Formidable	15,000	2	1902

The Nineteenth-Century Revolution in Naval Architecture

The nineteenth century saw a revolution in the construction and design of naval vessels, with fundamental changes in material, means of propulsion and the power of offence and defence.

Means of Propulsion: Sail to Steam

1821   The Royal Navy purchased its first steamer, a paddle-tug called the *Monkey*.

By 1840 about one-fifth of the ships in commission were steamers.

1845   The screw ship *Rattler* was victorious in a duel with the paddle steamer *Alecto*.

Improved versions of the screw replaced the paddle wheel.

1861   Oct: H.M.S. *Warrior* completed both with steam power and as a full-rigged sailing ship.

1870   Sep: H.M.S. *Captain* capsized in a storm off Finisterre. The disaster showed that rigging was not compatible with reducing freeboard to a minimum above the water-line to present the smallest target to enemy guns.

1873   Apr: H.M.S. *Devastation* completed with only a small signalling mast.

Basic Material: Wood to Iron

1839 The Admiralty ordered the first iron naval steamer, the *Dover*.

But there was a reaction against iron ships. Experiments conducted in 1846 with the ship *Ruby* at Portsmouth showed that in battle, iron plates were likely to splinter and difficult to plug.

1846 The Whig government ruled that iron frigates previously ordered should be converted into transports.

1853 Nov: The Russian annihilation of the Turkish fleet at Sinope demonstrated conclusively the destructive effect of shell-fire on wooden ships.

1861 Oct: Completion of the first British armoured iron ship, H.M.S. *Warrior*.

1866 The policy of building wooden ironclads and armouring existing wooden hulls was finally abandoned.

Armament

During the nineteenth century solid roundshot was replaced by the hollow shell filled with explosive or incendiary material; such developments in ordnance necessitated the adoption of armour for ships.

1838 Sep: The Admiralty decided it must follow the French decision of 1837 in favour of using shell-guns on ships of the line and frigates.

1855 Production of the Armstrong gun: new construction, rifled barrel, shell-firing, breech-loading.

The Admiralty introduced the Armstrong gun in 1858, though the breech-loading principle was not finally adopted until the 1880s.

1866 Feb: H.M.S. *Albert* completed, the Navy's first iron turret ship. It had become impossible to protect a whole ship with heavy armour, so hitting-power was concentrated in the central part, with as wide an arc of fire as possible.

1873 Apr: H.M.S. *Devastation* completed as a turret ship with 12-in. armour over the central part of the hull. With its emancipation from sail (referred to above) it has been called the true prototype of the modern warship.

1881 H.M.S. *Inflexible* completed with 24-in. armour.

1885 H.M.S. *Benbow's* 16·5-in., 110·5-ton breech-loaders were the culmination of the increase in size and power of ordnance.

These were found to be unnecessarily large as improved thinner armour was being used to cover a greater area as a defence against the small-calibre quick-firing gun.

In the Royal Navy of the 1890s, first-class battleships were equipped with 13·5-in., 67-ton breech-loaders (Royal Sovereign class), or with 12-in., 46-ton breech-loaders (the Majestic and later classes). By 1905 the thickness of armour plates was about what it had been thirty years before, from 6 to 12 in.

SELECT BIBLIOGRAPHY*

1. *General Military*
   Barnett, Correlli, *Britain and Her Army* (London, 1970)
   Bond, B. J. (ed.), *Victorian Military Campaigns* (London, 1967)
   Callwell, C. R. *Small Wars* (London: H.M.S.O., 1896; 3rd ed., 1906)
   Fortescue, Hon. J. W., *A History of the British Army*, vols. XI–XIII (London, 1923–30)
   Luvaas, Jay, *The Education of an Army: British Military Thought, 1815–1940* (London, 1964)
   Sheppard, Major E. W., *A Short History of the British Army* (London, 1926)
   Woodham-Smith, Cecil, *The Reason Why* (London, 1953)

2. *Army Administration*
   Biddulph, Sir Robert, *Lord Cardwell at the War Office* (London, 1904)
   Bond, B. J., 'The Effect of the Cardwell Reforms in Army Organisation 1874–1904', *Journal of the Royal United Services Institution* (Nov 1960)
   'Prelude to the Cardwell Reforms, 1856–1868', *Journal of the Royal United Services Institution* (May 1961)
   Dunlop, Colonel J. K., *The Development of the British Army, 1899–1914* (London, 1938)
   Hamer, W. S., *The British Army: Civil–Military Relations, 1885–1905* (Oxford U.P., 1970)
   Omond, Lieut-Col. J. S., *Parliament and the Army, 1642–1904* (Cambridge U.P., 1933)

3. *Navy*
   Bartlett, C. J., *Great Britain and Sea Power, 1815–1853* (Oxford U.P., 1963)
   Clowes, Sir W. L., *The Royal Navy: A History* (London, 1903)
   Marder, A. J., *Anatomy of British Sea Power: A History of British Naval Policy in the Pre-Dreadnought Era, 1880–1905* (London, 1940)
   Richmond, Sir Herbert, *Statesmen and Seapower* (Oxford U.P., 1946)
   Schurman, D. M., *The Education of a Navy: The Development of British Naval Strategic Thought, 1867–1914* (Univ. of Chicago Press, 1965).

*A comprehensive bibliography on the nineteenth-century Armed Forces may be found in *A Guide to the Sources of British Military History*, Ed. Robin Higham (Univ. of California Press, 1971).

11   Education

Ministerial and Departmental Arrangements

England, Wales and Scotland

1839   By Order in Council, a Committee of the Privy Council on Education set up for England and Wales. The Lord President was the active and responsible minister.

1853   Creation of a Department of Science and Art within the Board of Trade, to superintend scientific work and expenditure on government-aided schools of design.

1853   Creation by statute of a permanent Charity Commission, with powers to review the workings of charitable trusts and endowments, including those providing education. Three of the Commissioners were salaried; the fourth, unpaid, was expected to be a member of the Government and after 1856 was usually the Vice-President of the Committee of Council. The Charity Commission reported to the Home Secretary, but looked to the Lord Chancellor for legal advice and assistance.

1856   By Order in Council, the Department of Science and Art and the Education establishment of the Privy Council Office, now known as the Education Department, were linked under the Lord President of the Council and a newly-created Vice-President of the Committee of Council on Education, who spoke for education in the Commons but did not normally sit in the Cabinet.

1869   Creation by statute, for a limited period, of three paid Endowed Schools Commissioners, to review educational endowments. Any proposals for reorganisation had to be submitted to the Education Department.

1872   A Committee of Council on Education for Scotland, including both Lord President and Vice-President, was set up.

1874   When the powers of the Endowed Schools Commissioners lapsed, they were transferred by statute to an enlarged Charity Commission. Since the Education Department was still to review new schemes, the Vice-President undertook not to sit as an active member of the Commission.

1885   The Secretary of State for Scotland replaced the Vice-President as the responsible minister for Scottish education in the Commons and the section of the Education Department establishment dealing with Scotland was transferred to the Scottish Office.

1887   By statute, the unpaid member of the Charity Commission was to be an M.P. holding *no* other office of profit under the Crown.

1900   By statute the Education Department and the Department of Science and Art were amalgamated into one department under a Board of Education, with a President.

1900–03   The Charity Commissioners' powers to deal with educational endowments were transferred to the Board of Education.

Ireland

1813   By statute, a Board of Commissioners to review and regulate endowed schools created.

1831   On the initiative of the Chief Secretary and the Lord Lieutenant, a Board of Commissioners for Irish national education was created. All were initially unpaid, but arrangements were made in 1839 to pay one Resident Commissioner. Appointments were made by the Lord Lieutenant.

1844   Board of Commissioners for national education incorporated by Charter and thereby given a permanent existence.

1878   Creation of Board of unpaid Commissioners for intermediate and secondary education.

Ministers Principally Concerned with Education

W = Whig; C = Conservative; L = Liberal

Lords President

1839	M of Lansdowne (Lord Pres. since Apr 1835) (W)
Sep 1841	Ld Wharnecliffe (d. Dec 1845) (C)
Jan 1846	D of Buccleuch (C)
Jul 1846	M of Lansdowne (W)
Feb 1852	E of Lonsdale (C)
Dec 1852	Earl Granville (W)
Jun 1854	Ld John Russell (resigned Jan 1855 in protest against Govt decision to refuse inquiry into Crimean mismanagement) (W)
Feb 1855	Earl Granville (W)
Feb 1858	M of Salisbury (C)
Jun 1859	Earl Granville (W)
Jul 1866	D of Buckingham (C)
Mar 1867	D of Marlborough (C)
Dec 1868	Earl de Grey (created M of Ripon 1871, resigned Aug 1873 on conversion to Roman Catholicism) (L)
Aug 1873	H. A. Bruce (Ld Aberdare) (L)
Feb 1874	D of Richmond (C)
Apr 1880	Earl Spencer (from Apr 1882 also Viceroy of Ireland; in

Mar 1883 relinquished Lord Presidency to concentrate on Irish affairs) (L)

Mar 1883	Ld Carlingford (L)	Apr 1864	H. A. Bruce (W)
Jun 1885	Vt Cranbrook (C)	Jul 1866	Henry Corry (C)
Feb 1886	Earl Spencer (L)	Dec 1868	W. E. Forster (entered
Aug 1886	Vt Cranbrook (C)		Cabinet Jul 1870) (L)
Aug 1892	Vt Kimberley (also Secretary of State for India and inactive on education questions) (L)	Mar 1874	Vt Sandon (C)
		Apr 1878	Ld George Hamilton (C)
		May 1880	A. J. Mundella (L)
		Jun 1885	Hon. Edward Stanhope (in
Mar 1894	E of Rosebery (also Prime Minister) (L)		Cabinet) (C)
		Sep 1885	Sir Henry Holland (C)
Jun 1895	D of Devonshire (C)	Feb 1886	Lyon Playfair (L)
		Aug 1886	Sir Henry Holland (C)
	Vice-Presidents	Jan 1887	Sir William Hart Dyke (C)
Feb 1857	W. F. Cowper (W)	Aug 1892	A. H. D. Acland (in Cabinet)
Apr 1858	C. B. Adderley (C)		(L)
Jul 1859	Robert Lowe (resigned Mar	Jul 1895	Sir John Gorst (C)

Departmental Heads

Secretaries to the Committee of Council on Education, England and Wales

1839	Sir J. P. Kay-Shuttleworth
1850	R. R. W. Lingen
1870	Sir F. R. Sandford
1884	Patric Cumin
1890	Sir G. W. Kekewich

Secretaries to the Committee of Council on Scottish Education

1873	Sir F. R. Sandford
1884	Patric Cumin
1885	Henry Craik

Secretaries of the Science and Art Department

1853	Lyon Playfair and Henry Cole

1858	Henry Cole
1874	Sir F. R. Sandford
1884	Sir John Donnelly

Secretary to the Endowed Schools Commissioners

1869–74	H. J. Roby

Resident Commissioners for Irish National Education

1839	Alexander Macdonnell
1872	Sir P. J. Keenan
1894	C. T. Redington
1899	W. J. M. Starkie

Elementary Education

N.B. In England, Wales and Ireland elementary education was not education for the youngest age group; it was education for the children of the labouring poor. The term 'primary education' did not come into general use until the early 1900s. Secondary education, for most of the century, meant middle-class education. These distinctions were not, however, as sharp in Scotland.

England and Wales
Major Inquiries, Commissions, etc.
SC = Select Committee RC = Royal Commission
Abbreviated titles, where possible, are those given in Fords' *Select List of Parliamentary Papers*, 1833–99. Where an inquiry has

been associated with a particular politician, the name is given in brackets.

1818	SC Education of the Poor (Brougham), P.P. (1818) iii
1846–7	RC Education in Wales, P.P. (1847) xxvii
1859–61	RC State of Popular Education in England (Newcastle), P.P. (1861) xxi
1865	SC Constitution of the Committee of Council, P.P. (1865) vi, (1866) vii
1883–4	SC Education, Science and Art (Ministerial Responsibility for Votes), P.P. (1884) xiii
1886–8	RC Elementary Education Acts (England and Wales) (Cross), P.P. (1886) xxv, (1887) xxix, xxx, (1888) xxxv, xxxvi and xxxvii.
1897–8	Special Reports on Educational Subjects, P.P. (1897) xxv, (1898) xxiv and xxv.

Legislation

1870	Education Act (Forster's) provided for national inquiry into school supply; election of school boards in districts where school provision inadequate or a majority of the ratepayers requested it; school boards to be rate-aided with powers to build schools and compel attendance.
1876	Education Act (Sandon's) created school attendance committees for districts where there were no school boards. These were committees of the borough council or local sanitary authority and could take powers to compel attendance.
1880	Education Act compelled all school boards and attendance committees to make attendance bye-laws.
1891	Assisted Education Act made available a capitation grant of 10s. to all schools, thereby enabling most of them to cease charging fees.
1893	Education (Blind and Deaf Children) Act, made possible the establishment of special schools for the blind and deaf.
1899	Board of Education Act.

Grant Aid and the Structure of Local Administration

The provision of elementary schools during the eighteenth century was entirely a voluntary activity.

1809	Foundation of what was to become the British and Foreign School Society, encouraging the foundation of schools which gave undenominational religious teaching.
1811	Foundation of the National Society for the Promotion of the Education of the Poor in the Principles of the Established Church.
1833	Government grant of £20,000 to aid school building, distributed through the agency of the two societies.

1839   Grants increased; creation of inspectorate attached to Committee of Council.

1846   Series of Privy Council Minutes establishing a pupil-teacher system; grant incentives for the apprenticeship of children of 13 and over to existing teachers, with scholarships to the Normal or training schools, run by the two societies.

1849   Catholic Poor School Committee formed, as national co-ordinating committee for Roman Catholic schools.

1862   The 'Revised Code' of grant regulations inaugurated the system of payment by results: all grants except building grants replaced by a capitation grant, a portion of which depended on the child's regular attendance, the rest on his performance in examinations in the three Rs each year, conducted by the inspector.

1870   Voluntary schools and new board schools constituted a dual system, each board and each voluntary school committee of management dealing directly with Whitehall. Voluntary schools received no rate aid and no more building grants. After 1871 an increased amount of money was made available in annual grant.

1890–5   Payment by results gradually dismantled, replaced by a system approximating to block grants.

Scotland

Major Inquiries, etc.

1837–8   SC Education in Scotland, P.P. (1837–8) vii

1865–8   RC Schools in Scotland (Argyll), P.P. (1865) xvii, (1867) xxv, xxvi, xxvii and xxix.

Legislation

1838   Education (Scotland) Act made available government funds for the foundation and support of additional parish schools.

1861   Parochial and Burgh Schoolmasters Act relieved schoolmasters from religious tests and transferred the examination of their qualifications from the presbyteries to the universities.

1872   Education (Scotland) Act put all burgh and parish schools under the control of locally elected rate-supported boards, with powers to compel attendance.

1889   Local Government (Scotland) Act allowed surplus on probate duties to be used to enable schools to cease charging fees.

Grant Aid and the Structure of Local Administration

By the end of the eighteenth century few parishes or burghs in Scotland were without schools, controlled by the heritors, kirk sessions, presbyteries or town councils, and supported from local funds.

1838	Grants for building and maintenance of additional parish schools.
1839	Creation of an inspectorate of schools.
1862	Introduction of a version of payment by results.
1872	School boards replaced heritors, etc., as local authorities.
1874	Separate Code of grant regulations for Scotland began a shift away from payment by results.

Ireland

Major Inquiries, etc.

1806–12	Reports of Statutory Commission of Inquiry into Irish Schools, P.P. (1813–14) v.
1824–7	Reports of a further Statutory Commission, P.P. (1825) xii, (1826–7) xii and xiii.
1828	SC on Reports on Irish Schools, P.P. (1828) iv
1868–70	RC Primary Education (Powis), P.P. (1870) xxviii

Legislation

1875	National School Teachers (Ireland) Act allowed the raising of local rates to support national schools.
1892	Education (Ireland) Act enabled certain customs and excise revenues to be used to enable national schools to cease charging fees, and made attendance compulsory.

Grant Aid and the Structure of Local Administration

A number of voluntary school societies were active in Ireland at the end of the eighteenth century.

1800–31	Government grants made to a number of voluntary societies, most notably the Kildare Place Society (1816–31) and the Association for Discountenancing Vice (1800–31).
1831	All grants unified into a single fund, at the disposal of the Lord Lieutenant, advised by the Commissioners for national education. Grants could be made for building, maintenance and teachers' salaries. Because these national schools were intended to be interdenominational, a number of voluntary societies and individual patrons still continued to support denominational voluntary schools. The Commissioners, aided by an inspectorate, dealt directly with individual school managers and patrons.
1871	A version of payment by results introduced.

Average Number of Children in Attendance at Inspected Day Schools, 1850–1900

('000s)

Year	England and Wales	Scotland	Ireland
1850	(1851: 250)	28	(1852: 283)
1860	751	133	263
1870	1,152	198	359
1880	2,751	405	469
1890	3,718	513	489
1900	4,666	626	478

1. There are no reliable series of figures before 1850.

2. Besides children in attendance at inspected schools, there were an unknown number of children attending private schools of various kinds. These probably diminished sharply in the last three decades of the century.

3. Source for English, Welsh and Scottish figures: B. R. Mitchell and H. G. Jones, *Second Abstract of British Historical Statistics* (Cambridge, 1971) pp. 212–14.

4. Source for Irish figures: D. H. Akenson, *The Irish Education Experiment: The National System of Education in the Nineteenth Century* (London, 1970) pp. 276, 321, 346.

Secondary or Intermediate Education

England and Wales

Major Inquiries, etc.

1861–4   RC Revenues and Management of Certain Schools and Colleges (Eton, Winchester, Westminster, Charterhouse, St Paul's, Merchant Taylors, Harrow, Rugby and Shrewsbury) (Clarendon), P.P. (1864) xx and xxi

1865–7   RC Schools Inquiry: Schools not comprised within the Two Recent Commissions on Popular Education and on Public Schools (Taunton), P.P. (1867–8) xxviii

1871–5   RC Scientific Instruction and the Advancement of Science (Devonshire), P.P. (1871) xxiv, (1872) xxv, (1873) xxviii, (1874) xxii, (1875) xxviii.

1880–7   Intermediate and Higher Education in Wales (Aberdare), P.P. (1881) xxxiii

1882–4   RC Technical Instruction (Samuelson), P.P. (1882) xxvii (1884) xxix, xxx and xxxi

1893–5   RC Secondary Education (Bryce), P.P. (1895) xliii, xliv, xlv, xlvi, xlvii, xlviii, xlix, (1896) xlvi.

Legislation

1853   Charitable Trusts Act created a permanent board of Charity Commissioners to review all charities.

1869   Endowed Schools Act created a body of commissioners with power to review and revise educational endowments.

1874   Endowed Schools Act transferred the powers of the Endowed Schools Commissioners to the Charity Commission.

1887   Charitable Trusts Act enlarged powers of Charity Commission.

1889   Intermediate Education (Wales) Act allowed Welsh county councils to establish and support intermediate schools and initiate schemes for the reorganisation of educational endowments.

1889   Technical Instruction Act allowed county councils to use excise surplus (whisky money) to support technical instruction.

Grant Structure and Local Administration

Secondary schools were not aided by regular government grant until after the Education Act of 1902. Some of the scientific work done in the higher standards of elementary schools, in some endowed grammar schools and in private schools was aided by Science and Art Department grants from 1853 on, under a version of payment by results.

Scotland
Major Inquiries, etc.

1865–7   RC Schools in Scotland (Argyll) included a report on middle-class schools, P.P. (1867–8) xxix

1873–4   RC Endowed Schools and Hospitals (Scotland), P.P. (1873) xxvii, (1874) xvii, (1875) xxix

1884–9   RC Educational Endowments (Scotland), P.P. (1884) xxvii, (1884–5) xxvii, (1886) xxviii, (1887) xxxiii, (1888) xli, (1889) xxxii.

Legislation

1887   Technical Schools (Scotland) Act enabled county councils to spend excise surplus in supporting technical education.

1892   Education and Local Taxation Account (Scotland) Act made available funds for secondary education to be administered by committees representing both school boards and county councils.

Grant Structure and Local Administration

Before regular government aid was given in 1892, a number of the aided burgh schools had given quite advanced teaching. In addition, Scottish schools were eligible for Science and Art Department grants.

Ireland
Major Inquiries, etc.

1806–12   Statutory Commission of Inquiry into Irish Schools, P.P. (1813–14) v

1835–8   SC on Foundation Schools and Education in Ireland, P.P. (1837–8) vii

1854–7   RC Endowed Schools (Ireland), P.P. (1857–8) xxii

Legislation

1813   Endowed Schools (Ireland) Act created a board of commissioners to regulate the affairs of endowed schools.

1878 Intermediate Education (Ireland) Act created a commission to act as an examining body for all intermediate schools, supported by funds from the late established Church. They had no power to found schools.

Grant Aid and Structure of Local Administration

There was no regular grant aid to secondary or intermediate education in Ireland except through the medium of Science and Art Department grants.

Attendance at Secondary Schools

There are no reliable series of figures before 1900.

Higher Education

England and Wales

Major Inquiries, etc.

1850–2 RC Oxford University, P.P. (1852) xxii
1850–2 RC Cambridge University, P.P. (1852–3) xliv
1872–3 RC Universities of Oxford and Cambridge, P.P. (1873) xxxvii
1871–5 RC Scientific Instruction and the Advancement of Science (Devonshire), P.P. (1871) xxiv, (1872) xxv, (1873) xxviii, (1874) xxii, (1875) xxviii
1880–1 Intermediate and Higher Education in Wales (Aberdare), P.P. (1881) xxxiii
1888–9 RC London. University for London: whether any and what kind of new university or powers is or are required for the advancement of higher education in London (Selborne), P.P. (1889) xxxix

Legislation

1854 Oxford University Act ⎱ began the process of
1856 Cambridge University Act ⎰ strengthening central organs of government in the universities.

1871 University Tests Act abolished all religious tests.
1877 Universities of Oxford and Cambridge Act diverted some college revenues for university purposes.
1899 University of London Act enabled London to become a teaching as well as an examining university.

Foundation of Institutions of Higher Education besides Oxford and Cambridge

1826 University College, London
1828 King's College, London
1832 Durham
1836 London University given charter to act as an examining body

1851   Owen's College, Manchester
1871   Newcastle
1872   Aberystwyth
1874   Leeds
1874   Mason College, Birmingham
1876   Bristol
1877   Nottingham
1879   Firth College, Sheffield
1881   Liverpool
1883   Cardiff
1883   Bangor
1892   Reading
1893   Exeter
1893   University of Wales given charter as examining body for three Welsh colleges

Higher Education for Women
1848   Bedford College, London
1868   Institution of Cambridge Higher Local examinations for women
1869   Girton College, Cambridge
1871   Newnham College, Cambridge
1878   London degrees open to women
1879   Somerville College and Lady Margaret Hall, Oxford
1881   Cambridge Tripos examinations formally open to women

Grant Aid
1839   Small government grant to central administration of London University in recognition of its special role as an examining body both in the U.K. and the Empire.
1883   Treasury grants to Welsh colleges begun.
1889   Treasury grants to English institutions other than Oxford and Cambridge begun.

Scotland
Major Inquiries
1830–1 RC State of Universities of Scotland, P.P. (1831) xii
1836–7 RC Universities of Scotland, P.P. (1837) xxxv, xxxvi, xxxvii, xxxviii
1878   RC Universities of Scotland, P.P. (1878) xxxii, xxxiii xxxiv, xxxv.

Legislation

| 1858 | Universities (Scotland) Act | made each of the four universities (St Andrews, Glasgow, Aberdeen and Edinburgh) into self-governing corporations. |
| 1889 | Universities (Scotland) Act | |

Grant Aid

1831   Crown obligations to Scottish higher education dating from before the Act of Union placed on parliamentary vote.

1889   Annual Treasury grants begun.

Ireland
Major Inquiries

1852–3   RC State Discipline, Studies and Revenues of the University of Dublin and of Trinity College, P.P. (1852–3) xlv

1857–8   RC Queen's Colleges at Belfast, Cork and Galway, P.P. (1857–8) xxi

1884–5   RC Queen's Colleges in Ireland, P.P. (1884–5) xxv

Foundation of Institutions besides Trinity College, Dublin

1795   Maynooth

1849   Queen's Colleges at Belfast, Cork and Galway

1850   Queen's University given charter as examining body for the three colleges

1880   Royal University of Ireland

Grant Aid

1845   Grant to Maynooth made permanent. Grants to Queen's University and the Royal University from their foundation.

Higher Education: Numbers of Students

No regular and reliable series of figures before the foundation of the U.G.C. after the First World War.

Total Government Expenditure on Education, Science and Art in the U.K., 1800–1900

	(£000,000)
1800	(1802: 0·06)
1810	0·11
1820	0·09
1830	0·10
1840	0·17
1850	0·37
1860	1·27
1870	1·62
1880	4·0
1890	5·8
1900	12·2

SOURCE: B. R. Mitchell and Phyllis Deane, *Abstract of British Historical Statistics* (Cambridge, 1962) pp. 397–400.

SELECT BIBLIOGRAPHY

E. L. Woodward, *The Age of Reform, 1815–1870* (Oxford, 1938)

R. C. K. Ensor, *England, 1870–1914* (Oxford, 1936)

B. R. Mitchell and Phyllis Deane, *Abstract of British Historical Statistics* (Cambridge, 1962)

B. R. Mitchell and H. G. Jones, *Second Abstract of British Historical Statistics* (Cambridge, 1971)

D. H. Akenson, *The Irish Education Experiment: The National System of Education in the Nineteenth Century* (London, 1970)

A. S. Bishop, *The Rise of a Central Authority in English Education* (Cambridge, 1971)

Sir L. A. Selby-Bigge, *The Board of Education* (London, 1927)

Robert O. Berdahl, *British Universities and the State* (Berkeley, Calif., 1959)

George S. Pryde, *Scotland from 1603 to the Present Day* (London, 1962)

J. Kerr, *Scottish Education* (Cambridge, 1910)

Gillian Sutherland, *Elementary Education in the Nineteenth Century* (London; Historical Association, 1971)

P.P. (1897), xxv: *Special Reports on Educational Subjects*, vol. I.

12   The Press

National Daily Press

1. The Courier (1792–1840)

Proprietors/Editors:	1792–9	John Parry & 24 shareholders; J. Thelwall, editor
	1799	Daniel Stuart, proprietor
by	1811	Peter Street, co-proprietor & editor
	1822–7	W. Mudford, editor
	1828	Eugenius Roche, editor/shareholder
	1829	John Galt, editor
c.	1832	James Stuart, editor/manager
	1837	Laman Blanchard, editor

Subsequently sold to a Conservative syndicate, and expired 1840.
Politics: Whig/Liberal.

2. Daily Chronicle (1855–1930)

Proprietors/Editors:	1855	*Business and Agency Gazette* (weekly advertiser); conducted with *Clerkenwell News*
	1866	*Clerkenwell News & London Times* (daily)
	1870	*London Daily Chronicle & Clerkenwell News*
	1876	*Daily Chronicle*, purchased by Edward Lloyd; Robert Whelan Boyd, editor
	1892	Frank Lloyd, proprietor with brothers, Arthur, Herbert & Harry; Alfred Ewan Fletcher, editor
	1899	W. Fisher, editor
	1902	R. Donald, editor

Politics: Liberal/Radical.

3. Daily Express (1900–   )

	1900–2	A. Pearson, proprietor/editor

Politics: Independent/Conservative.

4. **Daily Graphic** (1890–1926)

1890	W. L. Thomson, proprietor
1891–1907	H. Hall, editor

Politics: Independent/Conservative.

5. **Daily Mail** (1896–   )

	A. Harmsworth (Ld Northcliffe), proprietor for Associated Newspapers Ltd
1899	T. Marlowe, editor

Politics: Independent/Conservative.

6. **Daily News** (1846–1930)

Proprietors/Editors:

	Bradbury & Evans + 100 shareholders led by Sir Thomas Paxton. Charles Dickens, editor; Henry Wills & Frederick Knight, sub-editors. Charles Wentworth Dilke, manager to 1849.
Feb 1846	Forster, editor
Autumn 1846	Eyre Evans Crowe, editor
1852	Frederick Knight Hunt, editor (H. Martineau, correspondent)
1854	William Weir, editor
1858	Thomas Walker, editor
by 1870	Samuel Merley & Henry Labouchere, proprietors; Frank Harrison Hill, editor
1886	Henry Lucy, editor
1901	Daily News Ltd, proprietors; G. Cadbury, chairman

Politics: Radical.

7. **Daily Telegraph** (1855–   )

Proprietors/Editors:

Jun 1855	*Daily Telegraph and Courier*: Col. Sleigh, proprietor; Thornton Hunt, editor
Autumn 1855	Mr Levy, printer & proprietor/editor (first penny daily)
1857	*Daily Telegraph*
1885	Sir J. M. LeSage, editor

| by | 1888 | Edward L. Lawson (Levy's son) & (Sir) Edwin Arnold, proprietors. |
| by | 1900 | Ld Burnham & family, proprietors |

Politics: Originally Radical; Independent by 1820; Conservative after 1843.

8. Financial News (1884–1945)

| | 1884 | H. Marks, proprietor/editor |
| | 1898 | Financial News Ltd; H. Marks, chairman |

Politics: Independent/finance.

9. Financial Times (1888–   )

| | 1888 | Financial Times Ltd, business syndicate |
| by | 1901 | W. Lawson & A. Murray, editors |

Politics: Independent/finance.

10. Morning Advertiser (1794–   )

Proprietors/Editors:

	1794	Incorporated Society of Licensed Victuallers
c.	1850–70	J. Grant, editor
	1871	Col. Richards, editor
	1894	F. Doney, editor

Politics: Independent/Conservative.

11. Morning Chronicle (1769–1862)

Proprietors/Editors:

1769–89	W. Woodfall, printer/proprietor/editor, *Morning Chronicle & London Advertiser*
1789	James Perry, proprietor/editor (Gray partnership)
1817	John Black, editor
1821	William Clement, proprietor
1834	Sir John Easthope, proprietor
1843	O'Doyle, editor
1847	D of Newcastle, Gladstone, Sidney Herbert, proprietors; J. D. Cook, editor
1854	Sergeant Glover, proprietor
1862	Expired under a Mr Stiff

Politics: Whig/Liberal to 1847, then Peelite (Lib/Con).

12. **(Manchester) Guardian** (1821–   )
  Proprietors/Editors: 1821   John Edward Taylor,
                                   proprietor; Jeremiah Garnett,
                                   editor
                         1855   became a daily
                         1872   C. P. Scott, editor
  Politics: Independent/Liberal.

13. **Morning Herald** (*a*) (1780–1869)
  Proprietors/Editors: Rev. Henry Bate (Dudley),
                                   proprietor/editor
                                   Alexander Chalmers, editor to *c.*
                                   1829, *Morning Herald & Daily
                                   Advertiser*
              c. 1820   16 shareholders led by a Mr
                                   Thwaites Wright, editor
                    1843   sold to Edward Baldwin
              c. 1857   sold by Charles Baldwin to
                                   James Johnson & John Maxwell;
                                   David Morier Evans, editor; sub.
                                   paper to *The Standard*
                    1869   expired
  Politics: Originally Radical; Independent by 1820; Conservative
  after 1843.

14. **Morning Herald** (*b*) (1892–1900)
  Proprietors/Editors: 1892   Morning Newspaper Company;
                                   D. Murray, editor
                         1898   *London Morning Herald*
                         1899   *Morning Herald*
                         1900   merged with *Daily Express*
  Politics: Independent.

15. **Morning Leader** (1892–1912)
  Proprietors/Editors: 1892   Colman family, Norwich; E.
                                   Parke, editor
                         1912   merged with *Daily News* as *Daily
                                   News and Leader*
  Politics: Liberal/Radical.

16. **Morning Post** (1772–1937)
  Proprietors/Editors: 1772   12 shareholders led by James
                                   Christie, Tattersall & John Bell;
                                   Rev. Henry Bate (Dudley),
                                   editor

1780	Tattersall, proprietor; William Jackson & John Taylor, editors
1795	Peter & Daniel Stuart, proprietors
1799	Coleridge, literary editor
1803	Nicholas Byrne, proprietor/editor
1817	Eugenius Roche, editor
1833	C. E. Michele, editor
1849	Peter Borthwick, editor
1852	Algernon Borthwick, editor (Ld Glenesk, 1895)
1876	Algernon Borthwick, owner/editor
1882	William Hardman, editor
1897	J. Dunn, editor to 1905

Politics: Conservative.

17. **The Standard** (1827–1917)

Proprietors/Editors: 1827	Charles Baldwin, *Evening Standard*; Dr Giffard, editor; Alaric Watts, sub-editor with Dr Maginn
1857	sold to James Johnson & Maxwell of *The Herald*; 2nd issue a daily, *Morning Standard*; Capt. Hamber, editor
1870	additional *Evening Standard*; Charles Williams, editor
1874	W. H. Mudford, editor; proprietor in 1878, Curtis editor
1897	S. Pryor, editor
1900	G. Curtis, editor

Politics: Conservative.

18. **The Times** (1785–   )

Proprietors/Editors: 1785	John Walter, *Daily Universal Register*
1788–1908	changed to *The Times*; Walter family, proprietors
c. 1812–15	Dr (Sir) John Stoddart, editor
1815–41	Thomas Barnes, editor
1841–77	J. T. Delane, editor
1877–84	Thomas Chenery, editor
1884–1912	G. Buckle, editor

Politics: Independent/Conservative.

National Sunday Newspapers

1. The Examiner (1808–1880)

Proprietors/Editors:	1808	John & Leigh Hunt, manager & editor
	1821(?)	Dr Fellowes, proprietor
	1826	Albany Fonblanque, editor; 1830, proprietor
	1849	John Forster, proprietor; Dudley Castello, editor
	1867	sold to Torrens
	1873	sold to P. A. Taylor
	1874(?)	Ld Rosebery, proprietor; William Minto & Robert Williams, editors
	1880	expired

Politics: Liberal/Progressive.

2. Illustrated London News (1842–   )

Proprietors/Editors:	1842	H. Ingram, M. Lemon, N. Cooke & W. Little, proprietors; 'Alphabet' Bailey, editor
	1848	Charles Mackay, editor
	1860	W. Ingram, proprietor to 1900
	1887	John Latey, editor

Politics: Independent/Conservative.

3. News of the World (1843–   )

Proprietors/Editors:

1843–55	John Browne Bell
1855–77	John William Bell
1877–91	Walter John Bell & Adolphus William Bell
1891–1941	Lascelles Carr, proprietor; Sir Emsley Carr, editor (nephew)

Politics: Liberal/Independent.

4. Observer (1791–   )

Proprietors/Editors:	1791	W. S. Bourne & W. H. Bourne
	early 19th c.	William Innell Clements, proprietor; Vincent Dowling, editor
	c. 1850	Lewis Doxat, proprietor; Edward Dicey, editor
	c. 1870	Julius Beer, proprietor; Rachel Beer, editor
	c. 1897	F. A. Beer, editor

1905   sold to Alfred Harmsworth
Politics: Independent/Conservative.

5. **Reynolds Newspaper** (1850–1967)
Proprietors/Editors: Originally a radical weekly, later
                                  an organ for socialism and the
                                  co-operative movement
            1879   J. Dicks & family, proprietors
            1894   W. Thompson, editor

6. **The People** (1881–   )
Proprietors/Editors: 1881   offshoot from the *Globe*
                                  (weekly); W. Madge & Sir G.
                                  Armstrong, proprietors; Dr
                                  Sebastian Evans, editor
Politics: Radical.

7. **The Spectator** (1828–   )
Proprietors/Editors: 1828   Mr Day, proprietor, financed by
                                  Hume & Benthamites; R. S.
                                  Rintoul, editor
            1858   Meredith Townsend & Richard
                                  Holt Hutton, proprietors
            1898   Spectator Ltd; J. St L. Strachey,
                                  proprietor/editor to 1925
Politics: Liberal/Radical.

8. **Sunday Dispatch** (1800–1961)
Proprietors/Editors: 1800   Robert Bell, proprietor/editor,
                                  Bell's Weekly Dispatch
      c.   1833   James Harmer, proprietor; W.
                                  J. Fox, editor, *Weekly Dispatch*
            1875   Ashton Wentworth Dilke,
                                  proprietor (died 1883)
Politics: Liberal/Radical.

9. **Sunday Illustrated News** (1842–1931)
Proprietors/Editors: 1842   E. Lloyd, *Lloyd's Weekly London
                                  Newspaper*
            1852   D. Jerrold, editor
            1857   Blanchard Jerrold, editor
      by   1887   T. Catling, editor
Politics: Independent/Liberal.

10. **Sunday Referee** (1877–1939)
Proprietors/Editors: 1877   I. Ostrer, owner; printed by
                                  Daily News Ltd; Henry
                                  Sampson, editor
Politics: Radical.

11. **Sunday Times** (1822–   )

Proprietors/Editors: 1822   D. W. Harvey (M.P. Colchester & Southwark)

        late 1820s   Mr Valpy, proprietor; Clarkson, editor, succeeded by Graspey to 1845

        1845–72   Levy, T. E. Smith & Sarle successive proprietors; Barnett editor on his death, 1872

        1872   F. Beer, editor

        1904   H. Schmidt amalgamated it with his 1897 *Sunday Special*

Politics: Liberal to 1845, then Conservative/Independent.

12. **Weekly Times (and Echo)** (1847–   )

Proprietors/Editors: 1847–84   a Saturday paper

        1884   J. Passmore Edwards, proprietor; amalgamated with his *Weekly Echo* as the *Weekly Times and Echo*, a Sunday paper, companion to Edward's *Evening Echo*

Politics: Radical.

London Evening Newspapers

1. **The Echo** (1868–1905)

Proprietors/Editors: 1868   Messrs Cassell, Petter & Galpin, proprietors; Arthur Arnold, editor

        1874   sold to Albert Grant, who sold to John Passmore Edwards; subsequently sold to Andrew Carnegie (New York) ànd back to Edwards

        by 1900   Consolidated Newspapers proprietors

        1898   W. Crook, editor

        1900   T. Meech, editor

        1901   P. Alden, editor

Politics: Radical originally; by 1900 Independent/Progressive.

2. **Evening News** (1880–   )
Proprietors/Editor: 1894   A. Harmsworth, proprietor for Evening News Ltd
                 1896   W. Evans, editor
Politics: Conservative.

3. **Globe** (1802–1921)
Proprietors/Editors: 1802   G. Lane & booksellers' consortium, to rival the *Morning Post*
                 1803   *The Traveller*, Col. Torrens & Walter Coulson, proprietors/editors
                 1823   Torrens amalgamated *The ˙Globe and Traveller*, Gibbons Merle, editor
        by 1871   (Sir) G. Armstrong, proprietor/editor; Madge, manager
                 1905   P. Ogle, editor
Politics: Radical to *c.* 1866, then Conservative.

4. **Pall Mall Gazette** (1865–1923)
Proprietors/Editors: 1865   G. Smith, Elder & Co., proprietors; Frederick Greenwood, editor (later of *St James's Gazette*)
                 1880   Henry Yates Thompson, proprietor (Smith's son-in-law); John Morley editor, subsequently proprietor
                 1883   William Thomas Stead, editor
                 1892   W. Astor Ltd, proprietor; E. T. Cook, editor
                 1896   Sir D. Straight, editor
Politics: 1865–80 Conservative; 1880–92 Liberal; after 1892 Liberal/Conservative.

5. **The Star** (1856–1960)
Proprietors/Editors: 1856   *Morning Star & Evening Star*, Cobden & friends, proprietors; Samuel Lucas, editor, succeeded by Justin McCarthy to 1869
                 1869   both papers absorbed in *Daily News*

1887	*The Star* owned by Daily News Ltd
1891	E. Parke, editor

Politics: Liberal/Progressive.

6. **The Sun** (*a*) (1792–1870)

Proprietors/Editors:	1792	William Pitt & friends; George Rose, editor
	1815–16	William Jerdan, editor & co-shareholder with John Taylor
	1816	John Taylor, proprietor/editor
	1825	Murdo Young, proprietor; Deacon, editor
	1850–70	Charles Kent, proprietor/editor

Politics: Government organ to *c*. 1815; thereafter Liberal.

7. **The Sun** (*b*) (1893–1906)

Proprietors/Editors:	T. P. O'Connor & H. Bottomley; T. P. O'Connor & T. Dahle, editors

Politics: Labour.

8. **St James's Gazette** (1880–1905)

Proprietors/Editors:	1880	Hucks Gibbs, proprietor; Frederick Greenwood, H. D. Traill & Adam Gielgud, editors & joint proprietors
	1888	E. Steinkopff, proprietor; Sidney J. Low, editor
	1897	H. Chisholm, editor
	1903	W. Dallas Ross & A. Pearson, proprietors; R. McNeill, editor 1900–3

Politics: Conservative.

9. **Westminster Gazette** (1893–1928)

Proprietors/Editors:	1893	Sir G. Newnes; J. Spender, editor

Politics: Liberal.

Provincial Newspaper Press

(All newspapers recorded were still circulating in 1900; the date of establishment is given. C = Conservative, L = Liberal; I = Independent.)

BATH—*Bath Journal* (Keene's) (1742) (L) weekly; *Bath Chronicle* (1757) (C) weekly; *Bath Herald* (1792) (L) daily after 1858; *Bath*

Daily Chronicle (1877) (C), merged 1900 with *Bath Argus* (1870) (C) as daily and evening respectively.

BIRMINGHAM—*Aris' Birmingham Gazette* (1741) (C) weekly; *Midland Counties Herald* (1836) (I) bi-weekly; *Birmingham Daily Post* (1857) (L); *Birmingham Daily Gazette* (1862) (C); *Birmingham Daily Mail* (1870) (L).

BRADFORD—*Bradford Observer* (1834) (L) daily in the late 1860s, changed to *Yorkshire Daily Observer* 1901; *Bradford Daily Telegraph* (1868) (L); *Bradford Citizen* (1884) (C) weekly; *Bradford Mercury* (1890) (L) weekly.

BRIGHTON—*Brighton Herald* (1806) (L) weekly; *Brighton Gazette* (1821) (C) bi-weekly; *Brighton Guardian* (1827) (C) weekly; *Sussex Daily News* (1868) (I).

BRISTOL—*Bristol Times and Mirror* (1714) (C) daily in 1858, as was *Bristol Mercury* (1790) (L); *Western Daily Press* (1858) (L); *Bristol Observer* (1859) (I).

CAMBRIDGE—*Cambridge Chronicle and University Journal* (1744) (C) weekly; *Cambridge Independent Press, University and Huntingdonshire Herald* (1807) (L) weekly.

CANTERBURY—*Kentish Post* (1717) (I) weekly, became *Kentish Gazette and Canterbury Press* in 1768; *Kentish and Canterbury Chronicle* (1768) (L) weekly; *Kent Herald* (1792) (L) weekly; *Kentish Observer and Surrey and Sussex Chronicle* (1832) (C) bi-weekly.

CARLISLE—*Carlisle Journal* (1798) (L) bi-weekly; *Carlisle Patriot* 1815 (C).

DARLINGTON—*Darlington and Stockton Times* (1847) (C) weekly; *Northern Echo* (1869) (L) daily; *North Star* (1881) (C) weekly.

DERBY—*Derby Mercury* (1732) (C) weekly; *Derby Reporter* (1823) (L) weekly; *Derby Daily Telegraph* (1879) (L); *Derby Express* (1884) (C) daily.

DONCASTER—*Doncaster Gazette* (1786) (L) weekly; *Doncaster Chronicle* (1836) (C) weekly; *Doncaster Argus* (1898) (L) weekly.

EXETER—*Trewman's Exeter Flying Post* (1763) (C) weekly; *Western Times* (1828) (L), became *Daily Western Times* in the 1860s; *Devon Weekly Times* (1861) (L).

HALIFAX—*Halifax Guardian* (1832) (C) weekly; *Halifax Courier* (1853) (L) weekly; *Halifax Evening Courier* (1892) (L) daily.

HUDDERSFIELD—*Huddersfield Weekly Chronicle* (1850) (C) weekly; *Huddersfield Weekly Examiner* (1851) (L); *Huddersfield Daily Chronicle* (1871) (I/C).

HULL—*Hull Daily Mail* (1787) (C) daily in 1860s as was the *Eastern Morning News* (1794) (I); *Hull Daily News* (1852) (L); *Hull and Lincolnshire Times* (1857) (C) weekly.

IPSWICH—*Ipswich Journal* (1720) (C) weekly; *Suffolk Chronicle* (1810)

(L) weekly; *Suffolk Times and Mercury* (1854) (L) weekly; *East Anglian Daily Times* (1874) (I).

LEEDS—*Leeds Mercury* (1718) (L) daily in 1861; *Yorkshire Weekly Post* (1754) (C) weekly; became *Yorkshire Post* (1866) (C) daily; *Leeds Weekly Express* (1857) (L); *Leeds Daily News* (1872) (C); *Leeds Evening Express* (1867) (L) daily.

LEICESTER—*Leicester Journal* (1753) (C) weekly; *Leicester Chronicle* (1810) (L) bi-weekly; *Leicester Advertiser* (1842) (C) weekly; *Midland Free Press* (1855) (L) weekly; *Leicester Daily Post* (1872) (L); *Leicester Daily Mercury* (1874) (L).

LINCOLN—*Lincolnshire Chronicle and General Advertiser* (1832) (I) tri-weekly; *Lincoln Gazette and Times* (1859) (I) bi-weekly.

LIVERPOOL—*Liverpool Courier* (1808) (C), became *Daily Courier* 1863; *Liverpool Mercury* (1811) (L) daily in 1857; *Liverpool Daily Post* (1855) (L); *Liverpool Porcupine* (1858) (I) weekly.

MANCHESTER—*Manchester Guardian* (1821) (L) daily in 1855; *Manchester Courier* (1824) (C) daily in 1861; *Manchester Weekly Times* (1856) (I); *Manchester Evening News* (1868) (I); *Manchester Evening Mail* 1874 (C); *Manchester Sunday Chronicle* (1885) (I) weekly.

NEWCASTLE-ON-TYNE—*Newcastle Courant* (1711) (I) weekly;' *Newcastle Weekly Chronicle* (1764) (I) weekly; *Newcastle Journal* (1832) (C), *Daily Journal* in 1861; *Newcastle Daily Chronicle* (1858) (I); *Newcastle Daily Leader* (1885) (L).

NORTHAMPTON—*Northampton Mercury* (1720) (L) weekly; *Northampton Herald* (1831) (C) weekly; *Northampton Daily Chronicle* (1880) (C); *Northampton Daily Reporter* (1880) (L).

NORWICH—*Norwich Mercury* (1714) (L) weekly; *Norfolk Chronicle* (1761) (C) weekly; *Norwich News* (1845) (L) weekly; *Eastern Daily Press* (1870) (L); *Norfolk Daily Standard* (1885) (C).

NOTTINGHAM—*Nottinghamshire Weekly Express* (1710) (L); *Nottinghamshire Guardian* (1846) (C) weekly; *Nottingham Daily Express* (1860) (L); *Nottingham Daily Guardian* (1861) (C).

OXFORD—*Jackson's Oxford Journal* (1753) (C) weekly; *Oxford Chronicle* (1837) (L) weekly; *Oxford Times* (1862) (C) weekly.

PLYMOUTH—*Plymouth Herald* (I), *Plymouth Journal* (L) and *Plymouth Times* (C), 1820, 1820 and 1832 respectively, all weeklies, expired before the turn of the century. *Western Daily Mercury* (1860) (L); *Western Morning News* (1860) (I) daily.

PORTSMOUTH—*Hampshire Telegraph* (1799) (L) weekly; *Portsmouth Times* (1850) (C) weekly; *Hampshire Post* (1874) (I) weekly; *Evening News* (1877) (L) daily; *Southern Daily Mail* (1884) (C).

SHEFFIELD—*Sheffield Register* (1787) (L) weekly, became *Sheffield Iris* 1794, expired 1848; *Sheffield Mercury* (1807–48) (C) weekly; *Sheffield and Rotherham Independent* (1819) (L) daily in 1861;

Sheffield Daily Telegraph (1855) (C); *Yorkshire Evening Telegraph and Star* (1887) (I) daily.

SOUTHAMPTON—*Hampshire Advertiser* (1823) (C) bi-weekly; *Hampshire Independent* (1835) (I) weekly; *Southampton Times and Hampshire Express* (1860) (L) weekly; *Southampton Observer and Hampshire News* (1867) (C) weekly.

WORCESTER—*Berrow's Worcester Journal* (1690) (C) weekly; *Worcester Herald* (1794) (I) weekly; *Worcester Chronicle* (1838) (L) weekly; *Worcester Daily Times* (1879) (C); *Worcester Echo* (1877) (L) daily.

YORK—*Yorkshire Chronicle* (1772) (I) weekly; *Yorkshire Weekly Herald* (1790) (L) became *Daily Herald* 1874; *Yorkshire Gazette* (1819) (C) weekly; *York Evening Press* (1882) (L) daily.

Wales

BANGOR—*North Wales Chronicle* (1807) (C) weekly.

CARMARTHEN—*Carmarthen Journal* (1810) (C) weekly.

CARNARVON—*Carnarvon Herald* (1831) (L) weekly.

CARDIFF—*Cardiff Times* (1857) (L) weekly; *Western Mail* (1869) (C) daily; *South Wales Daily News* (1872) (L); *Cardiff Evening Express* (1886) (C) daily.

NEWPORT (Mon)—*South Wales Times and Star of Gwent* (1829) (C) weekly; *South Wales Daily Star* (1877) (C); *South Wales Daily Argus* (1892) (L).

SWANSEA—*Cambrian* (1804) (L) weekly; *Herald of Wales* (1847) (I) weekly; *Swansea Journal and South Wales Liberal* (1848) (L) weekly; *Cambria Daily Leader* (1861) (I); *South Wales Daily Post* (1861) (C).

Scotland

ABERDEEN—*Aberdeen Weekly Journal* (1748) (C); *Aberdeen Weekly Free Press* (1806) (L), *Daily* in 1853; *Aberdeen Journal* (1876) (C) daily; *Aberdeen Evening Gazette* (1881) (L) daily.

GLASGOW—*Glasgow Herald* (1782) (I) daily in 1859; *North British Daily Mail* (1847) (L); *Glasgow Weekly Herald* (1864) (I); *The Bailie* (1872) (C) weekly.

DUNDEE—*Dundee Advertiser* (1801) (L) daily in 1861; *Dundee Weekly News* (1855) (L); *Dundee Evening Telegraph* (1877) (L) daily.

EDINBURGH—*Edinburgh Caledonian Mercury* (1660) (L) bi-weekly in 19th century; *Edinburgh Weekly Journal* (*c.* 1744) (C) bi-weekly in 19th century; *Edinburgh Advertiser* (1764) (C) bi-weekly; *Scotsman* (1817) (L) daily in 1855; *Scottish Guardian* (1870) (I) weekly; *Edinburgh Evening News* (1873) (I) daily.

PERTH—*Perthshire Courier* (1809) (I) weekly; *Perthshire Constitutional and Journal* (1832) (C) bi-weekly; *Perthshire Advertiser* (1829) (L) tri-weekly.

N. Ireland

BELFAST—*Belfast News Letter* (1737) (C) daily in 1857; *Belfast Northern Whig* (1824) (L) daily in 1857; *Ulster Echo* (1874) (L) daily; *Belfast Evening Telegraph* (1870) (C) daily.

Newspaper Legislation, Taxes and Prices[1]

Until the middle of the nineteenth century, newspaper proprietors were obliged to pay stamp, advertisement and paper duties. Together they comprised what Radicals criticised as 'taxes on knowledge', resulting in small circulations of expensive newspapers. Their complete abolition by 1861 made possible the cheap, daily provincial newspaper. Three distinct phases are discernible:

(a) To 1836.   The dear, taxed newspaper, and the fight of the 'unstamped'.
        1833 reduction of advertisement duty
        1836 reduction of stamp duty

(b) 1836–55.   Lower tax, lower newspaper prices and increased circulations.
        1853 abolition of advertisement duty
        1855 abolition of stamp duty

N.B. Until *c.* 1855, London had a monopoly of 'dailies'; provincial papers were usually weekly issues.

(c) 1855–1900. The penny daily, large circulations, rise of the provincial daily, morning and evening, and the beginning of the 'popular' press.

Stamp Duty (per paper)		Advertisement Duty (per advertisement)		Paper Duty (per lb.)	
1789–1797	2d.		2s. 6d.		
1797–1815	3½d.		3s. 0d.	1803–1836	3d
1815–1836	4d.	1815–1833	3s. 6d.		
1836–1855	1d.	1833–1853	1s. 6d.	1836–1861	1½d.
1855	*Abolished* 1852		*Abolished*	1861	*Abolished*

Effect on Prices

The Times	1821	7d.	1861	3d.
The Guardian		7d.		1d.

[1]Based on A. P. Wadsworth (see bibliography).

Newspaper Circulations

Statistics of any reliability are almost impossible to come by for the nineteenth-century press. Stamp returns to 1855 provide clues for general approximations only, while the later claims of editors are always suspect of the salesman's exaggerations. A general assessment is here given, based on the various sources listed in the bibliography.

(a) 1800–1850. London daily papers averaging 2,500 per day.
London weekly papers ranging between 25,000 and 100,000 per week.
Provincial weekly papers averaging 1,000–3,000 per week at least.

(b) 1850–1900. London daily papers reaching $\frac{1}{2}$ million mark per day by 1900.
London weekly papers reaching the 1 million mark per issue.
Provincial daily papers ranging between 20,000 and 50,000 per day.

N.B. The highest figures are given; many papers, especially in the provinces, had much smaller circulations.

BIBLIOGRAPHY

No attempt has been made in this survey to cover the radical presses, particularly the famous 'unstamped'. Sources marked thus * below, should be consulted for this information.

A. Andrews, *The History of British Journalism*, 2 vols. (London, 1859)

*A. Aspinall, *Politics and the Press, 1780–1850* (London, 1949)
'The Circulation of English Newspapers in the Early Nineteenth Century', *Review of English Studies*, XII (1946)
'The Social Standing of Journalists at the Beginning of the Nineteenth Century', ibid. (July 1945)

H. R. Fox-Bourne, *English Newspapers*, 2 vols. (London, 1887)

J. Grant, *The Newspaper Press*, 3 vols., (London, 1871–2)

W. Hindle, *The Morning Post, 1772–1937* (London, 1937)

*P. Hollis, *The Pauper Press* (O.U.P., 1970)

H. W. Massingham, *The London Daily Press* (London, 1892)

S. Morison, *The English Newspaper, 1622–1932* (Cambridge, 1932)

C. Peabody, *English Journalism and the Men who Have Made It* (London, 1882)

D. Read, *Press and People, 1790–1850* (London, 1960)

*J. H. Rose, 'The Unstamped Press, 1815–1836', *English Historical Review*, XII (1897)

The Times, *History of the Times*, 5 vols.

A. P. Wadsworth, 'Newspaper Circulations, 1800–1954', *Transactions of the Manchester Statistical Society* (1954–5)

*W. H. Wickwar, *The Struggle for the Freedom of the Press, 1819–1832* (London, 1928)

DIRECTORIES

C. Mitchell, *Newspaper Press Directories, 1846–1900* (London)

Street, *Newspaper Directory, 1899* (London)

13 Religion

Introductory Note

Statistics of religious practice have customarily received a bad press, often being dismissed by historians and sociologists as too unreliable to be useful. While in some cases this attitude appears to be based simply upon a prejudice against the ecclesiastical character of the data, in others it rests upon more substantive grounds. Until the beginning of the present century, in certain denominations, the returns from which published statistics were abstracted were often incomplete, and there has always been scope for error or exaggeration at several stages in the collection and collation of the material. These deficiencies clearly invalidate any uncritical use of the religious statistics presented in the following tables, but they are deficiencies which are equally characteristic of much of the secular statistical evidence about nineteenth-century society. Taken as a whole, religious statistics of the nineteenth century are neither distinctly more nor distinctly less reliable than other types of statistical data about the period. They do, however, vary considerably from denomination to denomination in accuracy and completeness. Methodist membership figures constitute some of the earliest and most reliable statistical series available to students of British society: tightly-knit connectional organisation was a guarantee of virtual completeness, and Methodist polity, by providing for the quarterly review of commitment among members, also ensured a minimum of distortion due to merely nominal attachment. But even within religious traditions much less statistically oriented than Methodism, figures were compiled and published which (examined in the context of other forms of evidence) can add significantly to the understanding of nineteenth-century religion and society.

Despite the comprehensive and careful survey of religious facilities and religious behaviour during the Government's Census of Religious Worship in 1851, the most useful indices of religious practice remain the official statistics published by the Churches and denominations themselves. The very uniqueness of the 1851 Census was one of its limitations. There has been no subsequent nationwide survey of religious attendance with which to compare it. Denominational series, in contrast, can be linked in time series. In many cases the following tables summarise on a decennial basis annual time

217

series which can be used for the fairly precise analysis of trends of religious growth.[1] While definitions of membership are too varied for the data of one organisation to be compared on any absolute basis with those of many other bodies, growth trends often can be compared. It is noteworthy (to take a single example) that the sharp rise in the number of Anglican churches and resident clergy around 1840 coincided with a definite deceleration of Methodist, Congregational and Baptist growth in England. The figures reflect an important aspect of the relationship between Establishment and Noncontormist worship in the nineteenth century, and one which would be much less easily perceived or documented on the basis of non-quantitative evidence.

The sources acknowledged in connection with the tables constitute the basic sources of nineteenth-century religious statistics. Other contemporary surveys of religious practice include: C. Booth, *Life and Labour of the People in London*, 3rd Series, *Religious Influences* (London, 1902); British Weekly, *Religious Census of London* (London, 1886); A. Hume, *Remarks on the Census of Religious Worship for England and Wales, with Suggestions for an Improved Census in 1861, and a Map Illustrating the Religious Condition of the Country* (London, 1860); A. Mearns, *The Statistics of Attendance at Public Worship, 1881–82* (London, 1882); R. Mudie-Smith, *The Religious Life of London* (London, 1904); and J. Rankin, *A Handbook of the Church of Scotland* (Edinburgh, 1888).

The important secondary sources on nineteenth-century religion include: D. H. Akenson, *The Church of Ireland* (Yale U.P., 1971); C. K. Francis Brown, *A History of the English Clergy, 1800–1900* (London, 1953); S. C. Carpenter (*Church and People, 1789–1889* (London, 1933); O. Chadwick, *The Victorian Church*, 2 vols. (London, 1966, 1970); R. Currie, *Methodism Divided* (London, 1968); J. R. Fleming, *A History of the Church in Scotland, 1843–1874* and *1875–1929* (Edinburgh, 1927 and 1933); J. D. Gay, *The Geography of Religion in England* (London, 1971); R. T. Jones, *Congregationalism in England* (London, 1962); J. D. Walsh and G. V. Bennett (eds.), *Essays in Modern Church History* (London, 1966); and E. J. Watkins, *Roman Catholicism in England from the Reformation to 1950* (Oxford, 1957).

[1]With Dr R. Currie, of Wadham College, Oxford, the authors are engaged in a 'Statistical Survey of Religion in Britain since 1700', a project supported by the Social Sciences Research Council and designed to collect and analyse all available quantitative evidence about religion in modern Britain. The results of the research will be published in due course.

Some Major Events in Nineteenth-Century Religious History

1828   Repeal of Test and Corporation Acts
1829   Catholic Emancipation
1831   Formation of Congregational Union of England and Wales
1836   Ecclesiastical Commission; Tithe Commutation Act
1838   Pluralities Act and (1838–9) Church Building Acts
1843   New Parishes Act ('Peel's Act'); 'Disruption' in Scotland (Free Church of Scotland formed)
1845   Newman joins Catholic Church
1847   United Presbyterian Church of Scotland formed
1849   Wesleyan schism precipitated by expulsions from Conference
1850   Catholic Hierarchy restored in England
1859   C. Darwin, *Origin of Species*; 1859–60: Widespread Revivals
1868   Church Rates abolished
1871   Irish Disestablishment
1876   Presbyterian Church of England formed
1880   Burials Act
1888   Lambeth Quadrilateral
1900   Free Church of Scotland and United Presbyterian Church of Scotland unite

TABLE 1

Marriages by Manner of Solemnisation in England and Wales, 1844–1901

Year	All Marriages	Church of England	Catholic Church	Other Sects	Civil Marriages
1844	132,249	120,009	2,280	6,515	3,446
1851	154,206	130,958	6,570	9,865	6,813
1861	168,627	135,902	7,769	13,667	11,289
1871	190,112	144,663	7,647	19,424	18,468
1881	197,290	140,995	8,784	22,456	25,055
1891	226,526	158,439	9,517	27,761	30,629
1901	259,400	172,769	10,624	35,030	41,067

SOURCE: *Annual Reports of the Registrar-General of Births, Deaths and Marriages in England and Wales.*

TABLE 2

Marriages by Manner of Solemnisation in Scotland, 1855–1901

Year	All Marriages	Church of Scotland	Free Church of Scotland	United Presbyterian Church	Catholic Church	Episcopal Church	Other Churches	Civil Marriages
1855	19,680	8,879	4,665	2,952	1,826	350	999	9
1861	20,896	9,332	4,969	2,925	1,806	386	1,453	25
1871	24,019	10,985	5,404	3,325	2,087	551	1,562	105
1881	26,004	12,179	5,402	3,088	2,537	695	1,684	419
1891	27,696	12,698	5,415	3,207	2,692	788	2,050	1,119
1901	31,387	14,167	8,669		3,184	942	2,473	1,952

NOTE: The Free Church and the United Presbyterian Church merged in 1900 to form the United Free Church.

SOURCE: *Annual Reports of the Registrar-General of Births, Deaths and Marriages in Scotland.*

TABLE 3

Attendance at Religious Worship in England and Wales, 31 March 1851

Religious Organisations	Places of Worship	Number of Sittings	Attendants		
			Morning	Afternoon	Evening
Church of England	14,077	4,922,412	2,371,732	1,764,641	803,141
Presbyterians	160	83,863	46,744	9,236	23,084
Congregationalists	3,244	1,002,507	515,071	228,060	448,847
Baptists	2,789	705,663	353,061	219,407	337,614
Wesleyans	6,579	1,361,443	482,753	376,202	654,349
New Connection Methodists	297	91,716	36,428	22,391	39,222
Primitive Methodists	2,871	369,216	98,001	172,684	229,646
Bible Christians	482	60,341	14,655	24,002	34,038
Wesleyan Meth. Association	419	90,789	31,922	20,888	40,170
Wesleyan Reformers	339	57,126	30,018	15,841	44,286
Quakers	371	89,551	14,016	6,458	1,459
Unitarians	229	63,770	27,612	8,610	12,406
Calvanistic Methodists	828	198,242	79,728	59,140	125,224
Catholics	570	164,664	240,792	51,406	73,232
Total	34,467	9,467,738	4,428,338	3,030,280	2,960,772

NOTES: 1. The Calvinistic Methodist Connection subsequently adopted the title 'The Presbyterian Church of Wales'. Its members were not regarded as 'Presbyterians' for the purposes of the Census.

        2. The totals (above) include not only the organisations listed, but also numerous small bodies and isolated congregations.

SOURCE: 'Report on the 1851 Census of Religious Worship', *Parliamentary Papers* (1852–3), LXXXIX, Table A, pp. clxxviii–clxxix.

TABLE 4

Attendance at Religious Worship in Scotland, 1851–1891

Year	Church of Scotland	Free Church of Scotland	United Presbyterian Church	Other Protestant Churches	Catholic Church	All Denominations
1851	351,454	292,308	159,191	97,120	43,878	943,951
1876	377,179	262,466	147,048	94,017	61,732	942,442
1881	318,106	255,290	135,968	95,630	64,904	870,528
1891	265,451	236,806	119,768	96,318	55,381	773,724

NOTE: The figures are for the best-attended services in each place of worship.
SOURCES: 'Report on the 1851 Census of Religious Worship: Scotland', *Parliamentary Papers* (1854) LIX 301–46; R. Howie, *The Churches and Churchless in Scotland: Facts and Figures* (Glasgow, 1893) p. 118.

TABLE 5

Professed Religious Adherence in Ireland, 1834–1901

(Irish Census Returns)

Year	Total Population	Catholics	Church of Ireland	Presbyterians	All Other Denominations
1834	7,954	6,436	853	643	22
1861	5,799	4,505	693	523	77
1871	5,412	4,151	668	498	96
1881	5,175	3,961	640	471	104
1891	4,705	3,550	601	447	112'
1901	4,459	3,309	581	443	126

NOTES: 1. The above figures are in 000's.
   2. The 1834 figure for other denominations excludes, and the figures for 1861–1901 include, Methodists.
   3. The 1834 figure for total population represents 'Total of Abstract' (the total population in Ireland according to the Census of 1841 was 8,175,238).
SOURCE: *Parliamentary Papers* (1863) LIX, (1902) CXXIX.

TABLE 6

Irish Priests and Clergymen: Parliamentary Returns, 1851–1901

Year	Roman Catholic	Church of Ireland
1851	2,464	1,786
1861	3,014	2,265
1871	3,136	2,221
1881	3,363	1,828
1891	3,502	1,734
1901	3,711	1,617

SOURCE: *Parliamentary Papers* (1856) XXXI, (1863) LIX, (1882) LXXVI, (1902) CXXIX.

TABLE 7
The Church of England, 1831–1901

		Clergy of the Church of England				
Year	Churches and Chapels	Resident	Non-resident	Curates	Estimated Total	Easter Day Communicants
1831	11,883	4,649	4,983	4,373	14,005	–
1841	12,668	6,699	3,736	4,743	15,178	–
1851	14,077	8,077	2,952	4,935	16,194	–
1861	14,731	–	–	–	17,966	–
1871	15,522	–	–	5,500	19,411	–
1881	16,300	12,495	1,063	6,150	20,341	–
1891	16,956	12,770	1,008	6,557	22,753	1,490,000
1901	17,368	–	–	7,059	23,670	1,945,000

NOTES: 1. Figures for estimated total clergy 1851–1901 include, as well as curates, a small proportion of unbeneficed clergy.
2. Figures for churches and chapels 1881–1901 are estimates based on data relating to church building.
3. Figures for 1881 (above) on resident and non-resident clergy and curates relate to 1883.
4. On Easter Day 1885 there were 1,384,000 communicants at Anglican services.
SOURCES: *Parliamentary Papers*; *Convocation of Canterbury Report, 1876*; *Church of England Yearbooks*; *Facts and Figures about the Church of England*; J. J. Halcombe (ed.), *The Church and her Curates* (1874).

Archbishops of Canterbury and York and Bishops of London, 1831–1901

Archbishops of Canterbury

1828	William Howley
1848	John Bird Sumner
1862	Charles Thomas Longley
1868	Archibald Campbell Tait
1883	Edward White Benson
1897	Frederick Temple (to 1902)

Archbishops of York

1807	Vernon Harcourt
1847	Thomas Musgrave
1860	Charles Thomas Longley

1862	William Thomson
1891	William Connor Magee
1891	W. D. Maclagan (to 1908)

Bishops of London

1828	Charles James Blomfield
1856	Archibald Campbell Tait
1868	John Jackson
1885	Frederick Temple
1897	Mandell Creighton (to 1901)

TABLE 8
The Episcopal Church in Scotland, 1851–1901

Year	Clergy	Members	Communicants
1851	137	–	–
1855	165	38,113	14,234
1861	162	–	–
1871	190	–	
1881	240	70,847	–
1891	276	91,740	35,593
1901	361	127,093	46,922

SOURCES: *Annual Reports of the Representative Church Council of the Episcopal Church in Scotland*; *Scottish Ecclesiastical Journal* (Dec 1856); *Reports of the Scottish Episcopal Church Society*.

TABLE 9
**The Catholic Church in England and
Wales, 1840–1901**

Year	Estimated Catholic Population	Churches and Chapels	Priests
1840	700,000	469	–
1851	900,000	597	826
1861	1,250,000	798	1,177
1871	–	947	1,551
1881	1,353,575	1,175	1,979
1891	1,357,000	1,387	2,604
1901	–	1,536	3,298

SOURCES: *Catholic Directory*; H. Thurston, 'Statistical Progress of the Catholic Church', *Catholic Emancipation, 1829 to 1929* (London, 1929); *The Month*, no. 59 (Feb 1887).

TABLE 10
**The Catholic Church in Scotland,
1827–1901**

Year	Estimated Catholic Population	Churches and Chapels	Priests
1827	70,000	–	–
1841	–	66	81
1851	–	97	118
1861	–	195	165
1871	310,789	222	207
1881	321,008	286	301
1891	352,749	329	351
1901	432,900	351	476

SOURCES: The figure for 1827 is from *The Irish National Almanack for 1851*; the figure for estimated Catholic population for 1871, which relates to 1876, is from Howie, *Churches and Churchless*; all other figures are from *Catholic Directories for the Clergy and Laity in Scotland*.

TABLE 11
**The Church of Scotland,
1833–1901**

Year	Congregations	Communicants
1833	1,067	–
1841	1,210	–
1851	1,183	–
1868	1,254	422,357
1871	–	436,147
1881	1,587	528,475
1891	1,696	599,531
1901	1,780	661,629

NOTES: 1. At the 'Disruption' of 1843 the number of
congregations adhering was 754.

2. Figures for congregations for 1881 and 1901
relate to 1884 and 1898 respectively.

SOURCES: *Church of Scotland Magazine*, I (1834); *Church of
Scotland: Assembly Papers*; *Yearbooks of the Church of Scotland*.

TABLE 12
The Free Church of Scotland, 1844–1901

Year	Churches	Clergy	Members and Gaelic Adherents	Sunday School Scholars
1844	621	583	–	50,472
1851	837	736	198,941	99,090
1863	904	885	245,210	116,778
1876	984	1,014	263,520	135,695
1881	1,052	1,097	312,429	152,101
1891	1,089	1,169	337,331	164,954
1896	1,107	1,163	287,612	160,054

NOTES: 1. In 1876 almost all 'Cameronians' (Reformed Presbyterians) joined
the Free Church. The *Reformed Presbyterian Magazine* had stated
their membership as 7,134 in 1874.

2. The membership figure given for 1851 relates to 1848.

SOURCES: Free Church of Scotland, *Proceedings and Debates*; Howie, *Churches
and Churchless*; *Original Secession Magazine*.

TABLE 13
The United Presbyterian Church of Scotland, 1856–1901

Year	Congregations	Communicants
1856	449	142,956
1861	474	154,037
1871	503	163,030
1881	551	174,557
1891	571	185,298
1896	580	194,463

NOTE: The United Presbyterian Church was formed in 1847 by the union of the United Secession Church with the Relief Church of 1761. In 1900 it merged with the Free Church (see Table 11) to form the United Free Church of Scotland. Figures given are for Scotland only (i.e. they do not include the English congregations which withdrew from membership in 1876, the year of English Union).

SOURCE: *Proceedings of the Synod of the United Presbyterian Church.*

TABLE 14
The Presbyterian Church of England, 1876–1901

Year	Congregations	Communicants	Elders	Sunday School Scholars
1876	258	46,540	1,291	45,741
1881	275	56,399	1,593	64,830
1891	290	66,774	1,900	79,697
1901	326	78,024	2,303	81,967

NOTES: 1. The Presbyterian Church of England was formed in 1876 from a union of the Presbyterian Church in England (which was in association with the Church of Scotland) and the English Synod of the United Presbyterian Church of Scotland. These bodies, which had been set up in the 1830s mainly by Scottish emigrés, had attracted remnants of the earlier indigenous English Presbyterianism (which had virtually disappeared by the early nineteenth century). From a combined membership of fewer than 10,000 in 1838, they expanded to have about 15,000 members between them in 1851, 27,000 in 1860, and 38,000 in 1870.
2. The term 'communicants' frequently was used interchangeably with 'members' in the official records of the Church.

SOURCE: *Minutes of the Synod of the Presbyterian Church of England.*

TABLE 15
The Presbyterian Church of Wales, 1838–1901

Year	Churches	Ministers	Communicants	Adherents
1835	427	–	37,576	106,750
1851	828	–	52,600	–
1861	–	–	90,560	–
1871	1,050	449	93,276	245,316
1881	1,179	610	119,355	274,605
1891	1,271	687	137,415	288,185
1901	1,374	834	160,333	323,951

NOTES: 1. 'Adherents' includes 'Communicants'.
2. The figure for communicants for 1851 relates to 1848.
SOURCES: *The Record*, 26 Sep 1839; *Protestant Dissenters' Almanack* (1849); T. Rees, *History of Protestant Nonconformity in Wales*, 2nd ed., (1883); *Blwyddiadur y Methodistiaid Calfinaidd* (for all data from 1871).

TABLE 16
The Presbyterian Church of Ireland, 1840–1901

Year	Congregations	Ministers	Communicants
1840	433	430	185,000
1870	551	627	123,441
1881	560	626	103,548
1891	558	637	102,735
1901	573	662	106,070

NOTE: Presbyterianism, established in Ireland with the plantation of 1610, was concentrated largely in Ulster.
SOURCES: J. M. Barkley, *A Short History of the Presbyterian Church in Ireland* (Belfast, 1959); *Reports of Proceedings of the ... General Presbyterian Council*.

TABLE 17
**Wesleyan Methodism in Great Britain,
1831–1901**

Year	Ministers	Members	Sunday School Scholars
1831	736	249,119	–
1841	978	328,792	–
1850	1,217	358,277	–
1861	918	319,782	536,313
1871	1,251	347,090	638,606
1881	1,510	380,956	829,666
1891	1,588	424,220	938,372
1901	1,675	454,982	965,057

NOTES: 1. 'Ministers' excludes probationers and super-
numeraries.
2. The Wesleyan Connection lost an estimated
100,000 members in the early 1850s through
schism. Membership was 302,209 in 1851 and
260,858 in 1855.
3. The figure for Sunday School scholars for 1861
is an 1863 figure.
SOURCE: *Minutes of Wesleyan Methodist Conference.*

TABLE 18
**Wesleyan Methodist Membership in England, Wales,
Scotland and Ireland, 1831–1901**

Year	England	Wales	Scotland	Ireland
1831	232,883	12,842	3,962	22,470
1841	305,682	19,287	3,823	27,268
1851	334,458	19,720	4,099	21,107
1861	291,288	24,025	4,469	23,551
1871	319,495	22,139	5,456	20,005
1881	349,695	26,365	4,896	24,237
1891	387,779	29,762	6,679	25,365
1901	412,194	34,411	8,191	27,745

NOTE: The figures for 1851 (above) relate to 1850.
SOURCE: *Minutes of Wesleyan Methodist Conference, Minutes of the Methodist Church in Ireland.*

TABLE 19

Membership of Major Non-Wesleyan Methodist Bodies, 1831–1901

Year	Bible Christians	Methodist New Connection	Primitive Methodist Connection	United Methodist Free Churches	Wesleyan Methodist Association	Wesleyan Reformers
1831	6,650	11,433	37,216			
1841	11,353	20,506	75,967		22,074	
1851	13,324	16,962	106,074		20,557	45,000
1861	16,866	22,732	127,772	52,970		
1871	18,050	22,870	148,597	61,924		
1881	21,209	25,797	169,422	65,067		
1891	25,608	28,756	181,167	67,200		
1901	28,315	32,324	188,683	72,568		

NOTES: 1. The figures relate to Great Britain, although each body was concentrated overwhelmingly in England.

2. The Wesleyan Methodist Association, which broke away from the Wesleyan Connection in 1837, and the Wesleyan Reformers, who seceded after the Conference expelled leading ministers in 1849, merged in 1857 to form the United Methodist Free Churches.

SOURCE: *Minutes* of the various Conferences.

TABLE 20

Congregationalism in England, 1830–1900

Year	Churches	Members
1830	1,141	–
1840	1,323	135,000
1850	1,465	165,000
1860	1,607	180,000
1870	1,845	–
1880	2,013	190,000
1890	3,413	–
1900	3,326	257,435

NOTES: 1. The membership figure for 1840 has been extrapolated from the 1838 membership; the figure for 1860 relates to 1863.

2. Congregationalism lost congregations and members to the resurgent English Presbyterianism during the 1860s and 1870s.

3. The figures for churches for 1890 and 1900 include, and the earlier figures exclude, branch churches.

SOURCES: *Congregational Year Books*; *The Record*, 26 Sep 1839; *Protestant Dissenters' Almanacks*.

TABLE 21

Congregationalism in Wales, 1815–1901

Year	Churches	Members
1815		23,600
1838		43,000
1848		60,000
1861	636	97,647
1870	878	–
1882	883	116,618
1890	1,010	130,112
1901	1,255	149,778

NOTE: The figures on churches for 1890 and 1901 include, and the earlier figures exclude, branch churches.

SOURCES: 'Report of Royal Commission of 1906 on the Church of England in Wales', *Parliamentary Papers* (1910) XIX 153; *Protestant Dissenters' Almanack*; *Congregational Year Books*.

TABLE 22

Congregationalism in Scotland and Ireland, 1861–1901

Year	Scotland		Ireland	
	Churches	Ministers	Churches	Ministers
1861	101	–	30	–
1871	102	107	28	25
1881	103	121	31	20
1891	101	109	29	27
1901	208	200	44	29

NOTE: The figures for 1901 include branch churches under 'churches', and retired ministers and ministers without pastoral charge under 'ministers'.

SOURCE: *Congregational Year Books*.

TABLE 23
Baptist Churches in England and Wales, 1833–1900

Year	Churches	Ministers	Membership		
			England	Wales	Total
1832	1,240		70,000	20,000	90,000
1838	1,426		100,000	25,000	125,000
1851			140,000	35,000	175,000
1863	2,268		153,000	51,085	204,000
1870	2,421	1,670	170,380	60,000	230,000
1880	2,453	1,805	200,713	80,500	281,000
1890	2,673	1,767	225,000	91,479	316,000
1900	2,611	1,902	239,114	106,566	346,000

NOTES: 1. The figures aggregate Particular and New Connection General Baptist data. The two bodies merged in the Baptist Union in 1891.
2. Statistical returns to the Baptist Union were never comprehensive during the nineteenth century. The above figures for Wales for 1851, 1870 and 1880, and for England for 1890, have been extrapolated from incomplete returns.
3. The figures for churches for 1832 include an estimate for Welsh Baptist churches. There were 1,042 English Baptist churches in 1832.
SOURCES: *Baptist Magazine*; *The Record*, 26 Sep 1839; *Baptist Hand-Books*; *General Baptist Hand Books*; *Protestant Dissenters' Almanack*.

TABLE 24
Baptist Churches in Scotland and Ireland

	Scotland		Ireland	
Year	Churches and Chapels	Members	Churches and Chapels	Members
1868	208	6,855	66	1,354
1871	220	8,873	75	1,434
1882	196	9,875	58	1,521
1891	233	12,304	56	1,847
1901	268	17,266	64	2,649

SOURCE: *The Baptist Handbook.*

TABLE 25

Year	Unitarians Ministers	Society of Friends (Quakers) Members	Moravian Brethren Members	Churches of Christ Members	Salvation Army Corps Outposts and Societies	Mormon Church Members
1837	–	–	5,000			600
1841	–	16,277	–	1,300		5,814
1851	–	–	4,955	2,081		32,894
1856	320	14,530	5,133	2,103		22,502
1866	339	13,786	5,500	3,616		10,782
1876	357	14,441	5,604	4,903	29	5,408
1881	355	15,113	5,515	6,451	251	5,180
1886	–	15,453	5,647	7,672	1,006	3,588
1891	350	16,102	5,541	9,511	1,213	2,875
1896	354	16,674	5,866	10,834	1,375	2,726
1901	368	17,476	5,950	12,224	1,431	4,487

NOTES: 1. The figure for the Moravian Brethren for 1837 relates to 1835.
2. Corps, outposts, and societies in the Salvation Army are centres of work.
3. The figure for the Salvation Army for 1876 relates to 1877 (May) and that for 1891 to 1893.
4. Mormon losses during the second half of the nineteenth century resulted largely from migration to the United States.

SOURCES: *Whitaker's Almanack*; *Fraternal Messenger* (Moravian); *The Moravian Almanack*; *Protestant Dissenters' Almanack*; *Extracts from the Minutes of the London Yearly Meeting of Friends*; *Churches of Christ Yearbook and Annual Report*; R. Sandall, *The History of the Salvation Army*, vol. II. (London, 1950); *Salvation Army Yearbook*; data on the Church of Jesus Christ of Latter-day Saints (Mormons) supplied by the Official Archivist of the Church, Salt Lake City, Utah, U.S.A.

14   Population

England and Wales

| Year | Population | | | Increase in Decennial Period | Number of Families | Average Number of Persons in each Family | Number of Inhabited Houses |
	Males	Females¶	Total				
1801	4,254,735	4,637,801	8,892,536	–	1,896,723	4.69	1,575,923
1811	4,873,605	5,290,651	10,164,256	1,271,720	2,142,147	4.74	1,797,504
1821	5,850,319	6,149,917	12,000,236	1,835,980	2,493,423	4·81	2,088,156
1831	6,771,196	7,125,601	13,896,797	1,896,561	2,911,874	4·77	2,481,544
1841	7,777,586	8,136,562	15,914,148	2,017,351	Not stated	Not stated	2,943,945
1851	8,781,225	9,146,384	17,927,609	2,013,461	3,712,290	4·83	3,278,039
1861	9,776,259	10,289,965	20,066,224	2,138,615	4,491,524	4·47	3,739,505
1871	11,058,934	11,653,332	22,712,266	2,646,042	5,049,016	4·50	4,259,117
1881	12,639,002	13,334,537	25,974,439	3,262,173	5,633,192	4·61	4,831,519
1891	14,052,001	14,949,624	29,002,525	3,028,086	6,131,001	4·73	5,451,497
1901	15,728,613	16,799,230	32,527,843	3,525,318	7,036,868	4·62	6,260,852

Scotland

Year	Males	Females	Total	Increase	Families	Average	Houses
1801	739,091	869,329	1,608,420	–	364,079	4·42	294,553
1811	826,296	979,568	1,805,864	197,444	402,068	4·49	304,093
1821	982,623	1,108,898	2,091,521	285,657	447,960	4.67	341,474
1831	1,114,456	1,249,930	2,364,386	272,865	502,301	4·71	369,393
1841	1,241,862	1,378,322	2,620,184	255,798	550,428	4·76	–
1851	1,375,479	1,513,263	2,888,742	268,558	600,098	4·81	370,308
1861	1,449,848	1,612,446	3,062,294	173,552	678,584	4·51	393,220
1871	1,603,143	1,756,875	3,360,018	297,724	740,748	4·54	412,185
1881	1,799,475	1,936,098	3,735,573	375,555	812,712	4·60	§739,005
1891	1,942,717	2,082,930	4,025,647	290,074	876,089	4·59	§817,568
1901	2,173,755	2,298,348	4,472,103	446,456	967,200	4·62	§926,914

Ireland

Year	Males	Females	Total	Increase	Families	Average	Houses
1801	–	–	*5,395,000	–	–	–	–
1811	–	–	*5,937,000	–	–	–	–
1821	3,341,926	3,459,901	6,891,827	–	1,312,032	5·18	1,142,602
1831	3,794,880	3,972,521	7,767,401	965,574	1,385,066	5·61	1,249,816
1841	4,041,049	4,155,548	8,196,597	429,196	1,472,739	5·57	1,328,839
1851	3,212,523	3,361,755	6,574,278	1,622,319	1,204,319	5·44	1,046,233
1861	2,837,370	2,961,597	5,798,967	775,311	1,128,300	5·14	995,156
1871	2,639,753	2,772,624	5,412,377	386,590	1,067,598	5·07	961,389
1881	2,533,277	2,641,559	5,174,836	237,541	995,074	5·20	914,108
1891	2,318,953	2,385,797	4,704,750	470,086	932,113	5·05	870,578
1901	2,200,040	2,258,735	4,458,775	245,975	910,256	4·90	858,158

†United Kingdom

1801	–	–	15,895,956	–	–	–	–
1811	–	–	17,907,120	–	–	–	–
1821	10,174,863	10,718,716	20,893,584	–	4,253,415	4·91	3,572,232
1831	11,680,532	12,348,052	24,028,584	3,135,000	4,799,241	5·01	4,100,753
1841	13,060,497	13,670,432	26,730,929	2,702,345	Not stated	Not stated	–
1851	13,369,227	14,021,402	27,396,629	659,700	5,516,707	4·97	4,694,570
1861	14,063,477	14,864,008	28,927,485	1,536,856	6,298,408	4·59	5,127,881
1871	15,301,830	16,182,831	31,484,661	2,557,176	6,857,362	4·59	5,632,682
1881	16,972,654	17,912,194	34,884,848	3,400,187	7,440,978	4·69	§6,484,632
1891	18,314,571	19,418,351	37,732,922	2,848,074	7,939,203	4·75	§7,139,643
1901	20,102,408	21,356,313	41,458,721	3,725,799	8,914,324	4·65	§6,045,924

NOTE. The figures in the above table are exclusive of the Army and Navy for the years up to 1831, inclusive.

*Approximate.

†Exclusive of the Isle of Man and Channel Islands.

¶The excess in the number of females is partially attributable to the fact that men serving in the Army, Navy, and the Merchant Service, abroad, are excluded from the reckoning.

§A different method of arriving at the number of houses in Scotland from that previously used was adopted in 1881. In that year and at the subsequent enumerations every dwelling with a distinct outside entrance, or with a door opening directly into a common stair, was treated as a house.

Population of the Principal Towns ('000s)

	1801	1811	1821	1831	1841	1851	1851	1861	1861	1871	1871	1881	1881	1891	1891	1901	1901
Aberdeen	27	35	44	57	63	72	72	74	74	88	88	105	106	125	125	154	154
Bath	33	38	47	51	53	54	54	53	53	53	53	52	52	52	52	50	50
Belfast	—	—	37	53	70	87	87	122	122	174	174	208	208	256	273	349	349
Birkenhead	—	—	—	3	8	24	25	38	38	45	66	84	84	100	100	111	111
Birmingham	71	83	102	144	183	233	233	296	296	344	344	401	437	478	478	522	523
environs of Birmingham later incorporated (b)	—	—	—	—	—	—	—	—	—	91	91	145	—	156	156	238	238
Blackburn	12	15	22	27	37	47	47	63	63	76	83(a)	101	104	120	120	128	129
Blackpool	—	1	1	1	2	3	3	4	4	6	—	14	14	24	24	47	47
Bolton	18	25	32	42	51	61	61	70	70	83	—	105	105	115	156	168	168
Bournemouth	—	—	—	—	—	—	—	—	—	6	—	—	19	38	38	47	47
Bradford	13	16	26	44	67	104	104	106	106	146	147	183	194	216	266	280	280
Brighton	7	12	24	41	47	66	66	78	78	90	93(a)	108	108	116	116	123	123
Bristol	61	71	85	104	124	137	137	154	154	183	183	207	207	222	289	329	339
Cambridge	10	11	14	21	24	28	28	26	26	30	30	35	35	37	37	38	38
Cardiff	2	2	4	6	10	18	18	33	33	40	57	83	83	129	129	164	164
Carlisle	9	11	14	19	22	26	26	29	29	31	31	36	37	39	39	45	45
Chester	15	16	20	21	24	28	28	31	31	35	35	37	37	37	37	38	38
Colchester	12	13	14	16	18	19	19	24	24	26	26	28	28	35	35	38	38
Coventry	16	18	21	27	31	36	36	41	41	38	38	42	45	53	59	70	70
Derby	11	13	17	24	33	41	41	43	43	50	61	81	81	94	94	106	115
Dudley	10	14	18	23	31	38	38	45	45	44	44	46	46	46	46	49	49
Dundee	26	30	31	45	63	79	79	90	91	119	119	140	140	154	154	161	161
Edinburgh (including Leith)	83	103	138	162	166	194	202	203	203	242	244	295	295	332	342	394	395
Exeter	17	19	23	28	31	33	33	34	34	35	35	38	37	37	46	47	47
Gateshead	9	9	12	15	20	26	26	34	34	49	49	66	66	86	86	110	112
Glasgow	77	101	147	202	275	345	357	420	420	522	522	587	587	658	658	762	776
environs of Glasgow later incorporated (c)	—	—	—	—	—	—	—	23	23	46	46	86	86	108	108	142	142
Greenock	17	19	22	27	36	37	37	43	43	58	58	67	67	63	63	68	68
Halifax	12	13	17	22	28	34	34	37	47(a)	66	66	74	81	90	98	105	105
Huddersfield	7	10	13	19	25	31	31	35	35	61	70	82	87	95	95	95	95
Hull	30	37	45	52	67	85	85	98	98	122	122	154	166	200	200	240	240

Ipswich	11	11	17	20	25	33	33	38	38	43	43	51	51	57	57	67	67
King's Lynn	10	14	12	13	16	19	19	16	16	17	17	19	19	18	18	20	20
Leeds	53	63	84	123	152	172	172	207	207	259	259	309	309	368	368	429	429
Leicester	17	19	26	41	53	61	61	68	68	95	95	122	137	175	175	212	212
Liverpool	82	104	138	202	286	376	376	444	444	493	493	553	553	518	630	685	704
environs of Liverpool later incorporated (d)	–	–	–	8	13	19	19	28	28	47	47	74	74	113	–	–	–
Luton	–	–	3	4	6	11	11	15	15	17	–	24	24	30	30	36	36
Macclesfield	11	15	21	30	33	39	39	36	36	35	35	38	38	36	36	35	35
Manchester	75	89	126	182	235	303	303	339	339	351	351	341	462	505	505	544	645
environs of Manchester	–	7	9	12	17	26	29	43	43	57	57	95	–	–	–	–	–
environs of Manchester later incorporated (f)	–	–	–	–	–	9	9	17	17	36	36	66	–	70	70	101	–
Middlesbrough	–	–	–	–	6	8	8	19	19	40	40(a)	55	55	76	76	91	91
Newcastle-upon-Tyne	33	33	42	54	70	88	88	109	109	128	128	145	145	186	186	215	247
Newport (Mon.)	–	–	–	–	10	19	19	23	23	27	27	35	38	55	55	67	67
Northampton	7	8	11	15	21	27	27	33	33	41	41	52	52	61	75	87	87
Norwich	36	37	50	61	62	68	68	75	75	80	80	88	88	101	101	112	114
Nottingham	29	34	40	50	52	57	57	75	75	87	139(a)	187	187	214	214	240	240
Oldham	12	17	22	32	43	53	53	72	72	83	83	111	111	131	131	137	137
Oxford	12	13	16	21	24	28	28	28	28	31	31	35	41	46	46	49	49
Paisley	25	29	38	46	48	48	48	47	47	48	48	56	56	66	66	79	79
Plymouth (including Devonport)	40	51	55	66	70	90	90	113	113	118	118	123	123	139	145	178	178
Portsmouth	33	42	47	50	53	72	72	95	95	114	114	128	128	159	159	188	189
Preston	12	17	25	34	51	70	70	83	83	85	88(a)	97	97	108	108	113	113
Reading	10	11	13	16	19	21	21	25	25	32	32	42	49	60	60	72	81
St. Helens	–	–	–	–	–	15	15	18	32	45	45	57	57	71	72	84	84
Salford	14	19	26	41	53	64	85	102	102	125	125	176	176	198	198	221	221
Sheffield	46	53	65	92	111	135	135	185	185	240	240	285	285	324	324	381	409
Shrewsbury	15	17	20	21	18	20	20	22	22	23	23	26	26	27	27	28	28
Southampton	8	10	13	19	28	35	35	47	47	54	54	60	60	65	82	105	105
Southend-on-Sea	–	–	–	–	–	–	–	3	3	5	5	8	8	12	13	29	29
South Shields	11	15	17	19	23	29	29	35	35	45	45	57	57	78	78	97	101
Stockport	17	21	27	36	50	54	54	55	55	53	53	60	60	70	70	79	93
Stoke-upon-Trent (g)	–	28	35	35	54	66	66	78	78	101	101	113	125	145	193	215	215
Sunderland	24	25	31	39	43	64	65	78	80	98	98	117	117	131	132	146	146

	1801	1811	1821	1831	1841	1851		1861		1871		1881		1891		1901	
Swansea	10	12	15	20	25	31	31	42	41	52	52	66	76	91	91	95	95
Tynemouth	13	18	23	25	25	29	29	34	34	39	39	44	44	47	47	51	51
Wakefield	11	11	14	16	19	22	23	23	23	28	28	31	31	33	39	41	48
Wallasey	1	1	1	3	6	8	8	11	11	15	15	21	21	33	33	54	54
Walsall	10	11	12	15	20	26	26	38	38	46	51	59	59	72	72	86	86
Warrington	11	13	15	18	21	23	23	26	26	32	32	41	43	53	55	64	64
Wigan	11	14	18	21	26	32	32	38	38	39	39	48	48	55	55	61	82
Wolverhampton	13	15	18	25	36	50	50	61	61	68	68	76	76	83	83	94	94
Worcester	11	14	17	19	27	28	28	31	31	33	33	34	40	43	43	47	47
Yarmouth	17	20	21	25	28	31	31	35	35	42	42	46	47	49	49	51	51
York	17	19	22	26	29	36	36	40	40	44	44	50	62	67	68	78	78

SOURCES: *Reports* of the censuses of 1851–1901. These are conveniently summarised in Mitchell and Deane, *Abstract of British Historical Statistics*, an invaluable compendium of statistical information.

Figures for the period 1801–51 (first column) are for the area of the towns in 1851. For the census from 1851 onwards two figures are given—the first as shown in the census for the year concerned (first column), and the second as shown in that census for the area of the town as given at the subsequent census.

(a) These figures are approximate, but are generally accurate to within 0·5 per cent.

(b) The parishes or townships of Aston, Handsworth, King's Norton, Northfield, and Yardley (except such parts as were already incorporated in Birmingham)—i.e. an area which at the end of the nineteenth century comprised Aston Manor county borough, Erdington, Handsworth, King's Norton, and Northfield urban district, and Yardley rural district. A part of the area was incorporated in Birmingham between 1881 and 1891, and the remainder between 1911 and 1921.

(c) The town of Pollokshaws and the parish of Govan—i.e. the area which at the end of the nineteenth century comprised the burghs of Govan, Partick, and Pollokshaws, and was incorporated in Glasgow between 1911 and 1921. Other areas, namely Crosshill, Govanhill, Maryhill, Hillhead, and Pollokshields, which were incorporated in Glasgow between 1881 and 1891, were previously classed as suburbs, and are here included with the city throughout.

(d) The parishes of West Derby, Toxteth Park, Walton-on-the-Hill, and Wavertree (except such parts as were already incorporated in Liverpool). The whole of this area was incorporated in the city between 1891 and 1901.

(e) The parishes of Blackley, Harpurhey, Crumpsall, Bradford, Moston, Newton, Openshaw, and Rusholme, all of which were incorporated in Manchester between 1881 and 1891.

(f) The parishes of Moss Side, Gorton, Levenshulme, and Withington (except such parts as were already incorporated in Manchester). A part of this area was incorporated in the city between 1881 and 1891 and the remainder between 1901 and 1911.

(g) The townships of Hanley, Longton, Stoke, and Burslem for the period 1811–91. Thereafter the urban districts of Fenton and Tunstall are included.

15　The Economy

Chronology of Economic Events

15 Sep 1830　Death of Huskisson at opening of the Liverpool and Manchester Railway.

29 Aug 1833　Bank Act passed, making Bank of England notes legal tender. Usury Laws attenuated.

2 Dec 1835　Brunel signs contract for the *Great Eastern*.

11 Jul 1836　Specie Circular in the U.S.A., curtailing boom and precipitating British crisis of 1837.

17 Jul 1837　Chartered Companies Act. Letters patent could be granted to some limited liability companies. Beginning of Victorian company legislation.

26 Sep 1838　Establishment of the Anti-Corn Law League.

11 Mar 1842　Reintroduction of income tax at 7d. in £ recommended by Peel in Budget speech. Tariff on 700 articles to be abolished, also.

29 Apr 1844　Conversion of National Debt from $3\frac{1}{2}$% to $3\frac{1}{4}$% and, then, 3% Stock set in hand by Goulburn's third Budget.

19 Jul 1844　Bank Charter Act. Separation of Bank of England's function into Banking and Issuing Depts. Fiduciary Issue limited to £14m.

9 Aug 1844　Railway Regulation Act. Gladstone's 'parliamentary' train. Treasury option to purchase railways at 25 years' profits. Beginning of interventionist railway legislation.

22 Nov 1845　Sir John Russell's 'Edinburgh Letter' in favour of Corn Law Repeal. Whigs as a whole moving towards same position.

27 Jun 1846　House of Lords pass Corn Law Repeal, following Irish famine.

25 Oct 1847　Bank Charter Act suspended by 'Open Letter' from Treasury. Crisis, following prosperity of 1844–7.

Apr 1848　John Stuart Mill's *Principles of Political Economy*.

Jun 1849　Repeal of Navigation Laws.

1 May 1851　Official opening of Great Exhibition.

18 Apr 1853　Gladstone presents first Budget. Retention of income tax, lowering level of exemption, extension to Ireland. Tariffs on 123 articles abolished.

237

10 Aug 1854	End of Usury Act.
13 Aug 1856	Bessemer process of steelmaking proposed to British Association.
12 Nov 1857	Bank Charter Act suspended by 'Open Letter' from Treasury. Crisis.
16 Nov 1860	Supplementary Convention, completing Cobden–Chevalier Treaty, signed. Highpoint of free trade.
15 Apr 1861	Gladstone's Budget abolishes the paper duties.
7 Aug 1862	Act for Incorporation, Regulation and Winding-Up of Trading Companies and other Associations. Climax of mid-Victorian company legislation.
11 May 1866	'Black Friday', after Overend & Gurney crash. Crisis, with Bank Rate staying at 10% for longest period in British history.
Nov 1873	Bank Rate at 9% for 13 days to meet shortage of cash through commercial failures.
2 Oct 1878	City of Glasgow Bank crash. Scotland badly affected, with many bankruptcies.
1879	Gilchrist–Thomas steel process. Harbinger of Britain's decline from supremacy in heavy industries.
1879	Henry George's *Progress and Poverty* published.
8 Feb 1886	Trafalgar Square riots. Protest against unemployment.
9 Mar 1888	Forthcoming conversion of the National Debt explained to House of Commons by Goschen. Saving of £1·4m. from Apr 1889, and of £2·8m from Apr 1903.
8 Nov 1890	Rumours of imminent Barings failure circulate in City. Bank of England organises rescue operation.
16 Apr 1894	Harcourt's reform of Death Duties in his second Budget.
1896	Beginning of period of gold abundance, with discoveries in South Africa and Alaska.

List of Selected Statistical Tables

(1) Net National Income at Factor Cost in £m.
(2) Income Tax: Standard Rate in £ on Incomes over £150 p.a.
(3) Rousseaux Wholesale Price Index
(4) Average Price of Wheaten Bread in London per 4lb loaf
(5) Index of Industrial Production (1831 = 100)
(6) Gross Income of Central Government in £m.
(7) Government Income as a percentage of Net National Income
(8) Pig Iron output in '000s of tons
(9) Steel output in '000s of tons

(10) Raw cotton consumption in millions of lbs
(11) Coal Production in millions of tons
(12) Total arable acreage (in '000s of acres)
(13) Number of cattle in '000s
(14) Number of sheep in '000s
(15) Yield on Consols
(16) Bank Rate: Maximum and Minimum Levels by year
(17) Terms of Trade (1880 = 100)
(18) Value of merchandise exports (in £m)
(19) Value of merchandise imports (in £m)
(20) Value of re-exports
(21) Average price of bar silver per oz
(22) World production of gold in fine oz
(23) World production of silver in fine oz
(24) British portfolio foreign investment by year (in £m)
(25) Receipts of goods traffic on railways in £m. (for United Kingdom)
(26) Miles of railway open
(27) Debt charges in £m
(28) Expenditure on Army, Ordnance and Navy (in £m)
(29) Expenditure on Civil Government (in £m)
(30) Receipts from Customs and Excise (in £m)
(31) Death Duties and Stamps (in £m)
(32) Land and Assessed Taxes (receipts in £m)
(33) Receipts from Property and Income Tax (in £m)

Year	(1) Net National Income at Factor Cost in £m	(2) Income Tax: Standard Rate in £ On Incomes over £150	(3) Wholesale Price Index (Rousseaux) (av. of 1865 and 1885 = 100)	(4) Av. Price of Wheaten Bread in London per 4lb loaf	(5) Index of Industrial Production (1831 = 100)
1830			109	10·5d.	—
1831	533		112	10·0d.	100.0
1832			109	10·0d.	99·2
1833			107	8.5d.	104·7
1834			112	8·0d.	110·9
1835			112	7·0d.	114·8
1836			123	8·0d.	126·6
1837			118	8·5d.	120·3
1838			119	10·0d.	131·3
1839			130	10·0d.	142·2
1840			128	10·0d.	139·1
1841	556		121	9·0d.	141·4
1842			111	9·5d.	134·4
1843		7d.	105	7·5d.	142·2
1844		7d.	108	8·5d.	160·2
1845		7d.	110	7·5d.	169·5
1846	562	7d.	109	8·5d.	168·8
1847		7d.	115	11·5d.	164·1

Year	(1) Net National Income at Factor Cost in £m	(2) Income Tax: Standard Rate in £ On Incomes over £150	(3) Wholesale Price Index (Rousseaux) (av. of 1865 and 1885 = 100)	(4) Av. Price of Wheaten Bread in London per 4lb loaf	(5) Index of Industrial Production (1831 = 100)
1848		7d.	110	7·5d.	179·7
1849		7d.	95	7·0d.	182·0
1850		7d.	95	6·75d.	182·0
1851		7d.	91	6·75d.	189·8
1852		7d.	94	6·75d.	201·6
1853		7d.	112	8·33d.	218·7
1854		7d.	125	10·50d.	221·9
1855	627	1s./2d.	125	10·75d.	217·2
1856	656	1s./4d.	124	10·75d.	239·1
1857	636	1s./4d.	127	9·00d.	249·2
1858	624	7d.	111	7·50d.	232·8
1859	647	5d.	115	7·50d.	254·7
1860	684	9d.	120	8·75d.	267·2
1861	717	10d.	115	9·00d.	262·5
1862	731	9d.	120	8·50d.	246·9
1863	748	9d.	121	7·50d.	260·2
1864	784	7d.	119	7·00d.	270·3
1865	811	6d.	117	7·50d.	288·3
1866	834	4d.	120	8·75d.	300·0
1867	828	4d.	118	10·25d.	295·3
1868	824	5d.	115	9·25d.	311·7
1869	855	6d.	107	7·75d.	317·2
1870	923	5d.	110	8·00d.	339·1
1871	982	4d.	115	9·00d.	360·2
1872	1,037	6d.	128	9·75d.	371·1
1873	1.131	4d.	127	8·00d.	383·6
1874	1,132	3d.	121	7·25d.	391·4
1875	1,085	2d.	117	6·83d.	385·2
1876	1,089	2d.	115	7·15d.	389·8
1877	1,096	3d.	110	8·13d.	400·0
1878	1,075	3d.	101	7·50d.	378·9
1879	1,024	5d.	98	7·13d.	361·6
1880	1,079	5d.	102	6·98d.	423·4
1881	1,118	6d.	99	7·04d.	426·6
1882	1,161	5d.	101	7·38d.	455·4
1883	1,190	6½d.	101	7·00d.	467·2
1884	1,142	5d.	95	6·78d.	452·3
1885	1,124	6d.	88	6·23d.	438·3
1886	1,140	8d.	83	6·25d.	428·9
1887	1,169	8d.	81	5·63d.	450·0
1888	1,251	7d.	84	5·69d.	483·6
1889	1,339	6d.	84	6·02d.	514·8
1890	1,405	6d.	87	6·00d.	511·7
1891	1,392	6d.	86	6·21d.	514·1
1892	1,367	6d.	82	6·23d.	491·4
1893	1,336	6d.	82	5·75d.	478·9
1894	1,383	7d.	74	5·48d.	508·6
1895	1,449	8d.	72	5·08d.	525·8
1896	1,477	8d.	73	5·09d.	553·1
1897	1,528	8d.	74	5·50d.	557·0
1898	1,610	8d.	78	6·02d.	577·3
1899	1,683	8d.	84	5·09d.	603·9
1900	1,768	8d.	91	5·23d.	603·4

	(6) Gross Income of Central Government in £m.	(7) Government Income as % of N.N.I.	(8) Pig Iron output in '000s of tons	(9) Steel output in '000s of tons	(10) Raw Cotton consumption in millions of lbs
1830	55·3		677		248
1831	54·5	10·2			263
1832	50·6				277
1833	51·1				287
1834	50·2				303
1835	50·4				318
1836	50·0				347
1837	52·6				366
1838	50·4				417
1839	51·3				382
1840	51·8		1,396		459
1841	51·6	9·3			438
1842	52·2				435
1843	51·1				518
1844	56·7				544
1845	58·2				607
1846	57·5	10·2			614
1847	58·2		2,000		441
1848	56·1				577
1849	57·8				630
1850	57·1				588
1851	57·1				659
1852	56·3				740
1853	57·3				761
1854	58·5		3,070		776
1855	62·4	10·0	3,218		839
1856	69·7	10·6	3,586		891
1857	72·2	11·4	3,659		826
1858	66·9	10·7	3,456		906
1859	64·3	9·9	3,713		977
1860	70·1	10·3	3,827		1,084
1861	69·7	9·7	3,712		1,007
1862	69·0	9·4	3,943		452
1863	68·8	9·2	4,510		508
1864	68·4	8·7	4,768		554
1865	68·7	8·5	4,825		723
1866	66·1	7·9	4,524		881
1867	67·8	8·2	4,761		967
1868	67·8	8·3	4,970		992
1869	70·8	8·3	5,446		939
1870	73·7	8·0	5,963		1,078
1871	68·2	7·0	6,627	329	1,207
1872	73·1	7·0	6,742	410	1,181
1873	74·7	6·6	6,566	573	1,245
1874	75·5	6·7	5,991	630	1,277
1875	73·6	6·8	6,365	708	1,229
1876	75·5	6·9	6,556	828	1,280
1877	76·8	7·0	6,609	887	1,230
1878	77·7	7·2	6,381	982	1,192
1879	81·2	7·9	5,995	1,009	1,150
1880	73·3	6·8	7,749	1,295	1,361
1881	81·9	7·4	8,144	1,778	1,430

	(6) Gross Income of Central Government in £m	(7) Government Income as % of N.N.I.	(8) Pig Iron output in '000s of tons	(9) Steel output in '000s of tons	(10) Raw Cotton consumption in millions of lbs
1882	84·0	7·2	8,587	2,109	1,458
1883	87·4	7·3	8,529	2,008	1,526
1884	86·2	7·6	7,812	1,774	1,481
1885	88·0	7·8	7,415	1,887	1,298
1886	89·6	7·9	7,010	2,264	1,450
1887	90·8	7·8	7,560	3,044	1,499
1888	89.8	7·2	7,999	3,304	1,525
1889	89·9	6·7	8,323	3,571	1,564
1890	94·6	6·7	7,904	3,579	1,664
1891	96·5	6·9	7,406	3,157	1,666
1892	98·6	7·2	6,709	2,920	1,548
1893	97·7	7·3	6,977	2,950	1,434
1894	98·4	7·1	7,427	3,111	1,603
1895	101·8	7·0	7,703	3,260	1,664
1896	109·4	7·4	8,660	4,132	1,637
1897	112·3	7·4	8,796	4,486	1,618
1898	116·1	7·2	8,610	4,566	1,761
1899	117·9	7·0	9,421	4,855	1,762
1900	129·9	7·3	8,960	4,900	1,737

	(11) Coal Production in millions of tons	(12) Total arable acreage ('000s of acres)	(13) Number of cattle in '000s	(14) Number of sheep in'000s	(15) Yield on Consols	(16) Bank Rate: Max. and Min. Levels in Year
1830					3·5	
1831					3·8	4–4
1832					3·6	4–4
1833					3·4	4–4
1834					3·3	4–4
1835					3·3	4–4
1836					3·4	5–4
1837					3·3	5–5
1838					3·2	5–4
1839					3·3	6–4
1840					3·4	6–5
1841					3·4	5–5
1842					3·3	5–4
1843					3·2	4–4
1844					3·0	4–2½
1845					3·1	3½–2½
1846					3·1	3½–3
1847					3·4	8–3
1848					3·5	5–3
1849					3·2	3–2½
1850					3·1	3–2½
1851					3·1	3–3
1852					3·0	2½–2
1853					3·1	5–2
1854	64·7				3·3	5½–5
1855	64·5				3·3	7–3½
1856	66·6				3·2	7–4½
1857	65·4				3·3	10–5½
1858	65·0				3·1	8–2½

	(11) Coal Production in millions of tons	(12) Total arable acreage ('000s of acres)	(13) Number of cattle in '000s	(14) Number of sheep in '000s	(15) Yield on Consols	(16) Bank Rate: Max. and Min. Levels in Year
1859	72·0				3·2	$4\frac{1}{2}-2\frac{1}{2}$
1860	80·0				3·2	$6-2\frac{1}{2}$
1861	83·6				3·3	8–3
1862	81·6				3·2	3–2
1863	86·3				3·2	8–3
1864	92·8				3·3	9–6
1865	98·2				3·4	7–3
1866	101·6				3·4	$10-3\frac{1}{2}$
1867	104·5		4,993	28,919	3·2	$3\frac{1}{2}-2$
1868	103·1	17,754	5,424	30,711	3·2	3–2
1869	107·4	17,671	5,313	29,538	3·2	$4\frac{1}{2}-2\frac{1}{2}$
1870	110·4	18,335	5,403	28,398	3·2	$6-2\frac{1}{2}$
1871	117·4	18,403	5,338	27,120	3·2	$5-2\frac{1}{2}$
1872	123·5	18,428	5,625	27,922	3·2	$7-3\frac{1}{2}$
1873	128·7	18,185	5,965	29,428	3·2	9–3
1874	126·6	18,089	6,125	30,314	3·2	$6-2\frac{1}{2}$
1875	133·3	18,104	6,013	29,167	3·2	6–2
1876	134·1	18,036	5,844	28,183	3·2	5–2
1877	134·2	17,984	5,698	28,161	3·1	5–2
1878	132·6	18,043	5,738	28,406	3·2	6–2
1879	133·7	17,809	5,856	28,157	3·1	5–2
1880	147·0	17,675	5,912	26,619	3·1	$3-2\frac{1}{2}$
1881	154·2	17,568	5,912	24,581	3·0	$5-2\frac{1}{2}$
1882	156·5	17,591	5,807	24,320	3·0	6–3
1883	163·7	17,320	5,963	25,068	3·0	5–3
1884	160·8	17,175	6,269	26,068	3·0	5–2
1885	159·4	17,201	6,598	26,535	3·0	5–2
1886	157·5	17,056	6,647	25,521	3·0	5–2
1887	162·1	21,178	6,441	25,959	3·0	5–2
1888	169·9	21,178	6,129	25,257	3·0	$6-2\frac{1}{2}$
1889	176·9	21,111	6,140	25,632	2·8	$6-2\frac{1}{2}$
1890	181·6	20,930	6,509	27,272	2·9	6–3
1891	185·5	20,613	6,853	28,733	2·9	$5-2\frac{1}{2}$
1892	181·8	20,442	6,945	28,735	2·8	$3\frac{1}{2}-2$
1893	164·3	20,280	6,701	27,230	2·8	$5-2\frac{1}{2}$
1894	188·3	20,342	6,347	25,862	2·7	3–2
1895	189·7	20,052	6,354	25,792	2·6	2–2
1896	195·4	19,909	6,494	26,705	2·5	4–2
1897	202·1	19,944	6,500	26,340	2·5	4–2
1898	202·1	19,814	6,622	26,743	2·5	$4-2\frac{1}{2}$
1899	220·1	19,704	6,796	27,239	2·6	6–3
1900	225·2	19,528	6,805	26,592	2·8	6–3

	(17) Terms of trade (1880 = 100)	(18) Value of merchandise exports (in £m)	(19) Value of merchandise imports (in £m)
1830	149·8	69·7	46·3
1831	138·1	71·4	49·7
1832	127·9	76·1	44·6
1833	123·3	79·8	45·9
1834	124·7	85·4	49·4
1835	122·4	91·2	49·0

	(17) Terms of trade (1880 = 100)	(18) Value of merchandise exports (in £m)	(19) Value of merchandise imports (in £m)
1836	124·5	97·6	57·3
1837	129·6	85·8	54·8
1838	119·6	105·2	61·3
1839	111·8	110·2	62·0
1840	105·1	116·5	67·5
1841	109·7	116·9	64·4
1842	105·4	113·8	65·3
1843	113·0	131·8	70·2
1844	116·1	146·0	75·4
1845	119·6	150·9	85·3
1846	115·1	148·6	75·9
1847	112·5	146·2	90·9
1848	121·7	151·0	93·5
1849	115·2	190·1	105·9
1850	111·1	197·3	100·5
1851	110·0	214·4	110·5
1852	104·9	219·5	109·3
1853	100·8	242·1	123·1
1854	94·6	115·8	152·4
1855	89·4	116·7	143·5
1856	91·6	139·2	172·5
1857	87·1	146·2	187·8
1858	98·0	139·8	164·6
1859	98·2	155·7	179·2
1860	94·9	164·5	210·5
1861	98·1	159·6	217·5
1862	105·8	156·2	225·7
1863	107·2	196·9	248·9
1864	104·7	212·6	275·0
1865	107·0	218·8	271·1
1866	110·0	238·9	295·3
1867	107·8	225·8	275·2
1868	100·3	227·8	294·7
1869	103·1	233·0	295·5
1870	102·3	244·1	303·3
1871	109·4	283·6	331·0
1872	113·0	314·6	354·7
1873	117·2	311·0	371·3
1874	113·2	297·7	370·1
1875	111·6	281·6	374·0
1876	105·4	256·8	375·2
1877	98·5	252·3	394·4
1878	102·4	245·5	368·8
1879	101·7	248·8	363·0
1880	100·0	286·4	411·2
1881	96·7	297·0	397·0

	(17) Terms of trade (1880 = 100)	(18) Value of merchandise exports (in £m)	(19) Value of merchandise imports (in £m)
1882	99·6	306·7	413·0
1883	98·5	305·4	426·9
1884	99·9	296·0	390·0
1885	102·5	271·5	371·0
1886	104·4	269·0	349·9
1887	106·4	281·3	362·2
1888	102·3	298·6	387·6
1889	103·0	315·6	427·6
1890	109·1	328·3	420·7
1891	107·4	309·1	435·4
1892	107·0	291·6	423·8
1893	109·3	277·1	404·7
1894	111·4	273·8	408·3
1895	110·8	285·8	416·7
1896		296·4	441·8
1897		294·2	451·0
1898	109·3	294·0	470·5
1899	112·2	329·5	485·0
1900	120·0	354·4	523·0

	(20) Value of re-exports (in £m)	(21) Av. price of bar silver per oz std.	(22) World production of gold in fine oz ('000s)	(23) World production of silver in fine oz ('000s)
1830	8·5			
1831	10·7			
1832	11·0			
1833	9·8			
1834	11·6			
1835	12·8			
1836	12·4			
1837	13·2			
1838	12·7			
1839	12·8			
1840	13·8			
1841	14·7			
1842	13·6			
1843	14·0			
1844	14·4			
1845	16·3			
1846	16·3			
1847	20·0			

	(20) Value of re-exports (in £m)	(21) Av. price of bar silver per oz std.	(22) World production of gold in fine oz ('000s)	(23) World production of silver in fine oz ('000s)
1848	18·4			
1849	25·6			
1850	21·9			
1851	23·7			
1852	23·3			
1853	27·7			
1854	18·6	61½d.	6,410	28,489
1855	21·0	61$\frac{5}{16}$d.	6,410	28,489
1856	23·4	61$\frac{5}{16}$d.	6,486	28,489
1857	24·1	61$\frac{3}{4}$d.	6,486	29,095
1858	23·2	61$\frac{5}{16}$d.	6,486	29,095
1859	25·3	62$\frac{1}{16}$d.	6,486	29,095
1860	28·6	61$\frac{11}{16}$d.	6,486	29,095
1861	34·5	60$\frac{13}{16}$d.	5,950	35,402
1862	42·2	61$\frac{7}{16}$d.	5,950	35,402
1863	50·3	61$\frac{3}{8}$d.	5,950	35,402
1864	52·2	61$\frac{3}{8}$d.	5,950	35,402
1865	53·0	61$\frac{1}{16}$d.	5,950	35,402
1866	50·0	61$\frac{1}{4}$d.	6,270	43,052
1867	44·8	60$\frac{9}{16}$d.	6,270	43,052
1868	48·1	60½d.	6,270	43,052
1869	47·1	60$\frac{7}{16}$d.	6,270	43,052
1870	44·5	60$\frac{9}{16}$d.	6,270	43,052
1871	60·5	60½d.	5,591	63,317
1872	58·3	60$\frac{5}{16}$d.	5,591	63,317
1873	55·8	59$\frac{1}{4}$d.	4,654	63,267
1874	58·1	58$\frac{5}{16}$d.	4,390	55,301
1875	58·1	56$\frac{7}{8}$d.	4,717	62,262
1876	56·1	52$\frac{3}{4}$d.	5,016	67,753
1877	53·5	54$\frac{13}{16}$d.	5,512	62,680
1878	52·6	52$\frac{9}{16}$d.	5,761	73,385
1879	57·3	51$\frac{1}{4}$d.	5,262	74,383
1880	63·4	52$\frac{1}{4}$d.	5,149	74,795
1881	63·1	51$\frac{11}{16}$d.	4,984	79,021
1882	65·2	51$\frac{5}{8}$d.	4,934	86,472
1883	65·6	50$\frac{9}{16}$d.	4,615	89,175
1884	62·9	50$\frac{5}{8}$d.	4,921	81,568
1885	58·4	48$\frac{5}{8}$d.	5,245	91,610
1886	56·2	45$\frac{3}{8}$d.	5,136	93,297
1887	59·3	44$\frac{5}{8}$d.	5,117	96,124
1888	64·0	42$\frac{7}{8}$d.	5,331	108,228
1889	66·7	42$\frac{11}{16}$d.	5,974	120,214
1890	64·7	47$\frac{11}{16}$d.	5,749	126,095
1891	61·9	45$\frac{1}{16}$d.	6,320	137,171
1892	64·4	39$\frac{13}{16}$d.	7,094	153,152
1893	58·9	35$\frac{5}{8}$d.	7,619	165,473
1894	57·8	28$\frac{15}{16}$d.	8,764	164,610

	(20) Value of re-exports (in £m)	(21) Av. price of bar silver per oz std.	(22) World production of gold in fine oz ('000s)	(23) World production of silver in fine oz ('000s)
1895	59·7	$29\frac{7}{8}$d.	9,615	167,801
1896	56·2	$30\frac{3}{4}$d.	9,784	157,061
1897	60·0	$27\frac{9}{16}$d.	11,420	160,421
1898	60·7	$25\frac{15}{16}$d.	13,878	169,055
1899	65·0	$27\frac{7}{16}$d.	14,838	168,337
1900	63·2	$28\frac{1}{4}$d.	12,315	173,591

	(24) British portfolio foreign investment in each year (in £m)	(25) Receipts of goods traffic on railways (in £m)	(26) Miles of railway open–in Great Britain
1830			
1831			
1832			
1833			
1834			298
1835			
1836			
1837			
1838			
1839			970
1840			
1841			
1842			
1843		1·4	
1844		1·6	2,236
1845		2·2	
1846		2·8	
1847		3·3	
1848		4·2	
1849		5·4	5,538
1850		6·2	
1851		6·9	
1852		7·7	
1853		9·2	
1854		9·7	7,157
1855		10·5	
1856		11·4	
1857		11·9	
1858		11·9	
1859		12·8	8,737
1860		14·2	
1861		14·7	

	(24) British portfolio foreign investment in each year (in £m)	(25) Receipts of goods traffic on railways (in £m)	(26) Miles of railway open–in Great Britain
1862		14·7	
1863		16·1	
1864		17·7	10,995
1865	42·5	18·7	
1866	25·2	20·1	
1867	18·4	20·8	
1868	29·1	Returns incomplete	
1869	21·9	21·4	13,170
1870	44·7	23·2	
1871	70·2	25·5	
1872	93·9	28·0	
1873	69·3	30·7	
1874	74·5	30·9	14,322
1875	46·1	32·1	
1876	30·4	32·5	
1877	19·4	32·8	
1878	31·7	32·3	
1879	30·5	32·3	15,411
1880	41·7	34·5	
1881	74·2	35·6	
1882	67·5	36·5	
1883	61·2	37·4	
1884	63·0	36·4	16,339
1885	55·3	35·6	
1886	69·8	35·1	
1887	84·4	36·1	
1888	119·1	37·5	
1889	122·9	39·7	17,152
1890	116·6	40·8	
1891	57·6	41·8	
1892	39·8	41·4	
1893	32·1	39·5	
1894	48·3	41·8	17,864
1895	77·7	42·5	
1896	68·5	44·6	
1897	78·4	46·2	
1898	76·6	47·6	
1899	78·2	50·4	18,524
1900	49·6	51·8	

	(27) Debt charges in £m	(28) Army, Ordnance and Navy, in £m	(29) Civil Government, in £m	(30) Customs and Excise, in £m	(31) Death duties and stamps, in £m
1830	29·1	15·2	5·4	40·2	7·4
1831	29·2	13·9	4·9	39·4	7·3

	(27) Debt charges in £m	(28) Army, Ordnance and Navy, in £m	(29) Civil Government, in £m	(30) Customs and Excise, in £m	(31) Death duties and stamps, in £m
1832	28·3	14·4	5·0	35·7	7·2
1833	28·3	13·8	4·7	36·4	7·2
1834	28·5	12·3	4·3	35·5	7·1
1835	28·5	12·1	4·6	36·1	7·2
1836	28·6	11·7	4·5	36·4	7·2
1837	29·4	12·1	4·7	38·8	7·4
1838	29·6	12·8	5·1	36·7	7·1
1839	29·4	12·6	5·5	37·2	7·2
1840	29·6	13·8	5·6	37·8	7·2
1841	29·5	13·9	5·3	38·3	7·4
1842	29·7	14·4	5·6	38·3	7·3
1843	29·6	14·4	5·6	36·2	7·2
1844	29·4	14·1	6·0	36·6	7·1
1845	30·6	13·5	5·9	38·5	7·3
1846	28·6	15·2	5·4	36·4	7·9
1847	28·3	16·4	6·3	37·2	7·7
1848	28·4	18·0	8·1	35·6	7·7
1849	28·7	17·0	7·2	37·8	6·8
1850	28·5	15·1	7·0	37·3	7·0
1851	28·3	14·7	6·8	37·3	6·7
1852	28·2	13·7	6·9	37·6	6·5
1853	28·1	15·3	6·6	37·8	6·9
1854	28·1	19·4	7·2	38·8	7·1
1855	28·0	27·5	7·7	38·5	7·1
1856	28·2	46·7	8·7	40·7	7·1
1857	28·8	33·5	8·4	41·8	7·4
1858	28·7	22·5	10·1	40·9	7·4
1859	28·7	20·7	9·1	42·0	8·0
1860	28·7	24·9	9·7	44·9	8·0
1861	26·3	28·3	10·7	42·7	8·3
1862	26·3	29·1	10·8	42·0	8·6
1863	26·2	28·7	10·9	41·2	9·0
1864	26·2	26·2	10·8	41·4	9·3
1865	26·4	25·9	10·2	42·2	9·5
1866	26·2	24·7	10·3	41·1	9·6
1867	26·1	25·8	10·5	43·0	9·4
1868	26·6	27·1	11·2	42·9	9·5
1869	26·6	26·9	12·0	42·9	9·2
1870	27·1	21·5	11·0	43·3	8·7
1871	26·8	21·1	12·0	42·8	8·4
1872	26·8	24·2	12·2	43·6	9·1
1873	26·8	23·1	11·8	46·9	9·2
1874	26·7	23·6	12·7	47·5	9·8
1875	27·1	24·5	13·6	46·7	9·8
1876	27·2	25·0	14·8	47·6	10·2
1877	27·4	25·5	14·9	47·6	10·2
1878	27·6	25·1	15·6	47·5	10·2
1879	28·0	28·7	16·6	47·7	9·9
1880	28·1	25·2	16·9	44·6	10·4
1881	29·2	25·2	17·4	44·5	11·1

	(27) Debt charges in £m	(28) Army, Ordnance and Navy, in £m	(29) Civil Government, in £m	(30) Customs and Excise, in £m	(31) Death duties and stamps, in £m
1882	29·4	26·3	18·0	46·5	11·4
1883	29·5	25·4	18·9	46·6	11·8
1884	29·1	26·8	18·7	46·7	11·6
1885	29·0	30·0	19·0	46·9	11·9
1886	23·5	29·7	19·2	45·3	11·6
1887	28·0	31·7	19·3	45·5	11·8
1888	25·5	30·5	19·7	45·2	13·0
1889	25·1	29·0	19·4	45·7	12·3
1890	24·5	32·7	17·1	47·6	14·1
1891	23·9	33·4	17·6	46·9	15·9
1892	23·7	33·2	19·0	50·1	16·5
1893	23·5	33·2	19·3	50·0	16·2
1894	23·4	33·4	19·7	49·8	16·2
1895	23·3	35·4	20·4	51·1	16·6
1896	22·8	38·2	21·2	52·6	21·5
1897	23·6	40·5	21·4	53·9	21·4
1898	23·6	40·2	22·9	55·4	23·0
1899	23·6	44·1	23·4	55·4	23·2
1900	23·2	69·6	23·9	61·4	27·0

	(32) Land and assessed taxes, in £m	(33) Property and income tax, in £m
1830	5·3	
1831	5·4	
1832	5·2	
1833	5·2	
1834	5·2	
1835	4·8	
1836	3·9	
1837	3·9	
1838	3·9	
1839	3·9	
1840	3·9	
1841	4·2	
1842	4·7	
1843	4·5	0·6
1844	4·4	5·3
1845	4·4	5·3
1846	4·4	5·2
1847	4·5	5·5
1848	4·6	5·6
1849	4·5	5·5
1850	4·5	5·6
1851	4·6	5·5
1852	3·8	5·4

	(32) Land and assessed taxes, in £m	(33) Property and income tax, in £m
1853	3·6	5·7
1854	3·3	5·7
1855	3·2	10·6
1856	3·1	15·1
1857	3·1	16·1
1858	3·2	11·6
1859	3·2	6·7
1860	3·2	9·6
1861	3·1	10·9
1862	3·2	10·4
1863	3·2	10·6
1864	3·2	9·1
1865	3·3	8·0
1866	3·4	6·4
1867	3·5	5·7
1868	3·5	6·2
1869	3·5	8·6
1870	4·5	10·0
1871	2·7	6·4
1872	2·3	9·1
1873	2·3	7·5
1874	2·3	5·7
1875	2·4	4·3
1876	2·5	4·1
1877	2·5	5·3
1878	2·7	5·8
1879	2·7	8·7
1880	2·7	9·2
1881	2·7	10·7
1882	2·7	9·9
1883	2·8	11·9
1884	2·9	10·7
1885	3·0	12·0
1886	2·9	15·2
1887	3·0	15·9
1888	3·0	14·4
1889	3·0	12·7
1890	3·0	12·8
1891	2·6	13·3
1892	2·5	13·8
1893	2·5	13·5
1894	2·5	15·2
1895	2·5	15·6
1896	2·5	16·1
1897	2·4	16·7
1898	2·4	17·3
1899	2·4	18·0
1900	2·5	18·8

Specimen Tariffs

Tea

1830–3	96% *ad valorem* if sold at under 2s. per lb.
	100% *ad valorem* if sold at above 2s. per lb.
1834–5	1s. 6d. per lb. on low quality tea, 2s. 2d. per lb. on medium quality tea and 3s. per lb. on high quality tea
1836–9	2s. 1d. per lb.
1840–52	2s. 1d. per lb., plus 5% *ad valorem*
1853	1s. 10d. per lb.
1854	1s. 6d. per lb.
1855–6	1s. 9d. per lb.
1857–62	1s. 5d. per lb.
1863–4	1s. per lb.
1865–89	6d. per lb.
1890–1900	4d. per lb.

SOURCE: *Customs Tariffs of the United Kingdom from 1800 to 1897*, Cmnd 8669, pp. 204–5.

Sugar

Tariff per cwt. of refined sugar from a foreign country:

1830–9	£8 8s.
1840–4	£8 16s. 4d.
1845	£8 8s.
1846–7	£1 8s.
1848	£1 6s. 8d.
1849	£1 4s. 8d.
1850	£1 2s. 8d.
1851	£1 8d.
1852	19s. 4d.
1853 to 5 Jul	17s. 4d.
1854 from 5 Jul to 2nd Aug	19s. 11d.
1854 from 2 Aug	17s. 4d.
1854	16s.
1855–6	
1857–63	18s. 4d.
1864–6	12s. 10d.
1867–9	12s.
1870–2	6s.
1873	3s.
1874	Duties repealed

SOURCE: *Customs Tariffs of the United Kingdom from 1800 to 1897*, Cmnd 8669, pp. 217–20.

No. of Joint-Stock Companies Registered Annually after 1862

1862	165	1867	479	1872	1,116
1863	790	1868	461	1873	1,234
1864	997	1869	475	1874	1,241
1865	1,034	1870	595	1875	1,172
1866	762	1871	821	1876	1,066

1877	990	1885	1,482	1893	2,617
1878	886	1886	1,891	1894	2,970
1879	1,034	1887	2,050	1895	3,892
1880	1,302	1888	2,550	1896	4,735
1881	1,581	1889	2,788	1897	5,229
1882	1,632	1890	2,789	1898	5,182
1883	1,766	1891	2,686	1899	4,975
1884	1,541	1892	2,607	1900	4,966

SOURCE: Cmnd 4954 *Statistical Tables 1854–1908* (1909).

Major Industrial Enterprises at the Turn of the Century*

Name of firm	Industrial group	Year of registration	No. of directors in 1905	Capital in 1905 (to nearest £1,000)
Imperial Tobacco Co.	Tobacco	1901	28	17,545
Watney, Combe, Reid	Brewing	1898	10	14,950
J. & P. Coats	Textiles	1890	16	11,181
United Alkali	Chemicals	1890	16	8,490
Calico Printers' Association	Textiles	1899	6	8,227
Vickers, Sons & Maxim	Steel, shipbuilding, armaments	1897	15	7,440
Fine Cotton Spinners' & Doublers' Assoc.	Textiles	1898	33	7,290
Associated Portland Cement Mfrs	Cement	1900	28	7,061
Bleachers' Association	Textiles	1900	50	6,820
Arthur Guinness	Brewing	1886	11	6,000
Sir W. G. Armstrong, Whitworth & Co.	Steel, shipbuilding, armaments	1897	15	5,316
Samuel Allsopp & Sons	Brewing	1887	7	5,095
Whitbread	Brewing	1889	11	4,767
Bass, Ratcliff & Gretton	Brewing	1880	8	4,640
Guest, Keen & Nettlefolds	Iron, steel, coal	1900	11	4,536
Dunlop Pneumatic Tyre Co.	Rubber tyres	1896	7	4,396
Bradford Dyers' Association	Textiles	1898	46	4,310
Barclay, Perkins	Brewing	1896	9	4,270
Bolckow, Vaughan	Iron, steel, coal	1864	7	4,246
Cannon Brewery	Brewing	1895	7	4,200
Wall Paper Manufacturers	Wallpaper	1899	17	4,141
Charrington	Brewing	1897	12	4,025
Lever Brothers	Soap	1894	4	4,000
Ind, Coope	Brewing	1886	9	3,698
Truman, Hanbury, Buxton	Brewing	1889	8	3,515
Mann, Crossman & Paulin	Brewing	1901	7	3,250
English Sewing Cotton	Textiles	1897	8	3,101
Peter Walker & Son	Brewing	1890	7	3,000
John Brown	Iron, steel, shipbuilding	1864	7	2,947
United Collieries	Coal	1898	8	2,843
Linen Thread	Textiles	1898	13	2,726
Cammell, Laird	Iron, steel, shipbuilding	1903	12	2,623
Maple	Furniture	1891	13	2,620
Salt Union	Chemicals	1888	7	2,600
Courage	Brewing	1888	5	2,500
Bovril	Meat extracts	1897	6	2,500
William Beardmore	Steel, armaments	1902	4	2,500
Huntley & Palmers	Biscuits	1898	9	2,400
Hoare	Brewing	1894	7	2,354
Brunner Mond	Chemicals	1881	15	2,299
Waring & Gillow	Furniture	1897	6	2,205

Name of firm	Industrial group	Year of registration	No. of directors in 1905	Capital in 1905 (to nearest £1,000)
Wigan Coal & Iron	Coal, iron	1865	6	2,193
City of London Brewery	Brewing	1891	5	2,127
British Cotton and Wool Dyers' Assoc.	Textiles	1900	34	2,070
Distillers' Company	Distilling	1877	14	2,049
Threlfalls	Brewing	1888	4	1,997
Wilson's Brewery	Brewing	1894	5	1,992
Yorkshire Wool Combers' Association	Textiles	1899	8	1,966
Reckitt & Sons	Starch, blacklead, blue	1878	10	1,950
Lister	Textiles (silk)	1889	6	1,950
J. & J. Colman	Mustard	1896	5	1,916
Dorman, Long	Iron, steel	1889	15	1,910

Total capitalisation of the top 50 ranking firms: £220,921,000
Average capital: £4,418,420.

*This table lists the 52 largest British companies engaged in the agricultural processing, extractive, and manufacturing industries operating within the United Kingdom. It is based on the following sections of *The Stock Exchange Year-Book for 1905* by Thomas Skinner: 'Rolling Stock Companies'; 'Brewery, Hotel, and Kindred Companies'; 'Iron, Coal and Steel Companies'; 'Miscellaneous Companies'.

BIBLIOGRAPHICAL NOTE: The essential and most readily available starting point for statistical material for this period is B. R. Mitchell and Phyllis Deane, *Abstract of British Historical Statistics* (Cambridge, 1962). For the figures in the above chapter we have (except where stated) relied heavily on their work. Their detailed bibliography is indispensable for any research student.

16 Trade Unions and the Co-operative Movement

Landmarks in Trade Union Development

1799 Passing of Combination Acts

1824 Repeal of Combination Acts, guided through Parliament by Francis Place

1825 Amendment Act, considerably modifying the 1824 Act

1826 The Journeymen Steam Engine Makers (the 'Old Mechanics') founded at Manchester

1829 National Union of Cotton Spinners founded by John Doherty

1831 Foundation of Society for the Protection of Labour Operative Builders Union established

1832 Rioting in Merthyr; town occupied by miners.
National Equitable Labour Exchange set up in London for the exchange of goods produced by co-operative production.

1833 Foundation of Grand National Consolidated Trades Union

1834 'Tolpuddle Martyrs'. In 1833, Loveless, an agricultural labourer and Methodist lay preacher, formed a 'Friendly Society of Agricultural Labourers' because the wages in his area, already lower than elsewhere, were being reduced. Because there was some form of initiation ceremony, six of them were arrested almost immediately charged with breaking the 1797 Act against Unlawful Oaths. The trial was rushed through before opposition could be organised. All six sentenced to be transported for seven years.
1836: free pardon granted
1839: by this time they were all back in England, though soon after they emigrated

1837 During a strike by the Cotton Spinners Association in Glasgow, a blackleg was shot. The leaders of the union were tried for conspiracy. Although no complicity in the murder was proven, they were sentenced to seven years' transportation.

1842 Plug Plot era; general strikes by cotton workers.
Miners Association led by Martin Jude led movement to improve conditions. 70,000 members in 1844.

1845 Formation of National Association of United Trades for the Protection of Labour

1851   Birth of 'New Model Unionism' with foundation of Amalgamated Society of Engineers. Membership grew from 12,000 in 1851 to 33,000 in 1868. It reached 52,000 in 1886 and 71,000 in 1891.

1853   Formation of the Amalgamated Association of Operative Cotton Spinners. In Preston, a seven-month strike of cotton workers was defeated in Feb 1854 by the importation of Irish labour.

1855   Friendly Societies Act, gave legal protection to the funds of societies with benefit functions

1858   Alexander McDonald founded National Miners' Association; Glasgow Trades Council formed

1859   Molestation of Workmen Act allowed peaceful picketing; major building strike in London

1860   Coal Mines Regulation Act passed. Foundation of London Trades Council and also Amalgamated Society of Carpenters and Joiners.

1864   National Conference of trade union delegates told in London to press for reform of Master and Servant Act

1865   Foundation of the Reform League, to win the franchise for the working class

1866   Short-lived United Kingdom Alliance of Organised Trades; 'Sheffield outrages' of Oct 1866. Appointment of Royal Commission to investigate trade unions. Hornby *v.* Close case; decision goes against the union.

1867   Partial Amendment of Master and Servant Act.
Unions still dissatisfied. Emergence of the 'Junta' (Applegarth, Allan, Coulson, Odger and Guile) to ensure trade union case favourably received by the Royal Commission. Frederic Harrison acted as union nominee on the Commission.

1868   Establishment of the Trades Union Congress, although no formal organisation yet created. First conference attended by 34 delegates, mainly from the provinces.

1869   Second annual Trades Union Congress met at Birmingham in August: attended by 40 delegates representing 250,000 trade unionists

1871   Passing of the Trade Union Act and the Criminal Law Amendment Act. Under these measures, the trade unions were given legal recognition and were enabled to protect their funds under the Friendly Societies Act. However, trade unionists were still liable to criminal prosecution under the 1825 Act, and picketing, even in its most elementary form, was again made illegal. The Parliamentary Committee of the

T.U.C. was established; formation of the Amalgamated Society of Railway Servants.

1872 Birth of Joseph Arch's National Agricultural Labourers Union; by 1873 it claimed 1,000 branches and 10,000 members. Its weekly journal, *Labourers Chronicle*, at one stage reached a circulation of 30,000.

1874 Alexander McDonald elected for Stafford and Thomas Burt for Morpeth. New Conservative Government appointed a Royal Commission on the Labour Laws.

1875 Two major Government measures were passed – the Conspiracy and Protection of Property Act and the Employers and Workmen Act. The first of these measures, in addition to making peaceful picketing legal, changed the law so that the law of conspiracy would in future not apply in trade disputes unless the actions concerned were criminal in themselves. Under the Employers and Workmen Act the penalty for breach of contract was limited to payment of civil damages.
Beginning of Henry Broadhurst's period as · T.U.C. Secretary.

1880 Passing of Employers' Liability Act; conversion of H. M. Hyndman to socialism and subsequent rise of the Social Democratic Federation

1886 National Federation of Labour established in Tyneside

1887 Keir Hardie launches attack on Broadhurst at T.U.C. Conference

1888 H. H. Champion publishes *Labour Elector*, advocating a policy of forming an Independent Labour Party; London women matchworkers strike at Messrs Bryant & May. Beginning of 'New Unionism'.

1889 Mar: Will Thorne began organising workers at the Beckton Gas Works in East Ham. Victory to reduce working day from 12 hours to 8 achieved in July. Aug: beginning of the London Dockers Strike. Dockers won 6d. per hour. Formation of Dock, Wharf, Riverside, and General Labourers Union with Ben Tillett as secretary. Foundation of the Miners Federation of Great Britain.

1890 Shipowners form a Shipping Federation, partly in response to 'New Unionism'

1892 At T.U.C., Keir Hardie carried a resolution instructing the Parliamentary Committee to draw up a scheme for a labour representation fund. Little action resulted.

1893 Birth of the Independent Labour Party. Establishment of the National Free Labour Association.

1896 Lyons *v.* Wilkins case; an injunction was granted to Lyons to prevent the Amalgamated Trade Society of Fancy Leather Workers picketing his premises. The Court of Appeal upheld the decision.

Creation of the Employers Federation of Engineering Associations.

1897   From Jul 1897 to Jan 1898 a national lock-out in the engineering industry. Unions forced to reduce demands. Formation of the Scottish T.U.C.

1898   West Ham was the first council to be controlled by Labour. Formation of the Employers Parliamentary Council.

1899   Formation of the General Federation of Trades Unions

1900   Formation in Jan of the Scottish Workers Parliamentary Elections Committee. Birth of the Labour Representation Committee in Feb.

1901   Taff Vale Judgment. Strike by Taff Vale railway workers because of the alleged victimisation of a signalman who had led a movement for a pay rise. Strike officially supported by the Amalgamated Society of Railway Workers. Picketing organised to prevent importing of blackleg labour. Ammon Beasley, the Taff Vale Co.'s General Manager, on the advice of the Employers Parliamentary Council, applied for a Government injunction against the picketing (see Lyons *v.* Wilkins). The trial continued even after the strike was settled. The Lords confirmed judgement of the court that an injunction could be granted and also that the funds of a trade union were liable for damages inflicted by its officers. The Railway Union therefore had to pay £23,000 to the Taff Vale Co.

Trades Union Congress

Date	Place of Meeting	Name of President	Chairman of Parliamentary Committee	Secretary to Parliamentary Committee	No. of Delegates	No. of Societies Represented	No. of Members Represented
1868	Manchester	W. H. Wood	No record of Chairmen of Parliamentary Committee	G. Howell	34	–	118,367
1869	Birmingham	T. J. Wilkinson		G. Howell	48	40	250,000
1871	London	Geo. Potter		G. Howell	50	49	289,430
1872	Nottingham	W. H. Leatherland	A. McDonald	G. Howell	77	63	255,710
1873	Leeds	W. Lishman	A. McDonald	G. Howell	132	140	730,074
1874	Sheffield	W. Rolley	A. W. Bailey	G. Howell	169	153	1,191,922
1875	Liverpool	J. Fitzpatrick	R. Knight	G. Howell	151	107	818,032
1875	Glasgow	J. Battersby	{ J. Kane / J. D. Prior }	H. Broadhurst	139	109	539,823
1876	Newcastle	J. C. Laird	J. D. Prior	H. Broadhurst	140	113	557,823
1877	Leicester	D. Merrick	J. D. Prior	H. Broadhurst	141	112	691,089
1878	Bristol	G. F. Jones	A. W. Bailey	H. Broadhurst	136	114	623,957
1879	Edinburgh	D. Gibson	J. D. Prior	H. Broadhurst	115	92	541,892
1880	Dublin	J. Murphy	H. Slatter	H. Broadhurst	120	105	494,222
1881	London	E. Coulson	W. Crawford	H. Broadhurst	157	122	463,899
1882	Manchester	R. Austin	T. Birtwistle	H. Broadhurst	153	126	509,307
1883	Nottingham	T. Smith	J. Inglis	H. Broadhurst	163	163	471,651
1884	Aberdeen	J. C. Thompson	A. W. Bailey	H. Broadhurst	142	126	598,033
1885	Southport	T. R. Threlfall	J. S. Murchie	Geo. Shipton	141	136	580,976
1886	Hull	F. Maddison	J. Mawdsley	Geo. Shipton	143	122	633,088
1887	Swansea	W. Bevan	J. M. Jack	H. Broadhurst	156	131	674,034
1888	Bradford	S. Shaftoe	G. Shipton	H. Broadhurst	165	138	816,944
1889	Dundee	G. Shipton	J. Swift	H. Broadhurst	211	171	885,055
1890	Liverpool	W. Matkin	E. Harford	C. Fenwick	457	311	1,470,191
1891	Newcastle	T. Burt	John Wilson	C. Fenwick	552	177	1,302,855

Date	Place of Meeting	Name of President	Chairman of Parliamentary Committee	Secretary to Parliamentary Committee	No. of Delegates	No. of Societies Represented	No. of Members Represented
1892	Glasgow	J. Hodge	J. Havelock Wilson	C. Fenwick	495	418	1,219,934
1893	Belfast	S. Monro	J. Burns	C. Fenwick	380	–	900,000
1894	Norwich	F. Delves	D. Holmes	S. Woods	378	179	1,100,000
1895	Cardiff	J. Jenkins	E. Cowey	S. Woods	330	170	1,000,000
1896	Edinburgh	J. Mallinson	W. Thorne	S. Woods	343	178	1,076,000
1897	Birmingham	J. V. Stevens	A. Wilkie	S. Woods	381	180	1,093,191
1898	Bristol	J. O'Grady	W. J. Davis	S. Woods	406	188	1,184,241
1899	Plymouth	W. J. Vernon	F. Chandler	S. Woods	384	181	1,200,000
1900	Huddersfield	W. Pickles	C. W. Bowerman	S. Woods	386	184	1,250,000

The Co-operative Movement

Chronology of Main Events

1832 Owenite Co-operative Congress in Manchester
1844 Rochdale Society of Equitable Pioneers established
1852 First Industrial and Provident Society Act passed
1853 Society for Promotion of Industrial and Provident Societies formed. Co-operative League founded.
1860 Pitman's *Co-operator* first published
1863 First Scottish National conference. *Scottish Co-operator* first published. C.W.S. founded, Manchester.
1867 Co-operative Insurance Company established
1868 Scottish C.W.S. founded, Glasgow
1869 First Co-operative Congress, London
1870 Central Board elected
1871 *Co-operative News* first published
1873 Edward Vansittart Neale becomes first General Secretary
1875 First Constitution of Co-operative Union
1881 Parliamentary Committee set up
1882 Co-operative Productive Federation formed
1883 Co-operative Permanent Building Society founded
1885 Union's first Education Committee formed
1886 Emile de Boyve (France) proposed international co-operative organisation at Plymouth Congress
1889 Co-operative Union registered
1892 J. C. Gray appointed General Secretary
1894 Irish Agricultural Organisation Society established, Dublin
1895 International Co-operative Alliance founded, London
1897 Irish Agricultural Wholesale Society established, Dublin
1898 Union's Central Education Committee set up
1900 Parliamentary Committee became Joint Parliamentary Committee
1901 Argicultural Organisation Society, England, established

17　The British Empire

Main Territories under British Rule by 1900

	Original Entry into British Rule and Status in 1900		Original Entry into British Rule and Status in 1900
Aden	Colony (1839) and adjacent Protectorate	Cape of Good Hope	Ceded Colony (1814)
Antigua	Colony (1663)	Cayman, Turks and Caicos Islands	Ceded (1670) Dependencies of Jamaica (1848)
Ascension	Admiralty administered territory (1815)	Ceylon	Ceded Colony (1802)
Australia	First settled 1788; 6 self-governing colonies (1855 and later)	Christmas Island	Annexed (1888)
		Cocos-Keeling Islands	Annexed (1857)
Bahamas	First settled 1646; Colony (1783)	Cook Islands	Protectorate (1888)
Barbados	Settled 1627; Colony (1662)	Cyprus	British administered territory (1878)
Basutoland	Protectorate (1871) Colony (1884)	Dominica	Colony (1763)
Bechuanaland	Protectorate (1885)	East African Protectorate	Protectorate (1895)
Bermuda	First settled 1609; Colony (1684)	Egypt	Occupied by British since 1882
British Guiana	Ceded Colony (1814)	Falkland Islands	Colony (1833)
British Honduras	First settled 1638; Colony (separated from Jamaica 1884)	Fiji	Colony (1874)
British North Borneo	Protectorate (1893)	Gambia	Settlement began 1618; Colony (1843) and adjacent Protectorate (1888)
British Solomon Islands	Protectorate (1893)		
British Somaliland	Protectorate (1887)	Gibraltar	Ceded Colony (1713)
Brunei	Protectorate (1888)	Gilbert and Ellice Islands	Protectorate (1892)
Burma	Indian Province (1852)		
Canada	Ceded Colonies from 1714 onwards; self-governing Federation (1867)	Gold Coast	Settlement began 1750; Colony (1821 and 1874)
		Grenada	Ceded Colony (1763)
		Hong Kong	Ceded Colony (1843)

	Original Entry into British Rule and Status in 1900		Original Entry into British Rule and Status in 1900
India	Settlement began 1601; Indian Empire (1876)	St Christopher (St Kitts) and Nevis	Colony (1625)
Ireland	Union with Great Britain (1801)	St Helena	Administered by East India Co. 1673;
Jamaica	Colony (seized 1655 and ceded 1670)	St Lucia	Colony (1833) Ceded Colony (1814)
		St Vincent	Ceded Colony (1763)
Labuan	Colony (1848) governed by North Borneo Company (1890)	Sarawak	Protectorate (1888)
		Seychelles	Dependency of Mauritius (1810)
Lagos	Colony (1861)	Sierra Leone	Colony (1808) and adjacent Protectorate (1896)
Leeward Isles	Colonies federated (1871)		
Malay States	9 Protectorates, 4 of which were federated	Singapore	Under Indian Government 1824; part of Straits Settlements (1867)
Maldive Islands	Protectorate (1887)	Southern	Chartered Company
Malta	Ceded Colony (1814)	Rhodesia	(1889)
Mauritius	Ceded Colony (1814)	Straits	
Montserrat	First settled (1642) as Colony	Settlements (Singapore,	Colonies (1867)
Natal	Colony (1843)	Penang, Malacca)	
New Zealand	Self-governing Colony (1854)	Sudan	Condominium with Egypt (1899)
Newfoundland	Settlement began 1623; Self-governing colony (1855)	Swaziland	Protectorate (1903)
		Tonga	Protectorate (1900)
		Trinidad and Tobago	Ceded (1802 and 1814) Colony (combined 1889)
Nigeria	Protectorates (1900)[1]	Tristan da Cunha	British settlement (1815)
Norfolk Island	Settled 1788; under New South Wales (1896)[2]	Uganda	Protectorate (1894)
		Virgin Islands	Colonies (1666)
Northern Rhodesia	Chartered Company Territory (1889)	Windward Isles	Colonies (1763 and 1814, federated in 1885)
Nyasaland	Protectorate (1891)		
Papua	Protectorate (1884)[3] Colony (1888)	Zanzibar	Protected State (1890)
Pitcairn	Settled 1790; Colony (1898)		

[1] Colony of Lagos joined Southern Nigeria 1906. Protectorates of Northern and Southern Nigeria joined 1914.

[2] Became dependency of Australian Government 1914.

[3] Administered by Australia since 1906. United with New Guinea 1940.

Chronology of Major Events, 1830–1900

1830 Colonisation Society founded by Gibbon Wakefield

1833 Renewal of the Charter of the East India Company. The Company ceased all trading operations and became purely an agency for the government of India. Abolition of slavery in the British Empire.

1834 Formation by Wakefield of the South Australian Association

1836 Beginning of the Great Trek. Foundation of South Australia.

1837 Foundation of the Aborigines Protection Society. Rebellion of Papineau and Mackenzie in Canada. Foundation of the New Zealand Association by Wakefield.

1838 E of Durham sent to Canada as Governor-General

1839 Publication of the Durham Report. Occupation of Aden. Beginning of First Afghan War, with British attempt to install Shah Sujah as ruler. Outbreak of First China War.

1840 Annexation of New Zealand; Treaty of Waitangi. Discontinuance of transportation to New South Wales. Canada Act; united Lower and Upper Canada (henceforth called Quebec and Ontario) under a single administration and legislature.

1841 James Brooke appointed Rajah of Sarawak

1842 Treaty of Nanking: China ceded Hong Kong and opened five 'treaty ports' to British trade–Canton, Amoy, Foochow, Ningpo and Shanghai. The Ashburton Treaty settled the Maine boundary. Representative government set up in New South Wales. France declared protectorate over Tahiti.

1843 Annexation of Natal. Annexation of Sind by an army under Sir Charles Napier.

1845 First Sikh War followed the death of Ranjit Singh

1846 Acquisition of Labuan. The Oregon Treaty. Earl Grey Colonial Secretary (to 1852)

1848 Annexation of the Orange Free State. Second Sikh War; Sikhs defeated at Gujerat; the Punjab annexed. Dalhousie began era of reform in India.

1849 Repeal of the Navigation Acts

1851 Discovery of gold in New South Wales (at Bathurst) and in Victoria (at Ballarat). Abolition of the New Zealand Company.

1852 Second Burmese War; Rangoon captured. Rangoon, and the surrounding province of Pegu, both annexed. Sand River Convention; Britain abandoned policy of attempting to control the trekkers.

1853 Representative government introduced in the Cape Colony

1854 The Bloemfontein Convention

1855 Separation of the War and Colonial Secretaries: a separate

Secretaryship of State for the Colonies was established. Responsible government granted to New South Wales, Victoria, South Australia and Tasmania.

1856　Annexation of Oudh by Dalhousie. Responsible government granted to New Zealand. Renewal of war with China.

1857　Mutiny in India; the rising began in Meerut in May, quickly spreading to Delhi. When the revolt was quelled, the Crown assumed direct control over India. The Company's rule came to an end. A Secretary of State for India was established, with a Council of India to advise him.

1858　Anglo-French forces defeated the Chinese and secured the Treaty of Tientsin. China repudiated treaty in 1859. British Columbia became a Crown Colony.

1859　Responsible government granted to Queensland on separation from New South Wales. Sir George Grey, Governor of the Cape Colony, proposed a plan for a South African Federation.

1860　Britain attained full Free Trade. Outbreak of series of Maori Wars in New Zealand occasioned by private purchases of land by the New Zealand Company in defiance of the Treaty of Waitangi.

1861　Annexation of Lagos. Parliamentary Committee urged that territories enjoying responsible government should provide more towards their own defence.

1864　Quebec Conference laid basis for the creation of the Dominion of Canada in 1867

1865　Colonial Laws Validity Act; made clear that colonial legislatures could pass acts contrary to the Common Law of England, but could not enact laws contrary to the acts of the Imperial Parliament applying to the Colony. Insurrection at Morant Bay heralded crisis in Jamaica; rule of Governor Eyre.

1866　Crown Colony government introduced for Jamaica

1867　British North America Act created the Dominion of Canada. The four federating provinces were Quebec, Ontario, Nova Scotia and New Brunswick.

1868　Granville, as Colonial Secretary, ready to facilitate separation of the colonies from Britain

1869　Suez Canal opened. Hudson's Bay Company surrendered its political and territorial rights to the Dominion of Canada; rebellion under Louis Riel in Manitoba.

1870　Discovery of Kimberley diamond fields; subsequent annexation of Griqualand West. Manitoba joined the Dominion of Canada

1871　Dutch ceded Gold Coast forts to Britain; entire Gold Coast under British rule. British Columbia joined the Dominion of Canada.

1872   Responsible government introduced in the Cape Colony

1873   Outbreak of Ashanti War, when Britain rejected Ashanti claim to the ceded Dutch fort of Elmina; punitive expedition under Garnet Wolseley dispatched. David Livingstone died. Prince Edward Island joined the Dominion of Canada. Kimberley instructed Governor of the Straits Settlements to restore order in Malaya.

1874   Treaties with chiefs of Perak, Selangor and Sungei Ujong, under which British Residents were to give advice to the Malay rulers. Fiji annexed.

1875   A High Commissioner for the Western Pacific appointed. Purchase of Suez Canal shares by Disraeli.

1876   Failure of Carnarvon's attempt at South African federation. Queen Victoria created Empress of India; widespread famine in southern India. Lytton appointed Viceroy.

1877   Annexation of the Transvaal

1878   'Dual Control' in Egypt. Annexation of Walfisch Bay in South Africa. Anglo-Russian crisis over Treaty of San Stefano. Indian troops moved to Malta. British occupation of Cyprus under Treaty of Berlin. Renewal of Afghan Wars.

1879   Murder of British Resident at Kabul; peace not restored until 1880, when independence of Afghanistan from both Russian and British influence recognised. Zulu War; Cetewayo's army defeated British at Isandhlwana; Chelmsford defeated Zulus at Ulundi.

1880   Gladstone's electoral victory in part a reaction to Disraeli's Imperial adventures. First Boer War began in Dec.

1881   Sir George Colley routed by Boers at Majuba Hill. The end result was that the Transvaal became, in effect, an independent republic under Paul Kruger as President, but subject to the 'suzerainty' of the Queen. Rising of the Mahdi in Sudan. Formation of the British North Borneo Company.

1882   First shipment of New Zealand meat in cold storage to Britain. Organisation of the Canadian prairie area into four territories of the Dominion; Alberta, Athabasca, Assiniboia and Saskatchewan. Revolt of Arabi Pasha in Egypt; rioting in Alexandria in Jun. In Jul a British fleet bombarded Alexandria; in Sept, Wolseley defeated Arabi at Tel-el-Kebir and captured Cairo.

1883   Defeat of British force under Hicks Pasha in the Sudan. Sir Evelyn Baring (Lord Cromer) appointed British Agent and Consul-General in Egypt. Publication of Sir J. R. Seeley's *Expansion of England*

1884   German annexation of part of New Guinea and of the Solomon Islands. Britain took possession of remainder of New Guinea. Representative government introduced in Jamaica. Foundation of the Imperial Federation League. Beginning of British rule in Somaliland. Suzerainty over the Transvaal abandoned; Transvaal recognised as the South African Republic. German annexation of Togoland, the Cameroons and South West Africa. Opening of the Berlin Conference.

1885   Death of Gordon in Khartoum in Jan. Annexation of Bechuanaland kept open the 'road to the north'. Crisis in Penjdeh, in the disputed boundary area between Afghanistan and Russian Turkestan. Gladstone indicated that Britain would fight if Afghanistan was invaded. Birth of the Indian National Congress. Dispute over Newfoundland fisheries. Discovery of gold in the Witwatersrand.

1886   Final annexation of Burma; Thibaw deposed. Completion of the Canadian Pacific Railway. As a consequence of Sir George Goldie's work, the Royal Niger Company received a charter for trade and government on the Lower Niger. Germany gained control of Tanganyika; end of Sir John Kirk's hopes of an Arab–African state under the authority of Zanzibar.

1887   The First Colonial Conference. Joint Anglo-French control of the New Hebrides.

1888   Charter granted to the British East Africa Company, largely a creation of Sir William Mackinnon. The Matabele ruler, Lobengula, granted Rhodes the exclusive right to work minerals in his dominion.

1889   Charter granted to the British South Africa Company. Crisis in Samoa, eventually resolved in 1899 when Germany and the United States divided the Samoan group, while Great Britain received the Tonga islands. Sir Henry Parkes, Premier of New South Wales, paved way for an eventual Australian Federation.

1890   Responsible government introduced in Western Australia. Anglo-German treaty on East Africa negotiated by Salisbury and Bismarck: Heligoland ceded to Germany, and Caprivi Strip granted to South West Africa, in return for abandonment of large German claims in Africa.

1891   Anglo-Portuguese treaty signed. Portugal recognised the new British Protectorate of Nyasaland and the British claim to the territory between the Zambezi and the Congo Free State (taken over by the British South African Company to become Northern Rhodesia).

1892   Indian Councils Act introduced first Indian members on to the Viceroy's Legislative Council. Gold found at Coolgardie in Western Australia; further discoveries at Kalgoorlie in 1893.

1893   Matabele War ended in conquest by the British South African Company; L. S. Jameson appointed Administrator of Southern Rhodesia. British Protectorate established over Uganda.

1894   Ottawa Conference provided for cable link between Canada and Australia

1895   Joseph Chamberlain appointed Colonial Secretary. Creation of Federated Malay States. End of the British East Africa Company with the establishment of the British East Africa Protectorate under the Crown. Growing discontent of the Uitlanders. Jameson raid launched from Pitsani into the Transvaal on 29 Dec.

1896   Surrender of Jameson's force to General Cronje on 2 Jan at Doornkop. Venezuela–British Guiana boundary dispute referred to arbitration. Discovery of gold on the Klondike river, a tributary of the Yukon in north-west Canada. Ashanti conquered, the monarchy abolished and a protectorate established. Egyptian army retrained by Sir Herbert Kitchener for reconquest of the Sudan.

1897   Sir Alfred Milner sent to the Cape as Governor and High Commissioner. Beginning of period of 'Indian unrest'. Second Colonial Conference held in London on occasion of Queen Victoria's Diamond Jubilee. Convention at Adelaide to prepare terms for an Australian Federation.

1898   The Khalifa defeated at Omdurman; Anglo-Egyptian condominium proclaimed over the Sudan. Crisis at Fashoda, with the arrival of a French force under Marchand.

1899   War declared in South Africa, 9 Oct. Three successive British defeats in Dec, at Colenso, Stormberg and Magersfontein

1900   British Parliament passed the Commonwealth of Australia Act, which was to come into being on 1 Jan 1901. Royal Niger Company lost its ruling powers to the Crown. Reinforcements sent to South Africa under Kitchener and Roberts. Relief of Mafeking, 17 May. Cronje's army captured at Kimberley; Kruger fled to Europe; annexation of the Boer Republics in Sept. Beginning of protracted war against Botha, de Wet and Hertzog. Peace eventually signed at Vereeniging (31 May 1902).

Colonial Governors, 1830–1900

Australia

New South Wales

1825	Lieut.-Gen. R. Darling
1831	Col. Lindsay (*Lieut.-Gov.*)
1831	Maj.-Gen. Sir R. Bourke
1837	Lieut.-Col. K. Snodgrass (*Lieut.-Gov.*)
1838	Sir George Gipps
1846	Sir Maurice O'Connell
1846	Sir Charles Fitzroy
1855	Sir William Denison
1861	Lieut.-Col. John Kempt (*Admin.*)
1861	Rt Hon. Sir John Young
1867	Sir Trevor Chute (*Admin.*)
1868	E of Belmore
1872	Sir Alfred Stephen (*Admin.*)
1872	Sir Hercules Robinson
1879	Sir Alfred Stephen (*Lieut.-Gov.*)
1879	Rt Hon. Sir Augustus Loftus
1885	Sir Alfred Stephen (*Lieut.-Gov.*)
1885	Ld Carrington
1890	Rt Hon. Sir A. Stephen (*Lieut.-Gov.*)
1891	Rt Hon. E of Jersey
1893	Sir F. M. Darley (*Lieut.-Gov.*)
1893	Sir Robert Duff
1895	Sir F. M. Darley (*Lieut.-Gov.*)
1895	Vt Hampden
1899– 1900	Rt Hon. Earl Beauchamp

Queensland

1859	Sir G. F. Bowen
1868	Col. M. C. O'Connell (*Admin.*)
1868	Col. Samuel Wensley Blackall
1871	Col. Sir M. C. O'Connell (*Admin.*)
1871	M of Normanby
1874	Col. Sir M. C. O'Connell (*Admin.*)
1875	William Cairns
1877	Col. Sir M. C. O'Connell
1877	Sir A. E. Kennedy
1880	Hon. Joshua Bell (*Admin.*)
1883	Sir Arthur Palmer (*Admin.*)
1883	Sir Anthony Musgrave
1886	Sir Arthur Palmer (*Admin.*)
1886	Sir Anthony Musgrave
1888	Sir Arthur Palmer (*Admin.*)
1889	Gen. Sir H. W. Norman
1896	Ld Lamington

South Australia

1836	Capt. John Hindmarsh
1838	George Milner Stephen (*Admin.*)
1838	Lieut.-Col. George Gawler
1841	Capt. George Grey
1848	Sir Henry Edward Fox Young
1854	Lieut.-Col. Frederick Holt Robe
1854	Boyle Travers Finniss (*Admin.*)
1855	Sir Richard MacDonnell
1862	Sir Dominick Daly
1868	Lieut.-Col. Hamley (*Admin.*)
1869	Rt Hon. Sir James Fergusson
1870	Major James Harwood Rocke (*Admin.*)
1872	Sir R. D. Hanson (*Admin.*)
1873	Sir Anthony Musgrave
1877	Hon. S. J. Way (*Admin.*)
1877	Sir William W. Cairns
1877	Hon. S. J. Way (*Admin.*)
1877	Sir W. F. D. Jervois
1878	Hon S. J. Way (*Admin.*)
1883	Sir W. F. C. Robinson
1889	Hon. S. J. Way (*Admin.*)
1889	Rt Hon. E of Kintore
1890	Hon. J. P. Boucaut (*Admin.*)
1893	Hon. S. J. Way (*Admin.*)
1895	Sir Thomas Fowell Buxton
1898	Rt Hon. S. J. Way (*Admin.*)
1899	Rt Hon. Ld Tennyson

Tasmania

1824	Col. George Arthur
1836	Lieut.-Col. K. Snodgrass
1837	Sir John Franklin
1843	Sir J. E. E. Wilmot
1846	Charles Latrobe
1847	Sir W. T. Denison
1855	Sir Henry Fox Young
1861	Col. Sir T. Gore Browne
1868	Lieut.-Col. W. C. Trevor
1869	Sir Charles Du Cane
1874	Sir Valentine Fleming (*Admin.*)
1874	Sir Francis Smith (*Admin.*)
1875	Frederick Weld
1880	Sir Francis Smith (*Admin.*)
1880	Lieut.-Gen. Sir J. H. Lefroy (*Admin.*)
1881	Maj. Sir G. C. Strahan
1887	Sir R. G. C. Hamilton
1893– 1900	Vt Gormanston

Victoria

1851	Charles Joseph Latrobe (*Lieut.-Gov.*)

1854	J. V. F. Foster (*Admin.*)
1854	Capt. Sir C. Hotham
1856	Maj.-Gen. E. Macarthur (*Admin.*)
1856	Sir Henry Barkly
1863	Sir C. H. Darling
1866	Brig.-Gen. G. J. Carey (*Admin.*)
1866	Rt Hon. Sir J. Manners-Sutton
1873	Sir W. Foster Stawell (*Admin.*)
1873	Sir G. F. Bowen
1875	Sir Redmond Barry (*Admin.*)
1875	Sir W. Foster Stawell (*Admin.*)
1876	Sir G. F. Bowen
1879	Most Hon. M of Normanby
1884	Sir W. Foster Stawell (*Admin.*)
1884	Sir H. B. Loch
1889	Sir William Robinson (*Admin.*)
1889	Rt Hon. E of Hopetoun
1895	Sir John Madden (*Admin.*)
1897	Rt Hon. Lord Brassey
1900	Sir J. Madden

Western Australia

1829	Capt. James Stirling (*Lieut.-Gov.*)
1832	Capt. Irwin (*Acting*)
1833	Capt. Daniel (*Acting*)
1834	Capt. Beete (*Acting*)
1834	Sir James Stirling
1839	John Hutt
1840	Lieut.-Col. Clarke
1847	Lieut.-Col. Irwin
1848	Capt. Charles Fitzgerald
1855	Arthur Edward Kennedy
1862	John Stephen Hampton
1868	Lieut.-Col. John Bruce (*Acting*)
1869	Frederick Aloysius Weld
1875	W. C. F. Robinson
1877	Lieut.-Col. E. D. Harvest (*Admin.*)
1877	Maj.-Gen. Sir Harry St George Ord
1880	Sir W. C. F. Robinson
1883	Henry Thomas Wrenfordsley (*Admin.*)
1883	Sir F. Napier Broome
1890	Sir W. C. F. Robinson
1895	Sir Alexander Campbell Onslow (*Admin.*)
1895–	Sir Gerard Smith
1900	

Bahamas

1829	Sir J. C. Smyth
1833	B. T. Balfour (*Lieut.-Gov.*)
1835	Lieut.-Col. Colebrooke
1837	Sir F. Cockburn

1844	G. B. Matthew
1849	John Gregory
1854	Sir A. Bannerman
1857	C. J. Bayley
1864	R. W. Rawson
1869	Sir J. Walker
1871	Sir G. C. Strahan
1873	J. P. Hennessy
1874	Sir W. Robinson
1880	T. F. Callaghan
1882	Sir C. C. Lees
1884	H. A. Blake
1887	Sir A. Shea
1895	Sir W. F. Haynes Smith
1898–	Sir G. T. Carter
1904	

Bermuda

1825	Sir H. Turner
1831	Sir S. R. Chapman
1839	Lieut.-Col. Reid
1846	Capt. C. Elliot
1854	Col. Freeman Murray
1861	Col. H. St George Ord
1867	Col. Sir F. E. Chapman
1870	Col. Sir T. Gore Browne
1871	Maj.-Gen. J. H. Lefroy
1877	Maj.-Gen. Sir R. Laffan
1882	Lieut.-Gen. Thomas Gallwey
1888	Lieut.-Gen. E. Newdigate-Newdegate
1892	Lieut.-Gen. Thomas Lyons
1896–	Lieut.-Gen. G. Digby Barker
1902	

British Guiana

1831	Maj.-Gen. Sir Benjamin D'Urban
1833	Maj.-Gen. Sir James Smyth
1838	Henry Light
1848	W. Walker (*Acting*)
1848	Sir Henry Barkly
1854	Sir P. E. Wodehouse
1861	W. Walker (*Acting*)
1862	Sir F. Hincks
1869	Sir John Scott
1873	E. E. Rushworth (*Admin.*)
1874	Sir J. R. Longden
1877	William Young (*Admin.*)
1877	C. H. Kortright
1881	William Young (*Lieut.-Gov.*)
1882	Sir Henry Irving
1887	Charles Bruce (*Lieut.-Gov.*)
1888	Rt Hon. Vt Gormanston
1893	Sir Charles Bruce (*Lieut.-Gov.*)

1893	Sir Charles Cameron Lees
1895	Cavendish Boyle (*Acting*)
1896	Sir A. W. L. Hemming
1898	Sir Cavendish Boyle (*Acting*)
1898–	Sir Walter J. Sendall
1901	

British Honduras

1830	Lieut.-Col. F. Cockburn (*Supt.*)
1837	Lieut.-Col. A. McDonald (*Supt.*)
1843	Col. C. Fancourt (*Supt.*)
1851	Philip Wodehouse (*Supt.*)
1854	William Stevenson (*Supt.*)
1857	Frederick Seymour (*Supt.*)
1864	J. Gardiner Austin (*Lieut.-Gov.*)
1867	J. R. Longden (*Lieut.-Gov.*)
1872	W. W. Cairns (*Lieut.-Gov.*)
1874	Capt. Mitchell (*Admin.*)
1874	Maj. Mundy (*Lieut.-Gov.*)
1876	Capt. Mitchell (*Admin.*)
1877	F. P. Barlee (*Lieut.-Gov.*)
1882	Sir R. W. Harley (*Lieut.-Gov.*)
1883	Henry Fowler (*Admin.*)
1884	R. T. Goldsworthy (*Gov.*)
1891	G. Melville (*Acting*)
1891	Sir C. A. Moloney
1897	E. B. Sweet-Escott (*Acting*)
1897–	Col. David Wilson
1903	

Burma
(*Chief Commissioners*)

1862	Lieut.-Col. A. P. Phayre
1867	Col. A. Fytche
1871	Hon. Ashley Eden
1875	A. R. Thompson
1878	C. V. Aitchison
1880	C. E. Bernard
	(C. H. T. Crosthwaite, *Acting* 1882–4)
1887	C. H. T. Crosthwaite
1890	Alexander Mackenzie
1892	Sir F. W. R. Fryer (*Acting*)
1894	Alexander Mackenzie
1895–	Sir F. W. R. Fryer (*Lieut.-Gov.*
1903	from 1897)

Canada

1867	Vt Monck
1868	Ld Lisgar
1872	M of Dufferin
1878	M of Lorne
1883	M of Lansdowne
1888	Ld Stanley of Preston

1893	E of Aberdeen
1898–	E of Minto
1904	

Cape of Good Hope

1828	Hon. Sir Galbraith Lowry Cole
1834	Lieut.-Col. T. F. Wade (*Acting*)
1834	Sir Benjamin D'Urban
1836	Sir Andries Stockenstrom (*Lieut.-Gov.*)
1838	Sir George Napier
1839	Col. John Hare (*Lieut.-Gov.*)
1843	Sir Peregrine Maitland
1847	Maj.-Gen. Sir Henry Pottinger
1847	Sir H. F. Young (*Lieut.-Gov.*)
1847	Lieut.-Gen. Sir Henry Smith
1852	Lieut.-Gen. Hon. G. Cathcart
1852	Charles Darling (*Lieut.-Gov.*)
1854	Sir George Grey
1861	Sir Philip Wodehouse
1870	Sir Henry Barkly
1877	Sir Bartle Frere
1880	Maj.-Gen. Sir H. H. Clifford (*Admin.*)
1880	Maj. Sir G. C. Strahan (*Admin.*)
1881	Sir H. G. R. Robinson
1889	Lieut.-Gen. H. A. Smyth (*Admin.*)
1889	Sir H. Brougham Loch
1895	Lieut.-Gen. W. H. Goodenough (*Admin.*)
1895	Rt Hon. Sir H. G. R. Robinson
1897–	Sir Alfred Milner
1901	

Ceylon

1824	Lieut.-Gen. Sir Edward Barnes
1831	Maj.-Gen. Sir John Wilson (*Lieut.-Gov.*)
1831	Rt Hon. Sir Robert Wilmot Horton
1837	Rt Hon. James MacKenzie
1841	Lieut.-Gen. Sir Colin Campbell
1847	Sir J. E. Tennent (*Lieut.-Gov.*)
1847	Rt Hon Vt Torrington
1850	C. J. MacCarthy (*Lieut.-Gov.*)
1850	Sir George William Anderson
1855	C. J. MacCarthy (*Lieut.-Gov.*)
1855	Sir Henry George Ward
1860	Sir C. J. MacCarthy
1863	Maj.-Gen. Terence O'Brien (*Acting*)
1865	Sir H. G. R. Robinson
1871	Rt Hon. Sir W. H. Gregory

1875	A. N. Birch (*Lieut.-Gov.*)
1877	Sir James R. Longden
1883	Sir J. Douglas (*Lieut.-Gov.*)
1883	Hon. Sir Arthur Gordon
1890	Sir Arthur Havelock
1896–	Rt Hon. Sir J. West Ridgeway
1903	

Egypt

1882	Rt Hon. E of Dufferin (*Special Mission*)
1883–	Maj. Sir E. Baring (*Agent and Con.-Gen.*)
1907	
1884	Rt Hon. E of Northbrook (*High Comm.*)
1885	Rt Hon. Sir H. D. Wolff (*High Comm.*)

Fiji

1874	Sir H. G. R. Robinson (E. L. Layard, *Admin.*)
1875	Hon. Sir A. H. Gordon
1878	Lieut.-Col. G. W. Des Voeux
1879	Hon. Sir A. H. Gordon
1879	J. B. Thurston (*Acting*)
1880	Sir G. W. Des Voeux
1885	W. McGregor (*Acting*)
1885	Lieut.-Gov. J. B. Thurston
1887	Sir C. B. H. Mitchell
1887	W. McGregor (*Acting*)
1888	Sir J. B. Thurston
1897	Sir H. S. Berkeley (*Admin.*)
1897–	Sir G. T. M. O'Brien
1901	

The Gambia

1829	Lieut.-Col. Alexander Finlay (*Lieut.-Gov.*)
1830	George Rendall (*Lieut.-Gov.*)
1840	Sir Henry Huntley (*Lieut.-Gov.*)
1843	Capt. H. F. Seagram (*Gov.*)
1843	E. Norcott
1844	Cdr. G. Fitzgerald
1847	Sir R. G. Macdonnell
1852	A. E. Kennedy
1852	Col. L. S. O'Connor
1859	Col. G. A. K. D'Arcy
1866	Admiral C. G. E. Patey (*Admin.*)
1871	T. F. Callaghan (*Admin.*)
1873	Sir C. H. Kortright (*Admin.*)
1875	Sir Samuel Rowe (*Admin.*)
1877	Dr V. S. Gouldsbury (*Admin.*)
1884	Sir C. A. Moloney (*Admin.*)
1886	Sir J. S. Hay (*Admin.*)

1888	Sir Gilbert Carter (*Admin.*)
1891–	Sir R. B. Llewellyn (*Admin.*)
1901	

Gold Coast

1874	Capt. George Strahan
1876	Sanford Freeling
1878	Capt. C. C. Lees (*Lieut.-Gov.*)
1879	Herbert Taylor Ussher
1880	Sir W. Brandford Griffith
1881	Sir Samuel Rowe
1884	William A. G. Young
1885	Sir W. B. Griffith
1895	W. E. Maxwell
1898	Sir F. M. Hodgson

Hong Kong

1843	Sir Henry Pottinger
1844	Sir John Davis
1848	Sir George Bonham
1854	Sir John Bowring
1854	Lieut.-Col. Caine (*Lieut.-Gov.*)
1859	Sir H. G. R. Robinson
1862	William T. Mercer (*Acting*)
1864	Sir H. G. R. Robinson
1865	W. T. Mercer (*Acting*)
1866	Sir R. G. Macdonnell
1869	Maj.-Gen. Whitfeild (*Lieut.-Gov.*)
1871	Sir R. G. Macdonnell
1872	Sir Arthur Kennedy
1877	Sir John Pope-Hennessy
1882	W. H. Marsh (*Acting*)
1883	Sir George Ferguson Bowen
1885	Maj.-Gen. W. G. Cameron (*Acting*)
1886	W. H. Marsh (*Acting*)
1887	Maj.-Gen. W. G. Cameron (*Acting*)
1887	Sir G. W. Des Voeux
1891	Maj.-Gen. G. Digby Barker (*Acting*)
1891	Sir W. Robinson
1898	Maj.-Gen. W. Black (*Acting*)
1898–	Sir H. A. Blake
1902	

India

(*Governors-General and Viceroys*)

1828	Ld William Cavendish Bentinck
1835	Sir Charles Metcalfe (*Acting*)
1836	Ld Auckland
1842	Ld Ellenborough
1844	Rt Hon. Sir Henry Hardinge
1848	E of Dalhousie

1856   Vt Canning (1858, *Viceroy*)
1862– E of Elgin
63
1864   Rt Hon. Sir John Lawrence
1869   E of Mayo
1872   Ld Northbrook
1876   Ld Lytton
1880   M of Ripon
1884   E of Dufferin
1888   M of Lansdowne
1894   E of Elgin
1899– Ld Curzon
1905

Lieut.-Governors of Bengal
1854   Frederick J. Halliday
1859   John P. Grant
1862   Cecil Beadon
1867   William Grey
1871   George Campbell
1874   Sir Richard Temple
1877   Hon. Ashley Eden
1882   A. Rivers Thompson
1887   Sir Steuart C. Bayley
1890   Sir Charles Alfred Elliott
1895   Sir Alexander Mackenzie
1898– Sir John Woodburn
1902

Governors of Bombay
1827   Maj.-Gen. Sir John Malcolm
1830   Lieut.-Gen. Sir Thomas Sidney
       Beckwith
1831   E of Clare
1835   Sir Robert Grant
1838   James Farish (*Acting*)
1839   Sir. J. Rivett-Carnac
1841   George William Anderson
       (*Acting*)
1842   Sir George Arthur
1846   Lestock Robert Reid (*Acting*)
1847   George Russell Clerk
1848   Vt Falkland
1853   Ld Elphinstone
1860   Sir George Russell Clerk
1862   Sir Bartle Frere
1867   Rt Hon. W. R. S. V. Fitzgerald
1872   Sir Philip Edmund Wodehouse
1877   Sir Richard Temple
1880   Rt Hon. Sir James Fergusson
1885   Ld Reay
1890   Ld Harris
1895   Ld Sandhurst
1900– Ld Northcote
1903

Governors of Madras
1827   Stephen Rumbold Lushington
1832   Lieut.-Gen. Sir Frederick Adam
1837   Ld Elphinstone
1842   Lieut.-Gen. M of Tweeddale
1848   Maj.-Gen. Rt Hon. Sir Henry
       Pottinger
1854   Ld Harris
1859   Sir Charles Trevelyan
1860   Sir Henry George Ward
1860   William Ambrose Morehead
       (*Acting*)
1861   Sir William Thomas Denison
1866   Ld Napier
1872   Ld Hobart
1875   D of Buckingham and Chandos
1880   Rt Hon. W. P. Adam
1881   Rt Hon. M. E. Grant Duff
1886– Rt Hon. Robert Bourke
1890
1891   Ld Wenlock
1896– Sir Arthur Elibank Havelock
1900

Jamaica

1829   E of Belmore
1832   E of Musgrave
1834   M of Sligo
1836   Lieut.-Gen. Sir L. Smith
1839   Sir C. Metcalfe
1842   E of Elgin
1847   Sir Charles Grey
1853   Sir Henry Barkly
1857   Sir C. H. Darling
1862   E. J. Eyre
1865   Lieut.-Gen. Sir H. K. Storks
1866   Sir John Grant
1873   W. A. G. Young (*Admin.*)
1874   Sir William Grey
1877   Sir Anthony Musgrave
1883   Gen. Sir H. W. Norman
1888   Sir Henry Arthur Blake
1898– Sir A. W. L. Hemming
1904

Labuan

1847   Sir James Brooke
1848   William Napier (*Lieut.-Gov.*)
1850   J. Scott (*Lieut.-Gov.*)
1856   Hon. G. W. Edwardes
1861   T. F. Callaghan
1866   Hugh Low
1867   Sir J. Pope-Hennessy
1871   Sir H. E. Bulwer

1875 Herbert Taylor Ussher
1879 Charles Cameron Lees
1881 P. Leys (*Acting*)
1888 A. J. Hamilton (*Acting*)
1890 C. V. Creagh
1895 Leicester Paul Beaufort

Leeward Islands

1871 Sir B. C. Pine
1873 H. T. Irving
1875 Sir George Berkeley
1881 Sir J. H. Glover
1884 Sir C. C. Lees
1885 Ld Gormanston
1888 W. F. Haynes Smith
1895– Sir F. Fleming
1901

Malta

1826 Maj.-Gen. Sir F. C. Ponsonby (*Lieut.-Gov.*)
1836 Maj.-Gen. Sir H. F. Bouverie
1843 Lieut.-Gen. Sir P. Stuart
1847 Rt Hon. R. More O'Ferrall
1851 Maj.-Gen. Sir W. Reid
1858 Lieut.-Gen. Sir J. Gaspard Le Marchant
1864 Lieut.-Gen. Sir H. Storks
1867 Gen. Sir Patrick Grant
1872 Gen. Sir Charles T. Van Straubenzee
1878 Gen. Sir Arthur Borton
1884 Gen. Sir John Lintorn Arabin Simmons
1888 Lieut.-Gen. Sir H. D'O. Torrens
1890 Lieut.-Gen. Henry Augustus Smyth
1893 Gen. Sir Arthur James Lyon Fremantle
1899– Lieut.-Gen. Sir Francis Grenfell
1903

Mauritius

1830 Maj.-Gen. Sir W. Nicolay
1840 Col. J. Power (*Acting*)
1840 Sir Lionel Smith
1842 Col. W. Staveley (*Acting*)
1843 Lieut.-Col. Sir W. M. Gomm
1846 Lieut.-Col. T. Blanchard (*Acting*)
1848 Lieut.-Col. H. L. Sweeting (*Acting*)
1849 Sir George W. Anderson

1850 Maj.-Gen. W. Sutherland (*Acting*)
1851 James Macaulay Higginson
1857 Maj.-Gen. C. M. Hay (*Acting*)
1857 Sir William Stevenson
1863 Maj.-Gen. M. C. Johnstone (*Acting*)
1863 Sir Henry Barkly
1870 Brig.-Gen. E. Selby Smyth (*Acting*)
1871 Hon. Sir A. H. Gordon
1874 Edward Newton (*Acting*)
1874 Maj.-Gen. Sir A. P. Phayre
1878 F. Napier Broome (*Acting*)
1879 Sir G. F. Bowen
1880 F. Napier Broome (*Lieut.-Gov.*)
1883 C. Bruce (*Acting*)
1883 Sir J. Pope-Hennessy
1886 Rt Hon. Sir H. G. R. Robinson
1886 Maj.-Gen. W. H. Hawley (*Acting*)
1887 F. Fleming (*Acting*)
1888 Sir J. Pope-Hennessy
1889 Sir C. C. Lees
1892 Sir H. E. H. Jerningham
1897 C. A. King-Harman (*Acting*)
1897– Sir C. Bruce
1900

Natal

1843 Col. Cloete
1845 Martin West (*Lieut.-Gov.*)
1850 B. C. C. Pine (*Lieut.-Gov.*)
1856 John Scott (*Lieut.-Gov.*)
1864 J. MacLean (*Lieut.-Gov.*)
1872 Anthony Musgrave (*Lieut.-Gov.*)
1873 Sir Benjamin Pine (*Lieut.-Gov.*)
1875 Maj.-Gen. Sir Garnet Wolseley (*Admin.*)
1875 Sir Henry E. Bulwer (*Lieut.-Gov.*)
1879 Gen. Sir Garnet Wolseley (*Governor*)
1880 Maj.-Gen. Sir George Pomeroy-Colley
1881 Brig.-Gen. Sir H. Evelyn Wood (*Admin.*)
1881 Maj.-Gen. Redvers Buller (*Admin.*)
1881 Maj.-Gen. Sir H. Evelyn Wood (*Admin.*)
1882 Sir Henry Bulwer
1886 Sir Arthur Havelock
1889 Sir Charles Mitchell
1893– Hon. Sir W. F. Hely-Hutchinson
1901

Newfoundland

1825	Capt. Sir T. Cochrane
1834	Capt. Prescott
1841	Maj.-Gen. Sir J. Harvey
1847	Lieut-Col. Sir J. G. Le Marchant
1852	Ker Baillie Hamilton
1855	C. H. Darling
1857	Sir Alexander Bannerman
1864	Anthony Musgrave
1869	Col. Sir Stephen J. Hill
1876	Sir John H. Glover
1881	Sir H. F. Berkeley Maxse
1882	Sir F. B. T. Carter (*Admin.*)
1884	Sir John H. Glover
1885	Sir F. B. T. Carter (*Admin.*)
1886	Sir G. W. Des Voeux
1887	Sir F. B. T. Carter (*Admin.*)
1887	H. A. Blake
1888	Sir J. T. N. O'Brien
1895	Sir H. H. Murray
1899–	Sir H. McCallum
1901	

New Zealand

1840	Capt. W. Hobson
1842	W. Shortland (*Acting*)
1843	Capt. Robert Fitzroy
1845	Sir George Grey
1854	Col. R. H. Wynyard (*Acting*)
1855	Col. Sir Thomas Gore Browne
1861	Sir George Grey
1868	Sir G. F. Bowen
1873	Rt Hon. Sir James Fergusson
1874	M of Normanby
1879	Sir H. G. R. Robinson
1880	Sir Arthur Gordon
1883	Lieut.-Gen. Sir W. F. D. Jervois
1889	E of Onslow
1892	E of Glasgow
1897–	E of Ranfurly
1904	

Sierra Leone

1830	Alexander Finlay (*Lieut.-Gov.*)
1833	Octavios Temple (*Lieut-Gov.-in-Chief*)
1835	H. D. Campbell (*Lieut.-Gov.-in-Chief*)
1837	Richard Doherty (*Gov.*)
1840	Sir John Jeremie (*Gov.-in-Chief*)
1842	George MacDonald (*Gov.-in-Chief*)
1844	W. Ferguson (*Gov.-in-Chief*)
1845	N. W. MacDonald (*Gov.*)

1852	A. E. Kennedy (*Gov.-in-Chief*)
1855	S. J. Hill (*Gov.-in-Chief*)
1862	William Hill (*Lieut.-Gov.*)
1862	Samuel Wensley Blackall (*Gov.*)
1868	Sir A. E. Kennedy (*Gov.-in-Chief*)
1872	J. P. Hennessy (*Admin.*)
1873	R. W. Keate (*Gov.-in-Chief*)
1873	George Berkeley (*Gov.-in-Chief*)
1875	C. H. Kortright (*Gov.-in-Chief*)
1877	Samuel Rowe (*Gov.-in-Chief*)
1881	A. E. Havelock (*Gov.-in-Chief*)
1885	Sir Samuel Rowe (*Gov.-in-Chief*)
1888	J. M. Maltby (*Admin.*)
1888	J. S. Hay (*Gov.*)
1891	Maj. J. J. Crooks (*Admin.*)
1892	Sir Francis Fleming (*Gov.*)
1893	Maj. J. J. Crooks (*Admin.*)
1894–1900	Col. Sir F. Cardew (*Gov.*)

Straits Settlements

1828	Mr Ibbetson
1833	K. Murchison
1837	Samuel Bonham
1843	Col. W. J. Butterworth
1855	E. A. Blundell
1861	Col. Cavenagh
1867	Maj.-Gen. Sir H. St G. Ord
1871	Lieut.-Col. A. E. H. Anson (*Admin.*)
1873	Sir A. Clarke
1875	Sir W. F. D. Jervois
1877	Col. A. E. H. Anson (*Admin.*)
1877	Sir W. C. F. Robinson
1879	Maj.-Gen. A. E. H. Anson (*Admin.*)
1880	Sir F. A. Weld
1887	Sir Cecil Smith
1893	W. E. Maxwell (*Admin.*)
1893	Lieut.-Col. Sir C. B. H. Mitchell
1898–1901	Sir J. Alexander Swettenham

Trinidad

1830	Maj.-Gen. Sir Lewis Grant
1830	Lieut.-Col. Doherty
1830	Lieut.-Col. Sir Charles Smith
1831	Maj.-Gen. Sir Lewis Grant
1833	Sir G. F. Hill (*Lieut.-Gov.*)
1838	Lieut.-Col. Mein
1839	Col. Sir E. M. McGregor
1840	Col. Sir Henry Macleod
1846	Ld Harris

1854	Sir Charles Elliott
1857	Robert William Keate
1864	J. H. T. Manners-Sutton
1866	Arthur Hamilton Gordon
1870	James Longden
1874	William Wellington Cairns
1878	Sir Henry Irving
1880	Sir Sanford Freeling

| 1885 | Sir Arthur Elibank Havelock |
| 1885 | Sir William Robinson |

Trinidad & Tobago

1888	Sir William Robinson
1891	Sir Frederick Napier Broome
1897–1900	Sir H. E. H. Jerningham

Bibliographical Note

No one source or type of source was used predominantly in compiling the information presented in this book. Rather the problem was to extract relevant material from a wide range of available sources. And this book is therefore the product of a large number of others. Variety of sources does not much matter in compiling lists of names: the greater the number of sources the greater the possibility of completeness and the less the chances of omission. But it does present serious difficulties for compiling data of appointment to office, since a range of possible days can be considered to be the date of appointment. Different sources cite different dates.

In compiling the lists of Ministries it proved uncommonly difficult to discover precisely when a man was appointed to an office and for how long he held it. In order to reduce this confusion and to standardise as far as possible the basis for the dates given in this book, the following plan was adopted. Wherever possible the date of appointment cited is that given by the *London Gazette* as the date of appointment to the office. The *Gazette* recorded the bulk of major appointments. It noted also appointments of junior Lords of the Treasury, of Officers of the Royal Household and (less regularly) of the Law Officers of the Crown.

The *London Gazette* was preferred to *The Times* as a source of appointments to office for various reasons. For the century as a whole it is more comprehensive. For the first part of the period *The Times* itself extracted its information from the *Gazette*, which is therefore more up to date. Further, in the matter of appointments *The Times* tended to confuse speculation with fact, as when it announced the appointment of Cobden to the Presidency of the Board of Trade in 1859. Trollope pertinently observed the shortcomings of *The Times* as a source of information on political appointments:

> *The Times*, in its second edition on the Thursday, gave a list of the Cabinet, in which four places out of fourteen were rightly filled. On the Friday it named ten places aright, and indicated the law officers, with only one mistake with reference to Ireland; and on the Saturday it gave a list of the Under Secretaries of State, and Secretaries and Vice-Presidents, generally with wonderful correctness as to the individuals, though the offices were a little jumbled. (*Phineas Finn*, Chapter IX)

There is a final reason for preferring the *Gazette* to *The Times*: for the nineteenth century the *Gazette* has a reasonably complete and accurate index. Palmer's *Index to 'The Times'* is impossible to use successfully in compilation work.

Unfortunately not all appointments were gazetted. Many junior Ministers went unrecorded. Therefore wherever possible official publications have been used to supplement the *Gazette*. The most valuable of these were:

The *Foreign Office List* (annually from 1806), the *Colonial Office List* (annually from 1862) the *War Office List* (annually from 1862) and the *India Office List* (annually from 1858). Additional information about the Post Office was derived from *The Post Office: An Historical Summary* (HMSO, 1911). Under-Secretaries at the Home Office were taken from Sir F. Newsam, *The Home Office* (London, 1954). The Prime Minister was gazetted as a Lord Commissioner of the Treasury. Dates cited in this book are those of the kissing of hands, and are taken from the *Letters of Queen Victoria*.

Three works in particular proved of immense and continuous value. Joseph Haydn's *The Book of Dignities* (London, 1890) is the only comprehensive work on appointments for this period; and despite errors and omissions remains the best single work of reference on offices and office-holders. Frederic Boase, *Modern English Biography: containing many thousand concise memoirs of persons who have died between the years 1851–1900* (Truro, 1892–1921), has concise and accurate information on a whole range of political appointments, and is especially strong on minor office-holders who are seldom recorded elsewhere. For certain appointments, additional information can be found in Haydn's *Book of Dates* (London, 1910). F. M. Powicke and E. B. Fryde's *Handbook of British Chronology* (London, 2nd ed. 1961) lists English Officers of State, some Irish and Scottish appointments, and very many ecclesiastical dignitaries. For reasons explained above, dates of appointment given in the *Handbook* often differ by a few days from those provided in this book.

Five other major sources were found on examination to be insufficiently precise for the purposes of compiling the lists of Ministries: *Whitaker's Almanac* (published annually from 1869); Dod's *Parliamentary Companion* (annually from 1832); the *Annual Register* (annually from 1758); *Who's Who* (annually from 1847) and the *Dictionary of National Biography*.

Valuable information on particular offices was found in the *Whitehall Series* and *New Whitehall Series* of monographs on Government Departments. The following in particular contain lists of office-holders: Sir J. Winnifrith, *The Ministry of Agriculture, Fisheries and Food* (London, 1962); Lord Bridges, *The Treasury* (London, 1964); Sir D. Milne, *The Scottish Office* (London, 1957); and Sir H.

Llewellyn Smith, *The Board of Trade* (London, 1928). Additional information on the Admiralty was found in J. M. Briggs, *Naval Administration 1832–97* (London, 1897) and in a Return published in *Commons Papers* 1854, XLII 95. Appointments to the Board of Customs, and to the Inland Revenue are in *Commons Papers* 1878, LXI 161.

Lists (not always accurate) are also to be found in Oliver and Boyd's *Edinburgh Almanac* (annually); Thom's *Dublin Directory* (annually); the *Royal Kalendar for 1871* (London, 1871); and in A. H. Dyke Acland and C. Ransome, *Handbook to Politics* (London, 1883).

Very detailed and exact information on certain offices and their employees is to be found in the following works on *Office-Holders in Modern Britain* compiled by J. C. Sainty:

I *Treasury Officials 1660–1870* (London, 1972)

II *Officials of the Secretaries of State 1660–1782* (London, 1973)

III *Officials of the Boards of Trade 1660–1870* (London, 1974).

Information on Parliament came from the *Lords Journals*, the *Commons Journals*, and various well-known works of Parliamentary history. Statistics on the sittings, etc., of the House of Commons were published at intervals throughout the nineteenth century and conveniently collected in *Commons Papers* 1881, LXXIV 109. Additional information is to be found in the so-called *Black Book* of the House of Commons compiled in 1913 by A. A. Taylor and generously made available by the Librarian of the House of Commons. Statistics on Parliamentary Questions are to be found in D. N. Chester and N. Bowring, *Questions in Parliament* (London, 1962).

The following works were of some value for specific pieces of information: *The British Imperial Calendar*; *Local Government Directory* (from 1872); *Constitutional Year Book*; F. C. Carr-Gomm, *Handbook of the Administration of Great Britain 1801–1900* (London, rev. ed. 1901); the Liberal Year Book; *Eminent Persons: Biographies reprinted from 'The Times' 1870–94* (London, 1892–7); the *Statesman's Year Book* (annually from 1864).

Despite all efforts, the date of some appointments to office proved impossible to determine. This explains various gaps in the lists. For the sake of clarity, *n.a.* ('not available') has been inserted in some cases, but not in all.